Strategies of Segregation

AMERICAN CROSSROADS

*Edited by Earl Lewis, George Lipsitz, George Sánchez,
Dana Takagi, Laura Briggs, and Nikhil Pal Singh*

Strategies of Segregation

RACE, RESIDENCE, AND THE STRUGGLE
FOR EDUCATIONAL EQUALITY

David G. García

UNIVERSITY OF CALIFORNIA PRESS

University of California Press, one of the most distinguished university presses in the United States, enriches lives around the world by advancing scholarship in the humanities, social sciences, and natural sciences. Its activities are supported by the UC Press Foundation and by philanthropic contributions from individuals and institutions. For more information, visit www.ucpress.edu.

University of California Press
Oakland, California

© 2018 by David G. García

Library of Congress Cataloging-in-Publication Data

Names: García, David G., author.
Title: Strategies of segregation : race, residence, and the struggle for educational equality / David G. García.
Description: Oakland, California: University of California Press, [2018] | Series: American Crossroads; 47 | Includes bibliographical references and index. |
Identifiers: LCCN 2017036818 (print) | LCCN 2017039459 (ebook) | ISBN 9780520969179 (Ebook) | ISBN 9780520296862 (cloth: alk. paper) | ISBN 9780520296879 (pbk. : alk. paper)
Subjects: LCSH: Mexican Americans—Education—California—Oxnard—History—20th century. | African Americans—Education—California—Oxnard—History—20th century. | Segregation in education—California—Oxnard—20th century. | Racism in education—California—Oxnard—20th century. | Racism—California—Oxnard—20th century. | School integration—California—Oxnard—History—20th century. | Mexicans—Political activity—California—Oxnard—20th century. | African Americans—Political activity—California—Oxnard—20th century. | Oxnard School District (Calif). Board of Trustees—Trials, litigation, etc.
Classification: LCC LC2688.O96 G37 2018 (ebook) | LCC LC2688.O96 G37 2018 (print) | DDC 379.2/630979492—dc23
LC record available at https://lccn.loc.gov/2017036818

Manufactured in the United States of America

26 25 24 23 22 21 20 19 18
10 9 8 7 6 5 4 3 2 1

Para mi mamá y papá
y para Nayeli y Enrique

The publisher and the University of California Press Foundation gratefully acknowledge the generous support of the Lisa See Endowment Fund in Southern California History and Culture.

CONTENTS

ILLUSTRATIONS

FIGURES

PREFACE

The story of how my family came to live in Oxnard, California, begins with my father, Lamberto M. García. Recruited as a bracero in the early 1950s, he temporarily worked in Texas, Arkansas, Michigan, and California. He lived in Oxnard for an extended time, at Campo Buena Vista, which by the late 1950s had become known as the largest bracero camp in the nation.[1] Two of his brothers also lived and worked there. The camp was located on Fifth Street, east of Oxnard Boulevard and a few miles from the predominantly Mexican community of La Colonia. As he recalled, the men were transported to and from the fields each day, and they ate, slept, and engaged in recreation at the camp. To purchase their clothes and shoes, they were driven to and from a bracero-contracted store on Oxnard Boulevard. The spatial containment of the braceros represented a continuation of policies and practices in the city that relied on Mexicans as a permanent source of labor, yet sought to restrict them to La Colonia.

My dad searched for additional opportunities beyond the bracero program and found a job as a carpenter. By 1971 he had secured our U.S. residency and saved up enough money to move our family to Oxnard. My mom, Guillermina Frausto García, worked as a homemaker and a sales representative for Tupperware, Jafra, and other companies. She taught me as a young boy how to navigate the city by bus and I translated as we carried out daily errands. Through these bus rides, I became more conscious of race and place. I noticed that Mexicans mostly lived east of the railroad tracks and Oxnard Boulevard. I also saw that the more affluent White people lived west and northwest of the railroad tracks. I could not have known at the time that this racialized geography had been purposefully designed to segregate Mexicans from Whites in housing and schools.

I vividly remember 1974 because that was the year I rode on a school bus across town to attend kindergarten at Marina West Elementary School. The year before, my parents had purchased a home on Colonia Road, in a housing tract called Rose Park. As my four older siblings recall, I was assigned to attend Marina West because my neighborhood school, Rose Avenue Elementary, was overenrolled. What they did not realize was that it was over-enrolled with Mexican and Black students. I now know that the bus I rode to kindergarten was part of a federal desegregation case affirmed in 1974, a ruling that aimed to remedy racial imbalance in Oxnard's elementary schools.

Though this book is not about me, the schooling, labor, and housing experiences of my family, friends, and generations of Oxnard residents resonate throughout the chapters. Originally established as a sugar-beet company town, Oxnard's narrative begins similarly to my family's story—with the recruitment of laborers, mainly immigrants from Mexico. With their work harvesting and processing sugar beets, walnuts, lima beans, barley, and other crops, these men and women contributed to the development and wealth of the city and the surrounding region. In return, these pioneer-laborers received very little access to opportunities for social or educational mobility for themselves or their families.[2] Oxnard's dual school system exemplified national policies "inducing, and even welcoming a certain class of people to perform the [nation's] cheap labor," while rejecting them "as ... resident[s] and citizen[s]."[3] School segregation exemplified this contradiction, not by accident but by design.

Indeed, a select group of women and men, whom I refer to as the White architects of Mexican American education,[4] constructed schools to reproduce the socioeconomic and racial hierarchy. Having grown up in Oxnard, I was familiar with these individuals' names because they are memorialized in the schools, streets, and parks of the city. I understand few readers outside of Oxnard may recognize their names. What is more important, and what I emphasize throughout the book, are their efforts to systematically subordinate Mexican American, and later Black, communities as a commonplace way of conducting business within and beyond schools. As a historian, I am driven to recover this complex narrative, and to reclaim it as a narrative not just about a community's subordination and undereducation, but also about its assertions of self-determination and resistance.

ACKNOWLEDGMENTS

This book is a product of community collaboration and support that came in different forms and at different stages of this work and my life. Thank you to all the interviewees and their families who graciously shared their memories and personal collections with me. Your voices bring this narrative to life and enrich the book. Thank you especially to Juan L. Soria's family for their enthusiastic support.

A special thank-you to my *compañera,* Tara J. Yosso, a gifted scholar and amazing mother to our children, Nayeli and Enrique. This book has been a family affair, sometimes with the kids joining us at the archives. They have heard us analyze this project endlessly, and they let us know our conversations are annoying. Still, I am deeply grateful for your willingness to talk through the details, and I know the book is all the better because of your critical insights and support. Thank you to all of my *familia,* especially to my *papá,* who offered valuable insights about this history, and to my *mamá,* rest in peace, who alongside my dad always emphasized the importance of education.

My sincere appreciation to George Lipsitz, who saw this project develop and provided insightful feedback from the start. I continue to benefit greatly from your generous mentorship and admire your commitment to social justice. Thank you to my doctoral advisor and friend Juan Gómez-Quiñones, who has supported me in all my research and teaching projects. You are a pioneer scholar-activist and I am humbled by the opportunity to work with and learn from you.

I am indebted to those who blazed scholarly trails with research on Chicana/o history and Communities of Color, including (but not limited to) George I. Sánchez, Ernesto Galarza, Thomas P. Carter, Albert Camarillo, Charles M. Wollenberg, Rodolfo F. Acuña, Guadalupe San Miguel Jr., Gilbert G. Gonzalez, Rubén Donato, Antonia I. Castañeda, Vicki L. Ruiz,

Richard R. Valencia, Martha Menchaca, Devra Weber, Tomás Almaguer, George J. Sánchez, Mario T. García, and William H. Watkins. A special thank-you to Rubén Donato, James D. Anderson, Christopher Span, and Joy Williamson-Lott for your scholarship, feedback, and for the invaluable advice in navigating academia. Thank you to Judge Harry Pregerson for providing access to the court archives, sharing your memories, and epitomizing why, as you said, "The best judges come from East LA."

Thank you to Natalia Molina, whose work inspires me, and whose critical feedback at an early stage of the manuscript helped me envision my contributions. To José M. Alamillo, Frank P. Barajas, and Luis H. Moreno, who are recovering our community histories with scholarship on Ventura County and Oxnard. Thank you all for sharing contacts, sources, and providing feedback at different points. A special thank-you to Louie Valdivia for introducing me to your family, who graciously shared their insights along with many of the classroom photos for the book. To Mario Rios Perez and Dionne Danns for providing feedback on Chapter 5, Victoria-María MacDonald for early feedback on Chapter 1, and Nancy Beadie for affirming my work with an invitation to serve on the *History of Education Quarterly* editorial board.

I am appreciative for the support shown to Tara and me from the many students at UCLA. To the students who participated in my research apprenticeship course, including Alma I. Flores, Tanya Gaxiola, Lluliana Alonso, Johnny "The Hurricane" Ramirez, Ryan E. Santos, and Michaela J. López Mares-Tamayo, I appreciate the space we shared to give each other feedback on our work and to keep our individual projects moving forward. I am grateful for the research assistance and feedback provided by Ryan E. Santos. You always made time to help me out on short notice when up against deadlines. I appreciate working with you and look forward to seeing your contributions to the field.

Thank you also to my colleagues and friends for their support: Dolores Delgado Bernal, Octavio Villalpando, Rebeca Burciaga, Maria Ledesma, Gaye Theresa Johnson, Yoon Pak, Ana Elizabeth Rosas, Laura K. Muñoz, Carlos K. Blanton, Irene Vásquez, Corina Benavides López, José Aguilar Hernández, Linda Chaparro, Enrique Alemán Jr., Sonya Alemán, Verónica Castillo-Muñoz, Gloria Toriche, and Tomás A. Carrasco, who introduced me to the amazing Carrasco family. Thank you to my friends of many years, Alberto Cervantes, José Rangel, Angel Colmenero, Carlos Arenas, Jose Cervantes, and Adalberto Huerta; I appreciate the many laughs.

Thank you to everyone at the University of California Press, especially Niels Hooper, who saw the potential in this manuscript and moved it forward, Bradley Depew for patience and quick replies to my barrage of first-time author queries, Jeffrey Wyneken for applying skill and care with detailed copyediting and for his encouraging enthusiasm about the manuscript, Dore Brown for keeping the project on track, Jolene Torr for working to ensure the book reaches a broad audience, the anonymous reviewers, and the UC Press Faculty Review Board, whose suggestions made this manuscript stronger. Thanks also to Victoria Baker for assistance with the index, to Veronica N. Velez for assistance in adapting the 1948 school map, to Nancy Lee Sayre for editorial support, and to Martin Gonzalez for research assistance toward the end of this project.

Thank you to the UC President's Postdoctoral Fellowship Program, which supported my transition into a tenure-track position at UCLA. Thank you to the Ford Foundation Postdoctoral Fellowship, which allowed me the time, during a crucial year, to work in the archives and conduct interviews. I am also thankful for the UCLA Hellman Fellows Program for recognizing the promise of my scholarship with timely support for my travel to the multiple archives, transcription of interviews, and other research expenses. The UCLA Chicana/o Studies Research Center also provided funding to cover travel and graduate student research assistance.

Thank you to all my UCLA colleagues, especially Daniel G. Solórzano, a kind and giving mentor. It is an honor to learn from and work with you. To Tyrone Howard, Douglas Kellner, Concepción Valadez, John Rogers, Marjorie Orellana, Robert Chao-Romero, Vilma Ortiz, Thomas M. Philip, and Robert Teranishi, thank you for being supportive at critical times. At the University of Michigan, I also encountered a great group of colleagues and students. I am especially grateful for the support from Deborah Loewenberg Ball.

Thank you to the many archivists and librarians at the National Archives and Library of Congress in California and Washington, DC; your work and expertise are so vital. Charles N. Johnson at the Museum of Ventura County patiently helped me locate many of the early photographs of Oxnard. Thank you to Superintendent Cesar Morales for providing me access to the Oxnard Elementary School District archives, and to Sylvia Carabajal for your kind assistance. To all those who forged paths toward educational equality, and those who continue the struggle, *gracias*.

c/s

Introduction

Every generation in the United States evolves and contributes to redefining their society and civic polity, whether done specifically and consciously or indirectly and inattentively but under conditions inherited from the past. . . . The present always converses with that past, here as elsewhere in the world, and so it is with Mexican Americans.

—JUAN GÓMEZ-QUIÑONES AND IRENE VÁSQUEZ, 2014

IN 1970, JUAN L. SORIA organized a class-action lawsuit on behalf of Mexican American and Black children attending segregated schools in Oxnard, a coastal city in Ventura County, about sixty miles north of Los Angeles, California.[1] According to the evidence described in the *Soria v. Oxnard School Board of Trustees* complaint, the district knowingly maintained de facto segregation in schools east and west of the railroad tracks for at least ten years. During the appeals process, the plaintiffs' lawyers recovered additional evidence going back four decades, which they argued demonstrated de jure origins of segregation in Oxnard schools. Even with historical evidence of intentional segregation from the 1930s, the *Soria* case did not fully uproot patterns of inequality long denied, ignored, and purposely hidden.[2] Focusing on the period between 1903 and 1974, this book examines designs for racially unequal schooling in Oxnard with the understanding that contemporary educational conditions for Mexican Americans continue to converse with this past.

A handful of scholars have produced most of what we know about Mexican American educational histories.[3] Focused on places in Texas, California, Arizona, New Mexico, and Colorado, these studies document the establishment of separate and unequal "Mexican" schools,[4] rationalized by openly racist, ethnocentric[5] claims of inferior intelligence, language, and culture.[6] This research has also shown patterns of schools limiting Mexican students to programs of academic remediation and industrial or vocational education.[7] Moreover, this scholarship has chronicled struggles over access to equal schooling for Mexicans in the United States, recovering significant elements of a community legacy of resistance to injustice.[8]

Acknowledging the contributions of these studies, scholars have called on the field of educational history to more fully account for the perspectives of women and People of Color, and to connect history to current educational research and policy.[9] For instance, attorney Leticia Saucedo of the Mexican American Legal Defense and Education Fund suggested historical research could more effectively demonstrate "patterns of discrimination in education" for the court, and should be utilized in legal rationales to "more clearly show the causal connection between current practices and past discrimination in education."[10]

As a site, Oxnard lends itself to original analysis of schooling discrimination and contributes to national discussions of racism, segregation, civil rights, community resistance, and educational policy.[11] My inquiry into Oxnard's educational past reveals four strategies of segregation that complicate previous narratives: (1) establishing a racial hierarchy, (2) building a permanent link between residential and school segregation, (3) utilizing a school-within-a-school model of racial separation, and (4) omitting a rationale for segregation. The scholarly literature on labor and housing has identified a racial hierarchy at play in the very structures of society, but for the most part these studies do not account for educational institutions. As I analyze schooling experiences in an agricultural town that grew into a *rurban*[12] city with a predominately Mexican population, I find that schools functioned as a central part of the establishment and reproduction of racial hierarchy.[13] I argue that residential and school segregation became interconnected "not by chance, but by design."[14] This finding expands on research that tends to focus "exclusively either on schools or housing,"[15] in Black and White, urban and suburban communities.[16]

Furthermore, my interpretation of Oxnard's narrative identifies the construction of a school-within-a-school model of segregation, which kept Mexican children in classes apart from Whites and Asians from kindergarten through eighth grade. Scholars most often consider this model to be a form of resegregation created after the U.S. Supreme Court's 1954 *Brown v.*

Board of Education desegregation ruling.[17] By chronologically repositioning the model to the first half of the twentieth century, I name it as a foundational form of segregation. Additionally, while scholars most often locate the emergence of the Asian American "model minority" myth after World War II, evidence from Oxnard suggests much earlier origins.[18] Moreover, I classify the Oxnard school board's omission of any rationale for segregation as strategic and distinct from other sites.[19]

In examining the strategies of segregation prior to the *Soria* case, I recover parallel and shared struggles for equality forged by Black and Mexican American residents, in housing and education. My analysis of their activism as neighbors committed to a common cause for desegregation contributes to what Natalia Molina describes as the treatment of "race as a relational concept," by focusing on "how, when, where, and to what extent groups intersect."[20] This approach enables me to more fully consider the continuities of networks employed by Mexican American and Black residents organizing against school segregation in 1963 and to recognize *Soria* as among the first school desegregation cases in the nation to be filed jointly by Mexican American and Black plaintiffs.[21] Their eventual success in garnering a court ruling for integration exposed a school system designed to reproduce racial inequality.[22] In the following chapters, I excavate these designs and consider the implementation of the strategies of segregation, taking into account the perspectives of students who experienced them firsthand. It is my sincere hope that unearthing this history offers new dimensions to understanding our collective past—and that in critical reflection we forge a new vision for our future.[23]

THE WHITE ARCHITECTS OF MEXICAN AMERICAN EDUCATION AND MUNDANE RACISM

The making of the City of Oxnard—the "sugar empire"[24] and a booming regional agricultural economy—relied on the turnover of the land to Whites, who in turn depended principally on Mexican labor.[25] Early Oxnard ran very much like other small agricultural towns in California, governed by an interconnected group of Whites, whose families were often "linked by marriage,"[26] fraternal bonds, and business partnerships. Drawing on William H. Watkins's analysis in *The White Architects of Black Education: Ideology and Power in America*,[27] I refer to these men and women as the White architects of Mexican American education.

To expose the ideological frameworks embedded in Black education over time, Watkins builds on the work of James D. Anderson, who examined some of the colonial imperatives reflected in the schooling of Blacks during and after Reconstruction.[28] Watkins offers a critical biographical account of a small group of wealthy, powerful White men who reproduce race and class inequality for Blacks not as a matter of course but as a carefully constructed project of racial supremacy.[29] In applying his insights to understand the designs, construction, and development of educational inequality for Mexican Americans in Oxnard, I unearthed a similar ideological architecture attributable to a small group of powerbrokers. Different from those elites in Watkins's study, however, this local Oxnard group included civic and business leaders, members of fraternal and social organizations, teachers, parents, and homeowners. These elite and ordinary men and women contributed to what Charles Mills has identified as a "racial contract," a tacit societal agreement to privilege Whites over "nonwhites," through the systematic "exploitation of their bodies, land, and resources, and the denial of equal socioeconomic opportunities to them."[30] For Oxnard's White architects, it was not a question of *whether* to segregate Mexicans but *how* to do so effectively and permanently. They held a vested interest in restricting Mexicans to manual labor, and to reproducing an undereducated, low-wage workforce. To systematize racial and class inequality in the city, the White architects deployed four strategies of segregation concurrently.

Establishing racial hierarchy. Whites positioned themselves at the top of the racial hierarchy, and structured in privileges for themselves in housing and schools to ensure generational transfer of wealth and power.[31] As early as 1917, the White architects criminalized Mexican students, claiming that the "personal health of the Mexican children" posed "a threat and menace to the welfare of the community," affecting "every child in school."[32] In the 1920s, school leaders publicly acknowledged a policy of segregating Mexican children while permitting Japanese and Chinese students to enroll in White classes.[33] School board minutes from 1937 and 1938 reiterate plans to maintain Asian children in White classes, unless "in the case of future emergency,"[34] and to grant enrollment exceptions for only "a few of the brightest, cleanest Mexican children."[35] Indeed, schools were designed to serve Whites, and Whites determined whether and how to educate any racial/ethnic group. During World War II, when Blacks became a larger percentage of the city and school population, the White architects sought to position them alongside Mexican Americans at the bottom of the racial hierarchy.

Building an interconnection between residential and school segregation. The White architects strategically underdeveloped the predominately Mexican neighborhood of La Colonia, east of Oxnard Boulevard and the railroad tracks, and used racially restrictive covenants to maintain the northwest side of the city as exclusively White. They adjusted school attendance boundaries to make these racial divisions appear natural. Their actions established an inextricable link between residential and school segregation.

Constructing a school-within-a-school model of racial separation. Pragmatic school segregation occurred within three elementary campuses from 1903 to 1939. During these decades, with very few exceptions, the school board maintained segregated classes, distinct recesses, and staggered release times for Mexican students. After the 1940 construction of an elementary school in La Colonia, the strategic school-within-a-school model of segregation continued in the west-side junior high schools.

Omitting a rationale for segregation. Within their meeting minutes, the school board methodically documented their actions to segregate Mexican children. Trustees sought out legal opinions, worked collaboratively with city powerbrokers, studied regional and national segregation efforts, and accommodated segregation demands of White parents. Notwithstanding their detailed accounting of these actions, the trustees' records did not disclose whether school officials expressed dissent, and did not mention any rationale for racial segregation. With these omissions, the school board portrayed the pursuit of segregation as a policy of consensus.

While members depicted themselves as objective, dutiful administrators, the board's strategies of segregation casually projected "contemptuous condescension" toward Mexicans and effectively normalized the disparate treatment of Mexican children.[36] Indeed, over time the White architects of Mexican American education engaged in what I have identified as mundane racism—the systematic subordination of Mexicans enacted as a commonplace, ordinary way of conducting business within and beyond schools. I utilize the term "mundane racism" to more precisely account for the ways racism took place in Oxnard, and to understand the system of prejudice and discrimination against Mexicans designed to reproduce inequality as a routine matter of course.[37]

The formation of Oxnard follows a complex narrative of colonization, dispossession of land, and relegation of Mexicans to the working class across California and the Southwest.[38] The Chumash peoples originally inhabited the lands that became part of California's central coast, including the Oxnard Plain.[39] In the 1700s and 1800s, they encountered devastating European diseases and violent colonization. In 1810, Franciscan missionaries and Spanish colonial soldiers attempted to completely remove the surviving Chumash from their lands and force them to live in Mission San Buenaventura.[40] The Spanish divided the area into five land grants over the next decades, which subsequently came under the ownership of an elite group of Mexican women and men, *Los Californios*.[41] By the turn of the twentieth century, Rancho El Rio de Santa Clara O La Colonia was partitioned into the land that would comprise most of the city of Oxnard.[42]

In the wake of the U.S.-Mexico War of 1846–48, a series of droughts, a changing economy, and the Land Act of 1851 facilitated the dispossession of Mexicans from their lands. Similar to other Native American groups, Mexicans resisted and contested this encroachment by White migrants, confronting violations to the Treaty of Guadalupe Hidalgo, pursuing litigation in defense of their land titles, and challenging underhanded real estate schemes, squatters, and violence.[43] Some tried to avoid White speculators by selling their land to more financially stable Mexican families.[44] Native American and Mexican women also utilized the courts to claim their property rights and protect their livelihoods.[45] Despite such persistent, time-consuming, and costly efforts, the majority of the original inhabitants of California were rendered effectively landless by the 1880s.[46]

Consistent with the practices of state and federal governmental agencies during the first half of the twentieth century, Oxnard officials "counted" Mexicans as racially White only when it benefited White interests.[47] School officials also knew that almost all children of Mexican descent were U.S. born. Still, for the overwhelming majority of Mexicans in Oxnard, as elsewhere, U.S. citizenship, light skin, and upper-class standing did not guarantee constitutional rights, let alone the civil rights and social privileges afforded to Whites.[48] Mexicans often received lower wages than Whites and tended to be limited to menial labor positions.[49] Individuals and institutions aimed to restrict Mexicans in all aspects of public life, barring them from serving as jurists, patronizing stores and restaurants, utilizing public facilities (e.g., restrooms, swimming pools, hospitals, cemeteries), and purchasing property or attending schools designated for Whites only.[50] Scholars have analyzed such contradictory treatment as a status of being considered legally White but socially Mexican.[51] Because Mexicans exerted their agency from the beginning,[52] Whites pursued policies and practices that aimed to position Mexicans as racial inferiors—tolerable as laborers but unworthy of anything more than second-class citizenship.[53]

Such were the mechanisms in motion in 1898 when Henry T. Oxnard and his brothers James and Robert gained partial control of the land grant Rancho El Rio de Santa Clara O La Colonia and established the American Beet Sugar Company (ABSC). They oversaw construction of a large refining factory east of Oxnard Boulevard, near what is now Wooley Road. To harvest and process the sugar beets, the ABSC recruited mainly Mexican and Japanese laborers.[54] In 1903, Oxnard became an incorporated city, and for all intents and purposes it was a company town. To facilitate transportation of the refined sugar, the ABSC coordinated the construction of a Southern Pacific Railroad spur line, which ran parallel to Oxnard Boulevard until Fourth Street, where it veered slightly east.[55] Except for a few small neighborhoods, such as Meta Street, the boulevard and railroad tracks geographically marked the emerging town's two distinct sections, west and east, which cultivated "discernable white and nonwhite social worlds."[56]

To the west, paved roads covered "all of the important residence and business streets"[57] and racially exclusive subdivisions designated for "first-class" White residential properties.[58] To the east, the increasing numbers of laborers and their families recruited to develop Ventura County's agricultural economy built their own housing or lived in factory-built homes. These predominantly Mexican residents had few options outside of this area because racial covenants restricted occupancy of the west-side properties to Whites only, well into the 1950s. Most of the east side lacked basic amenities such as paved streets, plumbing, and electricity for over four decades after the city's incorporation. Substandard living conditions mirrored often-exploitative working conditions, but did not go uncontested. Despite these structured inequalities, Mexican Americans in Oxnard contributed to "redefining their society and civic polity"[59] by organizing for improved working and living conditions, obtaining college degrees, and creating resilient communities.[60]

SOURCES, TERMS, AND THE LIMITS
OF THE ARCHIVES

I recovered and documented this complex narrative by engaging in the organic processes of archival and oral history research. For example, searching for references to Mexicans, Blacks, Asians, segregation, and schooling, I examined numerous collections within archives at the Oxnard Elementary School District, Oxnard Public Library, City of Oxnard, E. P. Foster Library, Ventura County Clerk and Recorder, Museum of Ventura County, Federal Records Center, U.S. Bureau of the Census, Library of Congress, National Archives, Cecil H. Green Library at Stanford University, California Digital Archive, and the Bancroft Library. From these and other sources, I considered school board and city trustees' meeting minutes, photographs, maps, local business directories, unpublished manuscripts and reports, flyers, pamphlets, correspondence, master's theses, doctoral dissertations, and government records, including census data, property deeds, original *Soria* case court filings, affidavits, depositions, and interrogatories. I also explored English- and Spanish-language newspaper archives, both local and regional, and newspaper clippings within several collections. I found a paucity of information preserved in these archives and collections about Mexican American schooling in Oxnard. My approach to the archives became not just a recovery of a narrative but also a critical reclamation of the silences within the publicly available primary sources.

The White architects' voices of domination figured largely in the local archives.[61] Reading their accounts in the school trustees' 1930s meeting minutes, for example, I identified practices of strategic silence and actions of disregard that effectively omitted Mexican American perspectives. For instance, from 1934 to 1939, the school board meticulously recorded a series of race-based enrollment changes and open forums in which White parents demanded segregation. These same minutes made no mention of whether any communication went out from the board to the Mexican parents before, during, or after the enrollment shifts took place. They also fail to record any rationale for segregation.

Though frustrated by the relative invisibility of Mexican Americans in the archives, I came to appreciate that these primary sources contributed to my analysis of racism as mundane, and to understanding discrimination through acts of commission and omission.[62] Some of the local sources reproduced racial myths similar to origin stories told about other California towns.[63] At the

city's fiftieth anniversary commemoration, the *Oxnard Press-Courier* celebrated the "ambitious and energetic" White farmers "mostly from Germany
and Ireland," who forged a "rising city" from what was once simply "an empty
plain."[64] Such romanticized accounts of "founding fathers" and "pioneer families" camouflage how this group of White immigrants came to acquire parcels
of the original rancho land grants. Though casually omitted from most public
records of the time, some of these violent confrontations could not be completely covered up. For instance, James Young Saviers, who sold the property
where the ABSC later built its factory, reportedly lost part of his chin "in a
skirmish with Indians," in 1860. He grew a long beard to conceal the scar.[65]

Indeed, the local newspaper provided a tremendous resource for me to
piece together a chronological narrative about the city and its schools, but also
exhibited patterns of omission and distortion that rendered Mexicans, and
especially Mexican women, all but invisible. *The Oxnard Daily Courier,* later
called *The Press-Courier,* rarely reported on the Mexican community, though
the criminal actions of Mexican men often made headlines.[66] When news
stories did refer to Mexican residents, they did so with the consistent racial
identifier (e.g., "Oxnard Mexican Murders Girl," "Mexican Stabbed in Alley
Brawl," "Mexican Girl Injured in Traffic Jam at Fire")[67] and regularly mis-
spelled their names within the story. Community activism by Mexican
Americans and Blacks in the 1960s received some news coverage, though usually the editors interjected their own oppositional bias and patronizing tone.

This narrative is enhanced by over sixty oral history interviews, including
many with women and men who attended segregated schools in Oxnard in
the 1930s, 1940s, and 1950s, and with organizers, teachers, and administrators
who worked in and around Oxnard schools during the decades of the 1960s
and 1970s.[68] The eldest was Ignacio S. Carmona, who was born in 1916 and
celebrated his one hundredth birthday in 2016.[69] The eldest woman, Mary
Valdivia Lamm, was born in Oxnard in 1924.[70] Eleven additional interviewees were born in the 1920s, and sixteen in the 1930s. These interviews enabled
me to recover some of the many perspectives missing from the official
archives,[71] and they shed much light on the daily complexities of navigating
race, class, gender, and space in Oxnard during the first half of the twentieth
century. Some also shared materials from personal collections, including
class pictures, yearbooks, and family history projects, which provided a tremendous resource in visualizing this history. I also interviewed lawyers
involved in the *Soria* case and the Honorable Harry Pregerson, who presided
over the case in the U.S. Central District Court of California. Taken

together, these oral histories brought further depth to my analysis of mundane racism as it evolved and was challenged in Oxnard. While space restrictions have not allowed me to quote directly from every interviewee, their memories certainly strengthened this book and helped me identify patterns of experiences over time.

Identifying appropriate terminology has presented a challenge. Recognizing the limits of language in accounting for the diversity of the communities I discuss, I use the term "Mexican Americans" to refer to men and women of Mexican origin or descent residing in the United States, regardless of U.S. citizenship status. I use "Mexican" synonymously with "Mexican American," though the latter became a more commonly used term during and after World War II. In the 1960s, I also interchange "Chicana/o" with "Mexican American," consistent with the terms used at the time.

OUTLINE OF BOOK

Chapter 1 identifies the strategies of segregation employed by the White architects early in Oxnard's history, focusing on the city's first mayor and school superintendent, Richard B. Haydock. I consider Haydock's public remarks about race and Mexicans alongside his foundational contributions in designing substandard living conditions for Mexican laborers and a segregated school system for their children. I argue that the racial hierarchy Haydock and the other White architects established in schools functioned to relegate Mexicans, with very few exceptions, to the bottom as a seemingly normal practice enforced well beyond the classroom.

Chapter 2 investigates the White architects' public and private actions to link residential and school segregation. Specifically, I expose the racial covenants burdening the west-side properties of the very school and city officials who designed the blueprints for school segregation, and argue that they colluded to discriminate against Mexicans in perpetuity.[72] I also analyze various oral accounts of Mexican women and men who recalled navigating racially segregated spaces in Oxnard from the 1930s to the 1960s.

Chapter 3 presents my close examination of the publicly documented blueprints for school segregation from 1934 to 1939, as Oxnard school officials formalized a school-within-a-school model of separating Mexican children from Whites.[73] Considering the school board meeting minutes during this six-year period, I follow the trustees' incessant tinkering with classroom racial composition and social interaction practices within schools. They adjusted residential enrollment boundaries between schools and swiftly accommodated White parents' demands for segregation. These board actions facilitated racially disproportionate attrition rates for Mexican students before high school.

Chapter 4 explores the evolution of the White architects' four strategies of segregation from 1939, when they sought voter approval to construct a school east of the railroad tracks, through 1954, when the U.S. Supreme Court ruled that racially segregated schools were inherently unequal and therefore unconstitutional. During this time, the school trustees constructed new schools that maximized the race, class, and east-west geographic divisions in the city and sought to normalize the undereducation of Mexican American children.

Chapter 5 analyzes the increasing demographic presence of Mexican Americans and Blacks in the decades after World War II and the collective actions taken by these communities to challenge disparate material conditions and treatment in the growing city. I discuss the formation of two groups, the Oxnard–Ventura County Branch of the NAACP and the Ventura County Chapter of the Community Service Organization, and follow the convergence of their efforts in 1963, when they mobilized a common cause for school desegregation.

Chapter 6 examines the remarkable aspects of the *Soria v. Oxnard School Board of Trustees* case, from the 1970 filing on behalf of Mexican American and Black plaintiffs attending Colonia schools, through the 1974 ruling by Judge Harry Pregerson. Following the case chronologically, I analyze how this collective effort to end de facto segregation in Oxnard was shaped by and contributed to struggles for desegregation at a national level. I call attention to the use of historical evidence showing discrimination with intent (de jure) and in effect (de facto), which exposed and disrupted the district's long-denied, persistent dual school system.[74]

The Epilogue considers what Oxnard's narrative tells us about the historical imperatives and experiences of our segregated past, and reflects on how these insights can bring more complexity to national discussions about race, schools, and equality.[75]

ONE

The White Architects of
Mexican American Education

The ignorant are allowed to live and breed under conditions that become a threat and a menace to the welfare of the community. Many cases of filth and disease and contagion are found by us in the school work. We suggest to these Mexican people that they care for themselves, but they do nothing. The personal health of the Mexican children in the grammar school affects every child in the school.

—RICHARD B. HAYDOCK, JANUARY 31, 1917

IN JANUARY 1917, SCHOOL SUPERINTENDENT and city trustee Richard B. Haydock[1] made a case for the appointment of a city policewoman deputy nurse, warning that the living conditions of Mexican families posed "a threat and a menace" to the larger school population. In December 1921, when he spoke to the Oxnard Rotary Club, Haydock framed his concerns about "local problems" with remarks about Blacks as a national problem, because, "be it ever so slight, even as in the octoroon, the unfortunate is still a negro.... Few men will say that the American for which we hope and pray can ever be made out of such stock."[2] These 1917 and 1921 newspaper accounts offer a unique vantage point from which to understand the collective project of White supremacy embedded in Oxnard's infrastructure and institutions from the city's founding.

As noted in the Introduction, the White architects of Mexican American education helped craft indelible patterns of racial segregation within and beyond schools.[3] For example, before establishing municipal elections, an elite group of White men appointed each other to serve on the Oxnard City Board of Trustees. Many of these powerbrokers served on the Oxnard School Board of Trustees and had connections with the town's main employer, the American Beet Sugar Company (ABSC).[4] Others conducted business with the schools, providing the land, building materials, and insurance for constructing and maintaining facilities. Some took on each of these roles simultaneously. White men also exerted influence as members of racially exclusive fraternal and civic organizations.[5] White women contributed to and led educational efforts, segregated social clubs, church activities, and volunteer organizations.[6] A small group of White women also wielded power as school leaders.[7]

Richard Thompson Ford has observed, "public policy and private actors operate together to create and promote racially identified space and the racial segregation that accompanies it."[8] This chapter's close examination of the White architects' public remarks and actions during Oxnard's formative years, from 1903 to 1930 in particular, demonstrates a carefully constructed, ideological architecture aimed to establish Whites at the top of a racial hierarchy. They sought to reproduce this hierarchy through the physical infrastructure of a city demarcated by racial spaces. They manufactured disparate schooling and housing conditions as a central component of these designs. West of Oxnard Boulevard and the railroad tracks meant White, first-class treatment and the promise of prosperity, while east meant Mexican, second-class treatment and little hope for social mobility.[9] The White architects' enactment of mundane racism shaped an interconnected residential and educational system of discrimination that persisted well beyond the 1930s.

In 1903, as the newly elected president of the city board of trustees (i.e., Oxnard's first mayor), Haydock began to oversee all aspects of city planning and school construction.[10] He led efforts to purposefully underdevelop what became the predominately Mexican east-side neighborhoods. He approved plans for substandard housing and neglected to extend basic municipal services such as sewage, electricity, and paved roads to this area. At the same time, he oversaw the development of upscale homes, a sewage and waste system, lighting, and street pavement for the west side of the city, where the White community lived.[11] He also helped plan and place the city's elementary schools west of the tracks, in close proximity to White neighborhoods. Oxnard Grammar School was constructed in 1908,[12] on Third Street between A and B streets, and enrolled a predominately White student population.[13]

Though the school board began recording meetings in 1916, the minutes remain sparse until 1923, when trustees Ben S. Virden, Dr. Harry M. Staire, and Roy B. Witman expressed anxiety about overcrowding.[14] Newspapers and other materials offer insights about the development of the town and schools during this time. Haydock's 1917 remarks, for example, set out a seemingly objective motion for a deputy policewoman nurse, but also offered an argument for segregation. Indeed, he complained, "these Mexican people"

FIGURE I. Oxnard Grammar School, circa 1908. Richard B. Haydock (top left corner). Courtesy of the Museum of Ventura County.

purposefully placed "every child in the school" at risk because of supposed contagious diseases. In his proposal to the city trustees, he noted, "We have laws to prevent the abuse of livestock . . . but the people are allowed to abuse themselves."[15] In acknowledging that poor parents with sick children would likely not be able to access a doctor, he expressed tolerance for Mexicans. Still, he likened these families to livestock. The city trustees reviewed no actual evidence to corroborate Haydock's presumption of a health "menace" emanating from the Mexican children. Even so, they approved his motion for a deputy policewoman nurse and "insisted that she be able to speak Spanish."[16] Haydock patronizingly noted that if special instruction did not work, he could legally deny Mexican children access to schools altogether: "If possible, these people ought to be taught better. The law provides for the exclusion from school of children infected with a contagion. If we enforce this rule nothing is done for the children."[17] Haydock's claim to be flouting the law by allowing contagious children to attend school belied his role in ensuring the district's funding based on daily attendance, as Mexicans comprised at least 40 percent of elementary school enrollments.

About three weeks later, in February 1917, Haydock selected Policewoman Eloise M. Thornton, a graduate nurse who had "organized school nursing in the city of Los Angeles" and had experience working with police, health, and school departments as a "probation and humane officer."[18] Her appointment, "as a deputy marshal and a deputy health officer,"[19] reified the shared belief among the White architects that educating Mexican children required policing. These unexamined beliefs effectively criminalized Mexican children and their parents.

In 1916, the White architects, led by school superintendent and city trustee Haydock and the president of the school board of trustees and city treasurer Virden,[20] had overseen construction of a new school to accommodate a growing student population. In 1917, the school trustees officially named this facility the "Haydock Grammar School," supported by a petition organized by landowner Charles Donlon. Over thirty people signed the petition "in recognition of the long years of able, faithful, and efficient educational work [Haydock] has done in this community."[21] When the Richard B. Haydock School opened in March 1917, on the corner of Wooley Road and C Street, it enrolled approximately two hundred upper- and lower-grade elementary students who lived in "the south part of town."[22]

Local claims about Mexican children being a "menace" within schools reverberated with regional and national nativist arguments to halt immigration from Mexico altogether.[23] However, these voices conflicted with those of industrialists and growers, whose successful lobbying between 1917 and 1920 facilitated increases of over seventy-three thousand temporary Mexican immigrants and more than one hundred thousand permanent Mexican immigrants throughout the United States.[24] The very low wages paid to Mexican farmworkers and the seasonal availability of employment meant that families often worked together and followed the crop harvests. Men, women, and children worked in the fields.

Ventura County school officials encouraged such work, knowing that child labor laws exempted agricultural work and that compulsory education laws exempted children working in the fields.[25] For example, in May 1917, the *Oxnard Daily Courier* updated readers about the notices sent out by Ventura County school superintendent James E. Reynolds for assistance in harvesting crops, stating: "More than 300 families in Ventura [C]ounty have responded favorably. . . . High school children generally are likewise responding in good shape to the request of the officials for aid in harvesting the crops of the county."[26] While the top educational official in the county encouraged children working in the fields, other local officials expressed concern about Mexican children not attending school regularly.

When Policewoman Thornton outlined her initial work in January 1918, she "told of the necessity of keeping the children in school, of poor housing conditions, and advised that only English be spoken to the children."[27] These brief remarks foreshadowed the complex structural inequality shaping Mexican children's experiences, which would not be sufficiently addressed by a policewoman nurse. By August 1918, her report to the city trustees demonstrated she had accepted Haydock's approach to ignore the conditions shaping schooling experiences and focus on Mexican children as the problem. As she discussed her efforts in "Teaching Foreign Children Our Ways," Thornton took on some of Haydock's patronizing tone, remarking, "the Mexican must learn to keep his word if he expects to get help when he needs it. . . . He is slow to learn some things."[28]

Thornton stepped down from the position after about one year, citing that she could not sustain her own health while engaging in such a difficult job.[29] Haydock complained of the problems occurring in her absence, "especially in connection with the grammar schools."[30] He noted several cases of "pinkeye" that caused students to be sent home from school, remarking: "If they had medical care, or any kind of attention . . . the children would soon be cured, and back to school. As it is they spread the disease and do not get cured easily."[31] Consistent with his previous comments, Haydock could barely muster empathy for the Mexican children, and remained principally focused on the average daily attendance funds these students represented.

DESIGNING POOR LIVING AND HEALTH CONDITIONS

Haydock, along with the other city trustees, actually contributed to the very conditions of "filth" they claimed occurred because of Mexican "ignorance." Two weeks after his motion for a policewoman nurse, in mid-February 1917, he and the city trustees confirmed street paving plans for the town. They purposefully designed the pavement plans to cover only the west side of Oxnard in the commercial and residential sections of the White community.[32] In the meantime, neither city nor school leaders made efforts to secure the safety of the Mexican children who walked daily on dirt- or mud-filled streets and across the railroad tracks to attend west-side schools. These actions and refusals to act exemplified the mundane disregard shown for the tax-paying Mexican community.

FIGURE 2 (top). West-side residences, Oxnard, circa 1920s. Courtesy of the Museum of Ventura County.

FIGURE 3 (bottom). East-side residences and outhouses off Fifth Street, Oxnard, circa 1940s. Courtesy of the Museum of Ventura County.

Another example came with the flu of 1918, when the newspaper confirmed that Mexicans were not admitted to St. John's Hospital west of the tracks. On November 4, 1918, *The Oxnard Daily Courier* reported front-page health updates about White residents recovering from the flu at St. John's Hospital, and in the next column over announced that Police Chief Murray had opened a "temporary city detention hospital to care for Mexicans stricken with the 'flu.'"[33] Reportedly, in a building on Seventh and Meta streets, east of the boulevard, "homeless and helpless" Mexican flu victims lay on donated cots and bedding, while Murray and an untrained, unnamed male citizen volunteer administered "heroic measures."[34] The article further noted that in the first night the makeshift facility served five patients, though one died because "some were too far gone. . . . The 'hospital' has been needed badly for several days."[35]

The same night the "hospital" opened, the city trustees directed firemen to wash some of the west-side streets and sidewalks, "as a precautionary health measure."[36] The following week, the superintendent of streets, Charles Green, received the assistance of "some 12 or 14 Mexicans" to clean "the alleys in the Mexican section of the city as a precaution against the spread of influenza, through unnecessary filth."[37] Praising their volunteerism, the newspaper recognized that "a great many Mexicans since the influenza epidemic started have been doing splendid work in co-operating with the city authorities."[38] The article did not explain why the city trustees directed firemen to clean the paved streets on the west side of town and left Green alone to sanitize the dirt alleys on the east side. This lack of explanation, and the evidence of Mexicans working to compensate for the lack of city resources or personnel hours, reflects the commonly held understanding that the east side simply would not receive the same treatment as the west side. City and school leaders rarely made public statements justifying this disparate treatment, but when they did, they usually identified Mexicans themselves as the problem. This attribution of blame functioned to absolve the companies recruiting and profiting from the low-wage labor Mexicans provided.[39]

In October 1919, the city's newly hired policewoman nurse, Mrs. May Webb, continued this pattern of casually blaming Mexicans regardless of the facts. She complained almost immediately of the conditions on the east side of town that she believed contributed to a potential health disaster: "If typhoid fever ever broke out in your city I don't see where it would stop on account of these swarms of flies," she declared, detailing, "the conditions here that draw flies and breed flies are 'simply terrible.'"[40] She publicly critiqued "housing conditions in some of the poorer quarters" as "terribly bad," and reminded the trustees that these problems lay "only two blocks from the main part of your city."[41] She also observed "bad" conditions west of the tracks, on C Street, and asserted, "You spend plenty of money . . . you have a good man on the job. It must be the fault of your people."[42] While detailing her observations, she expressed frustration that while she had expected to be a "nurse inspector," her work in Oxnard took on "more of a social service nature, to teach not only the minds but also the five senses," and "to teach common sense."[43] She condescendingly remarked, "Getting hold of the ever elusive Mexican children, whose parents have no conception whatever of the need of their children going to school," required her to be more of a truant officer than a nurse.[44]

Webb's claim that Mexicans were a problem shifted attention away from the infrastructure issues she had just outlined and back onto familiar ideological territory. In response, the city trustees took some blame for the "torn-up condition of the streets due to paving and gas improvements [on the west side]"[45] and thanked Policewoman Webb for her report. With their silence about the east side, they endorsed Webb's reasoning that lack of "common sense" on the part of Mexicans caused the "terribly bad" conditions.[46]

As Natalia Molina has explained, "Portraying people of Chinese, Mexican, and Japanese ancestry in Los Angeles as threats to public health and civic well-being obscured the real causes of communicable disease and illness— inadequate medical care, exposure to raw sewage, and malnutrition."[47] In Oxnard, as in Los Angeles and elsewhere, such institutionalized neglect toward Mexicans did not go unchallenged.

About a week after Policewoman Webb's report, at an October 1919 meeting of the Monday Club, Charles H. Weaver, an ABSC representative, discussed newly built houses for "foreign laborers,"[48] and work to promote Americanization by developing "a better understanding between the laborer and the beet growers."[49] Weaver's remarks about the "industrial standpoint" echoed the ABSC directive from the previous July, which had instructed factory managers and supervisors to treat the Mexican sugar-beet workers well, so they would continue to stay "loyal employees."[50] His anecdotal observation of "the necessity of these foreigners being taught some idea of thrift"[51] exposed the paternalistic approach of the ABSC. At the same meeting, Father Gorman spoke on behalf of Father Ramirez, a priest working "among the people of his nationality here in Oxnard," to convey his colleague's concern for "the necessity of understanding these people before you could expect to help them to become good American citizens."[52] Ramirez's call foreshadowed collective efforts to improve living conditions by working "among"

Mexicans. This contrasted with Weaver's call for understanding "between" the sugar-beet workers and their supervisors, which reified the unequal power dynamics between Mexicans and Whites. Such tensions of race and class, east and west, intensified as the Mexican population continued to grow in the city and schools.

Mexican labor indeed fueled tremendous growth and profit in the agricultural economy. Restrictions on Japanese and Chinese immigration and land ownership, and the revolution in Mexico, all contributed to higher numbers of Mexicans working in Ventura County fields, burgeoning packinghouses, and canneries.[53] U.S. Census records for Ventura County estimated that the population increased from 18,347 residents in 1910 to 28,724 in 1920.[54] During that same time, the city of Oxnard grew from a population of 2,555 to 4,417.[55] Historian Juan Gómez-Quiñones has noted that the peak in emigration from Mexico to the United States in the 1920s intensified anti-immigrant and "anti-Mexican rhetoric."[56]

In Oxnard, Whites employed anti-Mexican rhetoric when alluding to problematic social issues emanating from the east-side area, including hygiene and truancy. Without acknowledging the vested interest in maintaining the west side as exclusively White, these complaints about the Mexican community inadvertently exposed strategically constructed substandard housing east of the boulevard. The crescendo of voices blaming Mexicans as a problem in the 1920s enabled school officials to feverishly work toward complete segregation of Mexican children the following decade without any public rationalization.

WOMEN OF THE RED CROSS:
"WE ARE AFRAID OF NOBODY"

One notable challenge to the city trustees' refusal to understand and respond to the Mexican community's perspectives occurred during a "decidedly interesting and tense" half-hour meeting in 1920 between three women of the local Red Cross and the city trustees. Led by Mrs. Frank McCulloch, and including Miss Garrison, a nurse, and Mrs. Parker, an interpreter, these women had spoken with Mexican residents over a three-week period, as they had inspected each home and alley in the east-side area. They reported "terrible" housing conditions endured by Mexican laborers and their families.[57]

The newspaper detailed, "Needless to say they found lots of vermin, lots of flies and intolerable sanitary conditions in many places. But the good of the trip was found in the willingness on the part of the Spanish speaking population to co-operate with the Red Cross ladies, when they were shown how."[58] Here the reporter assumed most readers knew of the poor living conditions east of the boulevard (likely the Meta Street neighborhood) and presumed few would have considered the Mexican community's willingness to collaborate in forging a remedy.

The women described that a ditch on Eighth Street had become an open garbage dump, and that they gave instructions to the residents about how to cover the ditch and clean the area. They also instructed about sixty children how to dispose of the vermin in and around the dump. Considered in retrospect, this visceral detail exposed the city powerbrokers as "a threat and a menace" to Mexican schoolchildren, not the reverse, as Haydock had claimed a few years prior. As the Red Cross representatives expressed enthusiasm for the immediate, "gratifying results" of their visits, they framed the problem as one of inferior conditions, not inferior Mexican culture. McCulloch stated, "Recently we have been hearing lots about Americanization work among the foreigners ... but there is also lots to be done in Americanization with Americans, and that is where the work should start."[59] She went on to explain, "When the Mexicans were asked why they did not go to the landlord to have a window pane replaced, and sometimes all the window panes were found broken, and the holes nailed up but one, leaving the room dark and dismal, they were told that these tenants were afraid to ask for repairs, because when they did they often failed to get them, but the rent would be raised forthwith."[60] After confirming that she and the other women had the receipts of these higher rent bills in their possession, she continued: "All that these people want is to be shown how to be sanitary and to be treated like human beings. Treated in this way they respond, and it is up to the property owners to improve the conditions. We expect to notify the owners of the needed improvements, and will see to it that they make the places fit for human beings. We are no respecter of persons ... and we are afraid of nobody."[61]

Boldly asserting the human rights of Mexicans, McCulloch warned that she and her colleagues would not be intimidated in demanding safe, sanitary living conditions. The city trustees gave these women a few opportunities to demonstrate whether they indeed would back down. For instance, Nurse Garrison stated that within the adobe housing units of the ABSC, only three of the twenty-four toilets "were in good condition," and that during their visit they came across "a dead man, and the flies were bad."[62] City trustee Weaver, an ABSC supervisor, reportedly "arose a little hot under the collar" to challenge Garrison. He argued that the state inspectors "frequently commended the company for the way they looked after conditions there."[63] He suggested the responsibility for the nonworking toilets and the festering dead body lay with the residents, who, he reiterated, were provided housing without charge, exclaiming they lived "rent absolutely free."[64] The women of the Red Cross recognized that the ABSC intended to provide screens for the ABSC homes and that the city trustees planned for garbage removal, but they persisted in their critique, reiterating they would seek a remedy directly from the state housing commission if necessary.[65]

Mayor Herbert H. Eastwood positioned himself as unable to mitigate the situation, suggesting that the city trustees had no legal power to regulate housing conditions.[66] He also argued that landlords had their share of "troubles" attempting multiple times a month to collect rent on each residence. McCulloch countered, "Considering the investment made $3 a month on many of those shacks was big returns," and gave an example of "one small lot that brought the owner $25 a month in small rentals like that."[67] These interactions shed light on the city trustees' profit-driven paternalism, enabling overcrowded, "intolerable sanitary conditions" for Mexican residents. The city trustees, led by Mayor Eastwood, empathized with the landlords because they too were White landowners, real estate developers, growers, and representatives of the ABSC. They shared the perspective that Mexicans should be grateful for a job that provided them housing "rent absolutely free."[68] There is no record of Mayor Eastwood or the city trustees following through with their promise to review a list of offending landlords or to cooperate with the Red Cross efforts. A few months later, in February 1921, McCulloch resigned from "all committees of the local Red Cross and welfare work of the community on account of her [own] ill health."[69]

HAYDOCK'S "FUTURE AMERICAN"

Like Mayor Eastwood and the city trustees, Haydock exhibited a disregard for Mexicans. He reiterated these sentiments in a 1921 speech to the Oxnard Rotary Club.[70] Because his educational philosophy was not publicly recorded elsewhere, Haydock's 1921 remarks merit focused analysis. In line with the arguments of "scientific" racism and the eugenics movement,[71] he began with an assertion that the Puritans who landed on Plymouth Rock, Massachusetts, were "representative of the stock from which the pure American breed has sprung."[72] He referenced previous Rotarian discussions to explain that creating and maintaining the "purest breed" of dairy calves with "unquestioned pedigree" required a significant financial investment and the collective will to do so. He then connected this idea to schooling, assuring the audience that while he would support each child's aspirations, he also recognized that "some of these kids are going to become valuable assets, and some are going to become mighty expensive liabilities."[73] To drive home his point about the public's will to pay for high-quality education as one of the many challenges facing schools, he asserted, "The better the breed, the bigger and better the returns in every aspect."[74]

Haydock then discussed a recent report indicating that New Bedford, Massachusetts, had the country's highest rate of illiteracy. Referring to U.S. census data for 1919 and recalling his own trip to Boston a few years prior, he attributed the illiteracy rate to the influx of "foreigners" who did not speak English. He worried about the future of schooling in the United States given these realities: "I tell you it brings a touch of sadness to the man who traces his American ancestry back to preRevolutionary days; and it must bring misgivings to every American, even by adoption, who looks forward with real interest into the future of his country and its institutions."[75]

After these comments, he transitioned from the eastern region to the South, reflecting on the legacy of African slavery for the southern states and for the nation. He argued that the struggle to end slavery represented a "glorious victory for human rights," but warned, "Unto the last generation the sins of our forefathers will rest upon our children." To further this point, he explained:

> More than fifty years have elapsed since the black man was freed; yet a full billion dollars of the cost are charged on the books of the government against you and me. But that sinks into insignificance when we think of the more than seventeen millions of sons and daughters of these former slaves who are still with us and whose children will be with us to the end. What would we not give if the whole horrible story could be wiped out! How gladly would we double of [sic] treble the cost of the civil war if we could but remove every trace of Ethiopian blood from out [sic] national life. Be it ever so slight, even

as in the octoroon, the unfortunate is still a negro. Regrettable as this may be, it is nevertheless a fact. Few men will say that the American for which we hope and pray can ever be made out of such stock—that there can ever be a perfect fusion of black and white. And these few, if there can be any such, will not attempt to gainsay we have been set back generations in the development of our race and nation.[76]

While conveniently omitting the tremendous socioeconomic gains Whites and the country realized from slavery, he expressed fidelity to the concept of segregation, noting the futility of educating Blacks, or integrating them with Whites in the hopes of a "perfect fusion."[77] Why Haydock went into such detail about Blacks when there were only eight Black school-age children in the district at the time remains unclear. His racist remarks, however, expose the ideology undergirding his actions as a city and school official. Rather than make an explicit connection to Mexican children, he utilized these remarks to frame his subsequent discussion of "strictly local issues."[78]

Haydock asked his fellow Rotarians for their patience as he recounted figures of inconsistent attendance and low achievement, implying as a matter of fact that Mexicans were to blame for these patterns. He reported that he and the teachers had conducted a district-wide census of all the children ages three to seventeen in October 1920,[79] and found that of the 1,345 children counted, Whites comprised 53 percent and Blacks, Chinese, Japanese, and Mexicans made up 47 percent.[80] He further disaggregated these numbers to emphasize that Mexicans comprised 41 percent of the student population and that 60 percent of children ages three to seventeen had parents born outside the United States. "In other words," he explained, "the children whom it is our duty to prepare for American citizenship are preponderantly of foreign born parentage."[81] This highlighted the contrast between Haydock, who traced his "American ancestry back to preRevolutionary days," and the ostensibly foreign origins of most of the elementary schoolchildren in Oxnard.

Presenting anecdotal observations and "figures" as objective facts, Haydock noted cases of head lice, irregular attendance, and "retarded" promotion patterns—all problems supposedly attributed to Mexican children. Beyond this speech, public records fail to record any rationale for school segregation. Instead, Haydock and the other architects segregated Mexican children as a mundane practice. He concluded his speech by calling for Whites to pass on a hard work ethic to their boys: "We must teach the dignity of labor. We must do more than teach it: we must give it dignity; we must live it."[82] Haydock's "racially charged vision"[83] for education did not appear to extend dignity to Mexican laborers or their children.

THE MEXICAN COMMUNITY TAKES COLLECTIVE ACTION

About five months later, a group of thirty-three Colonia residents further exposed the institutionalized indifference toward Mexicans when they requested the city to move the dump away from their neighborhood. The newspaper reprint of their petition confirmed the Red Cross women's prior statement that when "treated like human beings" Mexicans would "respond."

Oxnard, Calif., June 1, 1922.

Members of the Oxnard City Council.

Gentlemen—We, the undersigned, residents and taxpayers of the city of Oxnard, and living in that section known as Colonia Home Gardens, due west and north of the city dumping grounds, do hereby respectfully petition the city council of Oxnard to declare the present city dumping grounds a public nuisance, unsanitary, and menacing to the health of the inhabitants in its near vicinity, and menacing as well to our livestock and garden plants, both of which are vitally essential and necessary to our peaceful endeavor of earning our living and sustaining the health of ourselves, our wives, our children, and others who may abide with us.

Not only has the city of Oxnard outgrown its present dumping facility, necessitating an immediate removal from its present location, but we declare said dumping ground unsightly, a breeder of disease, a menace to the health and to the moral stability of contentment to residents nearby. We therefore respectfully ask that the city council appoint a committee to investigate the truth of our grievance and to act upon our suggestion and the results of your committee's investigation with American fairness and Christian sympathy.

> *Signed, V. Zarate, C. Soutana, Juan Martinez, Jose Roduarte, Joes Martinez, Makule Chavez, Pedro Herrera, Cecilio Ybarro, Otancio Nilo, Jesus Morales, Fernando Jabalos, Jose Romero, Reyes Landon, Chas Martel, Pete Marrie, Y. Rubio, Josephine Andrade, Camile Herrera, Santiago Meredez, E. Rubio, A. Leon, Mrs. M. Silveria, Serapio Rivay, Pans Padille, Gil Razo, Jose Ramirez, Aurelio Moreno, John V. Sotelo, Amador Jimenez, Patricio Martinez, O. Cortez, Daniel Mendosa, Rito Gonzalez.*

After note—the above signatures are only those who are not living on the aforesaid tract. There is almost double the number who have lots and who will all, in the very near future make their residence with the others who have signed.[84]

Inserting their voices into the public record about living conditions in La Colonia, these Mexican women and men strategically asserted themselves as a legitimate, financially contributing, and demographically significant part of Oxnard. While the newspaper condescendingly headlined their letter "Colonia Gardens Folk Petition City Dads to Change City Dump,"[85] they positioned themselves as taxpayers and residents who requested consideration as equal citizens pursuing the "peaceful endeavor of earning our living and sustaining the health of ourselves, our wives, our children." These women and men understood the racial hierarchy, which identified Mexicans as the source of the problems in La Colonia. Their petition posed a direct challenge to Haydock's 1917 call for a policewoman nurse because Mexicans, he claimed, would otherwise "become a threat and a menace to the welfare of the community."[86] They declared the dumping facility as the "menace" to their "health and moral stability" and proposed that an investigation would corroborate their claims. Whereas Haydock had referred to Mexicans as livestock, the petitioners asserted their humanity, describing the dump as a threat to their livestock and livelihood. They also appealed to the moral conscience of the city trustees, requesting timely consideration based on "American fairness and Christian sympathy."[87] To avoid dismissal of their request as a concern of a small minority, the petitioners noted that imminent population growth in the area necessitated urgent action.

While it remains unclear whether the petition successfully elicited enough "American fairness and Christian sympathy" from the city trustees to remove the city dump from La Colonia,[88] a few months later, in December 1922, the newspaper confirmed persistent substandard conditions east of the railroad tracks: "Residents of the Colonia Home Gardens on the east side of the railroad tracks north of the Oxnard Municipal water works will soon have water service. . . . The W. H. Lathrop piece, between the Colonia subdivision and the railroad tracks will also be piped for water . . . the work of laying the pipes and putting in connections has just started. . . . The residents of that section are to pay for the installation of the pipe. They are still without electric service or sewerage."[89] The article offered no explanation for why the city trustees held east-side residents financially responsible, above and beyond their taxes, for infrastructure projects the city fully subsidized for west-side residents.

Records confirm that developers such as Walter H. Lathrop, who also served as a city trustee,[90] extended basic amenities to La Colonia only when profitable. As the demand for labor and subsequent need for housing continued to increase, the geographic containment of Mexicans east of the tracks became more complicated.

SEGREGATED PLAYGROUNDS

In addition to segregating Mexican families geographically, Whites sought ways to socially contain Mexican children through playground activities. In May 1923, the newspaper reported on plans for Oxnard Community Service to train "play leaders" from cities throughout Ventura County in "an all-round program of community recreation."[91] The wives of many city leaders, including Mrs. Matthew Lehmann, Mrs. Henry Levy, Mrs. Charles Donlon, and Mrs. Rudolph Beck, simultaneously announced that Community Service would initiate "recreation for women and girls."[92] These committees adapted regional programming that ensured leisure activities would be racially distinct for Whites and Mexicans.[93]

For example, a few months later, in July 1923, Mrs. Charles Weaver, who had previously led an ABSC Americanization committee, proclaimed that in response to a needs assessment survey of the Mexican community, and "in connection with the playground movement now underway in Oxnard," she would "organize a class in games and story-telling for Mexican children."[94] In 1924, Community Service established a dedicated recreational space on the corner of Saviers Road and Sixth Street, which reportedly attracted about two hundred children on an average day, even before the construction of a playground apparatus.[95] This was commonly known as the Mexican playground. Within three years, the ABSC donated land on Seventh Street to move and expand the space for inclusion of *rebote* (handball) courts, baseball stops, and a "play apparatus."[96]

For Mexicans, the playground became a site for community building and organizing.[97] The board of directors of Community Service elected Mexican men as playground directors, and Mexican residents volunteered for the tasks of building, maintaining, moving, and cleaning the playground.[98] They requested support to utilize the outdoor recreational areas for community musical endeavors, which led to the creation of a successful Mexican band, comprising men who labored in the sugar factory, and a Mexican girls' chorus.[99] Here men, women, and children cultivated their artistic talents and athletic skills and interacted in competitive and collaborative ways, beyond their roles as laborers.

For Whites, the space ensured the social separation of Mexican children from their own. Public writings about the Mexican playground suggest that Whites framed their efforts in supporting segregated recreational activities as altruistic contributions to pluralism. Tam Deering, a secretary of Oxnard Community Service, wrote in a nationally circulated magazine that the idea for the playground built on efforts "to overcome the indifference and more or less ill-feeling on the part of the Anglo-Americans toward the Mexicans."[100] He went on to critique "superficial methods of past Americanization work," noting that a more effective "means for fostering cooperation between the Anglo-Americans and Latin-Americans in Oxnard is to be found in the leisure time activities."[101] Six months later, in February 1924, the newspaper boasted that Oxnard Community Service had received national recognition by the Elks organization for playground activities, which ostensibly reduced crime:

> Oxnard, California, in the sugar beet section, has a bit of a problem in its Mexican inhabitants. Strangers in a land that was once theirs, they spent most of their leisure hours in poolrooms or the police court, until someone had the idea of building a court for their favorite game of rebote, the Mexican version of handball. Now the Mexican interpreters [*sic*] in the courts is on a permanent vacation and the beet growers go to the rebote courts instead of the employment agencies for extra men when harvest time comes around.[102]

Published as front-page news in *The Oxnard Daily Courier*, this article, touting recognition by a racially exclusive organization such as the Elks, exemplified the paternalistic ideology driving Haydock and the other White architects' efforts to contain and control the "Mexican problem."[103] Indeed, the playground reified racial segregation as a seemingly natural, everyday part of life in the city.

WANTED AS LABORERS, BUT NOT STUDENTS

By October 1923, the school trustees' minutes report "very badly crowded" conditions in schools requiring "immediate action."[104] In August of that year, the Oxnard Grammar School had burned down, and Theodore Roosevelt School was constructed on the same grounds, on Third Street between A and B streets.[105] In 1924, the school board oversaw the building of a third school, Woodrow Wilson School, on Palm Drive and C Street.[106] The board's minutes note ongoing concern about accommodating students within their three available facilities: Haydock, Wilson, and Roosevelt.

A January 1926 meeting of the Oxnard Parent-Teachers' Association (PTA) demonstrated that the White community shared this anxiety. *The Oxnard Daily Courier* reported on a meeting of approximately one hundred members of the PTA discussing the need to move forward on school segregation plans. A local minister, the Reverend Thomas Burden, led the meeting that night, and in his opening remarks explained: "Forty percent of Oxnard school children are of Spanish extraction, and the question here is an important one. Neighboring cities have dealt with the situation effectively by the separate school system. Santa Paula is a notable example."[107] For Burden and the PTA, the "question" of segregation appeared to be "an important one" simply based on demographics. The group understood that his reference to children of "Spanish extraction" meant Mexican.

In Santa Paula, an agricultural town about fifteen miles northeast of Oxnard, school officials and church leaders argued for segregating Mexicans based on supposed hygiene, language, and cultural needs. These unsubstantiated claims justified actions to segregate Mexicans within existing Santa Paula facilities, and complete segregation in the Canyon School, beginning in the 1925–26 academic year.[108] The main teacher of the Canyon School, Miss Dorothy Lewis, spoke to the Oxnard PTA about "her supervision of between 800 and 1000 Mexican pupils" in kindergarten through eighth grade in this facility, and "illustrated graphically with her talk what has been accomplished by separate schools."[109] Further inspired by the Santa Paula example and Burden's remarks, the PTA planned to assign a committee to "cooperate with the Oxnard school trustees in considering this matter as a constructive issue to be solved at once."[110]

Regional labor demands intensified "overcrowding" in schools and the pressure on the trustees to segregate Mexican children.[111] On Thursday, March 4, 1926, the Oxnard Chamber of Commerce adopted a resolution favoring "unrestricted immigration for Mexicans into this state, on the ground that the farmers would be crippled without Mexican labor."[112] Within the week, *The Oxnard Daily Courier* questioned the Chamber's position in relation to schools. Under the headline "Our Race Problem," the newspaper suggested that unrestricted Mexican immigration presented a greater threat than "the so-called Japanese menace," but "the danger ... is escaping our notice under the spur of present economic necessity."[113] The brief editorial continued, "It is quite probable that the Mexican birthrate is almost as large as the Japanese ... the adult population in Oxnard is probably two whites to one Mexican, and yet the ratio in grammar school enrollment is just reversed."[114] The newspaper editors urged resolute, concerted action from school officials: "For many years there has been a demand for segregation in our local schools, but conditions have not been such in the past as to justify the remark reported to have been made by Principal R. B. Haydock of the Oxnard grammar schools that he would be glad to provide separate schools for the white children providing the white people will furnish them."[115] This critique of Haydock articulated an expectation that city officials and school leaders would dedicate public resources to segregate Mexicans from Whites.

In November 1927, the PTA again met to talk about segregation, this time with the school board and Superintendent Haydock present. Together they discussed a ruling by the U.S. Supreme Court denying a Chinese American girl, Martha Lum, access to an all-White high school in Mississippi.[116] Oxnard's PTA president, Mrs. Sam Weill, explained that locally, "there is no objection to the Japanese or Chinese children, as they are cleanly and of a high standard of intellect. The school district does not have sufficient funds to completely segregate the Latin American children from the American children, but we have already accomplished separation in cases where particularly desirable."[117] This clarification established that the PTA and the district officials distinguished Mexicans as a separate and inferior class of children, and shared an understanding that complete segregation would be the goal, when funds became available. They extended the privilege of integration with Whites to Japanese and Chinese children, whom they perceived to be "cleanly and of a high standard of intellect."[118] Records show no evidence of how the district made these determinations, other than by race. Superintendent Haydock contributed to the conversation, noting that "states already have the power to decide the question of segregation, because each separate state has its own particular problems. The Supreme Court ruling does not change the situation in California."[119] Ventura County justice of the peace Judge C. J. Elliott also remarked that the current practice of separating Mexican children from Whites within the same facility represented the most feasible way to avoid integration. This pragmatic strategy delineated the racial hierarchy in schools, with Whites at the top and in the position to determine the racial order beneath them. Judge Elliott reassured the PTA: "It is the right thing to do, and it is to the advantage of both races to be separated up to about the eighth grade. Children of foreign parentage can be better educated when they have their own classes. It is not necessary to build separate buildings, having separate schoolrooms in the same school is sufficient."[120]

Taken together, Superintendent Haydock and Judge Elliott interpreted the school-within-a-school strategy as legally valid and within their authority. Knowing there were no provisions under California statutes to segregate Mexican children on the basis of simply being Mexican, Haydock, the PTA, and civic leaders such as Judge Elliott manufactured the myth that Mexican children posed an escalating racial threat in schools. Without substantiating repeated claims of lower intelligence and poor hygiene, they pursued a strategy of segregation that separated Mexican students as an ostensibly necessary, and even benevolent policy. Indeed, their sense of urgency to segregate increased in step with further growth of the city's Mexican population. U.S. Census records show that by 1930, Mexicans comprised at least 13,839 of Ventura County's 54,976 residents (approximately 25%).[121] By 1927, children of Mexican descent accounted for 34 percent of Ventura County's public and Catholic elementary school enrollments, while Japanese students represented a little over 1 percent.[122] Statewide, over 70 percent of Mexican elementary schoolchildren "were reported as born in the United States."[123] In Oxnard, the trustees recognized that Mexican students did indeed account for "about two-thirds" of the elementary school population, and that almost all of these children were U.S. citizens.[124] Race apparently trumped citizenship status for the trustees, who in violation of the law worked to "completely segregate" Mexican children.[125]

In 1927, when the House Immigration Committee in Washington, DC, held hearings about whether to include Mexico in the Immigration Quota Act, California representatives again argued against restricting Mexican immigration.[126] The Los Angeles Chamber of Commerce also urged Oxnard Chamber of Commerce members to write to their senators and congressmen, "requesting that they use every effort to defeat enactment of any legislation which would disrupt the present status of immigration between the United States and Mexico."[127] These growers and Oxnard business owners held a vested interest in unrestricted Mexican immigrant labor.[128] Like other towns and cities across the Southwest, Mexicans were welcomed to the extent that they continued to enable the accumulation of wealth for the nation, but they were never quite considered "fit to be citizens,"[129] or students.

School officials also contributed to this problem with inconsistent and insufficient provisions for children of migrant farmworkers. One researcher, Wilbur K. Cobb, observed that for Ventura County children who worked alongside their parents harvesting walnuts prior to 1928, "there had been no concerted effort to provide schooling facilities. Some districts provided rooms for these migratory children with a half-hearted program. Others treated them as unwanted, while one school known to the writer [Cobb] put up a big sign, 'No Migratory Children Wanted Here.'"[130] *The Oxnard Daily Courier* reported that some Ventura County schools incorporated walnut and bean "holidays" into their academic year, stopping classes for up to four weeks during the harvests.[131]

"LITTLE BITS OF MEXICANS"

In October 1927, Ventura County superintendent of schools Blanche T. Reynolds[132] warned growers and parents that the walnut harvest could no longer take priority over school.[133] She explained, "Hundreds of children are working in the walnut orchards, and this is plainly against the law."[134] In 1919, she asserted the need for Mexican children to attend school from an early age. Speaking to an audience of about seventy-five people at Oxnard Union High School, she introduced a keynote speaker by remarking that she had initially believed in prioritizing that "older Mexican children should be educated," and recounted examples of teenage Mexicans drawing pictures in a first-grade class.[135] Without explaining why these youth may not have previously attended school, she stated that the underenrollment of younger children in schools presented an even more pressing concern. She told the audience she had become "firmly convinced that the 'little bits of Mexicans' are of first importance, and a greater serious problem to the community."[136] Her demeaning reference to children as "little bits of Mexicans" typified Reynolds's mundane disregard for the Mexican community, evidenced in her words and deeds as the county's top education official.

Reynolds's invited lecturer, Dr. Frank Fielding Nalder from the University of California, further revealed the racist framework developing in Ventura County schools.[137] According to Nalder, "Norwegians and Danes were easily assimilated. They made our best citizens and many of our most prominent men are of this race. These people mix easily with Americans and quickly learn our language."[138] In contrast, he argued, southern European immigrants "do not assimilate so easily and have a tendency to keep in colonies."[139] He cited the 1910 census that "over five and a half million people over 10 years of age" did not speak, read, or write English, which he stated "constituted a real problem before this country."[140] He then applied his concerns to Oxnard, observing: "This morning in the grammar school I noticed one frail school teacher in charge of 45 Mexican children. As each Mexican child is as hard to teach as two Americans because the teacher has to first teach in Mexican and then in American, this was altogether a too hard job."[141] Titled "Education and Inheritance," Nalder's speech presented ideas that Haydock would affirm in his "Education and the Future American" speech three years later. Both presented ideology as fact and framed their observations of Mexicans in schools as local problems connected to nation, race, and culture.

Reynolds contributed significantly to casting Mexicans as racial problems that must be contained. Eight years after talking about "little bits of Mexicans," she spoke about the enforcement of compulsory education laws and her duty to ensure that Mexican children of migrant farmworkers received an education. Still, she complained, financially "this presents a real problem to us, not only to get these children into school, but to provide the schools for them."[142] She explained, "In some instances the parents are to blame, but in other cases employers of these children will be cited to appear before the labor commissioner on the charge of violating the state labor laws."[143]

Reynolds's October 1927 resolve to follow the law did not last long. Three months after asserting, "The Mexican child as well as others must be given an opportunity to receive an education. They are as much entitled to it as any," she told the Oxnard Rotary Club that Mexican immigration should be restricted altogether because "Mexican costs are too high."[144] Her January 1928 remarks before the club and its president, Superintendent Haydock, began with a plea, "Give us a chance to make proper American citizens out of the Mexicans by not flooding our country with them."[145] Reynolds reported that in the 1926–27 academic year Mexican children comprised 4,886 (33%) of the 14,887 total county school enrollments. She noted that accounting for Mexicans presented a unique challenge because, she claimed, "they scattered like quail when the officer came to see them."[146] Reynolds's dehumanizing reference to Mexicans as quails echoed her previous public remarks and realigned her with Haydock, who had likened Mexicans to "livestock."[147]

Reynolds expressed frustration that Mexicans burdened public resources at the expense of "American taxpayers." She estimated that since they accounted for 33 percent of the student population, at least one-third of the county's schooling budget went to Mexican children. She lamented that these "American" tax dollars spent educating Mexicans had to be directed toward fixing Mexican children's "handicap" in English and compensating for the delays in the migrant students' promotion to the next grade. Clearly conscious that Rotarian members included local growers and businessmen, Reynolds avoided mention of her recent cooperation with state authorities in citing employers who violated labor and compulsory school attendance laws. Instead, she sought to convince the group that the benefits of open Mexican immigration policies could not be reconciled with the detrimental impacts Mexicans caused to "Americans" in schools and beyond. She characterized Spanish speaking as a disadvantage and generalized that "the average Mexican child" took two years to complete one grade, which "drags down the average for the American child."[148] She went on to present data on the disproportionate incarceration and mental health hospitalization rates of Mexicans. As she continued to position her ideological arguments as facts, she warned that increased Mexican immigration would exacerbate children's academic underachievement and adult incarceration, leading to an inevitable "lowering by the Mexicans of the moral and health tone of our children, and of the general community."[149]

While Reynolds's position against Mexican children seemed to contradict her previous calls for their receiving access to education, her condescending tone of racial superiority remained consistent. Her comments reverberated with Haydock's 1917 arguments to the city trustees, warning that Mexican children posed an urgent "threat and a menace" to schools with their "filth and contagion and disease."[150] Reynolds concluded with more of the same contemptuous remarks: "Mexicans are not immoral . . . they are merely unmoral. They don't know any better . . . they will lower and undermine our lives and standards eventually if floods of them are let in in the future as at present."[151] *The Oxnard Daily Courier* reported that Reynolds's talk elicited "lively discussion" among the Rotarians and that club president Haydock postponed full deliberations "til a future meeting can take care of the question."[152] The newspaper did not report on those deliberations, and after this article rarely published civic or school leaders making such blatant assertions of White racial superiority over Mexicans.[153]

Though their bigoted views were not so publicly expressed on the front page of the newspaper, by 1930 the White architects had embedded their racist ideologies into public policies within and beyond schools. They strategically implemented separate and unequal treatment for children of Mexican descent as mundane educational practice. Indeed, the ideologies of Haydock, Thornton, Reynolds, and leaders of the PTA were deeply felt in the everyday schooling experiences of Mexican children.

"DRAW A CIRCLE IN THE DIRT"

So one day, I don't know what I said, anyways, it was a Spanish word, and oh God, you'd think I'd done away with the school or something. They put me on restriction. I had to get a rock, draw a circle in the dirt, and stand in the middle ... until the bell rang, and I felt like a weird person because, you know, everybody would come by and look at me, like I was on display. . . . And I felt like the ugliest, the dirtiest little girl around, you know, really bad. . . . I could have forgotten Spanish right then and there, but I thought, "no." [Laughs]

—ANTONIA ARGUELLES DILIELLO[154]

Antonia Arguelles (DiLiello) was born in Winfield, Kansas, in 1925 and enrolled in the second grade at Roosevelt School in 1932, after her family moved to Oxnard. In addition to segregated classrooms, distinct recess/lunch play areas, and public punishment for speaking Spanish, Antonia and other Mexican children who attended Oxnard schools in the 1930s were sent home at least ten minutes after White students each afternoon—to avoid potential interracial socializing.

Antonia remembered this scene over seventy years after it had occurred. She recognized that the punishment was intended to be memorable, to teach her a lesson about the error of speaking her language, even outside of class. She admittedly felt horrible, "like the ugliest, the dirtiest little girl around." Yet she also laughed, in retrospect, about the fact that she refused to forget Spanish. She went on to say that she and her friends learned to be "very careful" to avoid punishment. "By the time I got to Wilson School, I made sure if I spoke Spanish, it would be when none of the teachers were around."[155] Her narrative sheds much light on the ways Mexican American children confronted subtle and stunning racism in school.

Antonia's parents immigrated from Chihuahua, Mexico, to El Paso, Texas, in 1906. Her father, who had worked for a smelting company in Texas and as a railroad worker in Kansas, labored in the fields and in the street maintenance department for the city of Oxnard. In addition to being a homemaker, her mother worked seasonally pitting apricots and shelling walnuts. To financially contribute to the household, her two older brothers stopped attending school after junior high and started working full time. During the summers, the entire family camped in the nearby Conejo Valley Ranch to harvest and pit apricots.[156] Antonia remembered feeling conflicted about her family's social circumstances, which seemed to stand in stark contrast to what her teachers said made America great. She explained, "Going through school, we were made to believe that the country was beautiful and we had all of these things. Things that our parents couldn't afford."[157] To make sense of why her family was so poor in comparison to White families just across the tracks, she theorized that her father did not want to work hard enough. "I think that's when I decided my dad was lazy. 'Cause we didn't have the things they had. And so maybe because he's lazy we don't have the things they have, which is so sad."[158]

Years later, she realized that stereotypes about Mexicans likely reinforced what she learned at school, and contributed to her unsubstantiated belief that her dad was lazy. Eventually, as part of a family history project, she discovered evidence that her father had been commended for working in an "industrious and conscientious manner,"[159] and that he did so until personnel regulations necessitated his compulsory retirement at age seventy.[160] She expressed a sense of embarrassment that she did not fully appreciate this as a child. "I can remember my father going out clean, clean as a whistle, and coming back dirty from head to toe from working in the fields. I thought he was lazy, I really thought he was lazy! And I thought, my gosh, it's so sad, because that's the picture they give you and that's what you think."[161] In hindsight, she regretted being unable to see her father as the hard worker he was. Being publicly humiliated at school and "shunned" in places around Oxnard further distorted the "picture" Antonia held in her head and the shame she felt about her family and herself. As a child, Antonia could not shake the feeling that she was dirty and ugly. Indeed, the daily disparate treatment of Mexican American children such as Antonia sent insidious messages about race, class, and gender, which reverberated well beyond the classroom.

CONCLUSION

In this chapter, I analyzed the ways the White architects embedded their racial ideologies into the very structures, practices, and discourses of schooling in Oxnard from the city's founding. They divided the city by residence and race and according to an understood racial hierarchy. They intentionally established separate, unequal schooling and housing conditions for Mexican families. Their school-within-a-school strategy of segregation normalized discrimination against Mexican American students and aimed to limit their social mobility.

Antonia's voice and other oral histories throughout this book help to reassert the human experiences of mundane racism. Their collective memories complicate mainstream accounts of Oxnard's history that almost completely ignore those laborers and their families who contributed in multiple pioneering ways to the developing city. The resilience of Antonia, her peers, and the generations that followed contested the White architects' attempts to frame them as a health menace, a tax burden, and a race problem. In the next chapter, I consider experiences of Mexican youth as they navigated Oxnard's east-west "color-line."[162] I document the White architects' strategic interconnection of school and residential segregation, examining how these school and civic leaders codified their racist words through their property deeds.

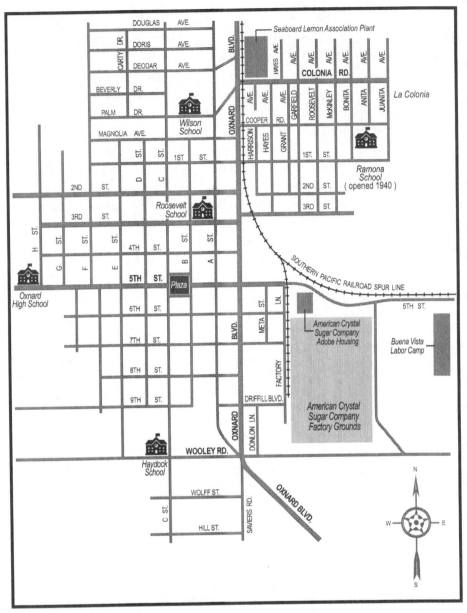

MAP I. Oxnard, California, circa 1950. Adapted from original by George W. Y. Moller. Not to scale. Courtesy of the Museum of Ventura County and Oxnard School District.

TWO

Pernicious Deeds

RESTRICTIVE COVENANTS AND SCHOOLS

It was kind of an unwritten rule that drew a line between White residents and Mexican residents. Some of those things are hard to pinpoint but they are understood. Most White residents lived in what is now known as the historical district, two-story homes, some of them. That district incidentally was near the Santa Clara church and schools. Mexicans lived in more moderate homes or rundown shacks and they were located in other parts of Oxnard, mainly around Meta Street. And then later, when Meta got filled, a new neighborhood developed called La Colonia, across the tracks where it was almost exclusively Mexican.

—MIGUEL ESPINOSA

MIGUEL ESPINOSA[1] WAS BORN IN VENTURA in 1933, and grew up in Oxnard keenly aware of the "unwritten," yet "understood" rule that geographically divided the city by race. As detailed in the previous chapter, from the city's founding, Haydock and other White architects strategically constructed La Colonia as a substandard place that housed a predominately Mexican population of factory laborers, field workers, and their families. At the same time, they developed Oxnard's west side to accommodate White supervisors, landowners, and school and civic leaders, replete with "first class" residences[2] and a business district that included all the amenities of a modern town (e.g., electricity, paved roads, sidewalks, gas, water, sewage, trash collection, street lights, and telephone service).

While Miguel may not have been privy to the racial covenants filed with the county clerk that restricted west-side properties, he and his peers who came of age during the 1940s learned their "place" in Oxnard by witnessing and experiencing limited access to White spaces well beyond schools. In this chapter, I expand on my examination of the White architects' strategies of segregation to analyze the interconnection they forged between school and residential segregation. Considering the link between these two seemingly discrete forms of discrimination[3] across four decades, from the 1920s through the 1950s, I explore the subtle and stunning spatial mechanisms of mundane racism in Oxnard.[4]

David Montejano has explained, "Residential segregation demarcated, in a highly visible way, the distinct social standing of Anglo and Mexican. . . . Segregated schools were a straightforward reflection of the racial divisions of farm towns."[5] In Oxnard, the White architects designed housing and school segregation to permanently limit the socioeconomic mobility of Mexicans. From the city's incorporation in 1903 until 1939, Oxnard had three schools for children in kindergarten through eighth grade: Richard B. Haydock, Theodore Roosevelt, and Woodrow Wilson. These schools were all located west of Oxnard Boulevard and the railroad tracks. The majority of Mexican families lived east of the tracks and the boulevard, but not by chance.[6] County records demonstrate extensive use of racially restrictive covenants by individual homeowners, mortgage companies, and land developers to prohibit Mexicans and other People of Color from purchasing, renting, and occupying properties west of the tracks. These racial restrictions contributed to a concentration of poverty on the east side and limited educational access for Colonia residents.[7] The relegation of Mexicans to substandard housing and segregated schooling conditions in Oxnard came to be "understood" as a mundane reality. Whites continually contributed to and enforced this "color-line."[8]

"NOT A SINGLE MEXICAN FAMILY"

On April 21, 1938, Alice Shaffer wrote a letter to the Oxnard School Board of Trustees, protesting a disruption of racial segregation that she and her neighbors had previously enjoyed. She urged the board to pursue the academic separation of Mexican children from Whites with more consideration for residential segregation: "About two years ago, Haydock Grammar School was taken away from the use of the American children and given bodily over to the use of Mexicans. . . . This leaves all of Oxnard, from fourth Street . . . to Hill Street, without a school for American children; and the children from the south part of town have to pass the Mexicans coming from the northerly parts of town on their ways to school."[9] Shaffer positioned herself as a representative for a group of concerned parents and neighbors as she demanded an explanation for the removal of White children from Haydock School.[10] Her letter revealed that she knew Mexicans were prohibited from living in her residential tract. She believed the school board shared this awareness and would subsequently understand her entitlement to racially exclusive schooling for her children. Her letter continued:

> We resent the implication that the Acre Tract is a Mexican district, inasmuch as there is not a single Mexican family living in the Acre Tract. Wolff Street is one of the finest streets in Oxnard, and there are good homes throughout this whole district. The fact that the Haydock School was close was one attraction to those who bought property and built homes in this locality, and we object to having to provide means to convey our children to a distant school, when there is a good one close at hand.[11]

Shaffer's street references and her grant deeds confirm she did in fact own properties in racially restricted neighborhoods, including the Wolff Hill Laubacher Subdivision.[12] Her resentment expressed her belief that the trustees had violated a tacit "racial contract" that she and her neighbors had bought into—that schools should serve Whites, not Mexicans. She insisted that the trustees prioritize the needs of White students, recommending, "If there is an urgent need to care for the Mexican Children, a school should be built in Colonia Gardens, or somewhere else in close proximity to their homes."[13] Unbeknownst to Shaffer, the board had previously fielded similar complaints from White parents.[14] Though they did not move to approve the construction of a new school east of the tracks for another year,[15] the trustees responded to Shaffer within a week.

Indeed, four days later, in a letter dated April 25, 1938, school trustee John H. Burfeind wrote, "The present School Board is not responsible for the schools being located where they are and the change that was made two years ago was at the request of a large group of parents living in your part of Town."[16] In fact, Burfeind had designed the very enrollment shifts Shaffer now protested.[17] He referred to these changes with a carefully worded note about the constraints under which the trustees functioned, trying to maintain a dual school system that privileged Whites in a heavily Mexican district. He wrote:

> At that time there were about three foreign children to one American in the Haydock School. This condition was what we attempted to overcome. About two-thirds of the youngsters going to our Schools today are of Mexican parentage. However, of this total there are only about sixty who are not American born and are legally entitled to all of the advantages of any other American citizen. Too, there are not enough American youngsters to fill any one of our Schools.[18]

According to Burfeind, the number of Mexican students had demographically necessitated the trustees' actions two years prior. Still, he also pointed out, the board had a legal obligation to educate Mexican children, regardless of citizenship. Burfeind went on to explain that in terms of the structure of the facilities, neither Roosevelt nor Wilson School could enroll students in kindergarten through eighth grade, so Haydock School represented the only option for enrolling all grades of Mexican children. Perhaps unsatisfied with the board's response, Shaffer began to sell her Hill Street properties in 1940.[19]

Though Burfeind's letter denied it, the school board, and certainly Superintendent Haydock, guided the location of the schools.[20] As outlined in the previous chapter, Haydock was the first mayor of Oxnard and then served as a city trustee for at least a decade, alongside city council members who also served as school board members. Burfeind's strategic positioning of the school trustees as neutral administrators belied the fact that they did indeed share knowledge of racially identifiable residential spaces. References to geographic locations permeate the board minutes in relation to race. For example, in September 1937, the board discussed the urgent need to relieve overcrowding in White classrooms while pursuing the complete segregation of Mexican students. They considered, "a. Enrollment by schools, b. By nationality; White, Oriental, Mexican, [and] c. By residence, north or south of Fifth Street."[21] The trustees' plan to utilize Fifth Street to determine school enrollments demonstrated their consciousness of residential segregation.[22] Ventura County records further show that these school board members did more than simply empathize with White parents who sought to avoid both social and academic integration with Mexicans.

"STRICTLY IN THE CAPACITY OF SERVANT"

Said property shall not, nor shall any interest therein, at any time, be leased, sold, devised, or conveyed to or inherited by or otherwise acquired by or become the property of a person whose blood is not entirely that of the Caucasian Race . . . but if persons not of the Caucasian Race be kept thereon by a Caucasian occupant, strictly in the capacity of servant of such occupant, such circumstances shall not constitute a violation of this condition . . . [which] shall be perpetual.

—GRANT DEED OF BEN S. VIRDEN, 1931[23]

The men who served as school trustees omitted their rationale for segregating Mexican children in their meeting minutes, but included very specific language in their property deeds. As school board president from 1916 to 1930 and city treasurer from 1910 to 1920, Ben S. Virden's record as a public servant was absolute, with a fixed beginning and end to his period of service. His grant deed, however, specified "perpetual" restrictions for non-Whites, except as servants.[24] Virden's colleague and successor as president, trustee Noble A. Powell, also bought property that prohibited sale, rental, lease, *occupancy, use,* or *inheritance* to non-Whites, unless they worked for the White property owner, as a condition held to be "perpetual and binding forever."[25] Likewise, trustee Roy B. Witman, the school board clerk from 1916 to 1930, bought property in a northwest subdivision, which prohibited ownership by "persons not of the Caucasian race" and specified "particularly that no part of the same shall be sold, conveyed, leased or rented to any person of the Negro, Japanese or Chinese race, or to any Mexican, Indian, or East-Indian."[26]

Property deeds, indentures, mortgage agreements, and maps from the Ventura County clerk and recorder demonstrate that what Miguel thought was an "unwritten rule" was actually a set of officially recorded real estate agreements binding most of the residential lots, tracts, and subdivisions west of Oxnard Boulevard and the railroad tracks. This evidence confirms that school board members, principals, and teachers bought, sold, and lived in properties bound by racial covenants. Some school officials directly challenged Mexican land holdings in court and others obtained or inherited lots from previous legal rulings.[27] They regularly conducted school business with other White immigrants, who likewise acquired partitions of land that they encumbered with racial restrictions. None of the school officials removed the racial covenants from their properties, as they profited from them and passed them on to their spouses and children.

While continuing the practice of omitting any rationale for separating Mexican children from Whites, Burfeind and his fellow school trustees Dr. Everett C. Beach, Dr. Ray Erwin Dockstader, and Elmer W. Power exercised their knowledge of Oxnard's racial geography to guide school segregation plans. Their designs for shifting school and class enrollments accounted for race and residence because they each endorsed and contributed to housing discrimination. These deliberate contributions to residential segregation complicate the notion that school segregation simply reflected established housing patterns beyond their control.

For example, school board president Dockstader's property prohibited sale or conveyance to "any person of the Negro, Japanese, or Chinese race, nor to any Mexican or Indian."[28] Racial covenants often specifically excluded Mexicans, despite the fact that Mexicans were considered White by law. Dockstader's deed also restricted the subdivision for use "exclusively as a first class residence property,"[29] reiterating the social location of Mexicans and other People of Color as distinct groups of second-class residents.

In addition to his personal residence, trustee Beach purchased large parcels of land from Eugene H. Agee, Adolph J. Carty, and Edwin L. Carty, who each integrated racial restrictions into individual deed grants within their tracts and filed long-term reservations, restrictions, and protective covenants to bind their entire subdivisions well into the 1960s.[30] Agee's "protective covenant" over Beach's property exemplified how U.S. citizenship did not necessarily ensure civil rights benefits for Mexicans: "No persons of any race other than the White or Caucasian race, nor any Mexican, Indian, or East Indian, nor any person who is a lineal descendant of the first or second degree of a person born in the Republic of Mexico, shall use or occupy any building, or any lot, except that this covenant shall not prevent occupancy by domestic servants of a different race domiciled with an owner or tenant."[31] Such reservations underscored the "racial contract" at play in Oxnard, where Whites accepted Mexicans as servants and expected future generations to remain in these roles.

Beach's colleague, trustee Power, bought and sold racially restricted properties from Walter H. Lathrop, a city councilman and land developer who constructed residences on both sides of the tracks—though his lots on the east side did not include running water, electricity, or sewage.[32] Power's westside Lathrop lot was amenity rich and racially exclusive. His additional westside property also denied rental, use, or occupancy to "any person not of the White or Caucasian race, except such as are in the employ of the owners or tenants of said lots residing thereon."[33]

Beach and his trustee colleagues also partnered, as an official policy-making body, with businessmen such as Agee and with civic leaders who bought, lived in, and sold properties with racial covenants intact.[34] Extensive use of racial restrictions, including by city trustees and mayors Herbert H. Eastwood[35] and Edwin L. Carty,[36] contributed to this legitimization of segregation in housing and schools. The business, civic, and social connections of these White architects helped establish and maintain the color line as seemingly natural and normal. Carty in particular exemplified the entrench-ment of White landowning farming families within this network. As the grandson of Doretta Maulhardt,[37] Carty inherited subdivisions once home to Chumash and Mexican pioneers, and maximized his family connec-tions to permanently prohibit People of Color from ever owning the land again.[38] He and Eastwood both served on the city council alongside their corporate land-developing partners Walter H. Lathrop,[39] Leon Lehmann,[40] and Thomas M. Hill.[41] Throughout the 1930s, this politically powerful group also included George Pryor,[42] Oxnard's chief of police, James J. Krouser, the publisher of *The Oxnard Daily Courier,*[43] and John Cooluris,[44] owner of the racially exclusive Oyster Loaf Café, where the school trustees held their daily meetings. Most of these men simultaneously held leader-ship roles in racially exclusive organizations (e.g., Rotary Club, Elks Club, Masonic Order).

Use of racial covenants extended beyond Oxnard's powerbrokers to also include schoolteachers and principals.[45] Bernice W. Curren, who served as the principal of Roosevelt School and later became a member of the Ventura County School Board, owned racially restricted property in the exclusive John B. Dawley Subdivision, located in front of Oxnard High School.[46] Likewise, Anna J. Sells, principal of Wilson School from approximately 1925 to 1929, and principal of Haydock School from 1930 to 1940, bought and sold racially exclusive property in Lathrop's co-owned Oxnard Development Company Subdivision—the same lot once owned by Eastwood.[47] When Clarence Brittell relocated from Hollister, California, to serve as superin-tendent of Oxnard schools from 1939 to 1949, trustee Beach sold him one of his racially restricted Carty tract properties.[48]

The highest-ranked educational leader in the region, Ventura County school superintendent Blanche T. Reynolds, likewise led by example, endors-ing segregation in word and deed. The conditions on her property included the same language as Virden's, permitting use only "if persons not of the Caucasian Race be kept thereon by a Caucasian occupant, strictly in the capacity of servant of such occupant."[49] Indeed, county records indicate that beyond the 1930s, school and civic leaders continued the widespread use of restrictive covenants, carrying on the pernicious goal of relegating Mexicans to perpetual second-class status.[50]

The filings of racial covenants from the late 1940s also reveal a sense of urgency on the part of White homeowners to codify discrimination despite the law. One of the first successful legal challenges to racial covenants occurred in 1943, in a case where a Mexican American family purchased a home in a racially restricted neighborhood in Fullerton, California, about ninety-three miles south of Oxnard.[51] The *Doss v. Bernal* case went on to bolster the 1948 *Shelley v. Kraemer* Supreme Court case, which ruled federal enforcement of all racial covenants to be unconstitutional.[52]

Despite these rulings, Carty and Agee each filed long-term covenants and restrictions lasting twenty-five to thirty years over their entire subdivisions. They further set the restrictions to renew automatically for successive periods of ten years unless two-thirds of homeowners voted otherwise. School trustee Burfeind purchased one such property in the Carty subdivision in 1948, which specified the extension of the racial covenants until at least 1972.[53] Likewise, Elliot B. Thomas, the principal of Wilson School from 1943 to 1956, owned multiple properties in the restricted Carty tracts until 1970.[54] In 1949, a year after the *Shelley v. Kraemer* case and while he served as acting superintendent of Oxnard schools, Thomas purchased another Carty lot that prohibited "any person whose blood is not that of the white or Caucasian race" to use or occupy the residence until 1978, unless "employed as servants by Caucasian owners or tenants actually residing on said lot."[55] Moreover, Effie Dunning, who served as the first woman on the Oxnard School Board of Trustees the previous decade, bought and sold properties in Agee's subdivision with the racial restrictions in the 1950s.[56] Similarly, Richard M. Clowes, who served as Oxnard Elementary School District superintendent from 1949 to 1960, bought and sold property in the northwest Carty subdivision, replete with racial covenants.[57]

By signing their deeds with racial conditions intact, school and city officials sought to systematically position People of Color subordinate to Whites. Their shrewd participation in a real estate market kept exclusive by racial covenants demonstrates this cabal did not view their status as school and civic representatives as a conflict of interest with their property holdings. Their pursuit of wealth accumulation for themselves and their descendants depended on an available pool of low-wage workers who had few options beyond ostensibly serving landowning Whites. Their vested interest, therefore, lay in maintaining a dual school system to undereducate Mexican children—simultaneously ensuring that these young people would one day face the same restrictions their parents knew in the west-side real estate market. These individual acts of racial discrimination carried over into the daily lives of the students "served" in Oxnard schools.

MEMORIES OF RACE AND SPACE

Until I die I'll say I'm glad that I grew up in Colonia, I am proud
that I grew up in Colonia.

—ANTONIA ARGUELLES DILIELLO[58]

Antonia, whose story of public punishment at Roosevelt School closed chapter 1, remembered La Colonia as a place she had to learn to appreciate. She
reflected with nostalgia on being surrounded by Mexican culture and people,
growing up on Hayes Avenue. Her father grew corn in their backyard and her
mother soaked the corn to prepare *masa* for tortillas. Like Miguel, she
described La Colonia as "all Mexicans in the neighborhood." She participated
in her parents' traditions from Mexico, such as serenades with *las mañanitas*
and *kerméses* and *jamaicas* (neighborhood celebrations). As a young adult, she
walked home from work at night in fear, not on the east side but on the west
side of the tracks. On the west side "it was quiet, quiet, no nothing. And once
I got across the railroad tracks [sighs, laughs], I was home. Music, aroma, you
know, I loved it!" In her sigh of relief and subsequent giggle, Antonia recognized that most people would not consider La Colonia a place that represented comfort, safety, family, and home. Though in hindsight she considered
herself fortunate to have come of age in such a culturally wealthy place, she
acknowledged the hard time she had as a child growing up in poverty, just
across the tracks from the economic wealth of the White west side.

My interviews with Mexican women and men who grew up in Oxnard in
the decades of the 1930s and 1940s show that from a young age, they were
very aware, even without public signs, of the geographic racial boundaries
that limited their mobility. They also recognized the power dynamics evident
in spaces and places throughout the city. As adults, they reflected on how
segregated spaces normalized disparate social and educational trajectories.
Though they and many of their parents were born in the United States, they
grew up with the mundane reality that Mexicans, regardless of citizenship
status, worked in manual labor, low-wage jobs in the beet sugar factory, in the
fields, and in canneries. For the most part, all family members contributed in
some way to support the household income because they all shared aspirations to social mobility. They witnessed intense economic pressures and
inferior educational conditions pushing out the majority of their peers and
older siblings before high school. Many felt school officials held low expectations for Mexican American students, and they too came to view high school
attendance as a privilege beyond their reach. Still, most of my interviewees

graduated from high school, and some also pursued college degrees. Regardless of their family's socioeconomic circumstances and their educational trajectories, they did not see themselves as victims. While acknowledging the obstacles, they never expressed a sense of resignation to the restrictions of race and space in the city. Their comments shed light on how they made sense of and navigated the subtle and stunning racial divisions they encountered as youth.

Antonia recalled street lamps and electricity throughout west-side residential streets and businesses, and in schools, while in La Colonia they relied on kerosene lamps. She remembered an open dump a few blocks from her house, and a big hole in her backyard, which functioned as a cesspool. She and other interviewees verified that their neighborhood lacked paved roads, sidewalks, or streetlamps, and very few had gas, sewage, running water, or telephone service.

Walking home from Roosevelt and Wilson schools with her sister during rainy seasons, Antonia explained, "going into Colonia, there were no sidewalks, we just had to slush our way through . . . slush, slush, slush all the way home."[59] Mary Valdivia (Lamm), who was born in Oxnard in 1924 and attended the same classes as Antonia through the eighth grade, remembered arriving to school "soaked" when it rained. Since it seemed to rain the first day of school each September, this usually meant that the students spent time drying their socks and shoes near the classroom heater, and started schoolwork the next day.[60]

Joe I. Mendoza, who was born in Oxnard in 1932, recalled that because there was only one road leading in and out of La Colonia, a stopped train on the railroad tracks sometimes cut off the community from fire and medical emergency services.[61] Multiple interviewees also confirmed that because of the high cost of a hospital visit and the record of racial exclusion at St. John's Hospital before World War II, most Mexican women in Oxnard gave birth at home, with the assistance of a midwife.[62] In Ernie Carrasco Jr.'s experience, Mexicans sought medical treatment only in emergencies, and only at Ventura County General Hospital. Ernie was born in 1941 in East Los Angeles and lived with his family in Texas until they moved to Oxnard in 1947, when he was in the first grade. "The big joke is that half of Oxnard was born in Ventura," he explained. "Hospitals were only for White people. It was an unwritten rule. You didn't go to St. John's. You went to the County."[63] With very little access to medical care, he remembered using "home cures."[64] Joe also recalled Mexican women and men regularly relying on "*curanderos* and *sobadores*" (healers following indigenous Mexican traditions) for everyday health concerns.[65] In addition to fashioning homemade remedies and seeking out community healers, Mexican women and men also exhibited self-reliance in the organization of mutual aid societies, civic action, and social groups to improve and make La Colonia their own.[66]

As youth, my interviewees recognized that the racial divide between east and west also demarcated the middle/upper class from the poor.[67] They knew that very few Mexicans broke the color line by purchasing a home west of the tracks. Antonia recalled:

> I think we all knew they wouldn't sell to us, so none of us tried to buy. But the Herreras were the first, maybe not the first Mexicans, but they bought a house. And it was an old rundown house. It wasn't anything fancy. I think it was on Magnolia. And the neighbors tried to remove her, but she said, "No, this is my house. I paid for it." They couldn't get her out. But the rest of us, I guess we just knew they wouldn't sell to us, so we would just build and rebuild.[68]

I asked Antonia if the Herreras were fair skinned, thinking that they may have "passed" for White.[69] She responded with a laugh, "No, but they had money." The Herreras, as Antonia recounted, owned a few stores in La Colonia. Still, these successful entrepreneurs were not welcomed in their attempt to build property assets on the west side. According to Antonia, the Herreras successfully broke through the color line only to end up living in an "old, rundown house," fighting White neighbors who "tried to remove" them.

Antonia and other interviewees presented vivid details of the geographic boundaries of La Colonia and of Mexican home ownership. She noted: "Colonia was from Third Street to Cooper Road, from Harrison to McKinley. That was Colonia. . . . Most of them, the ones that didn't want to live in Colonia, would buy between Wooley Road, Saviers Road, and Hill Street."[70] Dolores Ávila (Carrasco), who was born in Kansas in 1943 and raised in Oxnard, described her family's trajectory from a house on Hayes Avenue to a public housing project in Colonia to a home one block west of the tracks:

> The bathroom on Hayes was outside, we used to call it *el cuartito* [the little room]. . . . So when we moved to the projects, it was like, "Oh my God!" The girls had one bedroom and the boys had another bedroom and of course my mom [and dad] had their own bedroom. . . . And we had a bathtub. It was like heaven, like a miracle had happened. . . . [But they dreamed about being homeowners] so my brothers and my dad started saving money because we wanted to get out of Colonia and my dad wanted to buy a house.[71]

She continued, explaining the higher standard her parents were held to in qualifying for a house outside of La Colonia:

> I remember my dad telling me that they had saved $2,000 to buy a house. It was hard for a Mexican to buy a house uptown. All the Mexicans in those days were across the track, *que viene siendo Colonia* [which was basically Colonia]. He went to a realtor and she made it difficult for him, so he had to save more money. So, finally, we moved in 1952. We moved [to] 1411 California Street.[72]

Miguel Espinosa also attempted to purchase a place in the early part of the 1950s, "just across the railroad tracks," in the expanding southwest part of the city:

> I wanted to buy a home in the first Pleasant Valley Estates in Oxnard. . . . They flat denied me because they said, "We don't sell to Mexicans." . . . I went to the office right on the grounds where they were making the sales and I sat down and said, "I want to apply for a home." And they said, "We don't sell to Mexicans." Just like that. And I worked on the tract as a mason.[73]

Miguel took this rejection particularly hard as a Korean War veteran and as a skilled laborer who had helped construct the homes in that tract. "I can't purchase a home and I can't get a job because I'm Mexican. That's appreciation."[74] Indeed, the racially restricted covenants burdening most of the westside tracts established a pattern that with very few exceptions denied Mexicans homeownership outside La Colonia.[75] This mundane reality severely hindered the majority of Mexican families from accumulating wealth[76]—wealth that could also have facilitated increased educational access and opportunity for their children. Enforcement of the west side as a "first class" residential area also conferred second-class treatment upon Mexicans in social spaces and places.

"MEXICANS NOT ALLOWED, YOU JUST KNEW IT"

My interviewees shared vivid memories of subtle and stunning disparate treatment west of the tracks. Miguel explained, "You could sense a White supremacy environment in the atmosphere."[77] Antonia elaborated that on the west side "it was very noticeable. . . . *Más claro no canta un gallo* [A rooster doesn't sing any more clear]. . . . And they didn't have to say Mexicans not allowed, you just knew it."[78] In addition to the obvious residential segregation between La Colonia and the west side, she and other interviewees offered examples of Whites-only policies maintained in restaurants and retail stores along Oxnard Boulevard and throughout the west side. For example, Joe, Miguel, and other interviewees each recalled a segregation policy at the Strand movie theater on the corner of Fifth and C streets. "Mexicans had to go around the back and up the stairs to use the balcony," Joe stated.[79] Similarly, Antonia described limited access at the Oxnard Theater. An usher confronted her when she tried to use the water fountain, saying she was not allowed in that section. He monitored her until she returned to her seat. Antonia and her peers encountered racially exclusive policies firsthand, and at other times they avoided discriminating places based on word of mouth. "There was one place on Fifth Street almost close to the park where there was Mr. Wineman; he used to own a dress shop. But we never went in there because we didn't know if we were supposed to or not. And I guess it happened that some girls had gone in and weren't waited on, so after that they just never went, and so we didn't either."[80] She reiterated that business owners did not put up signs prohibiting Mexicans: "You just knew that you couldn't go in. Or you *shouldn't* go in, because they weren't going to wait on you anyways." This shared understanding led Mexican American youth to strategically navigate a complex social world of racial barriers, and to do so as part of their everyday routine. "We could go in and sit down. But they wouldn't serve us. So why even bother to go in? So we used to go to the hamburger stand right next door."[81]

Well into the 1950s Dolores remembered a particular "milk shop" that looked like the sort of diner portrayed in *Happy Days,* but she noted, "We never went in there, we just looked in [laughs]."[82] She continued, "For Mexicans, that's just the way it was ... there were certain places you just didn't hang out."[83] In Dolores's memory, this exclusive scene exemplified the outsider status of Mexican American youth in the city.

Referencing the Colonial House Restaurant, Antonia expanded on why Mexican Americans may have avoided testing the unwritten rule of segregation: "I don't know if we weren't allowed in there or we were too ashamed to go in there because we were afraid they might say that we couldn't go in."[84] Ernie echoed this understanding: "My father would never even think about going into the Colonial House. And that was in him. It was already in their mind that only the White people visit those establishments."[85] He and the other interviewees discussed the barriers against Mexicans as both real and perceived, raced and classed. In describing the Oyster Loaf Café on Oxnard Boulevard,

Antonia stated: "They wouldn't let us go in. We never tried it. . . . I suppose because it looked too fancy or somebody must have said, 'No, you can't walk in,' because we never tried it. And we couldn't have afforded it anyway."[86]

Ernie carried a similar awareness of where Mexicans could purchase a home: "We couldn't buy downtown. It was like a rule that was there that you didn't sell to Mexicans. It wasn't a written rule. You couldn't buy on F Street and all the nice places."[87] Dolores elaborated on the continuity of this reality when her family moved one block west of Oxnard Boulevard in 1952. Repeating my questions, she detailed:

> How did you know that you were not supposed to go? Who told you? It was just an understanding. . . . You didn't go to just any market. . . . They were all owned by Jewish people. When I lived on California Street, the name of the store was called the Palms. They were Jewish people. When we would walk in that store, we were *watched*. We never took anything, but we were watched. . . . There were certain stores that you didn't go to. You only went to the friendly stores. Even though they were owned by White people.[88]

Dolores remembered being policed by the owners of a local market in their new neighborhood, which led her family to find more welcoming "friendly stores." She continued, offering examples of those places: "My parents used to go to Safeway and A&P. And then *finally* we got La Perla! That was a Mexican store. My mom and dad went there and bought everything. The owners were Mexican, he and his wife."[89] Mexican businesses, including La Central Bakery, La Flor de Mayo, and La Perla, represented a tradition of independence and entrepreneurialism in Oxnard. These places catered to a Mexican clientele and contributed to affirming Mexican culture on the east side of the city.

In contrast, west-side spaces often represented racial exclusivity. As a young man, Joe experienced enforcement of this color line with a police-enforced curfew. He and his peers developed back-alley routes to avoid being caught on the west side of the tracks after dark. "We were not allowed to cross over the railroad tracks after sunset. We had to stay in the Colonia. And if the police caught you, they would bring you back and just dump you off there on the railroad track and call you all sorts of fun names and so forth. We always learned how to walk through the alleys."[90] His recollections about Oxnard as a "sundown town"[91] exemplified the gendered differences in the discrimination my interviewees encountered as youth. The men tended to reference physical confrontations and being considered a threat, whereas the women talked more about being socially shunned and rendered invisible. For example, Miguel recalled, "I had an encounter with the cops when I was very small, probably seven, eight years old."[92] He described walking down the block from his house to join some older boys who were playing in a building still under construction. "When I got there, on the front yard there was a coffee can with a rag in it, and I had just picked it up when a black and white police car arrived and they asked me what I was doing. They put me in the car and took me to jail. I was in jail until after dark, until my parents came and picked me up. That was all very confusing to me."[93] Though this incident occurred around 1940, it stayed with Miguel for decades. In hindsight, he felt that his very presence in northwest Oxnard would have likely been considered suspicious. "Mexicans were reluctant to even walk in that area and they probably didn't, because if they did maybe somebody would say something about it."[94]

Dolores talked about her struggle to make friends with White girls after her family moved west of the tracks. She described going out of her way to walk with White girls on their way to school, but "never once was I invited into the house, ever. So I used to think they were better than me, Mexicans are not the same."[95] Antonia had similar experiences as a teenager. At Oxnard High School, she made cordial acquaintances with White girls: "We would say hello and all that and talk to each other in class. But some of them would see you downtown and make like they didn't even know you."[96] These young women came to understand that friendships between White and Mexican youth had limits, based on race and evident in social space.

CONCLUSION

> Racialized space gives whites privileged access to opportunities
> for social inclusion and upward mobility. At the same time, it
> imposes unfair and unjust forms of exploitation and exclusion
> on aggrieved communities of color.
>
> —GEORGE LIPSITZ, 2011[97]

School and city officials maintained racial covenants on west-side properties, consciously seeking to contain Mexicans east of the tracks and Oxnard Boulevard. While growing their own personal assets, these leaders denied Mexicans and other Communities of Color the ability to accumulate and pass on wealth. In Oxnard, these seemingly private agreements, signed between individual property owners and mortgage companies, real estate agents, and loan officers, created a publicly understood racial hierarchy evident in social spaces throughout the city. Though they did not formally post signs prohibiting Mexicans from their businesses, Whites casually refused service and access to restaurants, theaters, shops, and other spaces throughout the west side. School officials, including teachers, participated in, profited from, and endorsed mundane racial discrimination against Mexicans. Indeed, the school trustees made many decisions about segregation while meeting in the racially exclusive Oyster Loaf Café.

Residential segregation and discrimination did not stop in Oxnard despite two U.S. Supreme Court rulings against racial covenants (*Shelley v. Kraemer,* 1948; *Barrows v. Jackson,* 1953).[98] Successful California lower court challenges to racial covenants (e.g., *Doss v. Bernal,* 1943) did not even receive coverage in the *Oxnard Press-Courier,*[99] likely because publisher Dan Emmett himself owned racially restricted property.[100] The illegality of residential discrimination did not seem to faze Oxnard city or school officials. Instead, they memorialized each other as city "pioneers," naming streets, schools, and parks after themselves (e.g., Bard, Brittell, Carty, Curren, Driffill, Eastwood, Haydock, Hill, Lathrop).[101]

Edward Soja has argued, "We must be insistently aware of how space can be made to hide consequences from us, how relations of power and discipline are inscribed into the apparently innocent spatiality of social life, how human geographies become filled with politics and ideology."[102] My interviewees shed light on the ways Mexican youth witnessed, endured, and navigated this inscription of hierarchy as a seemingly natural, everyday part of life in Oxnard. Mexican students who crossed the tracks from Colonia to the only three elementary schools available did so through neighborhoods bound by racial covenants. They observed two-story homes and various amenities lacking in their own neighborhood, such as sidewalks and electricity. They were also refused full access and service at many places where their White peers could "hang out"[103] as a matter of course.

Indeed, as Miguel indicated at the opening of this chapter, he and other Mexican youth may not have had written evidence to pinpoint the subtle and stunning "rule" of discrimination, but they clearly understood and felt it every day. In the next chapter, I discuss the "rule" of segregation in schools, where White students received "first class" status and treatment. By design, Oxnard's dual schooling system sent the same message as the racial covenants: Mexicans should remain "strictly in the capacity of servant."

THREE

"Obsessed" with Segregating Mexican Students

"Mr. Haydock, you don't seem to understand what these people want. They want complete segregation of the white children. Why can't that be done?" President Dockstader stated that the Board was in favor of the principle of segregation, although it might not be entirely practical at this time.

—OXNARD SCHOOL BOARD OF TRUSTEES,
MEETING MINUTES, 1936

THE EXCERPT ABOVE, FROM A NOVEMBER 4, 1936, meeting with school trustees, captured an exchange of words, and frustration, between a White father named Mr. Watts and school board president Dr. Ray Erwin Dockstader. Dockstader affirmed for Watts, and for the large group of White parents who participated in the forum that evening, that the school trustees shared their belief in racial separation of Whites and Mexicans but could not yet realize "complete segregation." Off the record, the school board, including Superintendent Haydock and trustees Dockstader, Dr. Everett C. Beach, John H. Burfeind, and Elmer W. Power, knew that most of the Mexican children already attended separate classes within the city's three schools—Roosevelt, Wilson, and Haydock. Until 1934, the trustees had not used the term "segregation" in their meeting minutes. This unacknowledged, but understood arrangement became more complicated between 1928 and 1938, because the number of Mexican schoolchildren increased significantly over this period.[1] Watts and the other White parents at the forum urged the board to enforce a stringent "color-line."[2]

This chapter analyzes the board's meeting minutes from 1934 to 1939 and shows that the White parents' demands helped to intensify segregation efforts precisely because the school trustees shared their disdain for Mexicans. Though they attempted to portray themselves as dutiful administrators without any particular agenda, their documented segregation plans during this six-year time period reveal the racism of their actions.

From 1934, when they first mentioned the word "segregation," through 1939, when they approved plans to construct an elementary school east of the railroad tracks, in the predominately Mexican area of La Colonia, the school trustees enacted four simultaneous and intersecting strategies of segregation: (1) Within Roosevelt, Haydock, and Wilson schools, they assigned students according to race, creating all-Mexican classes, and enforced social separation outside of class, institutionalizing a school-within-a-school model of segregation. (2) They formalized a racial hierarchy in schools that positioned Mexicans as an inferior group. (3) At the same time, they collectively created and fostered a permanent interconnection between racially restrictive housing covenants and school segregation.[3] (4) Though their minutes indicate Superintendent Haydock and the board of trustees were "obsessed with the subject of school segregation plans, and their implementation,"[4] these records do not make any mention of a rationale for their actions. Indeed, efforts to segregate Mexican students without a publicly articulated agenda and within seemingly integrated settings aimed to conceal the disparate treatment of Mexican children as mundane policy.

The crescendo of school segregation plans in the 1930s reflected a sense of urgency coinciding with a steady increase of Mexicans in the city and county. The 1930 U.S. Census reported 54,976 residents in Ventura County, which included 13,839 Mexicans.[5] While Mexican adults represented 25 percent of the county population, within the decade Mexican children comprised at least two-thirds of Oxnard elementary school enrollments.[6] These students endured the trustees' malicious agenda as mundane educational practice in Roosevelt, Wilson, and Haydock schools. The perspectives of some of these former students, woven throughout this chapter, shed light on the complex experiences and contestations of segregation not accounted for in the official school board records.

DESIGNING SEGREGATION TO ACCOMMODATE PARENTS' DEMANDS

As detailed in chapter 1, Oxnard's White architects made an ideological case for school segregation and set forth strategies of segregation well before 1930. The actual term "segregation" did not appear in the school board of trustees' meeting minutes until August 7, 1934. The note included a brief explanation that "complete segregation was impossible at the present . . . the matter was being handled in perhaps as satisfactory a manner as could be expected."[7] This initial use of the term and subsequent references to segregation did not include any of the ideological remarks school leaders such as Haydock, Reynolds, and the PTA had made earlier and likewise did not employ the racially restrictive language found in the trustees' property deeds. Instead, from 1934 to 1939 the trustees positioned most of their segregation efforts in relation to improving schooling conditions for White students. Their minutes treat the movement of Mexican students within and between schools as necessary and urgent, but do not explain why they needed to segregate these children or what they sought to accomplish with "complete segregation." Handling "the matter" occurred with immediate, deliberate actions that aimed to satisfy White parents.

For instance, in the first week of November 1936, Superintendent Haydock reported to the board that "three parents had come to him complaining of the small number of American [i.e., White] children in the Haydock School as compared with the number of Mexican."[8] He "immediately" compiled the number of children in all the classes at Haydock School from kindergarten through sixth grade, by the categories "American, Mexican, Oriental," and found 68 Whites, 214 Mexicans, and 10 Asian children.[9] Haydock was scheduled to report these figures to the board on November 4, but "when the meeting was called there were a large number of parents present and, instead of being a meeting for preliminary discussion, it became an open forum." Here the board suggested two plans to "group more of the American children together," which involved combining multiple grades in one classroom. The frustrated exchange of words that opens this chapter occurred during this meeting. Though Superintendent Haydock reminded parents that the board would "decide what should be done in the matter," the parents did not wait for the trustees to act.

Five days later, on November 9, the parents again appeared before the board and proposed the "transfer of all American children . . . at the Haydock School to their grades in the American classes at Roosevelt School. . . . To transfer the sixth grade intact, with their teacher, to Wilson School to make room available in the Haydock building: To transfer the all Mexican grades, with their teachers to the Haydock School."[10] Their statement verified that "all Mexican grades" already existed at both Roosevelt and Wilson schools. The minutes included a clerk's note in relation to the parents' recommendations, indicating that Haydock School had the capacity for eleven classrooms but that between the three schools there were twenty all-Mexican classes, "with a considerable number of Mexicans in some other classes."[11] In other words, President Dockstader and his colleagues confronted a structural problem in pursuit of "complete segregation" because there were too many Mexican children to contain within any one of the three existing schools in the district. Their accommodation of White parents led to their extension of the already established school-within-a-school model, and added momentum to the creation of an all-Mexican school.

Though the White parents persisted in recommending the placement of all-Mexican classes in Haydock School, they also recognized that this facility would not be sufficient to house the large numbers of Mexican students. To avoid compromise on their demand for "complete segregation," the parents asked the board to socially separate Mexican children from Whites at the other two schools through "staggered playground periods in the Wilson school—also if possible to release the American children ten minutes or so ahead of the Mexican children."[12] This arrangement proposed a formal expansion of the school-within-a-school model to include social segregation outside the classroom. Moreover, the White parents suggested "a school bond election as soon as possible to build a school east of Oxnard Boulevard for the convenience of the Mexican population."[13] With the exception of this last recommendation, which took a few years to implement, the trustees responded almost immediately to each of the White parents' demands.

The minutes evidence a shared understanding between White parents and the trustees. For example, the White parents' request for "the removal of American children and the sixth grade intact from the Haydock School"[14] implied there were no Mexican children enrolled in the sixth grade. No other note elaborated on this implication about student attrition. This omission exemplifies the process of normalizing dismal academic outcomes for Mexican students. It also demonstrates that the segregation already practiced in Oxnard's elementary schools functioned very well—to undereducate and push out the majority of Mexican students. In fact, Oxnard, like so many other school districts across the Southwest, did not maintain a segregation policy at the high school level because so few Mexican students persisted beyond primary school grades. In 1930, Ward A. Leis discussed this pattern from his survey of thirty-one school systems in four states bordering Mexico. Leis found twenty-one of them separated "the Mexican children entirely or in part from the whites for educational purposes."[15] He estimated

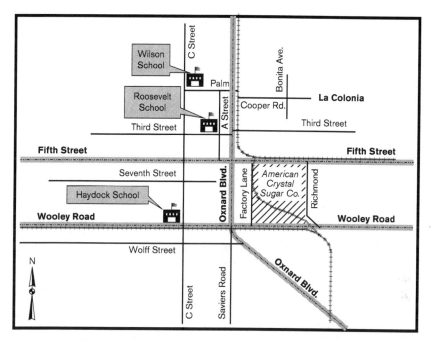

MAP 2. Oxnard's three elementary schools before 1940, all located west of Oxnard Boulevard and railroad tracks, away from La Colonia. Adapted from map published in "School Zones Are Outlined; Open Sept. 13," *Oxnard Press-Courier,* September 2, 1948, front page.

that 84.6 percent of schools in California practiced some form of segregation of Mexican students.[16] He calculated this number based on eleven of the thirteen school systems that responded to his survey, noting that three of them also segregated other nationalities along with Mexicans. Mexicans comprised an average of 90 percent of the student body even in these mixed segregated settings.[17] Leis further reported that two-thirds of all the school systems in California and the Southwest stopped segregating students by the sixth grade because, as school administrators explained, "by this time the Mexican language handicap has largely disappeared and his social adaptation has fitted him to go into the grades with the white children, provided he still remains in school. The large amount of dropping out at the end of the fourth, fifth, and sixth grades is also a factor in discontinuing segregation at these points."[18] The school trustees in Oxnard omitted any such explanations from their calculated plans. In their minutes, the fact that there were no Mexican children in the sixth-grade class at Haydock School did not merit mention.

On November 20, 1936, only eleven days after the White parents had presented their suggestions, the board met to review the new enrollments "in the different buildings, and for each of the classrooms under three general heads; American (white), Mexican, and oriental."[19] They concluded that further transferring of students between schools would only occur because of overcrowding of the White classes or if a family moved to a different part of town. These minutes reiterate that the trustees designed segregation for the benefit of White students. They also made a casual reference to why the trustees believed such separation to be necessary: "Overcrowded Mexican classes should be relieved by transferring some of the best to American classes that are smaller."[20] Using this phrase, "some of the best," without any explanation indicated the trustees' shared understanding that only certain Mexican children would be tolerated to sit next to White children.

Even as they swiftly accommodated the White parents' demands and exposed some of their views about Mexican students, the trustees attempted to position themselves as neutral administrators. By the spring of the 1936–37 school year, the minutes stated, "There seemed to be no agitation for further segregation of Mexican children and nothing further contemplated by the Board."[21] This lull in the segregation efforts did not last long.

At the onset of the fall semester in 1937, Superintendent Haydock and the school principals and teachers decided to group White children from two different grades together in the same class. By September 22, the trustees discussed a need to adopt "some definite plan"[22] for easing overcrowding in these White classrooms. They considered "possibilities of handling the situation in two different ways: a. The return of white children living in the south part of town to the Haydock School. [or] b. The complete segregation of Mexican children."[23] They developed a compromise that considered the fact that they had already transferred the White children out of Haydock School and did not have the facilities for complete segregation. The convenience of White students again took priority. Five days later, on September 27, trustee Burfeind outlined this plan, "calling for all 'Mexican' children living south of Fifth Street to attend the Haydock School, leaving all white and oriental children living south of Fifth Street in the Roosevelt and Wilson schools. The moving of Oriental children living south of Fifth Street to the Haydock School will be taken into consideration in case of future emergency, and no further shifting of pupils is intended."[24]

The plan aimed to reiterate the goal of placing as many Mexican children as possible at Haydock School, but offered no indication of what type of emergency might lead to Asians being segregated alongside Mexicans in that facility. Though Superintendent Haydock questioned whether all components of this plan could be adopted, three days later, on September 30, the board concurred that he and the teachers "could meet the situation in the way that seemed best as pupils return from the harvest season. The one point to be carried out as soon as convenient and with as little 'fuss' as possible was the transferring of Mexican pupils who live south of Fifth Street to the Haydock School."[25] In regard to Mexicans, apparently, "the case of future emergency" had already arrived.

The consistent reference to Fifth Street in relation to student placement discussions and acknowledgment of Mexican children working in the fields demonstrated the trustees' awareness of the racial dimensions of the local labor economy and their consciousness of residential segregation. Though some enrollment changes occurred immediately after the September 1937 meetings, three months into the school year, in November, Superintendent Haydock reported that Mexican enrollments had increased at all the schools, due to "the return of children from the walnut, prune, grape harvests etc."[26] Four classes at Roosevelt School counted over fifty students each. The trustees were frustrated at the ways these shifts undermined their efforts to segregate students.

Trustee Burfeind expressed some of this frustration in his correspondence with Alice Shaffer, who complained in April 1938 about the removal of "American" (White) students from Haydock School.[27] As discussed in chapter 2, Burfeind responded by explaining that the enrollment changes occurred at the behest "of a large group of parents living in your part of Town."[28] Though Shaffer and the parents she claimed to represent from her neighborhood south of Fifth Street may have disagreed with other White parents in 1936 about the specifics of how to keep Mexican children apart from their own, they shared a desire for complete segregation. Both groups also lobbied the trustees to build a school explicitly for Mexicans and suggested such a facility would be best located on the east side.[29] The White parents' repeated demands sought an urgent end to the permeability of the "color-line"[30] in schools.

"A FEW OF THE BRIGHTEST, CLEANEST MEXICAN CHILDREN"

The White architects' actions demonstrate they were actually "obsessed" with maintaining the "color-line."[31] At their September 13, 1938, meeting, the trustees decided on a plan to relieve the overcrowding at Wilson and Roosevelt schools. As in previous years, the expediency of implementing segregation focused on accommodating White students. The trustees recommended making another call for all children in the first through fifth grades residing south of Fifth Street to attend Haydock School. They also approved continued doubling up of two grade levels of White children into one class when the enrollment sizes permitted. In addition to keeping the "Mexican classes as such," the trustees agreed with "the placing of Oriental children in white classes that are not too large," and "the placing of some of the brightest and best of the Mexican children in white classes when the white class is small and the Mexican class is too large."[32] These notes reiterated the acceptance of Asian students in the White classes, and formalized the admission of Mexicans with the condition that these students be "some of the brightest and best." The record remains silent as to how the principals, teachers, and Superintendent Haydock would decide which Mexican students to bestow with these labels.

Three days later, on September 16, the principals and Haydock presented specific plans to reorganize class enrollments, and the trustees instructed Haydock "to take immediate steps to make the changes called for by the following Monday if possible."[33] This did not resolve the situation. By December 1938, the board again discussed how to avoid the overcrowded double-grade White classes in Roosevelt and Haydock schools. This time, Superintendent Haydock asked the teachers "to submit what they thought would be the best solution of the problem."[34] The teachers' plan called for "[White] classes of but one grade with a few of the brightest, cleanest Mexican children in each so as not to leave other classes excessively large."[35] The minutes did not detail how the teachers would operationalize "brightest, cleanest." The trustees' endorsement of this plan without any further explanation sheds light on the continuity of mundane racism.

Indeed, nothing about the teachers' plan was original. Eleven years earlier, *The Oxnard Daily Courier* reported on the PTA and other officials as they resurrected similar racial myths and blueprint designs for school-within-a-school segregation.[36] The trustees' inability to completely separate "the Latin American children" in November 1927 remained a problem in December 1938. Documenting their bigoted assumptions about Mexican children's hygiene and intelligence as a matter of fact, they positioned segregation as a common good. If, as they claimed, the brightest, cleanest, best Mexicans did indeed exist, these few children could be tolerated sitting next to White students—who of course, following this line of argument, were always superior to even the brightest, cleanest, best Mexicans simply by virtue of being White.

While systematically implementing racism as mundane educational practice, the trustees continually sought input from the White parents. At the December 21 meeting, they asked parents of students in double-grade White classrooms whether they preferred that their child remain in these large classes or whether they would prefer enrollment in single-grade classes "with approximately one-third of the classes consisting of the brighter and better class of Mexican children of the same grade."[37] The survey results showed White parents preferring the double-grade classrooms by a ratio of about two to one. A few weeks later, on January 10, 1939, a group of about thirty White parents agreed to entrust further segregation plans to the best judgment of the trustees and school officials. This marked the last time the board officially recorded their efforts toward "segregation" of Mexican students.[38]

Other records indicate the trustees kept the double-grade classes intact for the remainder of the school year. For example, on May 29, 1939, *The Oxnard Daily Courier* published alphabetical class rosters for third- and fourth-grade Gold Seal and Plain Seal reading certificate awards from the Oxnard Public Library. The first roster listed Miss Anderson's third- and fourth-grade students, which included no Spanish surnames. Below these awardees' names, Mrs. Arabella Owen's third-grade class and Miss Charlotte Reebe's fourth-grade class rosters each listed exclusively Spanish-surnamed students.[39] Indeed, the legacy of the trustees' 1930s obsession with segregation endured long after 1939. Oral accounts provide rare insight into Mexican students' daily experiences of this segregation—perspectives glaringly missing from the board's records.

A SCHOOL-WITHIN-A-SCHOOL

They were changing us around all the time ... [between] Haydock and Roosevelt and Wilson schools; we were always getting moved around. And I'm talking about colors and races.... [laughing] Those people [students] at Haydock probably didn't know where they belonged because they were moving them around all the time.... That's when I realized there were only two kinds of people, Mexicans and non-Mexicans, because they had every other ethnic group in the other [classes] except us.

—ANTONIA ARGUELLES DILIELLO[40]

For Antonia, school segregation was an everyday part of a normalized color line drawn between Mexicans and everyone else. Antonia enrolled at Roosevelt School in the second grade in 1932 (see chapter 1). She was traumatized when a school official publicly shamed her for speaking Spanish by forcing her to draw a circle in the dirt and stand in the middle of it. She continued in all-Mexican classes at Roosevelt through fourth grade. That year, 1934, her entire class was placed in a separate wooden structure located behind the main school building.[41] She explained that outside the classrooms, "We were segregated. The Anglos would play on this side and the Mexican children would play on this side."[42]

Antonia continued on to Wilson School from fifth through eighth grades, where she also attended all-Mexican classes. She and her peers ate in the section of the cafeteria designated for Mexicans, or walked home for lunch. They were also released later than the other children at the end of the school day. She remembered, "By the time we got out, there was nobody left."[43]

One incident in particular epitomized the color line between Mexicans and Whites at Wilson School. Antonia remembered feeling very sick and leaning over in a hallway, anticipating she might vomit. A White teacher, who saw her, ran in the other direction rather than lend a helping hand. Antonia's astonishment that a teacher would treat a young person so callously contributed to her belief that Whites did not care for Mexicans. "You get those little vibes here and there," she explained.[44]

Delia L. Hernandez was born in Oxnard in 1936 and attended Haydock School from fourth through sixth grades. There she was placed in a "sort of a hut" called the "Green House," which she understood to be a class for students who could not read.[45] She remembered her teacher was "always joking and nice,"[46] and her peers were Mexicans, mainly girls, and two Black girls. She noted there were no White students in the Green House. After Haydock, she continued on to Wilson School for seventh grade in the same class with peers who could not read. She was very conscious of her separation from the rest of the student body at both schools. "We had recesses different than all the other kids,"[47] she explained. She imagined the other students, Mexican and White, really enjoying Wilson School, whereas she felt isolated: "I didn't feel good. I felt that the other kids were more privileged to have more friends and more things to do than us ... I didn't feel very special in that school because I didn't know how to read. *Me sentía* [I felt] not a part of it."[48]

Delia felt tremendous pressure about the fact that she could not read, but did not want to be left behind as the oldest student in the class. She carried a

FIGURE 4. Theodore Roosevelt School, fourth-grade Mexican class, Oxnard, circa 1934. Mary Valdivia (bottom row, first on left), Antonia Arguelles (bottom row, second from left). This wooden building was located behind the stucco Roosevelt School. Courtesy of Mary Valdivia Lamm.

constant sense of anxiety in not knowing if she would be promoted to the next grade, and she carried this heavy burden alone. When I interviewed her in 2013, over sixty-five years later, she still felt conflicted about who was to blame for her situation: "It must have been partly my fault because I would get stubborn and not read. In a way, I think they should've told my mother or my older sister about me because my mother never scolded me and she never knew what was going on."[49] Delia recognized her mother and sister carried multiple work and family obligations, and believed this contributed to her situation not receiving much attention. By the end of seventh grade, she stopped attending school altogether and went to work in the fields. To her knowledge, her teacher had recommended she be promoted to the eighth grade. "He was nice. He let me slide, I passed."[50]

Reflecting on her teachers' actions, in the process of the interview, Delia began to reconsider whether she did indeed experience discrimination. "Well, now I think yes, because they should've really sat me down and said,

'You're going to stay here and you're going to learn how to read.' Or something. They never did that . . . maybe they didn't care."[51]

Though they may not have realized it at the time, Antonia and Delia were not alone in experiencing the daily acts of disregard for Mexican students. In his 1937 study of the influences of segregation on children's social attitudes, William A. Farmer surveyed students at six schools in Ventura County.[52] He found that "both Mexican and American [White] children in segregated schools felt that American children got more opportunities than Mexican children in school."[53] Even in integrated settings, he explained, most Mexican students believed that "teachers treat[ed] American children better than they [did] Mexican children."[54] Moreover, in one school that practiced 90 percent segregation, over 80 percent of the White students agreed with the statement, "Mexican children do not have the same rights as American children."[55]

Joe I. Mendoza viscerally remembered what this looked and felt like from fifth to eighth grade at Wilson School:

> Wilson had an office in the center [begins to sketch], then it had two wings that went off, and these classrooms were for Mexicans only and these classrooms for Americans only. Then out in the yard they had a white line painted. And we could only play on our side and Americans could only play on their side, and the bathrooms were on their side. And so we always used the trees, and I mean we used the trees for everything. It got bad, it was really bad. Then from here if you were lucky, there were very few of us who would graduate and go to Oxnard High.[56]

Given its almost grand outward appearance—with archways, large windows, and manicured landscaping—Wilson School did not look like a separate and unequal educational facility. As Joe described, however, structures and practices of segregation within the school fostered humiliating conditions that led to "very few" Mexican students persisting through the eighth grade.

Antonia further elaborated on the difficulty of persistence through Wilson School for Mexican boys: "By the time we got to eighth grade, every other boy was no longer with us."[57] She never quite understood why this happened, but she assumed the boys went to work in the fields. She expressed empathy for these young men, including her brothers, who had unrealized aspirations for attending high school, and she reminisced, "I remember most of these guys were really intelligent, like Tommy Estrada, Martin Muñoz, Albert [Valdez], and then Manuel."[58]

FIGURE 5. Woodrow Wilson School, Oxnard, circa 1939. Courtesy of Mary Valdivia Lamm.

In hindsight, Joe explained that he and his peers perceived segregation and the resulting high attrition rates as a very matter-of-fact part of growing up Mexican in Oxnard:

[Segregation] was the rule and so you just obeyed it. . . . It was normal. . . . It was accepted as a part of life, as who you were. That's your station, that's who you are. And that's it. . . . Walking to town you couldn't ride the buses. You didn't say "Oh, there goes the bus!" You just walk[ed] down the boulevard, that was it. . . . Dropping out was also acceptable. You had to go to work and that was it. Most of our classmates after sixth grade would drop out, very few would go—Out of a class of thirty there was maybe five or six of us that would go on to Junior High.[59]

Similarly, Antonia's classmate Mary Valdivia (Lamm) recognized segregation as a normal part of life. Though she attended Mexican classes at Roosevelt and Wilson, she did not consider this to be a significant part of her schooling experiences, and "never questioned it."[60] "We enjoyed going to school,"[61] she said. Mary remembered her teachers fondly and believed segregation was something imposed by White parents, remarking, "It [segregation] really didn't matter to me."[62] Upon her completion of the eighth grade, she "went to work" instead of continuing to Oxnard High School. She identified her own family circumstances as the reason for her limited schooling options.

While Mary gave segregation minimal consideration, Antonia and Joe viewed it as a significant, albeit mundane, part of their everyday life. Each

FIGURE 6. Woodrow Wilson School, seventh-grade Mexican class, Oxnard, circa 1937. Antonia Arguelles (bottom row, first on left), Mary Valdivia (second row from bottom, third from right), Mr. Hall (teacher, third row from bottom, left). This photo presents additional evidence that despite living in homes which often lacked electricity, running water, or gas, these children did not lack in hygiene. Courtesy of Mary Valdivia Lamm.

used the phrase "that's the way it was" when describing segregated schooling conditions. Antonia remembered that she hated going to school in Oxnard, but at some point, when she realized her family would never move back to her "beloved Kansas,"[63] she resolved to change her attitude. She began rationalizing the punishment she received for speaking Spanish at school and other incidents. Reflecting back, she recognized she had internalized the discrimination she experienced as somehow her fault: "I tried to be friendlier so I wouldn't have this horrible thing [feeling]. Well, because we're dirty—I'm dirty and ugly and they don't speak Spanish. I could find all kinds of excuses for whatever happened to me. I guess it was a defense mechanism, you know? Who cares."[64] Joe further reasoned that many of his peers were not "lucky" enough to survive the conditions of segregation.

While Antonia, Joe, Mary, and other Mexican youth tried to make sense of separate and unequal schooling conditions, the White architects left very little up to chance. In particular, the strategies of segregation implemented between 1934 and 1939 demonstrated a concerted effort to make racism appear normal. These tactics fostered Mary's perception that segregation "didn't matter,"[65] at the same time they led Antonia and Joe to explain hurtful incidents of discrimination as routine.[66]

OXNARD PARENTS CHALLENGE SCHOOL SEGREGATION

Though the school board documented the trustees' ongoing meetings with White parents, these records do not mention any direct communication with Mexican parents. One rare exception to this omission occurs in trustee Burfeind's 1938 correspondence with Shaffer, detailed in chapter 2. In explaining the board's rationale for transfer of Mexican students to Haydock School, Burfeind noted, "As a result of this change [in 1936], a Mexican Parent Teachers Association has been started and much good is coming from it."[67] Though I found no elaboration beyond this mention, Burfeind's acknowledgment of a Mexican PTA confirms that parents did indeed organize on behalf of their children's education.

Individual families also contested segregation. In looking at her fourth-grade class picture from Roosevelt School, Antonia remembered that at least two of her classmates' parents petitioned the school board to move their children out of the Mexican classes and into the White classes. She stated, "Sara Gonzales, her parents or her father, went to the school board and had them remove her. Anyway, by the time we got to Wilson School, she was no longer with us ... she went to the Anglo classes ... the other girl [whose parents petitioned the board] was Connie Diaz."[68] Eighth-grade class enrollments demonstrate that, indeed, these petitions were successful, as Consuelo ("Connie") and Sara were each enrolled in a White class.[69] Still, Antonia remembered feeling bad for students like Sara and Connie, imagining they may have felt extremely isolated in the White classes: "I used to often feel sorry for her [Sara]. I doubt if they [Sara and Connie] were ever invited to any of the Anglo parties. And the rest of us, the Mexicans, we were afraid to hang around with them; otherwise we'd be called—[It would have looked like] we wanted to sugar up to them. We wouldn't have anything to do with them either."[70] For Antonia, the transfer of students out of all-Mexican classes caused tension and sometimes ended friendships. She and her peers understood that they were perceived as somehow inferior to the students in the

White classes—including the few Mexicans. Indeed, students and their parents recognized the racial hierarchy being established by school officials.

The record shows one instance of a parent contesting segregation via legal counsel. On September 21, 1938, the trustees and Superintendent Haydock met with attorney Edward C. Maxwell, who explained "that he had been retained by Mr. Louis Carballo to protest against the recent changes in classes as they affected his own children, and that if some way could not be found to remove these objections the matter would be taken into court."[71] While discussing the Carballo complaint with the trustees, Maxwell expressed "as his opinion that segregation under certain circumstances is advisable and that he would not like to see the schools hampered in applying the principle along somewhat different lines."[72] It is not clear whether these "somewhat different lines" referred to residence, race, or some other distinctions. The trustees also sought the advice of Julien Hathaway, from the district attorney's office, but there is no record of a resolution to this threatened legal action.

Over seven decades later, an oral history interview of Louis Carballo's son, Richard, provides further insight into the details of this case. Richard, who was born in Oxnard in 1929 and attended Roosevelt School along with his sister Gloria, remarked: "I remember the segregation. I remember them segregating us. I remember Mom and Dad didn't want us to go with the Mexican people . . . so they kept us there at Roosevelt School."[73]

It remains unclear how Louis learned that his children were to be enrolled in segregated Mexican classes, but he took specific issue with the identification of his children as Mexicans in the first place. Richard explained, "We're Spaniards. Not that that makes any difference."[74] Louis immigrated with his family to California from Spain as a young boy and initially attended school in Lompoc before moving to Oxnard. He later married Ramona Ballesteros, who was born and raised in Oxnard. Louis became a successful businessman, and the couple had two children, Richard and Gloria.

Superintendent Haydock likely identified the Carballo children as Mexican on the basis of their surname.[75] When asked about whether his parents were upset about the board trying to segregate their children, Richard said: "Yeah, they were fueled! . . . It wasn't that they were against the Mexican people; it's just that they didn't want us to *mingle* with substandard [nervous laughter]— if that's what you want to call it—students."[76] His parents recognized the commonly held perceptions of Mexican children. They acted because they believed segregated, all-Mexican classes produced "substandard" students.

FIGURE 7. Theodore Roosevelt School, White class, Oxnard, circa 1938. Victoria Lee Haydock (teacher, top row center), Richard Carballo (third row from bottom, third from right), Robert Perez (third row from bottom, right of Richard, with glasses), Gloria Carballo (second row from bottom, second from right), Donna LaRue Ball (bottom row, second from right). This photo is additional evidence that Asian students (sitting on either side of Donna) were permitted in the White class. Courtesy of Richard Carballo.

Their father's threat of seeking a legal remedy likely extended his complaint to include the Carballo cousins Robert Perez and Lola Perez, who attended the White classes at Roosevelt and Wilson schools. The minutes note that a few days after the Carballo discussion, the trustees granted two other students slated to attend Haydock—Donna LaRue Ball and Lloyd Smith—"permission to attend Roosevelt School for what the Board considered good reasons."[77] Being White without a Spanish surname seems to have constituted the "good reason" for granting this enrollment exception. Ironically, Richard Carballo and Donna LaRue Ball became classmates.[78]

NORMALIZING RACIALLY DISPARATE OUTCOMES

The strategies of segregation facilitated disproportionate attrition rates for Mexican students before high school. In June 1939, when Mexicans comprised at least 67 percent of the Oxnard elementary schools, they comprised only 51 percent of the students promoted from the eighth grade.[79] Whites, who made up about 29 percent of the total elementary school population, were 41 percent of the 1939 eighth-grade graduating class. Similarly, students with Japanese or Chinese surnames, who represented less than 4 percent of the total elementary school enrollments, made up 8 percent of those promoted from the eighth grade that year.

A snapshot of the eighth-grade class of 1939 further confirms the school-within-a-school containment of Mexican students in kindergarten through eighth grades. Of the seventy-one students with Spanish surnames promoted from the eighth grade in 1939, sixty-seven were enrolled in the two Mexican classes, taught by Mrs. Beatrice Banner or Maurice E. Fox.[80] All the White and Asian students attended two eighth-grade classes, taught by either Harriet Puntenney or Laura S. Skilling.[81] Only four Spanish-surnamed students, all girls, were enrolled in these classes: Mary Martinez, Consuelo Diaz, Ruth Hernandez, and Sara Gonzalez.[82] As Antonia explained, Consuelo and Sara received access to these classes as a result of their parents petitioning the school board. Mary Martinez also likely enjoyed continued access because of her uncle Louis Carballo's previous complaint to the school trustees. These enrollment patterns indicate that segregation was almost complete through eighth grade and the few Spanish-surnamed students granted exceptions— per parent intervention—were successfully promoted alongside their White peers.

Indeed, the 1939 compromise of allowing "a few of the brightest, cleanest Mexican children" into the White classes seems to have permitted only two Spanish-surnamed girls in each of the two White classes at Wilson School. When Mrs. Skilling took her eighth-grade students on a picnic, Mary Martinez was the only Spanish-surnamed student who joined the party.[83] According to names listed in *The Oxnard Daily Courier*, no Asian-surnamed students participated.[84] This racial exclusivity typified the distinct social world White parents sought to construct for their children through segregated schooling conditions.

Though the newspaper did not report on it, Antonia talked about attending a picnic at the beach with her eighth-grade classmates and teacher, Mr. Fox, in 1939: "We had so much fun. I don't know if we went in cars or a bus. But the whole class went. We had a real good time."[85] She remembered this as the only time she and her classmates went with a teacher on a field trip. She went on to recognize: "I think my best teacher that tried to really get to us was Mr. Fox, our eighth-grade teacher. He would do this thing about letting us go ahead and write something. And then from that he could tell us what we wanted to be. And I remember he said that I had a background in medical terminology. So I ended up as a medical records technician."[86] For Antonia, Mr. Fox stood out as a teacher who tried to connect with her and help her and her peers envision a future. She recalled a couple of "very good teachers" but believed some of them, such as her third- and fourth-grade teachers, Mrs. Owen and Miss Reebe,[87] "could've cared less. If you learned, fine; if you didn't, they'd pass you on to another grade. But that's how it was. . . . Ms. Curren was very nice. She was my second-grade teacher. She was real helpful. We had Ms. Owen for third grade. She was very exact and if you didn't get good grades, you didn't get good grades. But you still got passed on."[88]

Following Antonia and her Spanish-surnamed (Mexican) peers from eighth grade in 1939 through high school graduation in 1943 sheds further light on the longitudinal effects of segregation. Of Oxnard High School's 105 graduates in 1943,[89] only seventeen bore Spanish surnames: one boy and sixteen girls.[90] Among the girls were Mary Martinez[91] and Consuelo Diaz. Of the other fifteen students, seven had been enrolled with Mr. Fox for eighth grade at Wilson School. None of the thirty-one students from Mrs. Banner's eighth-grade Mexican class in 1939 graduated from high school in 1943. Of the sixty-seven students promoted from the two Mexican classes at Wilson in 1939, only seven graduated from Oxnard High School four years later: one boy and six girls.[92]

From Antonia's perspective, even though Mexicans were integrated with Whites from ninth through twelfth grades, they faced significant academic and social-class barriers to high school graduation. Academic underpreparation figured large in her mind. "By the time we reached high school, so many of us were so far behind it was really pitiful," she explained.[93] She also described a dress code in effect at Oxnard High School, which required slacks, a collared shirt, and dress shoes for boys. Boys were not permitted to wear jeans or tennis shoes. Girls wore a blue or black skirt, a white blouse, and white socks. It remains unclear if these dress code regulations were enforced by school officials or whether they were informal expectations, but Antonia's brother, who owned only one pair of Levi's and one pair of work boots, felt compelled to leave high school after one semester. Antonia believed the high cost of the uniform may also have been a reason why very few other Mexican boys and girls continued on to Oxnard High School after eighth grade. Such clothes represented luxuries beyond the financial reach of many Mexican families. She recognized the high school uniform as a public symbol of education and was determined to acquire the attire so she could attain her diploma: "I remember two of my friends from Oxnard High, they had P-necklines. The ones that the sailors use now. And I thought, 'Oh boy! When I go to high school I'm gonna buy one of those and wear it.' Well, I bought it, but I didn't wear it. They weren't holding anybody to those blouses anymore. I was so disappointed. That meant education. I mean you stood out with a blouse like that."[94]

Around 1941 or 1942, Antonia explained, the dress code became less strict and boys began wearing jeans to school. "But by then my brother had gone off to war. So that was that."[95] Antonia promised her brother she would go to high school, but she carried a sense of guilt that she had an opportunity she felt he had been denied. "He was very proud of me when I graduated from high school,"[96] she said.

HAYDOCK'S LEGACY

Superintendent Haydock figured centrally in designing the real and perceived barriers to education that Mexican students such as Antonia confronted. While the trustees' minutes seem to position Haydock as a silent, dutiful administrator, his public remarks from previous decades belie any such characterization. As discussed in chapter 1, early on in his career Haydock expressed a "racially charged vision"[97] of public schooling that framed segregation as natural and necessary. This vision was manifest in the trustees' obsession with segregation from 1934 to 1939.

As superintendent for almost four decades, Haydock methodically implemented his anti-Mexican agenda, well aware that no California educational code or other legal statute allowed for the segregation of Mexicans in schools.[98] His 1917 claim that separate schooling was permitted for students "infected with a contagion," and his 1927 assertion that each state could segregate on the basis of their "own particular problems," demonstrated his ongoing consideration of the legally permissible grounds for segregating Mexicans from Whites. Analyzing the flurry of segregation plans enacted during the last six years of his tenure as superintendent reveals that Haydock sought to realize his vision for Mexican children before his retirement in 1939.

The continuities of his leadership in normalizing the segregation and undereducation of Mexican children contradict his treatment of Asian students. Haydock accounted for the number of "Oriental" children in the meeting minutes, but never sought to enforce the California State

Educational Code permitting separate schooling facilities for "children of Chinese, Japanese, or Mongolian parentage."[99] Instead, he and the trustees granted these students educational access and opportunities equal to Whites. This racial privilege in Oxnard schools contrasted with the discrimination that Asian communities endured in labor, immigration policy, and other aspects of life in the United States.[100]

On June 15, 1939, *The Oxnard Daily Courier* reported as front-page news that the Japanese community had honored Superintendent Haydock for affording them educational opportunities. In a ceremony recognizing Haydock's retirement, Japanese parents expressed their "deepest appreciation" for his treatment of their children.[101] A former student, George Yanaginuma, said Haydock "took a deep personal interest in the welfare of his students and encouraged them to pursue their studies in higher education."[102] In a bilingual ceremony with an audience of at least one hundred, one of the parents, W. Frank Takasugi, stated, "Through your kind effort and interest they have become useful citizens. . . . Many of them now are already doing very well for the betterment of their community life. . . . Some are already doctors and lawyers."[103] The newspaper's paraphrasing of Haydock's acceptance speech portrayed him as an egalitarian leader, who "always had an 'intense purpose' never to permit distinctions in dealing with school children. It made no difference to him whether they came from the homes of the poor or the rich, from American homes or those of foreign parentage. He considered it his duty to treat them without distinction."[104] Haydock's actual record reflected partisanship and discrimination. He not only permitted distinctions among children; he constructed a school system to maintain these distinctions for generations.

The Japanese parents publicly acknowledged Haydock's role in preparing their children for higher education and increasing their ability to contribute to "the betterment of their community life."[105] Conversely, Haydock led the charge for four decades to limit schooling opportunities for Mexican children, hindering their access to high school, let alone college, and restricting their ability to contribute to their community in roles beyond manual labor. Oxnard High School's 1939 graduating senior class reflects the consequences of his disparate designs for education. Among 105 high school graduates, only fifteen had Spanish surnames (14%). In contrast, eighty Whites (76%) and ten students with Chinese or Japanese surnames (10%) earned high school diplomas that year, including class valedictorian Naoyuki ("Nao") Takasugi.[106] These outcomes represent a complete inversion of the elementary

FIGURE 8. Oxnard High School graduation, 1939. Nao Takasugi delivering valedictory. Courtesy of the Museum of Ventura County.

school enrollment figures and provide further evidence of the opportunity gap for Mexican students.

Indeed, in Oxnard schools, Japanese and Chinese students received privileges elevating them to a contradictory status of a "model minority" decades before World War II.[107] For some Japanese American youth these academic benefits endured beyond their internment in 1942. For example, three years after his high school graduation, when the U.S. government relocated Japanese families in Oxnard for the duration of World War II, former valedictorian Nao Takasugi was pulled out of UCLA and sent to a camp in Gila River, Arizona. About one year later, with the assistance of a Quaker organization, he and other interned university students were granted security clearances to attend East Coast colleges.[108] After earning his baccalaureate and master's degrees, Takasugi moved back to Oxnard and went on to serve as a city council member, as mayor, and eventually in the California State Assembly.[109]

Most Mexican Americans who attended Oxnard schools in the 1930s and 1940s did not follow such an educational trajectory. Reflecting on growing up in La Colonia and navigating segregated schooling conditions, Joe explained that he and his siblings "had no vision of [higher] education" as a possibility for their future. Instead, they believed, "either you're going to pack the lemons at the packing plant or you're going to pick [in the fields]."[110]

These young people inherited a legacy of struggle. Many contributed to this collective struggle as laborers, entrepreneurs, active community members, and parents. Some became community organizers and civic leaders. A handful also pursued higher education.

Despite Haydock and the White architects' obsessed efforts to relegate them to a permanent, undereducated class apart, Mexican parents and youth held on to and passed on aspirations for a better future. Though Delia Hernandez never learned to read, she maneuvered successfully to provide for her family as a farmworker, factory laborer, and union leader. Antonia guided her three children through high school graduation, supporting her son through a baccalaureate degree and her daughter through a doctorate. Her love for learning drove her own pursuit of a university degree. Decades after graduating from Oxnard High School, she realized the full extent of the substandard schooling she and her peers had received: "By the time I got to Oxnard College, [when] I went back to school, one of the instructors said, 'You're in the ninth-grade level.' I said, 'What?'"[111] She took on the daunting task of mastering the remedial coursework and graduated from Oxnard College with honors. She went on to California State University, Channel Islands, where she excelled as a history major. Earning her baccalaureate degree at the age of eighty, Antonia had the last say to those Roosevelt School officials who sought to shame her by forcing her to stand in a circle in the dirt.

CONCLUSION

This chapter has chronicled the Oxnard school board's numerous enrollment adjustments planned and implemented from 1934 through 1939, when they appeared "obsessed" with school segregation.[112] Over this six-year period, the trustees formalized practices of separating Mexican children from Whites and Asians within the district's three facilities, Roosevelt, Haydock, and Wilson. This school-within-a-school model effectively contained the majority of Mexicans from kindergarten through eighth grades in distinct academic and social spaces. Some Mexican students who attended schools during this time period recalled feeling humiliated or isolated. While for the most part they remembered "nice" teachers, they also recognized that very few of their peers had an opportunity to continue their schooling beyond eighth grade. For these youth, "that's just the way it was." This normalization of disparate treatment and academic outcomes occurred not "by chance, but rather by design."[113] The trustees accommodated the demands of White parents in their methodical construction of racial hierarchy while making careful omissions in the meeting minutes. The next chapter considers how the trustees employed the strategies of segregation honed under Haydock's leadership toward their goal of "complete segregation" of Mexican students.

FIGURE 9. Antonia Arguelles DiLiello, Bachelor of Arts in History, California State University Channel Islands, 2006. Courtesy of Antonia Arguelles DiLiello.

FOUR

Ramona School and the
Undereducation of Children
in La Colonia

In spite of any and all excuses, the Spanish-speaking group is not
receiving a comparable education. . . . Then who has failed—the
child or the school? What of compulsory education? What of
the duty and responsibility of the State? What of the democratic
theory of education?

—GEORGE I. SÁNCHEZ, 1934

IN 1934, SCHOLAR GEORGE I. SÁNCHEZ questioned the long-term consequences of misusing intelligence tests to justify a "dual system of education" that discriminated against Mexican and Spanish-speaking children.[1]
He called the disparate schooling opportunities offered to these students in
cities and towns across the United States a "prostitution of democratic ideals
to the cause of expediency, politics, vested interests, ignorance, class and 'race'
prejudice."[2] Had Sánchez visited Oxnard in the 1930s, he would have seen
three elementary schools enrolling both Mexican and White students. Upon
closer examination, he would have certainly noticed that Mexican American
students endured separate and unequal educational conditions within those
schools. Indeed, without offering any excuse over the course of four decades,
Oxnard's White architects had steadfastly crafted segregated spaces that
effectively failed the majority of Mexican students.

When the trustees approved the construction of an elementary school in
La Colonia, in 1939, the dual school system in Oxnard became physically obvious. The decision to segregate Mexican children in this east-side school came
after six years of intense enrollment adjustments and readjustments within the
three west-side schools. By the end of the 1938–39 school year, tolerance for
Mexican children had almost completely eroded, to the extent that White
parents preferred to keep their children in overcrowded double-grade classes
rather than have them grouped with Mexican students. Superintendent

Haydock and the trustees had exhausted their plans and space, but had not given up on their desire for "complete segregation" of Mexican children.[3]

Building on discussions of race, space, and education in the previous chapters, and considering the ways population growth fueled segregation plans, I begin this chapter in 1939, when the trustees approved the first school in La Colonia. According to the U.S. Census, Oxnard was home to almost 8,519 residents by 1940.[4] Within the decade, the population grew to 21,567, spurred in large part by the increase of Mexican residents.[5] By 1954—the same year the U.S. Supreme Court ruled in the landmark *Brown v. Board of Education* desegregation case—the trustees had strategically positioned nine of the district's eleven schools west of Oxnard Boulevard and the railroad tracks in neighborhoods kept predominately White through racial covenants.

CONSTRUCTING AN EAST-SIDE SCHOOL

On June 27, 1939, without using the terms "Mexican" or "segregation," the board adopted a resolution to construct a school in La Colonia.[6] The motion called for a new building to help resolve the geographic "hazard" wherein "so many children must cross a railroad right of way and two heavily traveled streets in going to and from school."[7] The trustees further outlined the need for an additional facility based on "the increased enrollment in the primary school, known as Roosevelt School, [which] has caused cramed [*sic*] conditions to exist therein."[8] They set aside funds and mobilized for a special election to pass a bond measure that would facilitate the school's construction.

In the spring of 1939, *The Oxnard Daily Courier* embarked on a public campaign for an east-side school. For example, on May 2 the paper reprinted a letter from Ventura County superintendent of schools Wilbur K. Cobb to Oxnard's mayor W. Roy Guyer, asking for crossing guards to be assigned on Oxnard Boulevard.[9] Within five days, the paper printed the note of commendation given to Guyer from Cobb's office for "speedy action in safeguarding the lives of boys and girls in your community."[10] Two months later, in July, the paper ran a front-page story describing the proposed school as a safer option for the over "400 Mexican children [who] cross Oxnard Boulevard four times a day, imperiling their lives."[11] In September, the paper followed up with a report on the trustees' purchase of land for the school and included a short story about a kindergartener, Arthur Martinez, who had been hit by a car and broken his leg walking to Roosevelt School.[12]

The Oxnard Daily Courier took on a leading role in the campaign for a school bond to fund an east-side school. For example, an article on December 9, 1939, presented detailed building plans, reassuring potential voters, "The severely plain lines of the proposed school building in the Colonia Gardens section of Oxnard are meeting with the approval of many citizens of the district."[13] On December 11, four days before the special election on a $75,000 school bond issue, the newspaper dedicated a large portion of the front page to civic leaders' endorsements of the east-side school.[14] Some of the White architects endorsing the proposed facility included the head of the PTA and civic leaders Henry H. Eastwood, chief of police George Pryor, former school board president Roy B. Witman, and Oxnard Development Company president A. J. Dingeman.[15] The list did not include any Mexican residents. The day after the election, the newspaper reported the bond issue "passed by the margin of better than 10 to 1," and reprinted the thank-you note sent from the school board to *The Oxnard Daily Courier* for "assistance" in the campaign. The school trustees acknowledged, "The large majority given the bonds was in large part due to the fine publicity given by your paper."[16] Galvanizing around the building of an east-side school was in the interest of James J. Krouser, the publisher of *The Oxnard Daily Courier,* and many other civic leaders who maintained racial covenants on their west-side properties— and sought to keep the area exclusively White.

The successful campaign to fund a school in La Colonia under the pretext of keeping children safe helped the trustees deflect attention away from their previously stated goal of "complete segregation" for Mexican students. Despite repeated newspaper claims, the construction of Ramona was not about safety. Mexican children had walked across the boulevard and railroad tracks for over two decades with almost no assistance,[17] and those who continued on after elementary school in the 1940s would continue this dangerous trek—to school, home for lunch, and back again—at Wilson, Haydock, and Oxnard High schools. The White architects' feigned interest in the welfare of Mexican children echoed the patronizing remarks by Superintendent Haydock from 1917, when he nominated a deputy nurse to contain "cases of filth and disease and contagion" ostensibly found in Mexican schoolchildren.[18] Haydock's vested interest, then, to ensure Mexican students' daily attendance while providing them separate and unequal schooling remained consistent with the White architects' interests two decades later. Indeed, the construction of Ramona vindicated their previously failed attempts to create Haydock as a "Mexican" school. It also relieved the pressure to sustain and expand the school-within-a-school model of segregation within the over-crowded Roosevelt, Wilson, and Haydock facilities.

The school trustees took nominations for the new school name and decided on Ramona on a suggestion from "a taxpayer," who indicated the name would "tie-in with the rich Spanish history of California and the Spanish influence of the district surrounding the school."[19] The name reflected a romantic vision of Spanish-era California popularized by the 1884 Helen Hunt Jackson novel, and epitomized the mundane racism driving the school's construction. From the start, Ramona was designed to be inferior to the west-side schools. As reported by *The Oxnard Daily Courier,* "The proposed building is to have a concrete floor with stucco side walls and flat roof. The estimated cost per classroom is to be about $4,000 in comparison to the present Wilson building which was built at a cost of $7,500 per room."[20] This lesser amount was not adjusted for inflation, though Wilson School had been built fifteen years earlier.

The significantly reduced construction costs signaled the school trustees' urgency to build Ramona as a functional facility, without the amenities or design qualities of the three west-side schools. Trustee Beach stated, "This building will not be encumbered by elaborate 'gingerbread' designs nor will there be a place for ornate decoration."[21] Such decorations seemingly included trees. A note about air-raid drill procedures from January 22, 1942, confirms the differential design of Ramona School. The outline describes that "Regulations in this school are much different than for others due to construction of building: 1. Large wall space of glass. 2. No trees or other means of hiding building or children. 3. All children live within four blocks of building. 4. No traffic hazards."[22] With nowhere to take shelter on school grounds in the case of an air raid, students practiced drill instructions to "run home as fast as they can."[23]

Besides the minimalist construction budget and questionable quality of the facility itself, Ramona was designed to maximize the geographic containment of Mexicans east of the railroad tracks. A few weeks before Ramona School's opening in September 1940, the *Oxnard Press-Courier* outlined the new attendance boundaries: "All children living south of Fifth Street will attend the Haydock School in the first six grades. All children living north of Fifth Street and West of Oxnard Boulevard will attend the Roosevelt School in the first six grades. All children living east of Oxnard Boulevard and north of Fifth Street will attend the Ramona School."[24] These new school boundaries provided a concrete response to White parents' petitions in 1936 and 1938 for a social and academic "color-line"[25] between Mexican and White students. The school trustees' use of residential segregation as a guide to facilitate attendance divisions enabled the spatial expansion of the dual school system to appear geographically natural.

RESTRICTING EDUCATIONAL ACCESS:
A LONGITUDINAL STUDY

No Kindergarten

If the inferior physical facilities of Ramona School signaled educational disparity, the substandard quality of the academic program within the school confirmed that fact. A study by Domingo Martinez, a graduate student who became a teacher at Ramona, exposed multiple structural disparities leading to the undereducation of the predominately Mexican student body. To begin with, from the school's opening in 1940 until 1948, there were no kindergarten facilities provided. He noted, "Prior to this time, children were not admitted to school until they were of first grade age, at which time they were assigned to either pre-first or first grade."[26] Records remain unclear about the transparency of this policy. Some of my interviewees remember being in kindergarten at Ramona before 1948, but they were most likely in a "pre-first grade" class. Martinez's study spanned from 1941 to 1955, following the academic outcomes of 941 Mexican American students who attended Ramona through sixth grade and graduated from eighth grade at Wilson School. He analyzed the children in two distinct groups over the fourteen-year period. His "first period" included children who attended the "mixed" Roosevelt and "segregated" Ramona in the academic years 1941–42 through 1946–47. His "second period" referred to those who attended only the "segregated" Ramona School during the years 1947–48 through 1954–55.[27] Thirty-six percent of children from the first period and 69 percent from the second period did not attend kindergarten. He warned against making the presumption that these percentages reflected a problem of "strong family attachment, distance, lack of understanding of the kindergarten program, or indifference on the part of the parents."[28] Instead, Martinez argued, explanations for this pattern had to account for the fact that Colonia children were denied access to any kindergarten for almost a decade.

Records show that the school trustees' failure to include kindergarten facilities in Ramona's original design could have been corrected well before

1948. One year after the school opened, in 1941, the trustees made plans for three additional rooms at an estimated cost of $10,000.[29] Knowing that no kindergarten facilities were available for Colonia students, the trustees could have accommodated young children at Roosevelt. Instead, consistent with their colleagues from prior decades, the trustees chose to restrict rather than extend access for the mostly Mexican children east of the tracks. This policy decision shaped disparate academic outcomes for Mexican American students. Martinez found that the rate of sixth-grade completion corresponded with the rate of kindergarten attendance: a higher proportion of children who did not attend kindergarten did not complete sixth grade.[30]

Placement in Pre-first Grade

Martinez's study also showed a significant pattern of school officials assigning Colonia students to "pre-first grade," a class distinct from kindergarten for children deemed to be underprepared for first grade. Martinez found no records describing how school officials determined "pre-first grade" placements, but noted that most often the rationale seemed to be that they did not speak English. He found that 48 percent of children during the first period had been placed in "pre-first grade" and 41 percent in the second period.

As a tool employed exclusively for Mexican American children, the practice of enrolling students in an additional year of "pre-first grade" or "pre-primary" echoed segregation efforts aimed at Americanization from the early decades of the twentieth century. In Oxnard, preprimary classes followed Mexican student enrollments. Registration records show preprimary at Roosevelt from the 1929–30 through the 1939–40 school years. Roosevelt's discontinuation of preprimary occurred precisely when Ramona opened. Haydock, the school that trustees had attempted to designate for Mexican children, also maintained preprimary from 1929–30 through 1942–43. Ramona's preprimary began when the school opened in 1940 and continued into the 1950s.[31] The Ventura County director of curriculum instruction, Pauline Jeidy, described the use of "preprimary" classes in nine local school districts as a means of segregating Mexican American children for the purposes of teaching English and familiarizing them with the "Anglo-American" way of life.[32] Referring to considerations ostensibly initiated in 1942, she explained, "Segregation of the six-year-old Mexican-American children seemed necessary in the larger population centers because they had so little preparation for living with the Anglo-American children. . . . School administrators and teachers sincerely believed they could do more for the Mexican-American children by teaching them apart from the Anglo-American children. It was not their plan to cause the Mexican-American children to suffer disadvantages."[33]

According to Jeidy, as of 1947 the nine Ventura County districts she mentioned ended racial segregation of Mexican Americans but planned to continue "preprimary" segregation. For example, she explained that in nearby Fillmore, about twenty-four miles northeast of Oxnard, "the segregation of Mexican-Americans was discontinued this year," but went on to say that thirty-three first-graders "have been segregated until they learn the language, which requires about one year. This room for the Mexican children is called the preprimary room."[34] She noted that Fillmore's district superintendent planned to "establish a kindergarten conveniently located for the Mexican-American children" rather than continue with the preprimary class. Jeidy reported that Santa Paula also "dispensed" with segregation, but further elaborated that they did so because "the administration wanted all the children in the district to enjoy the same privileges and advantages."[35]

Noticeably absent from Jeidy's remarks was any mention of why these districts decided to end racial segregation, or more specifically how the timing of their policy changes coincided with the ruling for the Mexican American plaintiffs in the *Mendez v. Westminster* class action lawsuit. The case led to the removal of racial exclusions from the state education codes effective in 1947, and legally ended race-based segregation in California schools.[36] Still, segregation of Mexican students had never been legally codified in the state.[37] Inadvertently, her remarks made a few admissions as well. Specifically, Jeidy confirmed that additional districts throughout Ventura County did not offer kindergarten to Mexican American children until late in the 1940s, that school officials planned locations of facilities in segregated neighborhoods (often under the guise of convenience for the Mexican American community), and that segregated schooling conditions did indeed deny Mexican Americans "the same privileges and advantages" as Whites.[38]

The *Oxnard Press-Courier* further confirmed the racial makeup of Ramona's student body and the use of a "pre-primary" class as a form of remediation in April 1946:

> The 15-room school now can accommodate 540 pupils, all of whom come from either Mexican or Negro families living in the Colonia Gardens district.... Fifteen teachers are required to teach the classes which range from

the pre-primary through sixth grade. Stuart O. Streshly, principal of the school, said that usually the Mexican children entering pre-primary speak little or no English, and that a great deal of patience is required on the part of the teacher. However, once a knowledge of English is attained, the pupils are pushed along as fast as those of any other school.[39]

According to Martinez, not until 1952 did Ramona officials develop a "screening procedure" for placement of students in "pre-first grade." This assessment process included teacher observations, performance evaluation by all kindergarten teachers, and input from a consultant and the principal.[40] It is unclear whether the screening procedure was applied to students who attended kindergarten or those who were attempting to enroll in school for the first time at age six, or both. Martinez described the evaluating group as seeking to ensure that in addition to overcoming their ostensive "language handicap," children had "matured sufficiently" for "the program of a regular first grade."[41] He seemed optimistic about the screening procedure and the intentions of the evaluating committee, but his remarks expressed hesitation, noting that the new method still lacked "a scientific approach."[42]

High Retention Rates

As he further examined the educational experiences of the two student cohorts in his study, Martinez found that 21 percent of these Mexican American children had been retained sometime in their elementary school years, 12 percent in the first grade and 9 percent in other grades. He uncovered a significantly higher rate of retention at Ramona in comparison to Roosevelt. Ramona retained 16 percent of Mexican American students in the first grade and 13 percent of those in the second through sixth grades. Roosevelt retained 7 percent of Mexican American first-grade students and 3 percent of those in the other grades. Martinez did not mention whether any rationale had been recorded, academic or otherwise, for the retentions.

Martinez's exposure of multiple structural barriers refuted claims about cultural deficiencies leading Mexican Americans from Colonia to be over age and below grade level in reading, language, and arithmetic upon arrival to Wilson.[43] Despite the lack of academic preparation for Ramona students, close examination of Martinez's research also reveals much strength and resilience exhibited over a fourteen-year period by the 941 Mexican American children who successfully navigated through institutions designed to fail them and who graduated from the sixth and eighth grades. In doing so, these students attained a higher schooling level than most of the Spanish-surnamed population of Oxnard. Indeed, according to the 1950 U.S. Census, at least half of all persons of Spanish surname in Oxnard age twenty-five and older had completed less than 4.6 years of schooling—the lowest in the state.[44] The 1960 census showed median completion rates of 5.9 years.[45]

MEMORIES OF RAMONA SCHOOL

Ramona was all Mexicans. That was the segregation of the Colonia, the railroad tracks.... We were not allowed to speak Spanish, and in fact if you accidentally spoke it and a teacher overheard you, they carried these wooden paddles with them. Boy or girl, right there in front of everybody, they would just [make] you bend over, and they would swat you. So the discipline was really physical discipline; they never called your parents or anything else. Ramona School had very low expectations of us, it was primarily babysitting. In terms of what you learned, it was very simplistic.

—JOE I. MENDOZA[46]

By the time Joe graduated from the eighth grade, he had attended Roosevelt, Ramona, and Wilson schools and experienced segregation in each. Whereas at Roosevelt and Wilson he was placed in the all-Mexican classes, at Ramona in the early 1940s he attended alongside a student body which was in his words, "exclusively, totally Mexican."[47] In some ways, Joe's details about Oxnard's first east-side school echo accounts of cultural shaming and academic underpreparation experienced at the west-side schools. His remarks also shed light on the physicality of containment and control at the predominately Mexican American school. He mentioned that during his time there, he and other students brought lunches from home because there was no cafeteria. He recalled a blackboard in his classroom, but very few books. Decades later, witnesses in the *Soria v. Oxnard School Board of Trustees* trial gave testimony about classrooms featuring a single bare-bulb light fixture and floors appearing to be simply painted-over blacktop.[48]

Indeed, my interviewees had very few positive memories of Ramona School. Joe and other men I interviewed mentioned regularly experiencing and witnessing "physical discipline."[49] In addition to being "swatted" for speaking Spanish, Joe recalled that any student who attempted to skip out on school for the day, to work or just not attend, also received corporal punishment. He remarked, "They had a lady—I'm trying to remember her name—we all called her *la Bruja,* the Witch. She would drive this black Model-A Ford and she would drive around the Colonia. If she saw us, she'd bring us back to school. We'd get paddled and then sent into the classroom."[50]

Alex Quiroz, who was born in Camarillo in 1940 and raised in La Colonia, also remembered the physical discipline at Ramona. He explained that because he would talk a lot during class, "I used to get slapped a lot by the teachers. I had rulers broken on my hand because I spoke. I wasn't using bad language or anything, just talking to my classmates, and they would put you in front of the class and punish you."[51] He described himself as a "very curious" child, who would usually sit next to his kindergarten teacher. He enjoyed reading the "Dick and Jane and Spot" book she held up for the class, and recalled: "One day I asked her to lend me the book to take it home so I could read, and she laughed at me. She said, 'What do you mean read it?' I said, 'Yeah, I can read it.'"[52] In addition to having his teacher show disbelief in his academic capabilities, Alex soon realized she would not show any regard for his well-being:

> I was on the monkey bars and this kid—he was a year ahead of me at school— he grabbed my legs and I told him to let go. I couldn't hold on so I fell face first. So they took me to the nurse's room. They left me there and left me there, that's it. Nobody came. It was getting dark, so I went home and my mom and dad asked what happened, and right away they took me back and the principal was still in his office. I really don't know what was said, but I was totally ignored. I was all bloody and everything and I was just put in that room [and told,] "Just wait here." I was in kindergarten so I waited. And that was Mrs. Pollock. That's why I remember her name very well.[53]

Alex noted that his teachers at Ramona were all White women, whom he described as "dismissive" of him and his peers.[54] "We were just kind of warehoused there,"[55] he explained. The women I interviewed shared this sentiment. Many witnessed routine corporal punishment but spoke most about a climate of indifference and hostility.

Despite this harsh treatment, Alex excelled academically and even "skipped" from the third to the fifth grade. In his words, he "breezed through everything."[56] Over time, however, the daily stunning and subtle incidents he experienced at Ramona did diminish Alex's sense of enthusiasm for school. In the sixth grade, when he was placed in Mr. Domingo Martinez's class, he encountered for the first time a teacher trying to engage students. Speaking about Mr. Martinez, Alex acknowledged: "He tried, but at that time the boys were already very rambunctious. He tried to teach them about radios. So he brought a bunch of old radios and we took them apart. And he just gave up on us."[57] For Alex and his "rambunctious" peers, six years of containment and control at Ramona may indeed have been a difficult challenge for any one teacher to mitigate. By the time he started seventh grade at Wilson, he described matter-of-factly that he was a very good student, but he and his friends would "beat up" any of the White boys who tried to treat them as "less than."[58] Outside of Mrs. Pollock, Mr. Martinez was the only teacher whose name Alex remembered. He did not mention Mr. Martinez in relation to corporal punishment, and indeed this singular Latino teacher represented the only memory of Ramona he stated in somewhat positive terms. These moments in Alex's trajectory, from a "curious" child to a "rambunctious" preteen engaging in physical conflict with White students, shed light on some of the interpersonal influences of disparate treatment at Ramona School. Indeed, Domingo Martinez's study demonstrates that structural inequality at the elementary level led to low academic outcomes for the majority of Mexican Americans who persisted through eighth grade at Wilson.

Bedford Pinkard, who began attending Ramona School in the third grade, shed further light on the continuities of segregation for Colonia students.[59] Bedford, who incidentally remembered being paddled by the principal at Ramona, was born in Jacksonville, Texas, in 1930 and worked with his family picking lemons in Oxnard until his father found a job at the naval base in the early 1940s. They lived on Garfield Avenue in La Colonia, and he attended Ramona through the sixth grade as one of three Black children enrolled in the school at that time. He explained: "But once we arrived at Wilson School, the kids that came from Ramona School, they were segregated *in* the classroom. There was a row of seats—if you didn't have enough to fill a room there were certain rows of seats that you would sit in. You wouldn't sit next to the other [White] persons."[60] As he recalled the routine practice of grouping the few Black students with the Mexican students in designated rows apart from their White classmates, Bedford remarked: "I kind of knew what was going on and just accepted it and kept doing what I was supposed to be doing. . . . We didn't even mix with any [Whites] during PE."[61]

Robert Madrid, who was born in 1938, added nuance to the sense that disparate treatment was mundane. Considering his memories of being "disciplined for speaking Spanish" at Ramona and Wilson schools,[62] he explained that compliance was achieved through intimidation and force. He learned early on that his parents felt they could not advocate for him because they believed they did not have any authority to question the schools' English-only policy. Robert remarked, "so that's where I lost some of my Spanish."[63] By the time he and his peers matriculated to Wilson, he stated, they held a common understanding that anything they did to question school officials would result in punishment: "We had to learn how to say 'yes sir' and 'no sir' and move on, because it wasn't going to get us anyplace but a paddle on the butt."[64]

Though the trustees had realized much of their plan for "complete segregation"[65] with the construction of Ramona, their acceptance of a row or two of Colonia students into the White classes at Wilson suggests some pragmatic concessions in the 1940s. It remains unclear whether the Black and Mexican students admitted in the White classes went through any type of assessment, whether they needed to be identified as "the brightest, cleanest,"[66] as they had been the previous decade, or whether their placement was a result of what Bedford recalled as not having the numbers for "a complete class of kids from Ramona School."[67] Still, efforts to control racial mixing by maintaining separate physical education sessions for Mexican and Black children upheld the White parents' demands from previous decades for academic and social segregation.

CONTINUITIES OF MUNDANE RACISM AMID DEMOGRAPHIC CHANGE

After Ramona, the district did not build another school until after World War II. In the meantime, the city's population grew exponentially. The Bracero Program, initiated in 1942, facilitated huge growth for Ventura County[68] and for Oxnard. The Buena Vista Labor Camp, located east of Oxnard Boulevard on Fifth Street, became known as the largest labor camp in the United States.[69] Though recruited as temporary contract workers, braceros often established local relationships and many eventually brought their families from Mexico to Oxnard. By 1950, Spanish-surnamed (Mexican) residents comprised 7,155 (33%) of the city's population.[70]

In 1946, trustees oversaw construction of James Driffill School on Ninth Street, west of the boulevard.[71] A few weeks before the start of the 1948 school year, the *Oxnard Press-Courier* published an article outlining "geographical zones" for school attendance, including a new school, Elm School, also on the west side.[72] In 1949, Roosevelt School was replaced with another west-side facility, named Clarence Brittell School.[73]

Given the population growth of the city, and of La Colonia in particular, in November 1951 the trustees announced the anticipated completion of Juanita School, which was being constructed just one short block from Ramona School. Domingo Martinez became the founding principal of Juanita School. Similar to Ramona, Juanita was designed to underserve east-side students from the start. Superintendent Richard M. Clowes explained that the school would open in December in an effort to end double sessions at Ramona, and to provide a facility for the new 260-unit "low-rent" housing project in the east side, which was also near completion. In announcing the details about opening Juanita, Clowes inadvertently revealed that the school would be near capacity from the start: "The school has eight classrooms, two kindergartens, a cafeteria, and administrative offices. When the school is ready 120 kindergarteners, 180 first-graders, and 60 second-graders will be transferred from Ramona to Juanita School. . . . The total capacity of the new school is 420."[74]

Even as the trustees planned to enroll 360 students at Juanita—sixty shy of the facility's limit—they approved the hiring of extra teachers for Driffill School, on the west side of town, "where the number of kindergarten classes . . . jumped from an expected four to seven."[75] Indeed, double sessions started almost immediately after Juanita opened, and lasted for five years. In the meantime, in 1952, the pattern of building on the west side continued with Kamala School, and in 1954 the trustees approved three additional facilities, Bernice Curren School, Dennis McKinna School, and a replacement Haydock School.[76]

In November 1954, the *Oxnard Press-Courier* reported that about thirty second-graders who had been attending Juanita from 8:00 a.m. to 12:00 p.m. would transfer to Ramona, and be placed in a converted utility room.[77] Another thirty students, who had been attending Juanita from 12:30 to 4:40 p.m. each day, would now have a regular full-day schedule. The article noted that Juanita's last double session followed the end of double sessions across the district, which occurred weeks prior when the replacement Haydock School opened. The version of this story in the *Oxnard Press-Courier*'s weekly

Spanish edition differed from the English text. The Spanish version included quotes by Superintendent Clowes confirming that in the last five years the school trustees had approved the construction of 110 new classrooms to accommodate increasing district enrollments.[78] The Spanish-language article continued with Clowes encouraging La Colonia residents to vote in favor of upcoming school bonds so that as the district continued to grow, their children would not have to return to double sessions.[79] Framed in this way, the article confirmed that Clowes and the trustees had prioritized segregation for Colonia students, annually committing resources to build facilities on the west side of the city to accommodate population growth rather than easing persistently overcrowded conditions for east-side students. The trustees' inability to anticipate demographic change in relation to Mexican children was not new, but their refusal to respond equitably for east-side residents as compared to what they did for their west-side neighbors became even more apparent in the decade after World War II.

"YOU'RE IN THE WRONG SEAT"

As discussed in chapter 2, there was very little permeability of the east-west color line for Mexican and Black homebuyers before World War II. In 1952, the family of nine-year-old Dolores Ávila (Carrasco) finally negotiated their way out of La Colonia with a home purchase one block west of Oxnard Boulevard. This move meant Dolores would no longer attend Ramona, where she had been since kindergarten. Instead, for fifth grade she was enrolled at Elm School. She remembered:

> The first day that I went, I sat in the front row right by the teacher's desk, like what I was used to. So then class started, she introduced me and she said, "Children, we have a new student, her name is Deelores Aeeveela." I thought to myself, "That's not my name." My name was Dolores Ávila, but you didn't question, you didn't say nothing. So she says, "Deelores, I'm afraid you're in the wrong seat." And I thought, "Oh," you know, I got scared. She says, "Your seat is in the back, the last seat over there, the back row." I got up and got my little bag, my lunch, and I sat in the back. I felt like this [making a hand sign indicating she felt very little]. I was embarrassed. . . . I didn't understand why I couldn't sit in the front.[80]

Dolores felt conscious that she was the only Mexican in a class of all White students. She quickly recognized that she also stood out in terms of her academic preparation:

> After a few days, I realized they were *way* ahead of me in math, social studies, English, all the subjects. I was lost, and at Ramona School I was an "A" student. Well, they weren't A's in those days, it was a 1, a 1 through 5. I used to do my homework, I used to read, I used to do everything that I was told to, but I was lost. And I never said anything to anybody, not even my mom and dad.[81]

Dolores described feeling completely alone at Elm, and she was concerned that despite her best efforts she was not catching up to her White peers. Still, she did not talk with her parents about this situation. She recalled one incident of doing a "book report" for the first time, saying that her teacher, Mrs. Devore, "used me as an example in front of the class [of what not to do] and then she corrected, humiliated me. So I think that had a lot to do with my confidence going way down."[82] Describing herself as a younger child, living in La Colonia and attending Ramona, Dolores spoke about being outgoing, imitating the songs and dances she saw in the Shirley Temple movies, and doing well in school. Her sense of being special, talented, and smart was diminished in the transition to the predominately White neighborhood and school: "By the time I got to sixth grade, I was an average student. The highest grade on my report card was maybe a couple of B's and all C's. I was struggling, especially my reading. My reading and my math was really hard, and I don't know . . . in those days children didn't question anything, that was very disrespectful . . . so we just kept quiet and accepted any treatment you got."[83]

What Dolores could not have known was that many of her Mexican American and Black peers were also struggling in math and English. Not until the late 1960s would the California State Department of Education describe the Oxnard district's "tracking" pattern into junior high according to math and English "ability groups" as an indication of "unequal opportunity for minority group children."[84] By that time, Mexican Americans comprised 42 percent of the district but were only 11 percent of those "tracked" into the high-math group and 13 percent of those in high English. Black students, who were 13 percent of the district, made up slightly less than 4 percent of those tracked into the high-math and 5 percent of the high-English groups.

In contrast, White students, who comprised about 43 percent of the elementary district student population, comprised slightly more than 75 percent of the high-math and 74 percent of the high-English groups. Conversely, Mexican Americans were disproportionately overrepresented in the low-math and low-English ability groups, comprising 68 percent and almost 63 percent, respectively.[85]

Of course, the revelation that Mexican American and Black students were systematically denied equal access and opportunity came over a decade late for Dolores, who dealt in isolation with her feelings of inadequacy. As a child, she believed she deserved the "get to the back of the class" treatment she received at Elm. She recognized: "It affected me a lot. It made me feel like White people were better than me, smarter than me, had more than me."[86]

In sixth grade at Elm, with a new teacher, she began to make some friends with White girls. Midway through the year, another Mexican student, Dolores Rodarte, moved into her neighborhood. The two became best friends, and she started to feel less isolated. As she struggled in her new surroundings, she remembered timely *consejos* (advice) from her father:

> My dad used to say, "This is better for you. You need to go to school and learn something. [Take] your older sister Christina [for example]." I think she went up to maybe like in her freshman, sophomore [year], and she left school and went to work. So for the rest of her working days, she worked in *la chileria* [*chile* cannery]. So my dad used to tell the younger ones—I had three younger sisters—and myself, "You better *aplíquense en la escuela porque si no se aplican, allí van a trabajar en la chileria. O, van a trabajar en los files, de sol a sol*" [apply yourself in school or you'll have to go work in the *chile* cannery, or work in the fields, from sun up to sun down]. So my brother and I, Percy, we used to look at each other and say, "I don't want to work out in the fields. Well, you'd better get busy and finish that homework." We used to advise each other.[87]

Dolores had not shared her difficulties adjusting at Elm with anyone, and felt very encouraged in hearing her dad's aspirations for her and her siblings to carve out a life for themselves beyond the fields or factories of Oxnard through working hard in school. With clarity of vision and a sense that she was not alone, she worked alongside her brother to help realize their parents' hopes for a future of less hardship.

For junior high, Dolores was assigned to Haydock School, where she was again separated from White students. She was not clear about how she ended up in a class without any of her peers from Elm: "They put me in this class where I don't know anybody. All the Mexicans and Blacks were in one classroom, so I thought where's my [White] girlfriends from where I live, from my neighborhood? I don't know where they put them."[88] She asked her teacher why she was not in the same class as her friends, and he replied:

> "Oh, I don't know. Are they your neighbors?" He didn't believe that I lived in this neighborhood. And I go, "Yeah." [And he asked,] "Well, where do you live?" [I said,] "On California Street." [He asked again,] "And your friends?" [I said,] "Birch, Ash, Hemlock." [He responded,] "Ohhh ..." At the time I didn't know what he was realizing, but now I know he was realizing that I came from a White neighborhood and my friends were White.[89]

Though her teacher may have been surprised to learn Dolores and her family had crossed the "color-line,"[90] he did not question her placement in his segregated Mexican class. Indeed, her family's upwardly mobile social-class standing, which earned them a new address in a White neighborhood, did not garner her access to the White class. Despite being with a completely new group of students again, Dolores felt much less hostility at Haydock than she had experienced at Elm. In that segregated space, she began to recover her self-confidence. Remembering her teacher, she remarked, "He gave me a chance." Her teacher placed her in charge of monitoring other students when he stepped out, and this felt like a very affirming recognition for her: "I kind of started getting my confidence back, and my grades started improving because I was in the classroom where I was like one of the top, if not *the* top student. I got very good grades, *again*."[91]

This window into Dolores's experiences affirms the ways students, parents, and teachers employed agency in segregated spaces. Taken together, the memories of my interviewees demonstrate a pattern of a predominately White and female teaching staff who at best expressed very little care for Mexican students, and at worst engaged in stunning acts of disregard and public humiliation. A handful of male teachers stood out for my interviewees as creating more positive experiences for students. In chapter 3, Antonia referred to Mr. Fox in her eighth-grade Mexican class at Wilson as "the best teacher that tried to really get to us." Dolores positively remembered her teacher in the Mexican class at Haydock, reiterating, "He gave me a chance." Likewise, Alex described Mr. Martinez as the only teacher who "tried," and recounted an incident of his parents intervening on his behalf with the principal at Ramona. Such everyday expressions of caring and effective pedagogy cultivated students' resilience. They remained prominent in my interviewees' memories as exceptions to the commonplace demeaning treatment that they had come to almost accept.

IMAGES OF INEQUALITY

Archival photographs taken of Ramona, Juanita, and various west-side schools indicate the need for further research. For example, I found a series of pictures from Ramona, taken in the 1950s, portraying students in vocational classes. In a few of these photos, girls wear kitchen aprons in what appears to be a cooking/baking class.[92] Other photos show boys and one girl in a woodshop class. In yet another, girls and boys are digging the soil with long-handled hoes. I also found photos labeled "Ramona, 1952, Special Class," portraying individual boys and girls combing their hair or brushing their teeth.[93] I did not find any pictures with similar classroom activities at west-side schools. However, I did come across more than one photo of White students in an orchestra class at Wilson School. One picture also shows an Asian student in the class.[94]

There is also a peculiar presence of a chain-link, barbed-wire fence at both Ramona and Juanita in the 1950s—an image I did not see at any west-side school during any time period. For example, in the picture of Ramona students working with garden tools, the dirt they are tilling is in a relatively narrow space between the school building and a chain-link, barbed-wire fence. It remains unclear whether it was approved by district officials or installed by a neighboring facility as La Colonia grew around Ramona. In a photo of Juanita, a barbed-wire fence is visible from the sandbox in the kindergarten play area.[95] Another photograph captures the front of Juanita School, where students walk near or lean up against a chain-link, barbed-wire fence. The picture reveals a posted sign by the Oxnard City Parks and Recreation delineating hours for "Colonia Memorial Park." Further investigation may clarify how city officials rationalized such an enclosure of the park, and whether residents questioned the barbed wire, given that the fence ran directly up against an elementary school. Even without these details, the glaring barbed-wire fencing—found only at Ramona and Juanita schools—remains suspicious. These and the other photographs provide unique views into students' everyday experiences and offer a snapshot of the differential demarcation of schooling spaces from east to west.

FIGURE 10. Ramona School, fifth-grade students working with wood-shop tools, Oxnard, 1952. Courtesy of Oxnard School District.

FIGURE 11. Ramona School, sixth-grade students tilling soil near barbed-wire fence, Oxnard, 1952. Courtesy of Oxnard School District.

FIGURE 12. Juanita School, students leaning up against barbed-wire fence outside front entrance, Oxnard, 1952. Courtesy of Oxnard School District.

FIGURE 13. Woodrow Wilson School, White students and an Asian student in music class, Oxnard, 1952. Courtesy of Oxnard School District.

CONCLUSION

It is the summation of collective micro-offenses by the majority
that ignores the fact that a massive commitment is needed to
make the ghetto school fail.

—CHESTER M. PIERCE, 1970[96]

From its construction in 1939, Ramona School stood as a physical manifesta-
tion of a "massive commitment" to segregation. The geographic isolation of
Ramona, as Joe stated, "in the middle of a bean field,"[97] and the punitive, remedial treatment doled out to the majority Mexican American and few Black
students within its overcrowded classrooms represented a vision for education
four decades in the making. Indeed, in 1954, fifteen years after Superintendent
Haydock's retirement and even as the U.S. Supreme Court struck down the
legal doctrine of "separate but equal," Oxnard's strategies of segregation had
emerged as a seemingly natural and permanent dual school system.

On an everyday basis, Mexican and a few Black students experienced
Ramona as a series of subtle and stunning "micro-offenses," which aimed to
diminish their self-confidence and reduce their academic achievement.[98] In the
words of Joe and Alex, most teachers at Ramona held "very low expectations"
and seemed "dismissive" of Mexican students. Domingo Martinez's study
further verified that low expectations were not simply an expression of teachers' attitudes but were structurally manifest in the inferior academic program,
with long-term consequences. The "summation of collective micro-offenses" at
Ramona, and eventually at Juanita, resulted in significant academic underpreparation and attrition for Mexican children before sixth grade. Few students persisted to the junior high schools west of the boulevard and railroad
tracks, but those who did, endured containment within segregated classes and
racially separate rows within White classrooms.[99] In hindsight, the everyday
encouragement of parents, siblings, and a handful of teachers stood out for
interviewees as positive memories, though they did not eclipse the incessant
derogatory messages sent by racially disparate schooling conditions.

While Oxnard's two east-side elementary schools may have symbolized
the successful convergence of segregation strategies set in motion in prior
decades, these facilities also became physical evidence of the differential
treatment of Colonia students. The next chapter follows the population
growth of the Mexican and Black communities and their efforts to challenge
the trustees' "massive commitment"[100] to school segregation.

FIVE

A Common Cause Emerges for Mexican American and Black Organizers

Dear Sir. . . . Your editorial of March 8 raising the hue and cry of "outside interference" smacks of the time-worn plaint of newspapers and citizens in the deep South who hope to throw up a smoke screen so that the real issues cannot be seen.

—ALTHEA T. L. SIMMONS, REGIONAL FIELD
SECRETARY, NAACP, 1963

ON MARCH 18, 1963, ALTHEA T. L. SIMMONS, the field secretary for the western region of the National Association for the Advancement of Colored People (NAACP) wrote an editorial to *The Press-Courier* to "set the record straight"[1] about the desegregation proposal submitted to the Oxnard School Board two weeks earlier. Her statement put the trustees on notice that their denial of school segregation and refusal to take any responsibility to eliminate it reflected the same strategies of resistance that had "led to litigation" in other districts across the United States.[2] She also called out the newspaper for promoting a segregationist agenda. Just as Simmons and the members of the Oxnard branch of the NAACP linked local tactics of bigotry with "the deep South,"[3] they viewed the struggle to end school segregation in the district as part of a larger struggle for civil rights. Indeed, in Oxnard as in other cities across the nation, such organized struggle did not begin or end in 1963.

Between 1940 and 1970, Oxnard's population increased exponentially from 8,519 to 71,255 residents, and Mexicans accounted for much of this growth.[4] During this period, the city also became home to a significant number of Blacks. Whereas the 1940 U.S. Census counted only 28 Black residents, by 1950 there were 1,090 Blacks in a city of 21,567, comprising about 5 percent of the population.[5] Some of this population growth occurred because Oxnard's Port Hueneme, the only port between Los Angeles and San Francisco, became a naval base during World War II.[6] Many Black families relocated to Oxnard as part of the wartime economy.

As new neighbors in a growing city, Mexican Americans and Blacks shared the optimism and expectation of a more just society that many across the nation felt after making significant contributions to the "war for democracy."[7] Most found themselves living in La Colonia—whether they arrived home to the same muddy, unpaved streets and lack of municipal services they knew before having gone overseas to fight fascism, or whether they moved to Oxnard and encountered racial restrictions when attempting to rent or purchase a home west of Oxnard Boulevard and the railroad tracks. Being relegated to homes on the east side meant their children attended the overcrowded Ramona School or, after 1951, the overcrowded Juanita School. As noted in chapter 4, some students were shuffled back and forth between these two schools and placed in temporary or portable classroom spaces. Meanwhile, the pattern of placing new schools on the west side continued with Kamala in 1952, Curren and McKinna in 1954, and Norma Harrington School in 1955. Such disparate material conditions and treatment fueled racial tension—and collective action.

Indeed, the increasing demographic presence of Mexican Americans and Blacks in the city amplified the visibility of multiple forms of community activism, through church organizations, labor unions, civil rights groups, and local mutual aid societies.[8] In parallel and shared efforts, these neighbors contested unfair labor practices, inferior housing conditions, mistreatment by police, and unequal, racially segregated schools. This chapter follows some of the formation of Black and Mexican American organizations in Oxnard, and considers local, regional, and national intersections between organizers and organizations in 1963 in particular, when schooling emerged as a central site of struggle against racial inequality—a common cause—in the city.

THE FOUNDING OF THE OXNARD
BRANCH OF THE NAACP

Black residents, while small in number, contributed to community building in the Ventura-Oxnard area since at least the 1880s. The founding of the Oxnard–Ventura County Branch of the NAACP during an era of significant population growth provided a timely expansion of the networks and resources available to local organizers. Chartered on March 12, 1945, as the Oxnard Branch of the NAACP,[9] the group took on the specific issues of discrimination that emerged from the concerns voiced by its membership, many of whom also participated in other organizations (e.g., St. Paul's Baptist Church, Oxnard Negro Citizens Committee). Leroy A. Gibson Jr., who was born in Ventura in 1938 and grew up in the west Ventura neighborhood of Tortilla Flats, explained that the everyday unfair treatment in social spaces mobilized collective action in the Black community. Following in his father's footsteps, Leroy Jr. became a member of the NAACP in his early twenties. He recognized that the association brought local efforts wider recognition and a network of legal advocates, but he stated: "The grunt work was done by these different organizations, such as the Negro Citizens of Ventura County. It was done by some of the Urban League, it was done by at the time the A.M.E. church, and also the Baptist church."[10] From the perspective of being a member of one of the original Black families in Ventura County,[11] Leroy Jr. reflected on the multiple forms of advocacy taken up within organizations and the strengths of the networks involved: "You have to add the triangle of the churches, the private citizens club, and the NAACP as working as a unit. Because I remember my father, Leroy Sr., he was in all three."[12]

The advocacy of the Good Citizenship Club in Ventura exemplified some of these coordinated efforts of Black organizers and organizations. In October 1944, the group wrote a letter to the *Star–Free Press,* publicly calling on the Ventura City Council to utilize one of their existing buildings to establish a "Negro recreation center . . . for the benefit of Negro service men and others."[13] In their request for a leisure space for Black women and men, they observed, "There are no available places where this group of citizens may go and partake of a meal or refreshments or any other forms of recreation as other groups of citizens are so amply supplied with."[14] The group explained that previous petitions had been heard but not addressed by city leaders, resulting in devastating outcomes. They further described:

> It was brought to the attention of the council that there are some 30 or 40 negroes living in the rear of the colored A.M.E. church on Meta near Figueroa in a group of condemned and tumbled down shacks. It was stated that the conditions there were very unsanitary and that such conditions were a danger to the people, both to their health and to their morale. . . . Since the meeting of Oct. 2, two serious crimes have occurred in or around these shacks and in both cases the offenders have been sent to prison. . . . The law abiding colored citizens in Ventura feel both shocked and grieved; they feel that it is a stain on all the colored citizens living in the county of Ventura. They also feel that this might not have happened had conditions been otherwise, and that these men now languishing in prison might still be at liberty and supporting their respective families.[15]

In pressing the council to act, the editorial revealed that the A.M.E. church was already helping, albeit within limited means. The concerns of the Good Citizenship Club resonated with those expressed in 1922 by the thirty-three Mexican neighbors of Colonia Home Gardens. As discussed in chapter 1, these residents petitioned the Oxnard City Council to remove the town dump from their neighborhood as a "menace" to their "peaceful endeavor of earning our living and sustaining the health of ourselves, our wives, our children, and others who may abide with us."[16] The Good Citizenship Club similarly identified perilous living conditions as a prominent contributing factor to the crimes. They also expressed their concern that individual crimes committed by two Black men in Ventura would negatively influence the perception of all Blacks in the county. Still, they empathized with these individuals, noting that each lost his liberty and ability to provide for his family because of the city leaders' failure to act in a timely fashion. Their framing of the request as an appeal to the city council's sense of democratic and civic duty also reverberated in the Colonia residents' petition decades previously, when they had asked for urgent consideration based on "American fairness and Christian sympathy."[17] Similarly, the Good Citizenship Club quoted remarks by "a great and noble American, Wendell L. Willkie, 'that if they (meaning Negroes) have the right to die beside their fellow white citizens in the protection of liberty they have a right to live in and among them and enjoy that liberty."[18]

Even though they were fighting similar struggles decades apart, both groups astutely anticipated their petition might be dismissed for lack of numerically significant support. The 1922 Colonia residents noted that in addition to thirty-three signers, at least double that number of families would soon be impacted, and the 1944 group wrote, "This letter has the approval of the members and other Negroes of the Good Citizenship Club of Ventura."[19]

Indeed, Black organizers maximized regional networks and exhibited knowledge of the legal system to protest racism swiftly. For example, on March 21, 1946, a Los Angeles publication, the *Neighborhood News,* ran a front-page story about the forcible ejection of four Black patrons from the Oxnard Theater on the previous Sunday. Fred Tolsten, a Black man who unsuccessfully attempted to sit in the section designated for Whites, reported the incident to the Los Angeles Branch of the NAACP. The *Neighborhood News* ran the story under the heading "Prejudice in Oxnard Grows; Trouble Brews," and described it as evidence of "Race tension [which] appeared growing hourly in this small seaport town as the result of townsfolks decision to restore pre-wartime racial restrictive measures in public houses. The race bans in cafes and theatres hit all non caucasians, Negroes, Mexicans and orientals."[20]

Tolsten witnessed a Black woman being evicted by police as he entered the theater, and subsequently realized she had been removed "because she objected to the jimcrow [*sic*] set up."[21] He explained "racial tension is nearing a boiling point in the area," and he went to Los Angeles "to urge a strong inter-racial panel for Oxnard as a means to cure the existing conditions."[22] On April 4, 1946, the *California Eagle* newspaper reported, "Growing racial friction, which civic leaders assert is due to the large proportionate increase in the migration of southerners, both colored and white, to this community during the war years, broke out into the open recently punctuated by several anti-Negro and anti-Mexican episodes." This account detailed that four Oxnard residents, Allie Mae Beamon, Angeline Cole, Irene Turner, and Joe L. Bradford, entered the Oxnard Theater and "the usher tried to lead them to segregated seats. The women [and man] protested and insisted on sitting elsewhere."[23] The article further noted that a man named Richard Abrams, identified as "a prominent colored businessman, civic leader, and president of the local branch of the NAACP," called on the field director of the Los Angeles NAACP to present at an Oxnard branch meeting two weeks after the incident.

Within ten days, Abrams also wrote a letter to Noel Griffin of the NAACP in San Francisco, asking for funds to support filing a case in the Superior Court of Ventura County, noting: "This is a serious infraction of the rights of Negroes under Sections 51 and 52 of the Code of Civil Procedure of the State of California. The management of the theatre, the proprietor of the theatre, and the police officers should be sued."[24] Though the record remains unclear about whether the lawsuit went forward, the NAACP's capacity to consider such recourse would prove useful in its efforts to expose and challenge mundane racism in the city. As the Black community presence in Oxnard-Ventura became more pronounced in the years after World War II, organized calls for equal treatment and living conditions echoed the voices of their neighbors' past, but also expressed an increasing sense of urgency.

THE VENTURA COUNTY COMMUNITY SERVICE ORGANIZATION

Similar to their Black neighbors, Mexican American women and men in Oxnard often contributed to self-determination efforts through more than one organization, and took on various leadership roles within those groups. In 1946, for example, a group called Los Guardianes de La Colonia raised money for the Red Cross as they worked to address the lack of basic municipal services on the east side.[25] Previous Colonia residents' petitions reverberated in their efforts.[26] The newspaper reported, "Two streets, Harrison and Hayes, have been paved with all the lot owners on the streets paying the costs. According to Robert Hinostro, influential member of Los Guardianes, certain areas of Colonia are very unsanitary and unhealthy. A poor drainage system makes it impossible to leave Colonia on Second Street today, he said, since water is standing in the street."[27]

Across time and space, organizers confronted subtle, stunning disregard from city officials. The mundane racism shown to Mexicans seeking to better their living conditions in Oxnard in 1946 mirrored the indifference demonstrated toward Blacks asking for a safe community space in Ventura in 1944. Ultimately, the Oxnard City Council placed the onus on the taxpaying Colonia residents, charging them with enacting and financing their own community improvements.[28] Despite this disparate treatment, and just as their neighbors from prior generations had done, Mexican Americans exercised self-reliance and continued building up their community.[29]

Organizations evolved to be responsive to residents' concerns. For example, in the spring of 1958 Tony Del Buono, president of the Oxnard Civic Improvement Association (OCIA), and the Ventura County Human Relations Committee, arranged a town hall meeting, where at least three hundred participants discussed racial prejudice and discrimination in schools, employment, and housing.[30] The year 1958 also marked one of dramatic change in the city, with the shutdown of the American Beet Sugar Company factory and the designation of the Buena Vista Labor Camp as the largest bracero facility in the United States.[31] Nationally, labor organizers had vociferously challenged the bracero program, exposing its exploitative, unfair treatment of the workers. Oxnard activists contributed to these protests, specifically around the ways the program displaced local workers and normalized labor abuse considered intolerable in other industries. To this end, in late 1958 labor organizer César E. Chávez worked alongside Del Buono and members of the OCIA to create the Ventura County Chapter of the Community Service Organization.[32] Established in the wake of the unsuccessful campaign to elect Edward C. Roybal to the Los Angeles City Council, the CSO's platform focused on "educational reform, police malpractice, and an unresponsive municipal government."[33] This platform resonated deeply with Oxnard's Mexican American residents.

As a collective comprised of mainly Mexican American women and men, the Oxnard-based CSO mobilized on multiple levels toward the empowerment of Ventura County residents, with a special focus on La Colonia.[34] Its members collaborated with the established network of other local organizations to run an unprecedented voter registration drive and engage in house-to-house advocacy with farmworker families.[35] Del Buono served as CSO founding president and Juan "Big John" Soria was later elected president.[36] Born in Oxnard in 1932, Juan grew up in La Colonia.[37] He would go on to work with César Chávez organizing farmworkers.

When Juan ran for city council in 1960 and 1962, *The Press-Courier* editorialized about his CSO affiliation, claiming his organization of farmworkers conflicted with city interests.[38] Two failed attempts to win a seat on the council only strengthened Juan and the CSO's resolve to represent the interests of his Mexican American and Black neighbors. As his first wife, Julieta Flores Soria (Mendoza), recalled, their home often functioned as a central meeting place:

> *Aquí estaba siempre la casa llena de gente. . . . Aquí hacían las primeras juntas y todo. Aquí fue cuando ya empezó con César Chávez. . . . Habían muchas organizaciones de diferentes, y venían, y se juntaban aquí. No importa si fueron Chinos o Negros, venían a mi casa, y yo me ponía a concinar para darles de comer. Y también yo los acompañaba a las marchas.* [We always had a full house here. They held all the first meetings here. This is where Juan started working with César Chávez. There were many different organizations, and they came and met here. It did not matter if they were Chinese or Black; they came to my house and I got to work making them something to eat. I also went with them to the marches.][39]

Juan's bilingualism, interracial networks, and organizing skills, along with Julieta's work to provide a welcoming space, food, and extra blankets and pillows for overnight guests, exemplified what Leroy Gibson Jr. called the daily "grunt work" involved in creating change in Oxnard. Indeed, local organizers like Juan and Julieta bolstered the CSO's capacity to advocate for laborers and their families during this period. A persistent lack of political representation amplified the need for such advocacy across multiple fronts.

In December 1961, the CSO sponsored a meeting with city officials, where three hundred residents "voted unanimously to oppose any mass redevelopment" out of concern that such a federally subsidized, city-led plan would likely "leave hundreds homeless."[40] The CSO recognized that Colonia residents needed quality housing but also knew wholesale redevelopment plans rarely accounted for the interests of the residents themselves. The article quoted Chávez, who now directed the national CSO out of Los Angeles, making an argument against redevelopment. He offered, "We would rather see the old buildings condemned and the people given a chance to rebuild."[41] Given that the city council had regularly reneged on municipal responsibility for Colonia residents for decades, its pursuit of redevelopment appeared suspicious.

This suspicion was not unfounded. By December 20, 1961, the CSO vice president J. D. Rivera had presented a "strongly-worded plan" to the city council, asserting that "federal projects in other California communities have caused wide-spread displacement of residents. 'We know what these projects are and what they have done to our people in other cities, and we don't want that.'"[42] Community memory certainly contributed to the oppositional stance of Colonia residents and CSO organizers.[43] For example, the economically poor though culturally vibrant Tortilla Flats neighborhood in Ventura had been "wiped out" in the 1950s to make way for freeway construction.[44] Former residents such as Leroy Gibson Jr. believed the city planners purposefully designed the freeway to demolish the whole neighborhood:

> They could've went straight. They curved to make sure they got all of it. . . . It wiped out hundreds of families—dislocated them. Some of them, they replaced them over on a street called Ocean Avenue. . . . But mostly everybody got migrated here to Oxnard because they tore up our families. I mean it's the worst thing I've ever seen in my life, because you had breadwinners that are taking care of two generations and all of a sudden you come in and they just wash their house down and put a freeway over it. They have to scramble to where can they go, where can they qualify for housing. . . . We had to scramble. I came from Ventura to Oxnard in 1960.[45]

Oxnard organizers urging swift action to improve housing conditions remained skeptical about whether city officials had Colonia residents' best interests in mind. *The Press-Courier* took a stand seemingly in support of the CSO's position but still suggested federal funds could help ensure a well-researched strategy for moving forward: "The plan needs to get at the core of the problem, which is extreme overcrowding in certain sections of Colonia, making satisfactory conditions difficult to attain. That means sanitation is a problem. It means that family recreation space is not available. It means a hazard to health and morals. It means lack of privacy."[46] These observations by the newspaper editors in 1961 failed to mention that Colonia residents had been complaining about these very conditions for decades. Instead, the editorial attempted to recenter the public debate about how to improve housing conditions in La Colonia as a common problem endured by both Whites and Mexicans, and one that Whites would benevolently help Mexicans to fix. So while the CSO sought to insert some collective history into the discussion, *The Press-Courier* omitted any reference to the origins of Colonia's housing problems—the purposeful creation of the east-side neighborhood as substandard and the mundane disregard for the generations of families who lived there.[47]

The newspaper omission further framed the CSO as not fully understanding the complexity of the housing issue and lacking the patience required to enact change. In January 1962, for instance, city councilman Robert Howlett urged "that the Colonia blight problem be handled in a slow and sane manner."[48] According to Howlett, it was insane to advocate for prompt action. Consistent with the White architects past and current, he did not think it too much to ask Colonia residents to wait until they could more fully understand the problem, nor to ask those same families living in crowded, substandard homes to bear the brunt of the work to fix the problem. Still, as they had been doing since at least 1918, Colonia residents did take immediate actions to improve their neighborhood.[49] Individual homeowners sought "special permits" to improve their homes and complied with the CSO-sponsored "cleanup of the Colonia area through strict enforcement of the city housing code."[50]

These community-initiated efforts did not convince officials to be more swift and responsive to Colonia residents' concerns. Even during the CSO-led community cleanup in January 1962, urban renewal coordinator Henry Pollack complained that the preceding five months of study by the city committee were insufficient and that a "complete study" should precede any action in Colonia.[51] Meanwhile, one column over on the same newspaper page, the city named a new park after "Supervisor Edwin L. Carty."[52] This seemingly mundane announcement upheld the White architects' designs for racial inequality in the city. As a matter of course, they memorialized each other with ample "family recreation"[53] space on the west side, while they feigned ignorance, delayed action, and ultimately reneged on their obligation to create equitable living spaces east of the tracks.

Over the span of a few months in 1962, after the city rejected its plan for improving Colonia living conditions, the CSO began to view city leaders' arguments for a measured, well-studied remedy as a ruse to justify eventual redevelopment.[54] By October of that year, the head of the CSO's Colonia Civic Relations Committee, Alfred Contreras, accused the council of "purposefully sustaining a substandard section in the Colonia area 'as a show-case' to promote a federal renewal program."[55]

City leaders' tactics of repeatedly calling for studies and plans to remedy the housing crisis while ignoring the voices of Colonia residents reverberated in their strategies to maintain school segregation—a crisis simmering in the same pot as housing inequality. As examined later in this chapter, CSO members' recognition of these tactics, and willingness to, in *The Press-Courier*'s word, "blast" the city council, would serve them well in their confrontations with the school trustees on behalf of Colonia children.[56]

"YOU'RE OUT OF YOUR AREA": CONTINUITIES OF RACE AND PLACE

Colonia residents fought to rebuild their neighborhoods on their own terms at the same time as they sought an end to residential segregation, which had led to the concentration of poverty on the east side of the city. My interviewees who mobilized with the NAACP in Oxnard during the 1960s described this color line as reminiscent of racial discrimination in southern states and invariably linked to school segregation. For example, John R. Hatcher III, who transferred from a U.S. Air Force post in Savannah, Georgia, to Oxnard with his wife Joanne in 1964, described the regular practice of realtors directing Blacks away from homes on the west side: "I kept saying, 'Why are these people telling me to go to Colonia?' . . . It didn't look like the kind of area I wanted to live in. . . . [They said,] 'We have more houses in Colonia that would fit your needs.' I said, 'You don't know what my need is. My need is to get my kids in an area where they'll get a good school.'"[57] John was born in Birmingham, Alabama, in 1932 and went on to join the NAACP. He believed the prejudice of individual real estate agents reflected a tacit agreement to keep Blacks contained on the east side. He understood his purchase of a west-side home would mean his children could access "a good school,"[58] and was persistent in this pursuit. For instance, he remembered his loan was initially denied, so he went in person to the Veteran's Administration, and after being completely ignored by White personnel, he requested that a Black officer process his paperwork. Joanne Hatcher, who was born in 1928 in Columbus, Ohio, recalled her impression upon arrival to Oxnard: "I realized there was a lot of racism."[59] She worked as a licensed vocational nurse at a west-side community hospital and remembered that within one month of purchasing a house on Iris Street, south of Wooley Road and west of the railroad tracks, her "two neighbors on both sides put up 'for sale' signs."[60] John remarked that throughout the 1960s, Blacks seemed to be allowed on the west side as long as there was only one family per block: "That's the way the Blacks were separated, one on each street."[61]

Albert G. Duff, who was born in 1935 in Nashville, Tennessee, was working as a civil engineer at Douglass Air Force Base in Santa Monica before he moved to Oxnard in 1961. He recalled:

> We had problems finding housing. They wouldn't rent to us. We went through several situations. Calling, going by. It was a simple thing like, "Oh yeah, we have vacancy," on the phone. Get over there and they see us: "No, we just rented fifteen minutes ago." . . . It happened several times. It's obvious. See, we're from the area where we're familiar with that. It's a matter of survival where we come from in the South. "Separate but equal schools" but they weren't equal, that kind of thing.[62]

Margaret Tatum Potter was born in Camden, Arkansas, in 1925 and is also a lifetime member of the NAACP. She moved from Arkansas to Oxnard with her husband and newborn child in 1944. Her experiences during World War II demonstrate a continuity in Blacks being denied access to west-side properties: "When I went to the realtors inquiring to purchase property, they kept showing me lots and vacant property in the Colonia area. My husband and I told him we didn't want to purchase there. We wanted to purchase property on *this* [west] side of Oxnard."[63] She later confronted White real estate agents who refused to sell to Blacks in an area called Bartolo Square, south of Wooley and west of the railroad tracks: "When I told her we didn't want to buy in La Colonia, she called her manager. Because I wouldn't accept that fact that they wouldn't [let me] buy. So she called her manager, which was a male White man, and he said, 'Well the code says we cannot sell you any other place.' So we walked out of the place—out of the office."[64]

Most of my interviewees mentioned a significant individual—Black, White, or Mexican—who facilitated their successful purchase of a home on the west side. Margaret moved into Bartolo Square despite the "code," explaining, "We got in touch with a family that owned a lot and was willing to sell to us. . . . So we purchased a lot from person to person."[65] Bedford Pinkard, who as noted in chapter 4 was segregated into classes or in a row apart from Whites at Wilson School, was also barred from purchasing a home in the northwest area of the city. Eventually, his friend and real estate agent Richard Carballo brokered a deal so that Bedford was able to purchase a home in Bartolo Square. Albert finally found a couple who rented to him and his wife, Mexie, and they went on to buy their first west-side home from an acquaintance. John and Joanne broke the color line after a chance meeting with a woman on the street who was selling her house and had a background in real estate.

William L. Terry, who was born in St. Port, Louisiana, in 1930 and grew up in Northern California's Bay Area, moved to Oxnard in 1965, and regularly confronted the color line. He described a commonplace enforcement of geographic space as "strictly racism, because if you were caught in the north side [of] Oxnard and you weren't a maid, a butler, a gardener, something to do with the service of White people, you were stopped and asked, 'What are you [doing]? You're out of your area.'"[66]

For Black residents, many of whom had served in the armed forces and moved to Oxnard in the 1960s, repeated incidents of housing discrimination also conflicted with the expectation that California would be different from the South. Margaret Tatum Potter explained how racial restrictions in Oxnard triggered her memories of growing up in the South:

> I didn't feel too intimidated because of the fact I had come from Arkansas and that was quite prevalent there. I didn't anticipate running into that here, moving to California. We'd always heard, "Well California, there's no segregation, the schools," and blah, blah, blah, a lot of stuff. We'd been propped up that that didn't exist in California. "Oh, in California you can go to any restaurant," which after we came here we found that that was not true.[67]

She went on to describe many downtown establishments that did not serve Blacks. She noted that the Colonial House, a restaurant-hotel with a large advertisement of a grinning Black chef outside, "did not cater to Blacks either."[68] As discussed in chapter 2, similar to the way Antonia Arguelles (DiLiello) and other interviewees talked about businesses that did not serve Mexicans, Margaret explained: "We just never tried to break the barrier.... It was just common knowledge among Blacks.... When we found out they didn't want Blacks, we didn't want them to have our money."[69]

Mexie Duff was born in Nashville, Tennessee, in 1936 and was finishing her degree at UCLA when she and her husband, Albert, moved to Oxnard. She reiterated that their problems with finding a home on the west side were frustratingly reminiscent of the racism they encountered living in the South:

"It was a disappointment.... We expected a better situation. I did."[70] Still, the couple remained optimistic, working to create "a better situation" for themselves and others in their professional careers, and as members of the Bethel A.M.E. Church and the NAACP.

SCHOOL TRUSTEES: "BUSINESS AS USUAL"

In the spring of 1961, when the trustees decided to close Wilson School and open a new junior high school on the northwest side of the city, they set the stage for bringing racially segregated education to the center of public attention—and collective protest.[71] Designed to eventually accommodate 1,200 students, Fremont Junior High's initial buildings held a maximum capacity of 600 students and enrolled close to that level from the start, with 550 seventh- and eighth-graders in September 1961.[72] According to the district, at the onset of the 1962–63 school year, Fremont's student population was 52.4 percent Mexican, 31.6 percent White, 13.2 percent Black, and 2.8 percent Asian.[73]

The year after Fremont opened, the trustees took a page from their 1939 playbook, when they made the argument for building Ramona School. The board proposed construction of a new east-side junior high school in order to remedy overcrowding, reduce traffic hazards, and accommodate future population growth. By this time, in 1962, more and more students across the city had been placed in portable classrooms with increased student-teacher ratios, and many attended schools on double sessions or traveled past their "neighborhood school" to find enrollment space.[74]

In November 1962, before they even began to make the case for a new school bond, the trustees confronted "a new state ruling against segregated schools," which required "districts to pay close attention to the ethnic composition of an area when a new school is to be built."[75] Not surprisingly, the trustees decided to defy the regulation. Board president Mary Davis and Superintendent Harold DePue explained that despite the fact that "residents of Colonia are largely of Mexican and Negro descent," they interpreted the ruling as "a guide and not mandatory,"[76] and would therefore proceed to construct a school on land they had purchased five years earlier at the corner of Colonia Road and Rose Avenue—known as the Culbert site.

In choosing to bypass the state regulation, the trustees asserted that they knew best about how to ensure the welfare of all Oxnard children, on both sides of the boulevard and railroad tracks. The newspaper quoted school officials as recalling that "Colonia area parents objected" to the closure of Wilson and the opening of Fremont because it significantly increased the distance their children had to walk to school.[77] The proposed school, they argued, would initially enroll students from sixth through eighth grade but could potentially accommodate "overflow of lower grade children in Ramona and Juanita schools."[78] This new facility would ostensibly alleviate the "plague" of overcrowding on both sides of the tracks—but the emphasis seemed to be on freeing up seats on the west side. The newspaper further declared that shifting students to the new school would open up space for sixth-graders at Fremont and Haydock, which would in turn relieve cramped conditions for lower grades at McKinna and Curren. Admittedly, DePue estimated, even after opening the proposed east-side school, at least twenty-four classes would still run double sessions in the 1964–65 school year. It was not clear whether these classrooms would be on the west or east side of the city. In any case, the trustees found the dire state of current conditions compelling enough to go against the new state regulation. Trustee Robert E. Pfeiler stated, "We are not doing anything out of the ordinary in deciding to build a school where it's needed."[79] As the trustees moved forward with their plan to urge Oxnard voters to pass a $3.2 million bond in January 1963, trustee Henry Muller stated, "It should be business as usual."[80]

The Press-Courier bolstered the trustees' efforts with their own campaign, emphasizing race and space. On January 8, 1963, the newspaper printed three pictures and an article covering most of page six under a banner headline: "It Costs $5,000 for 305 Pupils to Ride to School."[81] The success of an upcoming school bond vote on January 22, the article explained, would "eliminate a $5,000 bill that goes down the drain each year to transport students far from their homes, across town to the Fremont Junior High School."[82] The captions under each photo referred to the cost on "taxpayers" to "haul" these "Colonia area students to and from school."[83] According to the newspaper, only passage of the bond and construction of an east-side junior high could eliminate this "permanent cost to the district's taxpayers."[84]

The school trustees had initiated busing when Fremont opened in 1961 because at least 150 Colonia students lived beyond the 2.5-mile state-allowed distance for walking to school. Within months, as the paper now explained, the Oxnard police recommended the rest of the 305 students also be bused because they presented "a serious traffic hazard" at the Oxnard Boulevard crossing and elicited "numerous complaints from residents in the north end of the city."[85] The newspaper did not identify the students by race or ethnicity. Instead, it printed three photos showing groups of Mexican and Black youth deboarding buses at Fremont. The pictures helped communicate to readers that "Colonia" meant Mexican and Black, and "north side residents" referred to Whites. In addition, the paper reported, "Police said homeowners complained over a huge mass of students marching to school at one time down their streets, straggling over lawns and creating other problems in their neighborhoods."[86] The choice of words here—"police," "huge mass," "marching," "straggling," "problems"—subtly underscored the need to contain Colonia students in order to enforce the racial rules in the city. *The Press-Courier*'s 1962 language utilized many of the same 1939 arguments to pass the bond that enabled the construction of Ramona: overcrowding, traffic safety, and neighborhood schools.[87] Their dismissal of Colonia residents as somehow not part of the "district's taxpayers" also echoed the 1928 claims of Ventura County superintendent of schools Blanche T. Reynolds when she warned that the costs of educating Mexicans in "American" schools were simply "too high."[88]

The immediate mobilization of White residents to pass the bond indicated many did indeed recognize the thinly guised racial agenda in progress. The day after the article about Colonia students as a taxpayer burden appeared, the newspaper ran a story announcing that fifty individuals had joined a "citizens committee for the elementary school bonds," headed by volunteer chairman and local medical doctor Charles Reach.[89] According to the article, the CSO had given "the bond issue a 'partial' endorsement" but asked the trustees to "build the proposed junior high school on the west side of Oxnard Boulevard and not on the site at Colonia and Rose roads."[90] The CSO's hesitation indicated their doubt that the plan accounted for the best interest of Colonia students.

"EDUCATION YES, SEGREGATION NO"

Over the next week, the CSO and the NAACP individually met with the school board and came together to discuss the possibility of a united stance.[91] At the joint meeting, the CSO announced its opposition to the bond. The NAACP scheduled a membership meeting to determine its position, noting it shared the concern that the school site location "would continue the segregation pattern in the Colonia area."[92]

On January 18, 1963, *The Press-Courier* moved coverage of the bond up from page 33 to front-page news with a report on a dialogue between Juanita School principal Jim Ingersoll, Harrington School principal Domingo Martinez, and the CSO.[93] CSO president Cloromiro Camacho argued that the construction of the "segregated" school would be "complete discrimination."[94] He asserted that Colonia students received inferior instruction because "good teachers" refused placements at Ramona or Juanita. CSO treasurer Eddie Flores further noted the problem of high teacher turnover rates in Colonia schools. Martinez could have cited his own master's thesis to bolster the CSO's claims about the repercussions of segregation at Ramona in particular, but instead he denied the CSO's accusations as unfounded.[95] He further retorted, "No child of Mexican descent is forced to go to a specific public school."[96] His colleague Ingersoll insisted that the district was "doing everything it possibly [could] to bring the best in education to the children of Colonia."[97] CSO vice president Al Contreras affirmed that he and the organization certainly shared the district's interest, "But there is a difference in one thing," he said. "Education, yes. Segregation, no."[98]

In an adjoining column, also on the front page, the headline read, "NAACP Joins Foes of Bonds."[99] The NAACP's position restated the shared concern that voting for the bond would be tantamount to a vote for segregation. The plan to construct the Colonia school, in the NAACP's opinion, was "not in keeping with the policies of our State Department of Education. . . . We support quality education for all children of Oxnard, however we cannot endorse segregation in any form."[100]

To minimize the impact of the public solidarity forged between the CSO and NAACP, *The Press-Courier* bombarded readers with articles and editorials portraying the school board members, west-side residents, and other White school and city leaders as completely taken off guard by the charges of segregation. This barrage of articles attacked the CSO in particular, highlighting perceived divisions among the members and former members, such as Ernestine Webb, who called on voters to pass the bond to avoid a "disaster" where children would "suffer."[101] With each article, the newspaper repeated that the CSO was a Mexican American organization. The weekend before the election, for example, the front page depicted two of these "foes," CSO officers Juan Olivarez and Eddie Flores, mapping out an "anti-school bond campaign," juxtaposed against Del Buono, who ostensibly pleaded with members to back the bond.[102] Alongside that front-page story, the paper attempted to question the authenticity of the CSO's advocacy and the veracity of its claims about Colonia schools, with the headline "CSO Officers Live outside Colonia Area."[103] In addition to listing the home addresses of the CSO leadership, the story detailed the number of children each officer had and the names of the schools they attended, showing that three of the six officers resided in the south end of the city and sent their children to schools outside of Colonia.[104] This revelation aimed to further position the CSO as disingenuous outsiders—a label later smeared on the NAACP.

Right through the day of the election, *The Press-Courier* framed advocates for the bond and school as informed, rational, and committed to the common good. On January 19, 1963, the newspaper editorialized about the CSO and NAACP's decision to oppose the bond as "A Sorry Mistake" because "There is not and has never been any 'discrimination,' on account of race or for any other reason in the Oxnard school system."[105] Three pages over, school board president Davis suggested that the de facto segregation, which the NAACP and CSO understandably could not endorse, was "unintentional segregation on the part of the school, but segregation because of the housing pattern."[106] She also trivialized their position: "They have a principle to defend. And we have a school system to run in the manner we feel is best for all children.... There are many educational advantages in having neighborhood schools."[107] In trying to convince readers and "foes" of the bond that school officials knew best, Davis suggested Colonia residents would come to appreciate being contained in their neighborhood. Still, her reference to the legal terms "de facto," "unintentional," "housing patterns," and "neighborhood schools" signaled Davis's awareness that desegregation was indeed much more than a matter of principle—it was a matter of law currently being contested in districts across California and the nation.[108] *The Press-Courier's* placement of a picture of sixty-four mainly White students sitting two per desk in their class at Curren School, next to Davis's statement, reinforced for readers what was really at stake in the election—the educational conditions for west-side (White) students.

On January 22, the newspaper placed five pictures of White women across the front page with the caption, "They're on the phone today to get voters to the polls for Oxnard school bond election."[109] On page 14, CSO president Camacho tried to counter the newspaper's attacks by reminding readers of the group's long-standing commitment to the betterment of Oxnard: "It was a long arduous task for us to oppose this bond issue.... We have in the past always supported not only school bond issues but all civic improvement programs.... As for the many members of our group that will not join us in opposition, we respect them and their democratic right of vote and freedom."[110] Meanwhile, on page 6, *The Press-Courier* relentlessly accused the NAACP and CSO of being "false prophets," whose opposition should be voted down "for the good name of Oxnard, for the future welfare of the children."[111] To further undermine the claims of racially disparate treatment in Oxnard schools, the editorial noted that "This charge violates the whole history of education in Oxnard. It could be that in one area more children of a certain racial group are found than in another. But never, in the history of the city, has that produced any sign or hint of discrimination."[112] Culled from a long tradition of distortion and omission, this blatantly false narrative aimed to limit the terms of the debate about schooling in Oxnard.

On January 23, *The Press-Courier* ran four articles under its banner front-page headline, "Bonds Win Heavily; New Schools Rushed," announcing the passage of the bond with 72 percent of the vote, well above the required two-thirds margin.[113] The front page also featured a table and short article detailing the outcomes from each precinct, highlighting that Colonia precincts recorded the lowest percentage of yes votes in the city: Ramona 45.8 percent, Juanita 55.4 percent, and Colonia Fire Station 44.3 percent.[114] The newspaper asserted the election counts represented "A Heartening Victory" against "malicious and unjustified racial antagonisms," even in "the distracted Colonia area, where the people were torn by misguided efforts on the part of two small groups."[115] In fact, a significant number of Colonia residents were not convinced that the trustees had their children's best interest in mind in proposing to contain them in racially segregated schools from kindergarten through eighth grade.

Four days after the election, the newspaper reported that the NAACP had requested a school board hearing and that even Del Buono believed "the proposed school would result in de facto segregation."[116] Taken together with the percentage of protest votes by Colonia residents, Del Buono's remarks confirmed that despite the election outcome, the NAACP and CSO had successfully disrupted "business as usual."[117]

FEIGNING IGNORANCE
TO ENFORCE SEGREGATION

On January 30, 1963, eight days after the election, the front page of *The Press-Courier* read: "Colonia Area School May Violate Law: Oxnard Board Seeks

Answer from State."[118] Facing now the request from both the NAACP and CSO for a hearing, the school trustees decided to seek counsel from the California State Board of Education. Though they would not admit to it yet, with their inquiry the trustees officially recognized segregation as more than "a matter of principle."[119] The same leaders who a few months earlier had determined that the state's regulation about locating new schools in segregated neighborhoods "did not apply"[120] to Oxnard now stated, "It is entirely possible that we may be breaking the law."[121] The trustees wanted to hear from a legal authority about whether opposition groups could obtain an injunction to prevent the district's proposed construction, what could happen if the community boycotted the school after it was constructed, and which entity, the state or the district, retained the power to decide ultimately if the school should be built at all. Trustee Thomas E. Millham suggested the board seek guidance to better understand and clarify eight specific "controversial points":

1. What is segregation, and how is it defined?
2. What is "de facto" segregation? Is it always an evil? Can it, or must it be prevented?
3. What constitutes a segregated school, and do any exist in our district today?
4. What is meant by an "ethnic group?"
5. What is a "minority group?"
6. Do the terms "minority group" and "segregation" apply equally to Caucasian as well as non-Caucasian?
7. What control does a local school board really have over the decision to locate a school where it will best serve the student population?
8. Is "local control" a reality or an illusion?[122]

These questions signaled the school trustees would proceed in much the same way as the city trustees had when confronted with protests against redevelopment in Colonia—they would feign ignorance, delay action, and ultimately renege on their obligation to create equal schooling conditions for Mexican Americans and Blacks.

Two weeks after the bond election, the newspaper ran a front-page banner headline, announcing president of the California State Board of Education Thomas W. Braden's response to the trustees' inquiries, "Colonia School May Break Rule, State Says."[123] Braden suggested that Oxnard school trustees seek legal counsel before proceeding with the proposed school site, which "would in effect create de facto segregation where it had not previously existed."[124] After hearing the state's reply, school board president Davis expressed regret that the board had not "considered all the facets."[125] Davis quickly backed away from the trustees' original position and admitted the NAACP did indeed "have a point. I don't think any of us really realized the implications."[126] Contradicting her previous statements and published thank-you letter to *The Press-Courier* on election day,[127] she declared, "I don't feel strongly about this. If we can't have a school there, we can do something else."[128] Taken together, the trustees' vote to ask the district attorney about the feasibility of their original plan and Davis's sudden willingness to be flexible offered at least two clues into the board's strategy. First, the trustees calculated that by feigning ignorance and pretending to be concerned about the perspectives of Blacks and Mexican Americans, they could call for repeated studies and forums, which would ultimately delay any action on integration. Second, they did not feel compelled to accept the assertions of the NAACP and CSO without obligation from a higher legal authority.

In contrast, at the February 5, 1963, board meeting the CSO and NAACP affirmed their willingness to work with the trustees to solve the segregation issue. On behalf of the CSO, Flores thanked the board for "taking preliminary steps towards the solution of the problem of providing school facilities for residents of the Colonia area."[129] NAACP representative John Mack reiterated: "We are not here to arouse emotions or serve as professional agitators as we have been referred to. . . . We want to affirm our commitment to eliminate all phases of segregation not only in our schools."[130] In addition, NAACP regional field secretary Althea T. L. Simmons requested permission to present "a plan to eliminate de facto segregation in the Colonia area."[131] These CSO and NAACP statements challenged Braden's statement that the proposed junior high school would somehow "*create* de facto segregation where it had not previously existed."[132] They contested the plan as an attempt to *extend* the "containment" of Mexican and Black students from kindergarten through eighth grade.[133] Indeed, while campaigning for a new east-side facility, the trustees and *The Press-Courier* had inadvertently drawn attention to the segregated conditions already in place at Ramona and Juanita schools.

On March 5, Simmons presented a statement to the trustees outlining three proposals to end segregation.[134] The first proposal suggested construction of a large junior high on the Culbert site, which could accommodate all the students previously attending Fremont. In this plan, elementary schools in the district would also be reorganized so that Juanita, Ramona, Brittell, and Curren would serve K–1 students and Fremont would become an elementary school serving grades 2–6. The second proposal offered a plan to "pair" the new east-side junior high school with Fremont, so that seventh-grade students would attend Fremont and eighth-grade students would enroll at the new east-side school. The third proposal presented the option of abandoning the Culbert site and constructing another facility adjacent or close to Fremont to enroll all students in seventh and eighth grades.[135] Simmons's five-page statement had been formulated by the organization's national legal advisor June Shagaloff and represented one of many integration proposals put forward to "city and county government and industry" throughout Southern California, "in line with 'stepped-up' demands for integration throughout the country in the field of civil rights."[136] Each of the Oxnard proposals challenged the east-west attendance boundary by referring to students as part of the "Culbert-Fremont" or "Fremont-Culbert" area. Moreover, the inclusion of Ramona and Juanita in their plans spotlighted the fact that these schools were already segregated.

Indeed, the NAACP had requested that the trustees release the student enrollment information prior to formulating their proposals. The newspaper subsequently published a chart confirming racial imbalance between east- and west-side schools.[137] Across the district in the 1962–63 school year, Whites comprised 48.6 percent and Mexican and Black students made up 48.6 percent. However, at Ramona, Whites were only 3.3 percent while Mexican and Blacks were 95.1 percent. Similarly, at Juanita, Whites were 2.9 percent and Mexicans and Blacks 95 percent. Meanwhile, White and Asian students (mainly Japanese) disproportionately attended the northwest schools.[138]

While the trustees pretended to know very little about segregation, *The Press-Courier* began to pose as a legal and educational expert. Three days after the March 5 school board meeting, the newspaper editorialized that the NAACP's "bad" proposals "should be disregarded."[139] In the paper's estimation, the NAACP wrongly sought to "target" Oxnard in a "campaign to end what it calls de facto segregation," without demonstrating that "children who go to schools in Colonia suffer educationally or in any other way."[140] The editors took issue with all aspects of the NAACP's plan, including the very basic fact that Simmons was not an Oxnard resident and that she identified Mexicans as "non-white," since the "U.S. Census does not so report them and they do not so consider themselves."[141] The newspaper questioned

TABLE 1. Oxnard Elementary School East-West Enrollment Pattern
by Race, Fall 1962

	White (%)	Mexican (%)	Black (%)	Asian (%)
East-Side Schools				
Juanita	2.9	75.6	19.4	2.1
Ramona	3.3	71.9	23.2	1.6
West-Side Schools				
Brittell	75.0	18.0	0	7.0
Curren	89.0	3.0	.4	7.6
Driffill	35.0	50.1	10.6	4.3
Elm	71.4	24.7	1.6	2.3
Fremont	31.6	52.4	13.2	2.8
Harrington	78.0	18.0	1.0	3.0
Haydock	56.0	35.0	7.0	2.0
Kamala	68.5	27.6	2.4	1.5
McKinna	67.8	18.5	12.3	1.4
District total	48.6	38.8	9.8	2.8

SOURCE: Adapted from table published in "'Minority Races' in Majority among Oxnard District Elementary Students," *The Press-Courier,* March 13, 1963, 5.

the applicability of integration designs originating in other cities and challenged the potential outcome of forcing taxpayers "to subsidize an arrangement that offers no apparent educational advantage."[142]

THE NAACP AND CSO CHALLENGE THE TRUSTEES' SMOKE SCREEN

Dear Sir.... During the last year, the NAACP's attack on public schools segregated-in-fact in the West and North has been extended to more than 70 cities in 15 states.... Continued evasion and inaction by school officials in some instances has resulted in litigation.... School officials may not be directly responsible for housing but they are responsible for the public schools they administer.

—ALTHEA T. L. SIMMONS, 1963[143]

Simmons debunked *The Press-Courier*'s claims and critiques of the NAACP plan with her own editorial on March 18, 1963. She began by explaining her role within a national organization, which encompassed thirty-four branches in Arizona, Nevada, and California, including the Oxnard branch.[144] She also framed the challenge to the east-side school site as part of a larger national strategy "to insure the end of all segregated public education in fact or by law by all means available."[145] While reminding readers that the NAACP had proudly argued the *Brown v. Board of Education* case to the U.S. Supreme Court in 1954,[146] she also revealed that the NAACP's statement to the California State Board of Education had helped to shape the statewide policy in effect as of November 1962. This of course was the regulation that the Oxnard school trustees had determined "did not apply" to them.[147] She went on to detail specific efforts to increase educational opportunities in Los Angeles and two court rulings in New York that promised to debunk the neighborhood school "defense," most often put forward in the "non-south" cases.[148] At this point in Simmons's editorial, the confluence of the CSO's struggle to improve housing conditions and the NAACP's struggle against segregation became clear. Indeed, she asserted, "It is the NAACP's intention to destroy this fiction, this myth—the neighborhood excuse."[149] She also discredited *The Press-Courier*'s claim that Mexican Americans would not be recognized alongside Blacks in a desegregation case: "We agree with the writer that the Census Bureau does not classify Mexican-Americans as non-white. They are classified, however, as a minority group, as are Negroes and others."[150] Indeed, she urged the implementation of the NAACP's proposals on behalf of Oxnard's "Negro and Mexican-American youngsters [who] are subjected to a segregated school environment," because "It has been clearly proven that youngsters subjected to such environment generally fail to achieve the inherent talent and ability which lies within them, despite the effort and ability put into the education program."[151]

In an attempt to undercut Simmons's rebuttal, *The Press-Courier* published a new editorial on the same page, under the headline "There Is No Deep South Bias Here."[152] The newspaper did not offer any evidence to counter Simmons's points but instead repeated the same blatantly false claim, "There is not and never has been discrimination in Oxnard."[153] Since World War II in particular, the paper argued, the district had aimed "to serve the children of expanding areas" with a "kindly policy observed over the years" that positioned new facilities "in such a way that no child would be forced to walk too far to school."[154] By asserting that residential segregation occurred naturally, the paper positioned school segregation as an unintended byproduct of a benevolent policy. In keeping with the patronizing tone of the White architects from previous decades, the paper chided the NAACP for being wrong and dishonest: "Everyone here knows that educational standards are as high in Colonia as elsewhere in Oxnard."[155]

Despite the newspaper's divisive tactics, the CSO and NAACP continued to pursue their common cause. When *The Press-Courier* reported on April 3 on district attorney Woodruff Deem's legal opinion about the trustees' proposal, readers were told the racial segregation accusation came from the NAACP without any mention of the CSO.[156] The front-page headline, "D.A. Ruling Backs Plan for Colonia Area School," also aimed to mislead readers. The subheading, "Board Advised to Study Race Issue," partially captured the directive of the actual finding by Deem, except for the fact that race was not simply *an* issue, but *the* issue in the plan. Deem wrote that constructing the east-side school "would probably be valid" if the trustees made an "exhaustive effort to investigate and evaluate all the facts, plans, and suggestions bearing on the problem."[157] In his opinion, part of fulfilling the requirement of making "a good faith effort to avoid de facto segregation" was keeping a "precise, clear and a full written record," which could be defended in a court if necessary.[158] He also reminded the trustees that "the law is unsettled on this matter."[159] For the CSO and NAACP, the suggestion to delay any action in order to conduct another study sounded familiar. Indeed, as the weeks and months passed in 1963, eight years after the U.S. Supreme Court ruling to desegregate "with all deliberate speed," the Oxnard school trustees aligned themselves with school boards across the country resisting integration by emphasizing "deliberate" over "speed."[160]

At the end of the month, on April 30, the school board called a special meeting to discuss the east-side school site plans and invited "interested citizens" from groups such as the Parent Teacher Associations at Juanita-Ramona and Fremont, the Oxnard Federation of Classroom Teachers, the Oxnard Police Department, the Oxnard Planning Commission, the NAACP, and the CSO.[161] At least sixty community members, parents, teachers, and principals joined the meeting. The statements from the NAACP and CSO reiterated their shared stance and, in the words of NAACP president Fred Brown, their "unequivocal opposition to segregation."[162] Brown reminded the trustees that the three NAACP-designed plans represented integration methods successfully used in New York, New Jersey, Michigan, Illinois, and Missouri. They resubmitted the proposals to the board along with a report for further consideration, titled *The Jim Crow School—North and West*.[163] Leo Alvarez, the vice president of the CSO, reportedly "attacked the city's zoning decision which permits small lots in the Colonia. These, he said, are part of the root of the segregation problem."[164] Community member Carlos Diaz affirmed the NAACP's argument: "The burden is on the school board to prevent a segregated school."[165] He then "warned" the trustees that proposing any new Colonia school, elementary or junior high, would face opposition.[166] Alvarez also told the board members, "Stop burying your heads in the sand. These racial problems exist."[167]

"MAYBE THE PEOPLE ARE HAPPY OVER THERE": THE STRUGGLE CONTINUES

On May 22, 1963, *The Press-Courier* ran a front-page banner headline, "Board 'Kills' Colonia School Plan: Segregation Controversy 'Settled.'"[168] The body of the article admitted that the board had only "unofficially killed" its plans, but gave no indication of who claimed the "segregation controversy" had been "settled."[169] The story continued, noting that the CSO and NAACP intervention brought the trustees to what board president Davis called "the moment of truth," because she and her colleagues "were unaware of the idea of de facto segregation as a deeply rooted problem until these organizations outlined their objections at various meetings."[170] The newspaper described trustees Davis, Pfeiler, Millham, and Marion L. Robbins agreeing to more deliberation, while Muller urged moving forward on the construction plans.[171] Though he stood with the majority of his colleagues, Millham reportedly expressed concern about breaking a "moral or ethical" agreement with voters who had passed the bond specifically targeted for building the school.[172]

On June 24, when the trustees unanimously decided to officially kill their plan, their carefully worded statement attributed this outcome to "many hours of study and deliberation," and not to the CSO or NAACP.[173] About one month later, the newspaper again placed the report of this decision on the front page, quoting Davis as acknowledging, "We made an error in judgement," and Muller explaining, "our decision was ill founded."[174] Millham further explained: "I never realized the magnitude of the de facto segregation problem. It obviously exists in the area of discussion."[175]

Though their records do not explain why, the trustees had a change of heart over the summer. On August 6, they made a formal retroactive correction to their June 24 meeting minutes, striking out the entire statement, "De facto segregation would occur by the containment of seventh- and eighth-grade pupils in a school with an enrollment predominately non-Caucasian."[176] The revised sentence read, "A majority of the board still believed that construction of a junior high school on the Culbert site had overtones of de facto segregation."[177] One would not need to step back too far from Oxnard to see the myriad of possible reasons for changing their wording. For example, three days after the June 24 meeting, the California Supreme Court ruled in favor of the Black plaintiff in the *Jackson v. Pasadena City School District* case. Jay R. Jackson Jr.'s challenge resonated strongly with the CSO and NAACP's struggle against the neighborhood school concept. In *Jackson,* the Court denied the school board's claim that they could not be held accountable for housing patterns, calling practices of drawing attendance zones around Black neighborhoods "a subterfuge for producing or perpetuating racial segregation in a school."[178] Moreover, the Court declared, "residential segregation is itself an evil. . . . The right to an equal opportunity for education and the harmful consequences of segregation require that school boards take steps, insofar as reasonably feasible, to alleviate racial imbalance in schools regardless of its cause."[179] Rather than face "the moment of truth,"[180] as Davis had indicated would be their course of action, the trustees decided to ignore the mounting evidence of racial imbalance in Oxnard and aggressively uphold the status quo.

In September 1963, just weeks after some 250,000 people garnered worldwide media attention for civil rights with the March on Washington for Jobs and Freedom, trustee Pfeiler made local headlines with his expression of doubt that the Supreme Court had ruled correctly on *Brown v. Board of Education.*[181] According to *The Press-Courier,* Pfeiler claimed segregation "may be harmful only in the mental attitudes it creates not in the level of education afforded segregated students. . . . The problem may be more spiritual than educational."[182] School board president Muller added to this official denial, stating, "I frankly have great difficulty to think we have a problem . . . 51 percent of the district's students are Mexican-Americans, Negros and Orientals who are not barred from enrolling in any school they wish if they live in the school's attendance zone."[183] Ignoring the testimonies of residents at the forum, the assessments conducted by the state and county officials, and the previous statements and reports submitted to the trustees, Pfeiler received Davis's support when he called for yet another study.[184] A survey, he suggested, would more effectively show whether Colonia parents were actually dissatisfied with the current educational conditions, because he "was not convinced that de facto segregation was harmful."[185] The trustees agreed to wait to conduct a parent survey until they received clarification about how the newly established California State Commission on Equal Educational

Opportunity might help solve the "problem of heavily minority group enrollment at Juanita and Ramona."[186] Pfeiler mused, "Maybe the people are happy over there."[187]

The board's defensive posturing and continued calls to study segregation served to delay action for Colonia residents.[188] As William L. Terry recalled, "The problem we had with integration was that the same people who segregate are put in charge of integrating, and they never really get anything done, 'cause they always want to protect their interest."[189] Ten months after the bond vote, racially disparate schooling conditions persisted, despite collective efforts for change. This reality may have felt especially daunting in October 1963, when the trustees unanimously voted to tell the NAACP they had "considered all aspects of the proposals to eliminate de facto segregation" and determined they were "not practicable or feasible to attempt in this district, and that no action will be taken to implement any of these proposals at this time."[190] Despite this setback, in her regional progress report Simmons emphasized the positive outcome of the NAACP efforts culminating in the district cancelling construction of the planned junior high school and petitioning the city council to "deny any more small lot low-cost housing tracts in Colonia, which 'attract low income groups to the area and increase our de facto segregation problem.'"[191]

For the NAACP and CSO, which had cast a public spotlight on the discrimination and segregation, the cancellation of the east-side school and inadvertent admission of de facto segregation did indeed represent significant outcomes. Having come together to challenge racial inequality in schools, these organizations continued protesting injustice on multiple fronts.[192] In October 1965, for example, May L. Davis reported on the NAACP Oxnard branch activities: "I enclose a few more clippings of our doings. The last ones showed that we had joined with the Mexican-American groups in our poverty area 'The Colonia' to push for civic improvement, and had sent a combined protest to OEO [Office of Economic Opportunity] because of a lack of [an] organizational representative on our Economic Action Commission."[193]

As the civil rights movements across the nation heightened, NAACP member and high school teacher Bert Hammond reaffirmed the need for continued collaboration: "The Mexican American community of Oxnard and Southern California . . . is being discriminated against and they are being deprived economically, just as the Negro is. . . . Things that cause one group to be deprived also affect the other. By joining together, we can help one another."[194] Albert also recalled the organic nature of the coalition building: "The president [of the

FIGURE 14. Juan L. Soria with members of the Oxnard-Ventura County Branch of the NAACP, early 1980s. Juan L. Soria (left), Fred Brown (middle), and John R. Hatcher III. Brown, Hatcher, and Frederick C. Jones (not pictured), each served as president of the NAACP. Hatcher was the presiding president at the time of my interview with him. Courtesy of Catalina Frazier Soria.

NAACP] at the time, Fred [Frederick C.] Jones, and Juan Soria were good friends.... I think there was some coming together. I think he came to several meetings of the NAACP, Juan Soria did."[195] Mexie confirmed, "I remember them working together ... each had their own, I guess, organizations, but they still were working together in a common goal."[196]

CONCLUSION

In this chapter, I recovered some of the parallel and shared struggles for equality among Mexican Americans and Blacks in Oxnard from the 1940s through 1963. During this time, the city remained divided by race and class, east and west. White parents continued to purchase property in exclusive northwest areas with the tacit assurance that they would not have Mexican or Black neighbors and that their children would attend school with very few Mexican or Black students. For the most part, Black and Mexican American parents remained restricted to living in La Colonia and sending their children to the overcrowded Ramona or Juanita schools. As residents in previous decades had done before them, these neighbors organized against disparate treatment in labor, housing, and education.

Two organizations in particular—the CSO and the NAACP—took on school desegregation as a central site of struggle for racial justice in 1963. Despite local newspaper distortions and school trustees' feigned ignorance, the CSO and NAACP stood united against the construction of a junior high school on the east side. Their collaboration brought elevated public attention to the ongoing segregation of Colonia children, even as the school trustees denied such conditions existed. The next chapter picks up this story at the close of the 1960s, when racial tensions had reached another boiling point in Oxnard and when Juan L. Soria coordinated a group of Mexican American and Black plaintiffs to take their common cause to federal court.

SIX

Challenging *"a Systematic Scheme of Racial Segregation"*

SORIA V. OXNARD SCHOOL BOARD OF TRUSTEES

> The Oxnard City Council and the elementary school district have been "censured and condemned" by the Mexican American Political Association for "strengthening" and "perpetuating" segregation in Oxnard.
>
> —JUAN L. SORIA, JANUARY 23, 1968

> Segregation has existed in Oxnard a great many years.... It is easy to feign blindness if one does not wish to see.
>
> —ELAINE COOLURIS, GERHARD ORTHUBER, AND LINO CORONA, MAY 6, 1969

ON FEBRUARY 20, 1970, ATTORNEYS from the Legal Service Center of Ventura County filed a class action injunction against the Oxnard School Board of Trustees in the U.S. Central District Court of California. Working out of an office on Cooper Road in La Colonia, attorney Gerhard (Gary) W. Orthuber and community organizer Juan L. Soria collaboratively developed a legal complaint that attempted to simultaneously challenge de facto and de jure segregation—charging the trustees of *knowingly* maintaining and *purposefully* perpetuating segregated schooling.

Gary, who moved to Oxnard in 1967, compared the racism in the city to "Mississippi in the 60s, [where] you had the iron clenched fist. Here you had a velvet glove over it.... [It was] made to look better," he said.[1] By the late 1960s, Juan and other community leaders, parents, and organizations had dedicated years to confronting this racism. Their efforts to end school segregation were apparent in the editorial pages of *The Press-Courier,* in presentations at city council and school board meetings, and in everyday advocacy efforts across multiple fronts.[2] The long-standing collaborations fostered

129

through social justice causes facilitated Juan's coordination of a group of Mexican American and Black plaintiffs to bring their protest to federal court.[3] The case was filed on behalf of ten children who attended one of Oxnard's three east-side elementary schools (Ramona, Juanita, Rose Avenue). Because Juan's nieces, Debbie and Doreen, were named as the lead plaintiffs, the case became *Debbie and Doreen Soria et al. v. Oxnard School Board of Trustees et al.*

By the beginning of 1970, despite intense public pressure to desegregate, the school trustees remained reluctant to implement any integration plans, even their own.[4] At their February 3, 1970, meeting, the trustees decided to enact only one piece of their master plan for integration: the removal of fourteen portables from Ramona School. Their agenda for the March meeting did not include further consideration of the plan.[5] Gary and Juan pursued the case outside of Ventura County because they recognized that the suit would challenge a powerful group of Whites who had a vested interest in maintaining racial segregation.[6]

Though triggered by a locally contentious matter, the *Soria* case reflected national concerns about race, schooling, and equality, concerns that remained largely unresolved sixteen years after the landmark *Brown v. Board of Education* ruling. In October 1969, the U.S. Supreme Court overturned a Fifth Circuit decision to delay integration in Mississippi, ruling that desegregation should commence "at once."[7] A deadline of February 1, 1970, had been set for six southern states, including Florida, where Republican governor Claude Kirk defied the Court in a televised standoff against "forced busing."[8] Meanwhile, Leon Panetta, director for civil rights in the Department of Housing, Education, and Welfare under President Richard M. Nixon, critiqued the idea that school segregation could only be challenged as de jure: "It has become clear to me that the old bugaboo of keeping federal hands off northern school systems because they are only de facto segregated, instead of de jure segregated as the result of some official act, is a fraud," he said. "Lift the rock of de facto and all too frequently something ugly and discriminatory crawls out from under it."[9] Nixon fired Panetta[10] during the same week in February 1970 that Gary and fellow attorney Michael Arthur Cohen filed the *Soria* complaint.[11] While the *Soria* plaintiffs took on the challenge of lifting "the rock of de facto," the school trustees aligned themselves with the Nixon administration and the community-based antibusing efforts gaining momentum across the country. Indeed, the *Soria* case eventually garnered Oxnard national attention as the first to confront the Nixon administration's busing moratorium.[12] The plaintiffs' lawyers, most of whom had been out of law school fewer than three years, took on these fierce opponents successfully with a legal weapon they did not initially consider—history.

Though years in the making, *Soria* emerged as a case from the civil rights movements and during the height of the Chicana and Chicano movement. As activists in Oxnard and across the nation mobilized for political representation, farmworker rights, educational opportunities, and other social justice causes,[13] *Soria* made its way to and through federal court. In this chapter, I concentrate on some of the remarkable aspects of this legal struggle, positioning the arguments employed by the defendant school trustees alongside those of the plaintiffs' lawyers, community organizers, and Judge Harry Pregerson. I begin in April 1969, when hundreds of Oxnard residents again advocated for school integration directly to the trustees. Following the case chronologically, I consider specific moments in time, such as the summer of 1971, immediately after Judge Pregerson issued his summary judgment for the plaintiffs, and the summer of 1972, when the U.S. Attorney General's Office sent its head civil rights attorney to intervene in support of the defendants' petition to stay the integration order. I also examine the legal rationales put forward by the trustees through their appeal to the Ninth Circuit in 1973, and their depositions after the case was remanded back to Judge Pregerson in 1974. These junctures showcase aspects of the *Soria* case never fully captured by the headlines or the court decisions. For a community long denied justice, they also highlight enduring victories: the public exposure of the racial ideologies guiding the trustees since Superintendent Haydock's era, and the disruption of their strategies of segregation.

THE BUREAU OF INTERGROUP RELATIONS' REPORT

As discussed in chapter 5, as of 1963 the trustees barely acknowledged segregation in Oxnard and remained unconvinced that it was a problem, let alone a problem they had a responsibility to fix. After dismissing the NAACP recommendations for desegregation in 1963 as "not feasible,"[14] the board proceeded with "business as usual,"[15] which meant ignoring state guidelines when choosing school sites to avoid racial imbalance. In 1964, citing overcrowding, they approved the location of Marina West Elementary south of Wooley Road and west of Oxnard Boulevard.[16] At the start of the 1965–66 academic year, Marina West's student body was 76.3 percent White.[17] That same year, the trustees opened Rose Avenue School, located east of the railroad tracks and adjacent to La Colonia.[18] There, White students initially comprised only 3.5 percent of enrollments, while Mexican Americans and Blacks made up 94.9 percent.[19] The following year, in 1966, the trustees opened Sierra Linda School in an emerging northwest residential area of Oxnard, north of Fremont Junior High.[20] From the start, 75 percent of children attending Sierra Linda were White.[21] The trustees' refusal to heed state statutes and recommendations from legal authorities had become increasingly apparent even to some district administrators.

For example, in October 1968, school superintendent Seawright H. Stewart prepared a forty-page report demonstrating the legal and research consensus on the value of integration, and encouraged the board to "re-examine its position and restate it in terms of the most recent thinking regarding equal educational opportunity."[22] Trustee Mary Davis received these materials with reluctance, and admitted, "I'm dragging my feet, because I haven't bought the argument that integration guarantees quality education."[23] After discussion, the board limited its action to a request for a study from the California State Department of Education's newly formed Bureau of Intergroup Relations. The tactical delay added fuel to the fire under the simmering pot of inequality.

Six months passed before the bureau's report arrived, at the end of April 1969,[24] and the trustees had taken no action on integration in the interim. The highly anticipated report summarized previous studies conducted by the district, and provided an overview on related desegregation jurisprudence, state policies on preventing and eliminating racial and ethnic imbalance in schools, and national research on racial disparities in schools (e.g., the Coleman Report, 1966).[25] The report then segued, "There is little need, however, to look to the 'Coleman Report' or other national studies for indicators of unequal opportunity for minority group children in Oxnard."[26] The bureau identified inequality in the "tracking" of Mexican American and Black children away from academic opportunities, including the disproportionate placement in the lowest "ability groups" for math and reading at Fremont and Haydock, and the overrepresentation of Colonia students in special education, remedial, and "standard" programs of study. These restricted opportunities, the bureau reiterated—not students' "intelligence and ability"—contributed to disparate outcomes, such as the high school graduation rate for Colonia residents being four times lower than for residents on the west side.[27] The report concluded with a recommendation that the Oxnard school board adopt a plan to eliminate racial and ethnic imbalance.[28] To assist in this process, the bureau proposed four possible integration plans, including closing Ramona and transporting its students to schools on the west side, and converting all K–5 elementary schools into facilities serving kindergarten and two other grades (e.g., K, 3, 4). The bureau suggested that the school board conduct a cost-benefit analysis of the alternatives and establish a timeline for their chosen plan by the fall of 1969.[29]

"CULTURAL CONTAMINATION"

Just as the bureau's findings and suggestions echoed previous studies, so too did the community response resonate with past discussions. At a three-and-a-half-hour board meeting held April 29, 1969, advocates for desegregation maintained that urgent action was necessary, and the trustees questioned the bureau's methods, conclusions, and recommendations for integration.[30] The *Ventura County Star–Free Press* reported on the "occasionally emotional, but orderly session" attended by over four hundred persons, including members from the NAACP, Mexican American Political Association (MAPA), and League of Women Voters, who "were predominately in agreement that segregation must cease so as to afford better educational opportunities for district pupils who are members of minority groups. But a few, all Caucasians, were vehemently opposed."[31] The article captured some of the tense debate between the participants, ending with Juan Soria plainly stating, "De facto segregation is shameful."[32]

The day after the board meeting, Oxnard resident Henry J. Johnson intensified the debate with an editorial in *The Press-Courier* claiming Black and Mexican students had inferior IQs, and warning that busing these children "would result in cultural contamination."[33] Johnson called on other residents who agreed with his views to "take the side of positive opposition to mixing culturally impoverished youngsters of doubtful intelligence with youngsters of centuries of Anglo-American culture behind them."[34] Within days, *The Press-Courier* published letters countering Johnson's racially inflammatory editorial.

In a May 4, 1969, editorial, William H. Thrasher and his wife, Margaret, declared, "The racist society must come to an end. . . . Ending de facto segregation, even if only in schools, is at least a start."[35] Two days later, Gary

Orthuber coauthored an editorial with Elaine Cooluris and Lino Corona debunking each of Johnson's assumptions, beginning with the myth of Whites' superiority. They wrote, "To attribute intelligence to race is one of the most unintelligent assumptions we have heard, especially coming from a person who considers himself a member of the 'superior Anglo culture.'"[36] Unequal academic achievement, they argued, resulted from institutional—not cultural—problems.[37] They questioned the veracity of claims by Oxnard residents and leaders that they had not previously seen segregation in the district until the bureau's report, remarking, "It is easy to feign blindness if one does not wish to see."[38]

Cooluris, Orthuber, and Corona concluded that those who opposed integration did so out of racial bigotry and in violation of the law. Their phrasing suggests that they shared a working knowledge of legal arguments in desegregation cases, which were making their way through the courts: "Under the California law, school boards have an affirmative duty to alleviate racial imbalance caused by residential segregation . . . busing is strictly a racial issue and . . . protests made against busing, for the reasons of economics, safety, or inconvenience are in effect prejudicial protests made against integration."[39] This editorial articulated some of the legal argumentation later employed by Orthuber and the other attorneys in the *Soria* case.

In addition to these public rejections of Johnson's claims, a White Oxnard high school student, Charles A. Brown, wrote a letter to the editor, declaring, "I have not, nor have any of my brothers, or sister, or friends been contaminated by any exposure to the, as Mr. Johnson says, 'culturally impoverished youngsters . . . of doubtful intelligence.'"[40] Forty-seven signatories endorsed Brown's rebuttal. Such demonstrations of support by Whites had not garnered much press attention in the past, and as the *Soria* case evolved, this advocacy became increasingly important. Despite the expanding network of support for integration, the board continued to find excuses for not moving forward.

About one month later, on June 3, Superintendent Stewart presented twelve integration plans to the school board—four from the bureau and eight of his own design.[41] Each of the twelve alternatives proposed "transportation" of students and weighed the "Best Features" and "Worst Features" in terms of who would bear the burden of integration, whether instruction articulation would be disrupted, and what would be the actual change to ethnic imbalance.[42] Despite this effort to forge a compromise, the trustees found problems with implementing any of the twelve plans. Trustee Pfeiler came up with a few distinct alternatives, such as voluntary busing of White kids to the east-side schools—an option he certainly knew most White parents would not choose. As he had done in 1963, he attempted to cast doubt as to whether Colonia parents really wanted integration, suggesting the board conduct a new survey and bus only those Colonia children whose parents requested that option. Loud moans from audience members indicated a collective sense that his recommendations for "dual school PTAs, joint Christmas programs, field day, athletic and scholarship competition" as means to "promote inter-racial understanding" were insincere at best.[43] Though Superintendent Stewart warned that the trustees could not postpone action "indefinitely," board president Muller suggested tabling integration plans for the summer as a "cooling off period."[44]

Muller's tactical delay did not temper expectations for integration advocates. In September 1969, at the start of the new school year, the *Ventura County Star–Free Press* reported on a board meeting under the headline "Oxnard Segregation Issue Boils Anew."[45] NAACP president Eddie London urged the board to revisit plans to desegregate, stating that "the problem still exists and it's not going to go away unless you solve it."[46] In the summer recess, two new trustees, Kenneth N. Tinklepaugh and Dr. J. Keith Mason, began their service on the board, and according to the newspaper they had not yet publicly revealed their positions about desegregation. In his statements at the meeting, London reportedly issued the board "a warning that 'outside forces' may compel the elimination of de facto segregation if the district does not."[47] *The Press-Courier* also took note of the NAACP leader's advisory statement and further described the new board president Pfeiler's dismissive and sarcastic response, "We'll get to all these things during the winter, and it will be a nice subject to keep us warm."[48]

Five days later, the NAACP's cautionary remark appeared less hypothetical, when *The Press-Courier* reported that the California State Attorney General's Office had requested "an immediate meeting for a discussion of de facto segregation in the district."[49] Pfeiler insisted—just as he had in 1963—that "de facto segregation will solve itself."[50] He further hinted that it was sensible to delay because a California proposition known as the "Wakefield Initiative Petition" was gathering signatures to stop busing altogether. At this point, Pfeiler's new colleagues, trustees Tinklepaugh and Mason, also revealed their opposition to "involuntary busing" as a means of integration.[51]

On October 7, 1969, the board officially acknowledged receipt of state deputy attorney Robert H. O'Brien's letter. Superintendent Stewart read it aloud, along with a request from the NAACP to place desegregation on the meeting agenda, and a letter from the president of Los Amigos, Frank Olivares, asking for "a timetable of actions to correct racial/ethnic imbalance."[52] *The Press-Courier* reported that Olivares also threatened to "invoke the assistance of the attorney general" if the trustees did not act.[53]

Two weeks later, the board agreed to place de facto segregation on their agenda.[54] At the October 21 meeting, trustee Tinklepaugh exposed his lack of basic understanding of the communities he was elected to serve. In a prepared statement that initially appeared to defend Mexican American students, he expressed indignation about the state's categorization of children, which "assumed any child with a Spanish surname is a disadvantaged minority group student."[55] However, he then facetiously "suggested the district would look considerably less bigoted if the state board would adopt a new ethnic classification 'Spanglos'—Anglos with Spanish surnames."[56] NAACP officer Ronald Govan took issue with Tinklepaugh's attempted joke, reportedly "scolding him for 'lampooning a very serious problem.'"[57] Although posed as humor, this was a serious attempt to delegitimize the standing of Mexican Americans as a racial/ethnic group, and in time became part of the legal arguments employed by the trustees as defendants. The NAACP's rapid reproach of Tinklepaugh indicated mounting frustration with the board's delay tactics.

Though patience was wearing thin, the persistence of individuals and groups demanding integration did push some of the board members to expose their racialized rationales for their opposition. For example, Tinklepaugh followed his condescending "Spanglos" remark with an assertion that "the problem was not ethnic balance but cultural deprivation, which could be best dealt with by special government programs working within the context of the child's own culture."[58] Indeed, community members and organizations exerted increasing pressure on the board over the 1969–70 school year, challenging the board at public meetings and through a letter-writing campaign.[59]

As they reported on this debate, the Oxnard and Ventura newspapers increased their front-page coverage of local and national mobilizations against integration. For example, California assemblyman Floyd Wakefield of Downey spearheaded a campaign in 1969 to require parental permission to bus students, aimed at ending "forced integration."[60] Both local papers published a series of stories about Kenneth Mytinger, an Oxnard resident leading efforts to gather signatures for the initiative to be placed on the November 1970 ballot.[61]

While the trustees who opposed busing sought to stall long enough for local or national momentum to sway in their direction,[62] support for integration received a boost at the end of October 1969, when the U.S. Supreme Court "unanimously ordered the immediate desegregation of Mississippi public schools."[63] Toward the end of 1969 in Oxnard, more support also emerged, when a number of White residents and predominantly White organizations publicly endorsed integration efforts in letters to the newspaper and the school board.[64] For example, Cloene I. Marson wrote a letter to *The Press-Courier* critiquing "Kenneth L. Mytinger and others like him" for apparent refusal to "accept the responsibilities and of helping reduce bigotry and foster unity."[65] She pointedly asked, "What is so threatening to Anglos about 'busing' that they must blind themselves to the educational, psychological, and social needs of their own and other children?"[66] Another editorial, by Christine E. Kennedy of Camarillo, questioned the trustees' contradictory stance of "encouraging the development of compensatory education" while ignoring "the need for desegregation."[67] "True democratic values can only be established in an integrated setting," she urged.[68]

Despite the U.S. Supreme Court and State of California rulings, most of the trustees remained staunch in their opposition. In November 1969, after the State Attorney General's Office again suggested the district was violating the law, trustee Thomas Kane asserted, "There is no immediate legal mandate that we do anything." His colleague, trustee John Marshall, agreed, "We're not legally obligated."[69] The NAACP did not relent in its efforts and organized a march to the school board for the first week in December. For the duration of the trustees' meeting, at least seventy-five protesters held signs demanding "Remove Bigots from the School Board," "Hear Us," and, referencing the demographic presence of Mexican Americans and Blacks in the district, "57% Say Now!"[70] The trustees also received at least fifteen new letters urging a resolution to de facto segregation.[71] The protestors' actions demonstrated that the common cause forged earlier in the decade had grown in strength and now included Mexican Americans, Blacks, and Whites collectively demanding change.

At the same time, Superintendent Stewart started seeking external perspectives from school leaders across the country regarding a nationally syndicated newspaper columnist's article, "Busing Students for Purpose of Race-Mixing Not Effective."[72] Stewart wrote to every person referred to in the publication, including the superintendents in districts from Chicago, Baltimore, and Minneapolis, and to James Farmer in the Department of Health, Education, and Welfare.[73] He explained, "Since this particular Paul Harvey column is being used to oppose our efforts toward integration, we would appreciate a clarification of your position concerning busing, and particularly, your position on school integration."[74] Each of the officials who responded to Stewart's request noted their remarks had been taken out of context or misquoted altogether. Farmer declared, "I am firmly opposed to segregation whether it be de jure or de facto. High-quality education in an integrated setting is imperative."[75]

Superintendent Stewart's November 1969 effort to dispute what he described as "a well-organized and vocal opposition to school integration"[76] offers insight into the contentious debate happening among and between Oxnard school officials—a struggle occurring in school districts and communities across the country. As in decades past, the trustees stayed current on court rulings and educational policies related to segregation. Indeed, by this point in time, the superintendent's office regularly clipped and saved news articles about desegregation and integration. Stewart's work gathering counterarguments against the board represented a distinct break from the era when Superintendent Haydock moved in lockstep with the trustees.

Records do not indicate when, how, or whether Stewart shared these endorsements for integration from a national sample of educators, but their opinions, taken together with the local voices of protest and the looming presence of the state attorney's office, certainly amplified the pressure on the Oxnard school trustees to change the status quo. Finally, in mid-December, the trustees unanimously approved a thirteen-point master plan for desegregation. NAACP president Eddie London reportedly acknowledged the milestone as "an important initial step."[77] "I'm glad to see they're taking some action," he said.[78]

London's guarded optimism was warranted. In January 1970, a split vote confirmed the board had not reached consensus on implementing even the most minimal aspect of their plan—the removal of fourteen portables from Colonia schools.[79] In the first week of February, they agreed to move the portables but then did not schedule further consideration of the other twelve points of the plan.[80] For a community that had long-engaged in struggles for equality within and beyond schools, this marked a breaking point.

FIGURE 15. Political cartoon depicting community frustrations about school segregation and other forms of injustice coming to a boil in Oxnard, 1969. Originally published in *Ventura County Star–Free Press,* April 13, 1969, C6. Courtesy of artist Dennis Rennault and the *Ventura County Star.*

MEXICAN AMERICAN AND BLACK STUDENTS
BECOME JOINT PLAINTIFFS

Defendant BOARD and each defendant, under color of their office and official duties, have consistently planned and sponsored racial discrimination in the DISTRICT.

—COMPLAINT FOR INJUNCTIVE AND DECLARATORY
RELIEF, FEBRUARY 20, 1970[81]

When Gary Orthuber and Michael Cohen signed off on the "Complaint for Injunctive and Declaratory Relief for Deprivation of Plaintiff's Rights to Equal Protection of the Laws and Due Process of the Law," the *Soria* case was already facing an uphill battle for at least three reasons. The U.S. Supreme Court had not yet ruled on a case applying the Fourteenth Amendment to Mexican Americans for the purposes of school desegregation, nor had it ruled on a case of school segregation occurring outside the South. In addition, rulings on desegregation cases making their way through the lower courts in 1970 showed inconsistency about whether plaintiffs needed to demonstrate that segregation was de jure (by law) rather than de facto (in fact) to be granted relief.

The plaintiffs' legal team paid almost no attention to the first issue, describing their clients as a class of "Mexican-American and Black children, citizens of the United States and the State of California, and residents of the Oxnard School District in Ventura County who attend predominately non-white schools within the district."[82] Positioning Mexican Americans as a defined racial group alongside Blacks, the attorneys argued that the plaintiffs represented a majority of the district (56%)—a majority, they alleged, that had been disproportionately placed in underresourced east-side schools as part of "a systematic scheme of racial segregation."[83] The legal strategy to stand together as Colonia classmates distinguished *Soria* as among the first desegregation cases in the nation to be filed jointly by Mexican American and Black plaintiffs.[84]

From the start, attorneys Orthuber and Cohen attempted to argue both de facto and de jure segregation simultaneously. This strategy considered the location of the case—in a state that did not mandate racial segregation—and recent court rulings that indicated this was an unsettled area of the law. The approach also anticipated the defendants' arguments. Orthuber and Cohen quoted from trustee Kane's remarks at the February 3, 1970, board meeting to highlight the particular brand of segregation—both de jure and de facto—present in the city. At the meeting, Kane expressed concern about the district being vulnerable to a lawsuit like *Spangler v. Pasadena City Board of Education*, which the federal court handed down on January 20, 1970. In the *Spangler* case, Judge Manuel Real treated the school board of Pasadena as "state actors," appointed officials responsible for implementing a public institution. He charged the board with taking "state action" by not making a "substantial effort" to alleviate the segregation of Black students.[85]

The *Soria* attorneys quoted Kane as admitting that he and his colleagues in Oxnard had not made what would be considered a "substantial effort . . . to solve the segregation problem . . . [so] if Judge Real ever comes up here, we're in for trouble!"[86] The plaintiffs' attorneys argued that because the trustees knew their master plan would likely be exposed as far less than "substantial" in the wake of *Spangler,* they strategically delayed its implementation altogether. In the May 22, 1970, amendment to the complaint, legal aid attorney Cohen clarified, "The Defendant Board and each of them, by reason of the foregoing affirmative actions have publicly and conclusively acknowledged their legal duty to maintain an integrated public school system, and their failure to so maintain such a system as alleged herein, creates the unlawful situation of de jure segregation in the district."[87]

From the start, the *Soria* attorneys sought to counter any claim the trustees could make about their legal obligation to desegregate. To frame this line of argument, they cited *Brown v. Board,* and the California Supreme Court's 1963 ruling in *Jackson v. Pasadena,* which compelled school boards "to alleviate racial imbalance in schools regardless of its cause."[88] Echoing some of the arguments presented in the *Jackson* case about whether the school trustees could be held accountable for residential segregation, Orthuber and Cohen described the board as "capitalizing on a clear pattern of de facto segregation" caused by restrictive racial covenants. Cohen went on to more specifically claim that the trustees "encouraged private individuals to racial discrimination in the sale and rental of housing in order to create and perpetuate racial segregation in the public schools."[89]

Date by date, Orthuber and Cohen described the trustees' purposeful avoidance of their obligation to desegregate and noted they "virtually ignored"[90] a series of integration proposals and "numerous statements, letters, etc. by concerned citizens."[91] These actions and inactivity amounted to "deliberate sabotage of all realistic efforts at achieving non-discriminatory education in the Oxnard School District, coupled with their intentional and total failure to adopt or implement a school desegregation plan."[92] Cohen then claimed that the trustees' deliberate and intentional actions carried deleterious effects for Mexican American and Black students. Because the trustees "have in the past and continue at present to provide unequal educational opportunity," Cohen argued, they "directly cause Plaintiffs to receive a lower quality of education and obtain lesser educational skills in Colonia schools than at other schools in the DISTRICT."[93]

Over the next year, the attorneys at the Ventura County Legal Service Center reached out to the Los Angeles-based Western Center on Law and Poverty. Working in collaboration, they developed a list of seventy-four findings of fact focused on four main issues: (1) the extent of the racial imbalance in the schools, (2) the creation and maintenance of facilities and busing between these facilities that perpetuated segregation, (3) the refusal (failure)[94] to remedy segregation despite many desegregation proposals put forward for consideration, and (4) the use of and reliance on residential segregation to exacerbate school segregation. The *Soria* case was assigned to Judge Harry Pregerson, Judge Real's colleague in the U.S. Central District Court.

INTEGRATE OR DEFEND SEGREGATION

On June 25, 1970, about one month after the plaintiffs filed the amendment to their complaint, attorney William A. Waters, the assistant counsel for Ventura County, sent a confidential letter to the trustees and superintendent Stewart. He and the county counsel asked the trustees to consider their next steps with the understanding of the probability that "the present litigation will result in a court order requiring your board to racially balance the schools in your system."[95] Waters explained that he and his colleagues came to this conclusion in studying recent legal cases focused on school integration. He outlined the legal rationales in cases of de facto or de jure segregation, noting, "the distinction is misleading. . . . For instance, where the neighborhood housing patterns were based on restrictive racial covenants, having nothing to do with any school board activity, the courts nevertheless hold that this was sufficiently de jure segregation to impose an affirmative duty on the school board."[96] Waters then gave examples of legal rationales in three California cases that the county counsel believed were most relevant to the present Oxnard case: *Brice v. Landis,* a federal case ruled on from the Northern California District Court in August 1969; *Spangler v. Pasadena,* a federal case ruled on in the Central District in January 1970; and *Crawford v. Board of Education of the City of Los Angeles,* which was ruled on in superior court in February 1970. Waters pointed out that in *Brice,* the court ruled that one-way busing of students "out of their neighborhoods and into the so-called, 'white' districts, was an unconstitutional manner of handling the problem of segregation."[97] This ruling, he suggested, meant that any proposed method of integration would need to avoid placing "too great a burden on minority students."[98] He went on to provide an overview of the relevant findings in the *Spangler* and *Crawford* cases, where "the Court went to great lengths to 'find' de jure segregation," focusing on effect regardless of intent. Taking these cases into account, then, he wrote, "the overwhelming trend is to require school boards to accomplish the complete, thorough and immediate integration of the schools in all areas and at all levels."[99] The counsel recommended that the trustees examine and correct any racial imbalance occurring as a result of "board action," including "determining school boundaries, transfer policies, transportation policies, faculty and staff assignment, hiring and promotion, and allocation of resources. . . . Such is the law and to do so would only strengthen your position in the pending litigation."[100]

The counsel offered three alternatives: voluntarily desegregate, integrate with court assistance, or "litigate the issue on its merits."[101] Waters further cautioned that if the school board decided to proceed with the case, it should be prepared for a costly litigation process, which was likely to end in a ruling for the plaintiffs.[102] Just as they had done with previous reports and recommendations, the trustees disregarded their attorney's advice.

"DE JURE OVERTONES"

On May 12, 1971, Judge Pregerson did what the defense counsel had foretold by issuing a summary judgment for the plaintiffs. The plaintiffs' legal team— Thomas Malley of the Legal Service Center, and Stephen Kalish and Peter Roos of the Western Center on Law and Poverty—had filed a motion for summary judgment "on the question of defendants' accountability for racial imbalance," and Judge Pregerson decided that the trustees did indeed bear responsibility for remedying de facto segregation: "It is agreed that the majority of the Oxnard Elementary Public Schools are segregated in fact . . . separate education for the Mexican American and Negro American students in the Oxnard Elementary Schools is inferior to education in racially balanced schools within the district . . . there are sufficient 'de jure overtones' established by the agreed-upon findings of fact . . . to entitle plaintiffs to relief."[103]

He reiterated that the defendant board had not disagreed with the findings of fact, but rather questioned the claim that the segregated conditions were a "result of concerted action" on their part. Just as the trustees' attorney Waters had anticipated, Judge Pregerson found that whether the board had caused the segregated conditions in Oxnard schools was not "a material issue." Instead, citing his colleague Judge Real's decision in *Spangler* and the California Supreme Court ruling in *Jackson,* Judge Pregerson held that the school board had "an affirmative duty" to offer the plaintiffs equal educational opportunities "with a racially balanced school system."[104] He asserted that this finding of accountability did not conflict with the U.S. Supreme Court's most recent decision in *Swann v. Charlotte-Mecklenburg Board of Education*.[105] Still, Judge Pregerson recognized, "there has been disagreement among the courts on the rule to be applied in this area."[106] He noted his application of the same standards applied in de facto segregation cases making their way through the courts in Colorado, Michigan, New York, and Illinois with his ruling of "sufficient 'de jure overtones' . . . to entitle plaintiffs to relief."[107]

By using this phrase "de jure overtones," Judge Pregerson accused the defendants of deliberately perpetuating segregation—a charge made by Juan Soria and MAPA three years previously. Pregerson identified intentionality in "such practices as Open Enrollment, Individual Intradistrict Transfer (or 'bussing'), location of new schools, placement of portable classrooms, failure to adopt proposed integration plans, and rescission of resolutions to relocate 'portables.'"[108] These actions and inactivity contributed to the problem of segregation rather than to the remedy. He concluded by encouraging the defendants to come up with an integration plan that eliminated racial imbalance "root and branch."[109]

The day after the decision was announced, newly appointed superintendent Doran W. Tregarthen released a public statement discouraging suggestions that community members could "flee from this ruling."[110] He expressed confidence

> that the people of Oxnard, after they have accepted the disadvantages inherent in total integration, will react in the finest tradition of community pride and service. We are going to be looked at by the nation. The way in which we respond will not only affect immediately the attitudes of our students, but will also be on display throughout the country. We must accept the fact that the court order is unpopular. It also, however, opens up opportunities for enriching experiences for our children.[111]

His remarks about integration being both a disadvantage and an opportunity for enrichment sent a mixed message that did not fully account for the sentiments of Oxnard residents who had long pressed the board to desegregate and provide an equal education to their children.

The newspaper explained that Judge Pregerson had given the board twenty days to generate plans, along with instructions that the proposals should not include "freedom of choice," voluntary busing, or "one-way busing" from Colonia to the west side.[112] The next day, *The Press-Courier* editors published a note to their readers applauding Tregarthen for responding to the situation with "wisdom and calm."[113] Calls for compliance in the wake of the court mandate sought to avoid a public confrontation such as those occurring in other parts of the nation.[114] Framing the *Soria* case around the presumptive concerns of the White parents relegated the plaintiffs' perspectives to the margins of the public debate.[115] Defiant government and school officials responded similarly on a national scale, treating Whites as the "silent majority," who opposed desegregation as an assertion of their rights rather than as the denial of the rights of Black and Mexican American children.[116]

In the months after the summary judgment, as the trustees hammered out the specific integration plans that would meet with the court's approval, they also strategized about how to appeal the court's decision. Their increasingly transparent effort to maintain White schools within a majority Mexican American and Black district did not go uncontested. In June 1971, for example, Albert G. Duff, who was serving on the executive committee of the NAACP, questioned the board's intentions in calling for a district-wide poll to determine parents' busing choices. "We wish to inform the general public, especially black people, that we are opposed to the board's decision to appeal, and we are equally opposed to the voluntary busing poll," he stated. "We as taxpayers will not stand idly by and allow the twisted logic of a few to continue the tragic results of a segregated system."[117] Indeed, Albert and other organizers in the city did not rest easy in the wake of the *Soria* case summary judgment. Rather, they stepped up their advocacy, recognizing the urgency of casting a critical light on board members' attempts to justify long-standing traditions that presumed public schools and public school officials only served Whites.

In July 1971, after a series of revisions, Judge Pregerson approved the district's "Amended Integration Plan,"[118] and ordered that the "defendants immediately and henceforth" implement it.[119] The plan called for pairing twelve racially imbalanced schools from kindergarten through sixth grades and implementing two-way busing.[120] The district attributed the plan to the Bureau of Intergroup Relations, but the NAACP had actually suggested the pairing design in 1963, based on the Princeton Plan. In addition, the district committed to increase the representation of racial and ethnic minority personnel at all levels of district staffing, provide staff in-service training and public relations programs in conjunction with desegregation, and modify the curriculum to include the history and contributions of racial and ethnic groups.[121] Furthermore, the district would be required to report to the court annually for seven years on the progress of the integration efforts.[122]

Busing opponents protested immediately and vociferously. *The Press-Courier* reported as front-page news a three-and-a-half-hour school board meeting, where "300 Turn Out to Oppose Forced Busing of Children: Board Affirms Decision to Appeal."[123] Using the phrase "forced busing" uncritically, the article portrayed the White parents as empathetic figures up against the court-mandated infringement of their rights.[124] The *Ventura County Star–Free Press* laid out the story in less distorted terms with a headline, "Busing Ultimatum: Foes 'Demand' Court Victory."[125] The article described heated exchanges between "angry parents," who "declared their unequivocal opposition to busing," and the school board, who despite threats from parents to recall their seats, voted 3–2 to heed the court-mandated plan for integrating kindergarten through sixth grade.[126]

A few days later, *The Press-Courier* published a letter from a White parent to the city council, which requested busing be placed on the ballot for the next election and cautioned that many parents were poised to boycott schools altogether.[127] Meanwhile, the *Ventura County Star–Free Press* editors affirmed their support for MAPA leader Vincent Godina, who had called on Democratic U.S. senator Alan Cranston and other officials representing Oxnard to speak out about the *Soria* case.[128] "We need somebody to make the kind of statement that will bring the community—black, brown, and white—together, Godina said. We concur. The failure of President Nixon and other figures on the national level to take leadership on this issue does not excuse local failures."[129]

On September 2, 1971, the week Judge Pregerson went on vacation, the attorneys for the trustees petitioned the Ninth Circuit Court of Appeals for a stay of the busing order pending their appeal of the district court's summary judgment.[130] Thomas Malley, attorney for the plaintiffs, suggested the trustees timed their request during this particular week in "an attempt to bypass Judge Pregerson."[131] Though the petition for a stay would be denied by the court, the board's stance against busing received timely affirmation by a visit from an antibusing activist, former Republican Florida governor Claude Kirk.

Kirk had garnered mass media attention for opposing busing for integration in his home state and named Oxnard as one of two "bulwarks" for a national campaign against "forced busing."[132] Leaders from Oxnard's newly formed Citizens Opposed to Busing (COB) group invited Kirk. The organization consisted mainly of White parents living on the west side of Oxnard, who had come together in the wake of the district court decision, and boasted a membership of 3,500.[133] COB members applauded trustee Mason's appointment as board president in July and expressed appreciation when the newly appointed trustee Kenneth Mytinger joined his colleagues to appeal Judge Pregerson's decision. Mason and Mytinger's public welcome of Kirk confirmed that they indeed shared the sentiments of the "angry parents" rallying at the school board meetings.[134] At a press conference with Kirk, Mason urged those organizing against busing to use legal means for expressing their protest. He then identified himself as a member of COB who, "speaking as a private citizen," would be working with the group to fight the district court's decision and those he called "guilt-ridden social do-gooders willing to trade dime store sensitivity training for a good education."[135] Mason's admission exemplified what the plaintiffs' original complaint argued, that "under color of their office," the trustees discriminated against Colonia children.[136]

Kirk amplified the already shrill voices of protest, declaring the district had been "defrauded of its constitutional right to trial."[137] *The Press-Courier* paraphrased him rallying COB with a motivational speech: "Oxnard may be small compared with the rest of the nation, he said, but so were Lexington and Concord, where the American Revolution started."[138] He then went further by saying, "My Lai was small too, but an atrocity was committed there, and the world got upset."[139] As if it were not horrific enough to equate busing with "an atrocity" of the magnitude of a war-crime massacre, Kirk accused the *Soria* attorneys of fraudulently contriving their plaintiff class. He declared that Mexican Americans could not be counted as a racial group because he "had never heard of a brown race's existence in a court decision. Blacks and whites, yes, the governor said, but not browns."[140] Local antibusing advocates did not publicly question Kirk's ignorant and inflammatory remarks.

Meanwhile, the school trustees' petition for a stay of busing also went after Judge Pregerson's summary judgment, arguing he improperly left them without an opportunity to contest the findings of fact during a trial. Their attorneys challenged Judge Pregerson's assertion that his ruling aligned with *Swann,* noting that the "touchstone" of that case was the issue of whether the school system "has been deliberately constructed and maintained to enforce racial segregation."[141] There was no evidence of such deliberate segregation, and no trial allowed for defendants to challenge the claim of their actions carrying "de jure overtones," the lawyers argued.

Though they were petitioning for a stay and not yet arguing their case on appeal, the defendants/appellants' attorneys gave a preview of some of their clients' objections to the district court ruling. Here they chided the *Soria* lawyers' oral arguments and questioned the vagueness of the plaintiffs' descriptions of housing and school discrimination. They went on to dispute the judgment based on the "epithet" of Oxnard schools being "segregated in fact."[142] Use of the "epithet" *segregation,* they argued, was not the same as establishing that Oxnard schools were indeed segregated, with children subjected to an inferior education. They accused the plaintiffs' lawyers of engaging in "emotional sloganeering" and asserted, "the terms 'segregation' and 'integration' are best eschewed. They are no more precise nor productive than 'justice' or 'evil.'"[143] The trustees' attorneys contended that to be fair, the plaintiffs should not make empty claims of "segregation," but rather bring evidence forward in a trial to demonstrate how children had been denied equal protection under the laws or equal access to educational opportunities.

In the full appeal of the case on its merits, they promised, the defendant board would also take issue with labeling "groups of Americans by their 'race,' 'color,' or 'surnames,'" as a discriminatory debasement of "the objectives of the civil rights advances of the past three decades."[144] With these arguments to stay the busing, the trustees' attorneys foreshadowed their clients' plans for an all-out challenge to court-ordered integration.

AFFIANTS FOR AND AGAINST BUSING

If the hopes which have arisen in the minority community as a result of finally attaining the first step toward justice in Oxnard (i.e.) equal schooling are to be dashed at this juncture, feelings of resentment, frustrations, anger and hatred may more sharply divide this community than the Southern Pacific Railroad Tracks and the four-lane boulevard which separates affluent homes in the white community from the crowded and neglected projects and multi-family dwellings in the Barrio.

—FRED JONES, PRESIDENT, NAACP, 1971[145]

In addition to asserting important legal arguments, *Soria* carried forward a common cause between Mexican Americans and Blacks. Notably, however, none of the groups who had mobilized collectively against school and residential segregation in the 1960s (e.g., CSO, MAPA, NAACP) officially participated as an organization in the *Soria* case. Still, footprints of these and other organizations who advocated for justice in Oxnard appeared in the facts presented by the plaintiffs, the legal rationales applied, and the specific considerations requested in fashioning a remedy. Fred (Frederick C.) Jones's affidavit, as president of the NAACP—submitted as part of the plaintiffs' response to the petition by the board to stay busing one week before the school year started in 1971—demonstrated multiple continuities in community advocacy networks over time in Oxnard. Ironically, none of these affiants were Mexican American. Jones and nine other Black and White parents, teachers, and community members presented the perspectives of west-side residents who opposed the stay and shared a commitment to integration. For example, William and Margaret Thrasher signed affidavits assuring the court that despite the intense opposition expressed by parents in the spring, they and many families on the west side were ready to participate in the integration program.[146] Margaret explained that a stay "would cause much confusion and unnecessary expense to the elementary district, as well as causing a reversal in the mellowing mood of the community."[147] Barbara Gardner, who taught at Harrington, noted concern that the stay was another example of "the students in the Oxnard Elementary School District . . . being victimized by School Board attempts to retain the vestige of a segregated school system in Oxnard."[148]

In contrast, the board members' affiants, such as trustee Mason, claimed the school district was the victim, unfairly "saddled with the burden of alleviating conditions that they did not condone, but actively sought to avoid."[149] Trustees Rachel Murguía Wong and Mary O. Davis specifically expressed support for integration but stood with trustees Tinklepaugh, Mason, and Mytinger in opposition to busing.[150] Davis claimed there would be "minimal, if any, objection to one-way busing," from the east side to the west side and expressed her feeling that the court order "indicts the school district and saddles it with the responsibility of rectifying poor urban planning," which she asserted, was not the fault of the school officials.[151] She attempted to reassure the court that while "there are segregationists and racists in Oxnard," even "firm believers in integration and equal opportunity" stood adamantly against two-way busing.[152]

Despite the board members' efforts to rationalize their stance against court-ordered busing, the last-minute attempt to stop busing in September 1971 did not work. The Ninth Circuit denied the motion on the first day of school.[153] Leading up to that day, the superintendent's office had engaged in extensive preparation, including having children ride the bus with their parents along the new routes. Assistant superintendent Norman Brekke told *The Press-Courier* that the district had also prepared a contingency plan, as it waited to hear about its stay petition.[154] In the meantime, the administration prepared a positive public announcement proclaiming, "A New Era for Oxnard Schools."[155] On the cover page of the report, a large group of smiling children stood together—Black, White, Asian American, and Mexican American. The inside included an overview of three national studies supporting school integration, updates on how teachers and class materials had been prepared over the summer, tables on ethnic distribution by school before and after busing, as well as maps and answers to frequently asked questions about the paired schooling assignments.

The week before school began, *The Press-Courier* reported a failed attempt to set the buses on fire and published subsequent remarks by Superintendent Tregarthen that he did not believe the crime was related to the integration order.[156] Indeed, given all the vociferous protests of spring and summer, Judge Pregerson himself traveled to Oxnard to witness the first day of school.[157] He remembered being quite pleased that from day one, the Oxnard Elementary School District commenced court-ordered busing among paired schools without incident.[158]

The trustees did not share Judge Pregerson's pleasure. A few days after the school year ended in June 1972, they directed their attorneys to request a rehearing of their petition to the Ninth Circuit to stay busing. The reconsideration, they argued, was warranted because President Nixon had just signed an eighteen-month moratorium on busing.

SORIA ATTRACTS "EYES OF THE NATION": TRUSTEES PETITION HIGHER COURT

Oxnard—the six letter word meaning a city of 78,208 population, 62 miles northwest of Los Angeles—enters the nation's vocabulary Thursday. It may not become a household term. But Oxnard—as in Soria v. Oxnard School District—will figure prominently in conversations of President Nixon and every other key figure in the national debate over court-ordered busing to achieve racial balance of students.

—HELEN REYNOLDS, AUGUST 9, 1972[159]

In the first weeks of August 1972, the Nixon administration dispatched the head of the U.S. Justice Department's Civil Rights Division, attorney David Norman, to argue alongside the trustees for the stay.[160] The Ninth Circuit had granted the U.S. government legal standing as an intervenor, because

Soria was the first case to test the constitutionality of the busing moratorium,[161] also known as the Broomfield Amendment.[162] The *Ventura County Star–Free Press* reported, "On Thursday at 2p.m. in the San Francisco Federal Court Building, the eyes of the nation will focus on the Oxnard Elementary School District."[163]

As the plaintiffs' attorneys Thomas Malley and Peter Roos prepared to argue in front of the Ninth Circuit, and against the U.S. government, they requested to extend the page length of the brief to fully capture "the complex issues" of a district that had "through a covert pattern of behavior over a number of years maintained a dual school system."[164] They further characterized the case law as "complex, due to the fact that the United States Supreme Court has not ruled on the constitutionality of factors constituting de jure or de facto segregation in a northern situation."[165]

Their extended brief challenged the Broomfield Amendment to the Emergency School Assistance Act of 1972 (ESAA), explaining, "The respondents can think of no compelling interest that calls for an automatic stay of an order enforcing the rights of minority children in a school desegregation case."[166] They went on to state, "The respondents believe that the reason that this section was enacted is because of the majority's dislike of busing for desegregation; but of course this is an invalid reason for depriving a class of citizens of their rights to equal protection."[167] Malley and Roos also questioned the retroactive application of the ESAA.[168]

When the Ninth Circuit denied the stay, on August 21, 1972, the trustees prepared a petition for a stay to the U.S. Supreme Court.[169] Three days later, Leonard H. Carter, regional director of the NAACP, confirmed that the NAACP legal team was ready to intervene in the case on behalf of the plaintiffs, should the U.S. Supreme Court agree to hear the appeal.[170] Terry J. Hatter Jr., the executive director of the Western Center on Law and Poverty, responded by forwarding to Carter the Ninth Circuit's decision on *Soria* and expressing appreciation for the commitments of the NAACP legal counsel, both national and regional.[171] He suggested they all coordinate directly through Peter Roos, the lead attorney for the plaintiffs. "We look forward to the NAACP joining us in this matter of importance to us all."[172] Carter subsequently forwarded the case and the letter from Hatter to NAACP general counsel Nathaniel Jones, who in turn sent the case to an attorney in Michigan, noting: "I think this Opinion has particular relevance for the Kalamazoo situation. I trust it proves helpful."[173] Indeed, the common cause of Mexican Americans and Blacks, almost a decade in the making in Oxnard, was poised to contribute to desegregation efforts at a national level. Over that time, the Oxnard school trustees' pretend obliviousness about segregation had evolved into vehement refusal to accept responsibility for its cause and belligerent avoidance of a remedy.

Eight days after the Ninth Circuit decision, the trustees did indeed petition the U.S. Supreme Court.[174] On September 9, 1972, two days before the scheduled start of the new school year, Justice William O. Douglas denied their petition.[175] One week later, attorneys for the school board filed a new petition with Chief Justice Warren Burger, which was also denied without an explanation.[176] The trustees then requested that Justice Lewis F. Powell Jr. refer their petition for a review by the full U.S. Supreme Court. On October 24, 1972, the U.S. Supreme Court denied the petition, which meant that Judge Pregerson's ruling would be upheld until the Ninth Circuit responded to their appeal.

THE QUESTION OF INTENT: DE FACTO EVIDENCE AND DE JURE HISTORY

> Appellants herein maintain that they were under no constitutional duty to affirmatively achieve any particular degree of racial or ethnic balance in any of their schools, and thus the failure to achieve such balance presents no constitutional infirmity... under the facts of this case, it is clear appellants and their predecessors have never maintained a "dual school system" with all the members of one racial or ethnic group being required to attend one set of schools pursuant to state statute or board policy.
>
> —BRIEF OF THE APPELLANTS (OXNARD SCHOOL BOARD OF TRUSTEES), MAY 1, 1972[177]

After three years of appeals and two and one half years of busing in the district, the *Soria* defendants remained defiant that they did not bear responsibility for segregation in Oxnard schools. Their attorneys highlighted social science that disputed previous research claims about desegregation improving the educational outcomes of Black students or significantly reducing intergroup conflict and prejudice.[178] Here they aimed to undercut "several educational and sociological findings" within Judge Pregerson's summary judgment, arguing that "sociological findings amount to mere guesses and... to decree major policy changes on mere guesses is undesirable."[179] This declaration—that social science should not be considered *real* evidence in court—echoed the defendants' previously brazen assertions before the Ninth Circuit that "the terms 'segregation' and 'integration' are best eschewed" for the purposes of the law.[180] This line of argumentation sought to delegitimize the plaintiffs' anticipated case in a trial, where the trustees ostensibly would object to every reference to segregation as an "epithet" and would question social science "guesses" about unequal schooling conditions. Furthermore, the appellants emphasized, many leaders in the "Chicano/Black" community had come to realize the problems with court-ordered integration.[181]

The appellants' attorneys took on the legal merits of the summary judgment by arguing that Judge Pregerson "failed to grasp the true meaning of *Brown I* that it is only where a school board intentionally maintains a dual school system that constitutional mandates are violated."[182] They also claimed *Swann* "is ruled immaterial here and the district court has intervened" erroneously because the board never "deliberately attempted to fix or alter demographic patterns to affect the racial composition of the schools."[183] In *Swann*, the U.S. Supreme Court unanimously found that although Charlotte, North Carolina, followed "a familiar phenomenon that, in metropolitan areas, minority groups are often found concentrated in one part of the city," this pattern did not necessarily mean the school board had intentionally discriminated against the plaintiffs.[184] The U.S. Supreme Court ruled that only a finding of a history of segregation shaping these patterns would obligate the school board to remedy the contemporary imbalance. In those cases, the justices asserted, "The court should scrutinize such schools, and the burden upon school authorities will be to satisfy the court that their racial composition is not the result of present or past discriminatory action on their part."[185]

The high Court's *Swann* decision also brought up the importance of history in relation to fashioning a remedy that is viewed by the defendants as "drastic," such as busing children between paired schools to accomplish integration.[186] "Absent a constitutional violation, there would be no basis for judicially ordering assignment of students on a racial basis. All things being equal, with no history of discrimination, it might well be desirable to assign pupils to schools nearest their homes. But all things are not equal in a system that has been deliberately constructed and maintained to enforce racial segregation."[187] In Oxnard, the trustee defendants/appellants interpreted *Swann* as a vindication of their case. They reasserted with confidence that their innocence extended back in time to include their predecessors, who also "*never* maintained a dual school system."[188] The lower court, they charged, had "erroneously applied the controlling law in finding certain 'de jure overtones.'"[189] This line of argumentation proved effective—at least for the moment.

On November 27, 1973, Judge Herbert Y. C. Choy wrote a decision on behalf of his colleagues on the Ninth Circuit, vacating Judge Pregerson's summary judgment and remanding the case back to the district court for a trial. The three-judge panel agreed that the "conclusion from the agreed-upon facts that the School Board's acts and omissions constitute 'de jure overtones' is inconclusive and vague on the question of the School Board's intent."[190] Despite awarding the board with the trial they had requested, the Ninth Circuit—for a third time—did not grant a stay of the busing order.[191]

As attorneys Herbert D. Nowlin from the Legal Service Center and Joel I. Edelman from the Western Center on Law and Poverty prepared the plaintiffs' case for a trial at the district court, history intervened. Sometime after receiving the November 1973 decision from the Ninth Circuit and before taking the depositions of school board members in September 1974, the school board minutes from the 1930s mysteriously surfaced. Though stories differ about when, how, and why these minutes had not been part of any initial filings or findings of fact put forward by the plaintiffs, the plaintiffs' attorneys seem to have been the last to know of their existence. This may have occurred because the case focused on existing school attendance patterns and failures of the defendant board to remedy racial imbalance in the years after *Brown v. Board of Education*—once the U.S. Supreme Court had ruled segregation to be unconstitutional. The initial requests had therefore focused on board meeting minutes for the academic years commencing in 1955–56 and through 1969–70. When Edelman and Nowlin "discovered" the 1930s minutes and entered them into the court record as evidence in 1974, the defendants' attorneys may indeed have regretted their insistence on a trial. In a 2010 interview, Nowlin recalled the presentation of the minutes into evidence before Judge Pregerson as "the most damning in the whole case for the school board."[192]

Having already attempted to dismiss the use of social science as "mere guesses,"[193] the trustees' legal team did not count on a confrontation with historical evidence. When or how these attorneys became aware of the 1930s minutes remains unclear, but the record does show that the trustees knew about the segregation policies documented in those minutes. Careful examination of *The Press-Courier*'s coverage of desegregation in October 1969 finds then–assistant superintendent for instructional services Norman R. Brekke at a presentation for the Community Action Commission, where he "pointed out that the Oxnard School District has been concerned with de facto segregation, from time to time, since the issue arose in the mid-1930s."[194] At a deposition in April 1974, plaintiff attorney Edelman asked Brekke, "Did you ever have occasion to review old board minutes with reference to segregated schools, or the whole subject of school segregation?"[195] Brekke responded, "I think I would have to answer that yes . . . the late or the middle 1930s."[196] Attorney William Waters interjected, "I'm going to object . . . I don't think it is relevant what happened . . . as to what the policy may or may not have been in this school district, when your pleadings are to the limited—to the period of 1954 to the present, or up to 1971."[197] When Brekke described segregation practices within schools, he gave away specific details while still trying to position himself as somewhat uninformed: "As I recall, the students in this building [where the deposition was being taken] . . . the Wilson Junior High School, were separated by racial and ethnic identification. They were racially and ethnically separated in some manner."[198] When pressed again for when the segregation practices occurred, Brekke stated: "I just recall only some discussions that were reported in the board minutes of the late 1930s, 1937 comes to mind. . . . This particular item was brought to my attention and I read it, and that is basically all I know."[199] Here, with his personal admissions, Brekke also implicated unnamed school officials as aware that the defense's claim to having "*never* maintained a dual school system"[200] was false.

Brekke indeed implied that the defendants had collectively and repeatedly lied about being ignorant of segregation. He and his colleagues did not disclose their knowledge of discriminatory policies and practices during the *Soria* case until specifically questioned under oath. In his deposition, Brekke further recognized that prior to his tenure as an administrator, the school board withheld evidence of racial imbalance from the public by marking many district-wide demographic studies confidential.[201] Since becoming superintendent, Brekke had insisted that school attendance data by race be made publicly accessible, yet he acknowledged that he had not ended other questionable practices regarding racial segregation, such as busing White children living east of Colonia past the east-side schools to attend Curren Elementary.

In his deposition, trustee Thomas Edward Kane defended the district's practices, arguing that segregation functioned as a benevolent tool, allowing the district to serve "children who needed special attention,"[202] such as those "most seriously handicapped by their educational background, or by virtue of the fact that they had recently migrated to California and didn't speak

English."[203] Upon further questioning, Kane conceded that he did not actually know what percentage of students had special needs or what particular programs would best benefit them.[204] Even without these facts, he expressed confidence that the benefits of segregation outweighed those of integration for Mexican American and Black students. When asked to explain what he meant by "a tension between integration and good education," Kane again made baseless claims by giving what he called a "philosophical answer":

> I am prepared to suggest that children who have come from homes where, for instance, there is no television, where there is no magazines, no books, where there is no parental help, where there is a poor diet, where there is an entirely different sort of mores, social graces, that these things represent obstacles as large to that child, nearly as the inability to speak English; that if they are going to live in our American society and compete in our American Society, that we have to somehow bring these children up to a level or standard equal to that of the other people in the community.[205]

In Kane's view, the school board kept Mexican American and Black children segregated for their own benefit, with an explicit goal of Americanizing them and bringing them "up to a level or standard equal to that of the other people in the community"—people who ostensibly had all the attributes necessary to "compete in our American Society."[206] Kane's unoriginal responses echoed the patronizing statements Superintendent Haydock made over five decades earlier about both Mexican and Black children.[207] A few additional questions from attorney Nowlin left little uncertainty about Kane's affinity toward Haydock's racial ideology as well: "Did the board ever ask for or receive information as to which Black and Mexican-American children did *not* need special education?" Kane answered as if the question were surprising: "Did *not* need special education? No, not that I am aware of." Nowlin followed up: "Are you operating under the assumption that most Black and Mexican-American children need special education programs?" Kane affirmed, "Yes."[208]

If Brekke's statements revealed that the board knew about the past district practices of segregation and Kane exposed their purposeful maintenance of segregation as a contribution to the common good, trustee Robert Pfeiler took a page from a past strategy playbook by feigning ignorance. As a board member from 1954 until 1971, he had been one of the most vocal antagonists of the NAACP and CSO efforts in 1963. Pfeiler also had perhaps the most extensive personal history with Oxnard schools.[209] The Pfeiler family was considered among the pioneer landowning families in Oxnard, and Robert went to Oxnard Grammar School, Haydock, and Oxnard High School, graduating in 1927.[210] Still, in 1974, he claimed: "The word segregation never came in my vocabulary until just recently. The word segregation was nil in Oxnard when I went to school."[211] After being asked about the various proposals to end racial segregation presented to the board from 1963 through 1971, such as those of the NAACP and the Bureau of Intergroup Relations, and the 1969 master plan, Pfeiler dismissively claimed amnesia: "I have forgotten all about this stuff. I am a busy man and these things I wipe off mind and I don't think about this, and I can't answer either way."[212]

Reflecting on his childhood and whether there was a separate school for Mexican Americans, Pfeiler described: "Oxnard was a Mexican town at that time [but] in the elementary level, I just can't remember. I'm sure we had Mexicans."[213] He did recall the name of one Black student who went to Haydock Junior High, "but the Mexicans I cannot remember," he said.[214] When Edelman asked him whether consideration of a student's race or ethnic background ought to be part of educational decision-making processes, he said, "Yes . . . by providing the necessary additional courses and teaching ratio that the ethnic people need; programs that these people need for a good education."[215] Pfeiler's tenure as a board member exhibited a continuity of disregard for Mexican American children.

Trustee J. Keith Mason seemed annoyed about being deposed, though his memory was markedly better than Pfeiler's. He admitted to being "very upset about the lawsuit. I was very upset about what we were being forced into."[216] Mason clarified that he opposed the court-ordered integration plan because he was against "forced busing."[217] "First of all, I think it is wrong, philosophically. I think it doesn't accomplish any goals. I think it is an expense that isn't warranted. That pretty much covers it at the time. Obviously now, it hasn't accomplished anything since it was instituted."[218] Mason went on to acknowledge that board members had discussed "some type of forced segregation," which he attributed to "the unprinted policy" of the district "many, many years ago."[219] He and his colleagues did not look further into the past, he explained, because "I think we all felt very strongly it had no effect on what the present situation was."[220] Mason showed his own ignorance in trying to drive home his point that court-mandated integration was unnecessary in Oxnard, unlike a place such as Los Angeles: "We don't have a ghetto-type situation like they reportedly have down there. The town of Oxnard is pretty well integrated voluntarily . . . there are all different colored peoples living in all different parts of Oxnard . . . without being obstructed."[221]

If the revelations in the depositions and the 1930s minutes were not enough corroborative evidence of the trustees' "systematic scheme of racial segregation,"[222] school board members and administrators further substantiated these findings with details of pernicious acts of racial discrimination during the three-day trial in September 1974. Indeed, in my 2014 interview with Judge Pregerson, he vividly remembered the trial: "In Oxnard, the people who ran the schools were very open to integration—all but the board of trustees. They were a bunch of rednecks up there."[223] Judge Pregerson specifically recalled the dramatic accusations of a district psychologist who had witnessed the trustees in social settings: "He knew them all well. Maybe they belonged to the same service club. He got up and testified as to each one separately and concluded that, as far as I can remember, that each one of them was a racist. They're sitting over there and he's telling them that. I thought that was pretty dramatic. He's looking them in the eye and telling them."[224] *The Press-Courier* coverage of the trial corroborated the judge's memory, but with less detail, noting Nowlin's questioning of Dr. William Berzman about the trustees' attitude toward integration.[225] Berzman, who had worked in the district as director of personnel from 1961 to 1973 before becoming a staff psychologist, reportedly testified that although the school board members would not admit it, their actions showed they "were in favor of segregation."[226] When Judge Pregerson pressed Berzman about whether "the same mentality of segregation found openly in 1930 board members existed in more subtle form with board members in the 1960s," he affirmed, "Yes."[227]

Former superintendent Harold R. DePue gave what the newspaper described as "the strongest testimony against the school district that board members had a definite segregationist policy" during the years he served, from 1961 to 1965.[228] DePue explained that his proposed agenda items pertinent to integration were scuttled, and eventually his contract was not renewed because the board did not want to "face the segregation problem."[229] According to the newspaper, Judge Pregerson interrupted some of DePue's testimony to read an excerpt of the 1930s board meeting minutes and asked if "the same fear of integrating schools" existed in the early 1960s.[230] DePue replied, "Yes . . . the whole question of desegregation became 'a no-no subject.'"[231]

Taken together, the depositions, testimony, and historical evidence presented at trial revealed the mundane use of strategies of segregation inherited from the past. Indeed, the school board shared a staunch determination to carry those designs for inequality into the future. Attorney Edelman recalled his sense that the trustees were "in total denial, denial of the reality and denial of the fact that there was actual bias . . . it didn't matter to them what was accurate, or it didn't matter to them that it was wrong. They didn't want to lose."[232]

"INTENTIONAL, DELIBERATE, PURPOSEFUL SEGREGATION"

In December 1974, three years after his summary judgment, Judge Pregerson rendered a decision for the plaintiffs and ordered that the integration plan "shall remain in effect."[233] Reflecting on the original findings of fact informing his summary judgment, he wrote, "those 'de jure overtones' appeared to represent visible branches which foreshadowed a hidden intent. But it took more digging by plaintiffs' attorneys to discover the School Board's minutes for the 1930s, whereby exposing the roots of the Board's discriminatory intent."[234]

Quoting from the "newly discovered" school board meeting minutes from 1934 through 1939, Judge Pregerson chronicled the board's "blatant intent to segregate Oxnard's elementary school children,"[235] charging them with being "obsessed" with keeping Mexican children separate from Whites. In addition, Judge Pregerson found it appalling that the board took "positive action to aggravate segregation" in the 1950s and 1960s, "under the guise of pursuing a neighborhood school policy."[236] During this time, he explained, in failing to take action on any of the integration proposals brought by groups such as the NAACP, the Bureau of Intergroup Relations, and legal authorities, the trustees violated Title VI of the Civil Rights Act, Title 5 of the California Administrative Code, and the California Supreme Court's ruling *Jackson,* all requiring "affirmative action to overcome effects of prior discrimination."[237]

These regulations, he noted, established the "affirmative duty" of the school board to integrate even if the plaintiffs had only presented evidence for their original complaints of de facto segregation. He cited the obligation to end "that *effect*" of discrimination, "regardless of the cause," as adherent with the U.S. Supreme Court's 1974 *Lau v. Nichols* ruling and the California Supreme Court's 1963 *Jackson v. Pasadena* decision.[238] In addition, Judge Pregerson reminded the Oxnard trustees that their appeal to the Ninth Circuit had led to the *Soria* plaintiffs substantiating the de facto case with de jure evidence. As a result, he concluded, the plaintiffs' attorneys had convincingly demonstrated that the dual school system in place before 1971, replete with its deleterious effects on Mexican American and Black children, "was caused by the School Board's intentional, deliberate, and purposeful policy of racial segregation."[239]

CONCLUSION

But what if the minutes had remained forgotten, these board decisions of 30 and 40 years ago hidden from view? ... The nation will not excise this debilitating prejudice until it acts with equal vigor against the unspoken injustices that are recorded in no board minutes.

—*LOS ANGELES TIMES,*
JANUARY 26, 1975[240]

In January 1975, the *Los Angeles Times* editorialized about Judge Pregerson's ruling in *Soria,* describing the historical evidence of segregation as "a shocking reminder of how some people viewed these matters only a few years ago," but calling on the courts to act with "equal vigor" in de facto cases as well.[241] The *Crawford* case, where the plaintiffs were heading to the California Superior Court without such evidence of intent to segregate, was certainly present on the editors' minds.[242] Indeed, the common cause of desegregation forged by Mexican American and Black plaintiffs in an elementary school district of 9,500 students had captivated local, regional, and national attention along its journey from the Legal Service Center office in La Colonia to federal court, to the Ninth Circuit Court of Appeals, and almost to the U.S. Supreme Court.

This chapter has analyzed aspects of the *Soria* case, which set out to reclaim the Fourteenth Amendment rights of Mexican American and Black children enduring overcrowded, segregated, substandard schooling conditions on the east side of Oxnard. By challenging persistent racial imbalance as discrimination, the plaintiffs protested generations of "unspoken injustices" at a time when the U.S. Supreme Court had not decided on whether de facto segregation, or segregation outside the South, merited judicial remedy. The plaintiffs' pursuit of these rights led to their unearthing the school board's historical obsession in the 1930s with "the matter" of segregation.[243] In doing so, the plaintiffs asserted that history matters. Their win in court led to the implementation of a decade of two-way busing, efforts to integrate classroom curricular materials, increased attention placed on the recruitment of Black and Mexican American personnel, and annual reports on the progress of the integration order.[244] The enduring victories of the case, however, lay in the exposure and disruption of deeply entrenched strategies of segregation, which had been long denied, ignored, and purposefully hidden.[245] Reflecting on *Soria* forty years later, Judge Pregerson smiled as he said: "I'm very proud of my rulings on that case. I'm glad my name came up on the wheel."[246]

Epilogue

The schools and courts themselves cannot eliminate segregation and racism . . . the ultimate question for the future is not whether court ordered busing is to continue, but whether the educational and judicial systems are to be part of any concerted and consistent national effort to end racism in America.

—CHARLES M. WOLLENBERG, 1976

LISTENING TO THE PAINED, but determined voices of those who attended schools in Oxnard generations before me has brought new depth and dimension to my understandings of race, residence, and the elusiveness of educational equality. These are the insights I share in this book. I have chronicled the structures, practices, and discourses shaping Oxnard elementary schools over a seventy-year period. During this time, the White architects designed the systematic subordination of Mexican Americans to appear as a commonplace, inevitable, everyday way of conducting business within and beyond schools. They embedded this mundane racism into the educational infrastructure from 1903 to 1939 by strategically institutionalizing a school-within-a-school model of racial separation, formalizing a racial hierarchy with Mexicans positioned as an inferior group, fostering a permanent interconnection between school and residential segregation, and omitting a rationale for segregation from their records.

By 1940, with the opening of Ramona School on the east side, the White architects expanded their strategies of segregation to more effectively contain Colonia children. In the decades after World War II, Mexican American and Black neighbors contested social inequality, and in 1963, mobilized by the CSO and NAACP, they forged a common cause in school desegregation. A little over a decade later, when Judge Pregerson wrote his December 1974 *Soria* opinion, he concluded that, indeed, school segregation in Oxnard had been deliberate.

Desegregation cases such as *Soria* each carry unique local histories shaping the questions of equality before the court, but legal remedies rarely account for the diversity and nuances of these narratives. While the *Soria* case grew out of struggles for justice in the fields and factories for generations of pre-dominantly Mexican agricultural workers, the legal case did not emphasize these characteristics as making Oxnard somehow distinct from other deseg-regation suits. Beyond the initial filings from the parents of the ten Mexican American and Black plaintiffs in February 1970, the affidavits in support of the integration order were all from Black or White residents, and the trial testimony focused on White school trustees and administrators. Even while the district court's opinion highlighted the trustees' plans to segregate Mexican children in the 1930s, the case materials did not record the perspec-tives of Mexican Americans from any decade.

What would have been different if the *Soria* case had more centrally accounted for Oxnard's history? Would this have helped to expose the board members' use of racially restrictive covenants as part of "a systematic scheme of racial segregation"?[1] What if the attorneys, for the plaintiffs or the defend-ants, had sought out experts on educational history? Whom would they have called on and what insights would these scholars' reports have provided?

Local histories remind us that narratives about race, schooling, and equal-ity are complex, sometimes contradictory, and never complete. With my analysis of parallel and shared struggles for social justice, I do not intend to imply that there were no conflicts between or among Mexican American and Black residents. Certainly, competition over minimal resources fostered divi-sions inside and outside schools. As Gaye Theresa Johnson argues, interracial tensions are part of reality but full consideration of the historical record dem-onstrates "there are far more examples of mutually meaningful Black-Brown antiracism struggles and radical creative affiliations. . . . Coalitions among oppressed minorities in California have always been present, even when they have not always ended in victory."[2] Recovering Oxnard's educational history enabled me to reclaim one example of a common cause for racially equal schools. Within this interracial alliance, there were undoubtedly some tense debates.

For instance, in June 1970, a few months after the court filing, Juan Soria was quoted by the newspaper explaining that for MAPA "Our first concern is not with integration, but with a proper education for our children . . . integration should be left to the courts and Colonia children provided with 'sensitive' and 'fearless' teachers."[3] Among activists and organizations fighting for social justice, debates over how to best achieve racial equality in schools had deep roots in California and across the nation.[4]

In December 1974, discussions of two-way busing all but eclipsed press coverage of the court-approved robust integration plan. The plan's objectives included the recruitment of racially diverse teachers, staff, and administrators, the incorporation of Black and Chicana/o histories in the curriculum, and the reframing of professional development around the cultural strengths of Communities of Color. These goals reflected some of the demands made by activists questioning the premise of integration altogether. In Oxnard as in so many other communities, even those residents mobilizing around desegregation recognized that integrating schools would not be the end of the struggle for educational equality. Indeed, veteran organizers did not become complacent with the court order. Some of the Black and Chicana/o activists of the 1960s and 1970s eventually navigated their way into roles as teachers, administrators, and school board members. For his part, Juan continued organizing in Oxnard until his passing in 1997.[5] A little over a decade later, a new generation of school trustees honored Juan's activism with a school in his name, Juan Lagunas Soria Elementary.[6]

MOVING BEYOND DISCIPLINARY BOUNDARIES TO EFFECT POLICY CHANGE

Four decades ago, Charles M. Wollenberg expressed concern that "California's long history of school segregation and exclusion has been virtually ignored by educators and historians, let alone politicians and the general public."[7] Since that time, some remarkable studies have contributed much to our knowledge of school segregation. Still, much of the research on segregation analyzes schools and housing separately and tends to focus on Black and White experiences in urban and suburban communities. Countless educational histories remain untold, in part because most doctoral programs in education do not train students to apply a historical lens in their work, and few history programs offer education courses as part of the doctoral curriculum. For students interested in remedying this gap, I hope this book demonstrates the possibility of bridging history with other disciplines and renews the urgency to reveal how history shapes contemporary schooling conditions.

We know segregation was present in over 80 percent of the school systems across the Southwest in the 1920s, but we know little of the strategies employed within those systems. Within and beyond California, we need researchers to excavate the historical function of schools in establishing and reproducing racial inequality. Local studies should account for the ways schooling is shaped by and contributes to a community's history. By positioning these narratives in conversation with regional and national studies, scholars can deepen our knowledge of race and schools across time and place. Researchers should also continue casting a critical light on where educational reform efforts converge—and, in the words of Kenneth B. Clark, should name contemporary conditions of "segregated schools and segregated housing . . . as lasting symbols of our history of racism."[8] This work can help recover the voices of those who came before us in this struggle.

Oxnard's narrative challenged me to work not just in between but also across and beyond disciplinary boundaries, to locate education in relation to housing and the law. This transdisciplinary approach enabled me to document voices ignored by the official archives and to identify intergenerational perspectives missing from contemporary educational policy discussions. Indeed, while we work to expand the reach of our inquiries, we should remain focused, as Richard Delgado and Jean Stefancic write, on "the particulars of lives lived at the margins of society," if we indeed seek to "introduce their views into the dialogue about the way society should be governed."[9] How, for example, might the accounts of my interviewees in Oxnard inform national policies?

In 2016, while Latinas/os comprised 25.9 percent of public school enrollments in the nation, 54 percent in California, and 57.7 percent in Ventura County, these children made up 92.6 percent of the Oxnard Elementary School District enrollment.[10] How might we apply historical insights to better serve these students? In my interview with Dr. Cesar Morales, the Oxnard School District superintendent in 2016, he reflected on the legacy of the *Soria* case as "a testament to the community of Oxnard's desire to have equity for all of its students, and we need to honor that by taking it a step further in not only ensuring equity in the educational experience but tying it to the purpose of . . . [attaining] a higher education." To realize this goal, he explained, educators need an "asset-minded perspective," recognizing that regardless of income or educational levels, "there are assets in [parents' and children's] local experience and in their cultural experience that they bring to the table."[11] This vision dramatically departs from the designs for inequality Superintendent Haydock and the White architects left for Antonia, Delia, Joe, and generations of their peers.

As we near the end of the second decade of the twenty-first century, we are still confronting the challenge of transforming systems of prejudice and discrimination that were designed to reproduce racial inequality as a matter of course. I offer this book on Oxnard's educational history, and the precious community memories it holds, as a contribution to carrying this cause forward.

Appendix

LIST OF INTERVIEWS CONDUCTED
AND CONSULTED

As noted in the introduction, space restrictions prohibited me from quoting every interview examined for this project. The list here includes interviews I conducted in collaboration with Frank P. Barajas or Tara J. Yosso for an earlier article publication, and existing interviews I gathered from various archival collections. I received approval for this research from the UCLA Institutional Review Board.

Harry C. Alford Jr.
Guadalupe Anguiano
Ana Del Rio Barba
Francisco S. Barba
Denise Carballo Beltran
Richard A. Carballo
Mary A. Martinez Carlyle
Ignacio S. Carmona
Ricardo Carmona
Ernie Carrasco Jr.
Dolores Ávila Carrasco
Edwin L. Carty
Ruth L. Chaparro
Robert Cheveres
Krista Comer
Gilbert G. Cuevas
Antonia Arguelles DiLiello
Albert G. Duff
Mexie Duff
Joel I. Edelman
Miguel Espinosa Jr.
John K. Flynn

Lamberto M. García
Leroy A. Gibson Jr.
Javier Gomez
Jess Johnny Granados
Jess Gutierrez
Joanne Hatcher
John R. Hatcher III
Delia L. Hernandez
Gene S. Kanamori
Mary Valdivia Lamm
Armando Lopez
Manuel M. Lopez
Robert Madrid
Thomas Malley
Joe I. Mendoza
Julieta Flores Soria Mendoza
Cesar Morales
Herbert D. Nowlin
Gerhard W. Orthuber
Sandra Peña
Manuel L. Perez
Virginia D. Perez
Bedford Pinkard
Margaret Tatum Potter
Harry Pregerson
Lylian Pressel
Mary Quintana
Alex Quiroz
Carmen Ramírez
Dennis Renault
Marty Renault
Peter D. Roos
Juanita L. Sanchez-Valdez
Catalina Frazier Soria
Isabel Soria
Juan L. Soria
Daisy A. Tatum
William L. Terry
Margaret Thrasher
Juanita A. Valdivia
Rachel Murguía Wong

NOTES

1. Richard Lyttle, "The Largest Labor Camp in Nation in Oxnard," *Oxnard Press-Courier,* March 6, 1958, 11.

2. Juan Gómez-Quiñones, *Mexican American Labor, 1790–1990* (Albuquerque: University of New Mexico Press, 1994).

3. Julian Samora, "Mexican Immigration," in *Mexican-Americans Tomorrow: Educational and Economic Perspectives,* edited by Gus Taylor (Albuquerque: University of New Mexico Press, 1975), 60–80, 62.

4. The term "the White architects" is inspired by the work of William H. Watkins, though I define and apply it differently in relation to Oxnard. See Introduction for further description. William H. Watkins, *The White Architects of Black Education: Ideology and Power in America, 1865–1954* (New York: Teachers College Press, 2001).

INTRODUCTION

Epigraph: Juan Gómez-Quiñones and Irene Vásquez, *Making Aztlán: Ideology and Culture of the Chicana and Chicano Movement, 1966–1977* (Albuquerque: University of New Mexico Press, 2014), xxix–xxx.

1. *Debbie and Doreen Soria, et al., v. Oxnard School Board of Trustees,* 386 F. Supp. 539 (U.S. Dist. 1974).

2. Here I paraphrase some of what Peter Linebaugh and Marcus Rediker observed in their comparison of the study of history with the study of ocean waves, and the length of their fetch. The wave's fetch refers to "the distance from its point of origin," which remains hidden under the ocean's surface for most of its journey. The fetch becomes "visible only at the end, when [the waves] rise and break." Linebaugh and Rediker assert that close examination of the fetch of history can surface "connections that have, over centuries, usually been denied, ignored, or

simply not seen, but that nonetheless profoundly shaped the history of the world in which we all of us live and die." Peter Linebaugh and Marcus Rediker, *The Many-Headed Hydra: Sailors, Slaves, Commoners, and the Hidden History of the Revolutionary Atlantic* (Boston: Beacon Press, 2000), 1, 7.

3. See, for example, Thomas P. Carter, *Mexican Americans: A History of Educational Neglect* (New York: College Entrance Examination Board, 1970); Rubén Donato, *Mexicans and Hispanos in Colorado Schools and Communities, 1920–1960* (Albany: State University of New York Press, 2007); Gilbert Gonzalez, *Chicano Education in the Era of Segregation* (Philadelphia: Balch Institute Press, 1990); Laura K. Muñoz, "*Romo v. Laird:* Mexican American School Segregation and the Politics of Belonging in Arizona," *Western Legal History* 26, nos. 1 and 2 (2013): 97–132; Guadalupe San Miguel Jr., "*Let All of Them Take Heed": Mexican Americans and the Quest for Educational Equality in Texas, 1910–1981* (College Station: Texas A&M University Press, 1987); Charles M. Wollenberg, *All Deliberate Speed: Segregation and Exclusion in California Schools, 1855–1975* (Berkeley: University of California Press, 1976). A few additional scholars have written books, articles, or book chapters contributing significantly to Chicana/o educational history. See, for example, Martha Menchaca, *The Mexican Outsiders: A Community History of Discrimination and Marginalization in California* (Austin: University of Texas Press, 1995); Jeanne Powers, "Forgotten History: Mexican American School Segregation in Arizona, 1900–1951," *Equity and Excellence in Education* 41, no. 4 (2008): 467–81; David Torres-Rouff, "Becoming Mexican: Segregated Schools and Social Scientists in Southern California, 1913–1946," *Southern California Quarterly* 94, no. 1 (2012): 91–127.

4. Richard R. Valencia, Martha Menchaca, and Rubén Donato, "Segregation, Desegregation, and Integration of Chicano Students: Old and New Realities," in *Chicano School Failure and Success: Past, Present, and Future,* 2nd ed., edited by Richard R. Valencia (London: Routledge, 2002), 70–113.

5. Martha Menchaca and Richard R. Valencia, "Anglo-Saxon Ideologies in the 1920s–1930s: Their Impact on the Segregation of Mexican Students in California," *Anthropology and Education Quarterly* 21, no. 3 (1990): 222–49.

6. See, for example, George I. Sánchez, "The Education of Bilinguals in a State School System" (Ph.D. dissertation, University of California, Berkeley, 1934); George I. Sánchez, *Forgotten People: A Study of New Mexicans* [1940] (Albuquerque: University of New Mexico Press, 1996); Menchaca, *Mexican Outsiders.*

7. See, for example, Carlos K. Blanton, "'They Cannot Master Abstractions, but They Can Often Be Made Efficient Workers': Race and Class in the Intelligence Testing of Mexican Americans and African Americans in Texas during the 1920s," *Social Science Quarterly* 81, no. 4 (Winter 2000): 1014–26; Carlos K. Blanton, "From Intellectual Deficiency to Cultural Deficiency: Mexican Americans, Testing, and Public School Policy in the American Southwest, 1920–1940," *Pacific Historical Review* 72, no. 1 (February 2003): 39–62; Gilbert Gonzalez, "Segregation of Mexican Children in a Southern California City: The Legacy of Expansionism and the American Southwest," *Western Historical Quarterly* 16, no. 1 (1985): 55–76; Torres-Rouff, "Becoming Mexican."

8. Guadalupe San Miguel Jr., *Brown, Not White: School Integration and the Chicano Movement in Houston* (College Station: Texas A&M University Press, 2001); Guadalupe San Miguel Jr., *Chicana/o Struggles for Education: Activism in the Community* (College Station: Texas A&M University Press, 2013); Guadalupe San Miguel Jr. and Richard R. Valencia, "From the Treaty of Guadalupe Hidalgo to Hopwood: The Educational Plight and Struggle for Equity for Mexican Americans in the Southwest," *Harvard Educational Review* 68, no. 3 (1998): 353–412; Richard R. Valencia, *Chicano Students and the Courts: The Mexican American Legal Struggle for Educational Equality* (New York: Routledge, 2008).

9. Rubén Donato and Marvin Lazerson observed fifteen years ago, "For all the tremendous growth in research on the educational histories of people of color, this area of inquiry remains very small, understudied, and insufficiently explored." Rubén Donato and Marvin Lazerson, "New Directions in American Educational History: Problems and Prospects," *Educational Researcher* 29, no. 8 (2000): 4–15, 8.

10. Leticia M. Saucedo, "The Legal Issues Surrounding the TAAS Case," *Hispanic Journal of Behavioral Sciences* 22, no. 4 (2000): 411–22, 420.

11. San Miguel, *Brown, Not White;* San Miguel and Valencia, "From the Treaty of Guadalupe Hidalgo to Hopwood."

12. Carey McWilliams wrote about Southern California as a "rurban" region that was "neither city nor country but everywhere a mixture of both." Carey McWilliams, *Southern California: An Island on the Land* (Layton, UT: Gibbs Smith, 1946), 12.

13. In documenting some of Oxnard's early labor history leading to the 1903 strike against the American Beet Sugar Company, Tomás Almaguer identifies a racial hierarchy at play in the city, noting, "The most obvious feature of this hierarchy was the residential segregation of the community and the organization of the local labor market in racial terms." He argues that Mexicans occupied a position along the hierarchy above Asians but still beneath Whites. However, he does not examine schools, and does not consider the development of this hierarchy much beyond 1903. My narrative expands and complicates his analysis. Tomás Almaguer, *Racial Fault Lines: The Historical Origins of White Supremacy in California* (Berkeley: University of California Press, 1994), 188.

14. See Christopher Ramos, "The Educational Legacy of Racially Restrictive Covenants: Their Long Term Impact on Mexican Americans," *The Scholar* 4 (2002): 149–84, 155.

15. Paul M. Ong and Jordan Rickles, "The Continued Nexus between School and Residential Segregation," *Berkeley La Raza Law Journal* 15 (2004): 51–66, 53; for some of the few exceptions to this pattern in the literature, see the papers published from a 1995 forum "In Pursuit of a Dream Deferred: Linking Housing and Education Policy" by the Institute on Race and Poverty and the University of Minnesota Law School, *University of Minnesota Law Review* 80, no. 4 (1996): 743–910. See also the volume of reprints and additional essays: john a. powell, Gavin Kearney, and Vina Key, eds., *In Pursuit of a Dream Deferred: Linking Housing and Education Policy* (New York: Peter Lang, 2001).

16. See Matthew D. Lassiter's essay introducing three distinct articles in a special section of the *Journal of Urban History* "exploring the interplay between educational policies and housing markets in metropolitan U.S. history during the twentieth century." These studies highlight what he determines to be a "disciplinary divide between the history of education and urban/suburban history," which he argues necessitates "a new methodological approach that recognizes the mutually constitutive nature of public education and private housing on the metropolitan landscapes of modern America." Matthew D. Lassiter, "Schools and Housing in Metropolitan History: An Introduction," *Journal of Urban History* 38, no. 2 (2012): 195–204, 196.

17. See, for example, Gary Orfield and Susan Eaton, *Dismantling Desegregation: The Quiet Reversal of Brown v. Board of Education* (New York: New Press, 1996).

18. Most of this research focuses on the Cold War period and tends to examine the construction of the model minority myth within a Black/White binary, arguing that Asians have been perceived and portrayed as acceptable to Whites because they are not Black. See, for example, Robert G. Lee, *Orientals: Asian Americans in Popular Culture* (Philadelphia: Temple University Press, 1999); Ellen D. Wu, *The Color of Success: Asian Americans and the Origins of the Model Minority* (Princeton, NJ: Princeton University Press, 2013). Oxnard's educational history challenges us to consider the perceptions and portrayals of Asians as acceptable to Whites because they are not Mexican.

19. See Menchaca and Valencia, "Anglo-Saxon Ideologies."

20. Natalia Molina explains that because "race is a mutually constitutive process," we can learn more from a relational approach to race, which attends to the intersectionality of group experiences. She distinguishes this from a comparative group analysis, which takes a compare-and-contrast approach. Natalia Molina, *Fit to Be Citizens? Public Health and Race in Los Angeles, 1879–1939* (Berkeley: University of California Press, 2006), 3.

21. Almost all past desegregation cases to this point had been filed on behalf of one group, Blacks or Mexicans, or treated as distinct cases by the courts. For example, in 1955, in El Centro, California, the NAACP and Alianza Hispano Americana of Imperial County each filed a separate lawsuit in federal district court. Their complaints were identical except that one referred to Mexican students (No. 1712-SD), and the other to Blacks (No. 1713-SD). These children attended two schools for Black and Mexican students, which were kept apart from ten other exclusively White schools. The two suits, one for Blacks and one for Mexican Americans, were initially rejected by the federal district judge and remanded to the county court. When the attorneys appealed this decision to the U.S. District Court of Appeals they also requested that the suits be consolidated. The case marked the first in California since *Brown v. Board* to challenge segregation. See "Segregation Challenged in El Centro," *Oxnard Press-Courier,* July 28, 1955, 2; *Romero v. Weakley, Burleigh v. Weakley,* 131 F. Supp. 818 (U.S. Dist. 1955). See further analysis in Guadalupe Salinas, "Mexican Americans and Desegregation," *El Grito: A Journal of Contemporary Mexican-American Thought* 4, no. 4 (1971): 36–58. See also Valencia, *Chicano Students and the Courts,* 55–56. The *Keyes v. School District No. 1, Denver, Colorado*

suit was filed in 1969, and the district court questioned the joint filing of "Hispanos and Negroes." When the U.S. Supreme Court ruled on *Keyes* in 1973, the justices reversed the district's decision and concluded "that the District Court erred in separating Negroes and Hispanos for purposes of defining a 'segregated' school." The high Court also cited the *Soria* case among the rulings establishing that "Hispanos constitute an identifiable class for purposes of the Fourteenth Amendment." See *Keyes v. School District No. 1, Denver, Colorado*, 413 U.S. 189, 195–98 (1973). The *Crawford v. Board of Education of the City of Los Angeles* suit was filed in 1963 on behalf of Black students, but before the case went to court in 1968, "Hispanic" students were added as plaintiffs. See *Crawford v. Board of Education*, Cal.3d 280, 302, 551 P.2d 28, 42 (1976).

22. For the purposes of this study, I try to be consistent with conveying the social and legal meanings of the terms "desegregation" and "integration" as the organizations, individuals, and courts referenced them at the time. The community aspirations fueling school desegregation efforts were never just about racial balance. Organizers often used the term "desegregation" interchangeably with "integration," and did not allow legal definitions to limit their demands for change. For example, Oxnard school desegregation advocates called for racially balanced school enrollments but also called for changes to the curriculum to incorporate the histories of different ethnic and racial groups, for the hiring of additional Black and Chicana/o teachers, staff, and administrators, and for professional development of teachers to become more responsive to students' cultural backgrounds. As elsewhere, some activists in Oxnard also questioned the premise that integration would increase equal educational opportunities.

23. Gómez-Quiñones and Vásquez, *Making Aztlán*.

24. "Sugar King Gave City Start: Henry Oxnard Created City in Building Sugar Empire," *Oxnard Press-Courier*, September 24 and 25, 1948, 1.

25. An article written by Mexican American businessman H. C. Palomino for the newspaper's special edition of the city's fiftieth anniversary acknowledged, "In every agricultural community in Southern California, there is always a great influx of Mexican labor. Oxnard is one of these places." H. C. Palomino, "Mexican-Americans Taking Even Greater Role in City," *Oxnard Press-Courier*, September 24, 1948, sec. E, 7.

26. "Four Daughters of Mike Kaufman Linked Families," *Oxnard Press-Courier*, September 24, 1948, sec. E, 3.

27. William H. Watkins, *The White Architects of Black Education: Ideology and Power in America, 1865–1954* (New York: Teachers College Press, 2001).

28. See James D. Anderson, *The Education of Blacks in the South, 1860–1935* (Chapel Hill: University of North Carolina Press, 1988).

29. Watkins's exposure of this complex and often contradictory ideological architecture also suggests its susceptibility to deconstruction. Watkins, *White Architects of Black Education*.

30. Charles Mills, *The Racial Contract* (Ithaca, NY: Cornell University Press, 1997), 11.

31. See Melvin Oliver and Thomas Shapiro, *Black Wealth/White Wealth: Toward a New Theory of Inequality* (New York: Routledge, 1994). George Lipsitz

also explains, "Net worth is almost totally determined by past opportunities for asset accumulation, therefore is the one figure most likely to reflect the history of discrimination." George Lipsitz, *The Possessive Investment in Whiteness: How White People Profit from Identity Politics* (Philadelphia: Temple University Press, 1998), 13–14.

32. "Policewoman Graduate Nurse for City Health," *Oxnard Daily Courier,* January 31, 1917, front page.

33. "Supreme Court School Ruling Affects Oxnard," *The Oxnard Daily Courier,* November 22, 1927, front page.

34. Oxnard School Board of Trustees meeting minutes, September 27, 1937. The Oxnard Elementary School District holds a microfilm copy of the board of trustees meeting minutes, hereafter referred to as "OSBT meeting minutes," with the date.

35. OSBT meeting minutes, December 12, 1938.

36. Chester M. Pierce explained: "It is from feelings of superiority that one group of people proceeds to brutalize, degrade, abuse, and humiliate another group of individuals. The superiority feelings and the accompanying contemptuous condescension toward a target group are so rampant in our society.... [But] most offensive actions are not gross and crippling. They are subtle and stunning." Chester M. Pierce, "Offensive Mechanisms," in *The Black Seventies,* edited by Floyd B. Barbour (Boston: Porter Sargent, 1970), 265–82, 265–66.

37. See David G. García, Tara J. Yosso, and Frank P. Barajas, "'A Few of the Brightest, Cleanest Mexican Children': School Segregation as a Form of Mundane Racism in Oxnard, California, 1900–1940," *Harvard Educational Review* 82, no. 1 (2012): 1–25. My definition expands on scholarly analysis of racism in U.S. society; for example, Derrick A. Bell, *And We Will Not Be Saved: The Elusive Quest for Racial Justice* (New York: Basic Books, 1987); Derrick A. Bell, *Faces at the Bottom of the Well: The Permanence of Racism* (New York: Basic Books, 1992); Manning Marable, *Black America* (Westfield, NJ: Open Media, 1992).

38. See, for example, Mario Barrera, *Race and Class in the Southwest: A Theory of Racial Inequality* (Notre Dame, IN: University of Notre Dame Press, 1979); Rodolfo F. Acuña, *Occupied America: A History of Chicanos,* 3rd ed. (New York: HarperCollins, 1988); Almaguer, *Racial Fault Lines;* Miroslava Chávez-García, *Negotiating Conquest: Gender and Power in California, 1770s to 1880s* (Tucson: University of Arizona Press, 2004); Laura E. Gomez, *Manifest Destinies: The Making of the Mexican American Race* (New York: New York University Press, 2007); Leonard Pitt, *The Decline of the Californios: A Social History of the Spanish-Speaking Californians, 1846–1890* (Berkeley: University of California Press, 1998); Frank P. Barajas, *Curious Unions: Mexican American Workers and Resistance in Oxnard, California, 1898–1961* (Lincoln: University of Nebraska Press, 2012).

39. The Chumash people lived throughout what are now known as Ventura and Santa Barbara counties. See further discussion by Barajas, *Curious Unions,* 13–15; Menchaca, *Mexican Outsiders,* 1–3. See also Elaine K. Garber, "Hueneme: Origins of the Name," *Ventura County Historical Society Quarterly* 12, no. 3 (June 1967): 11–15; Roberta S. Greenwood and R. O. Browne, "The Rise and Fall of Shisholop,"

Ventura County Historical Society Quarterly 12, no. 2 (February 1967): 2–5; Chester King, "The Names and Locations of Historic Chumash Villages," *Journal of California Anthropology* 2, no. 2 (1975): 171–79, 175.

40. Antonia I. Castañeda, "Sexual Violence in the Politics and Policies of Conquest: Amerindian Women and the Spanish Conquest of Alta California," in *Building with Our Hands: New Directions in Chicana Studies,* edited by Adela de la Torre and Beatríz M. Pesquera (Los Angeles: University of California Press, 1993), 15–33, 17–19; John R. Johnson and Sally McLendon, "Cultural Affiliation and Lineal Descent of Chumash Peoples in the Channel Islands and Santa Monica Mountains" (Santa Barbara, CA: Santa Barbara Museum of Natural History, 1997), 150; Holly Love and Rheta Resnick, "Mission Made Pottery and Other Ceramics from Muwu, a Coastal Chumash Village," *Pacific Coast Archaeological Society Quarterly* 19, no. 1 (1983): 1–11, 9; Rheta Resnick, "Subsistence Patterns at VEN-11, a Coastal Chumash Village" (master's thesis, California State University, Northridge, 1980), 21.

41. Rancho Las Posas, Rancho Calleguas, Rancho Santa Clara del Norte, Rancho El Rio de Santa Clara O La Colonia, and Rancho Guadalasca. For more detail about these land grants, see Barajas, *Curious Unions,* 22. See also Chávez-García, *Negotiating Conquest,* regarding the independence and wealth that land ownership enabled for Native American and Mexican women.

42. See Tomás Almaguer, "Class, Race, and Capitalist Development: The Social Transformation of a Southern California County, 1848–1903" (Ph.D. dissertation, University of California, Berkeley, 1979), 145; Robert G. Cowan, *Ranchos of California: A List of Spanish Concessions 1777–1822 and Mexican Grants 1822–1846* (Los Angeles: Historical Society of Southern California, 1977), 37, 63, 9–94; W. W. Robinson, *The Story of Ventura County* (Los Angeles: Title Insurance and Trust Company, 1950); Burgess McK. Shumway, *California Ranchos: Patented Private Land Grants Listed by County* (San Bernardino, CA: Borgo Press, 1988), 114–16; Howard F. Gregor estimated the size of Rancho Santa Clara del Norte as 13,989 acres and discussed the process by which much of this land became considered "public domain" (Howard F. Gregor, "Changing Agricultural Patterns in the Oxnard Area of Southern California" [Ph.D. dissertation, University of California, Los Angeles, 1950]); J. N. Bowman, "Prominent Women of Provincial California," *Southern California Quarterly* 39, no. 2 (1957): 149–66, 154.

43. Almaguer, "Class, Race, and Capitalist Development"; Almaguer, *Racial Fault Lines;* Douglas Monroy, *Thrown among Strangers: The Making of Mexican Culture in Frontier California* (Berkeley: University of California Press, 1993); Pitt, *Decline of the Californios;* Richard B. Rice, William A. Bullough, and Richard J. Orsi, *The Elusive Eden: A New History of California* (New York: McGraw-Hill, 1996), 335.

44. Frank P. Barajas and Tomás Almaguer each highlights this with the case of the Gonzales family selling their lands to Camarillo after a protracted legal battle and the strong-arm tactics of Thomas A. Scott. See Almaguer, *Racial Fault Lines,* 82–84; Barajas, *Curious Unions,* 29–30. County records include many property deeds referencing partitioned land from the *Scott v. Gonzales* case.

45. Chávez-García, *Negotiating Conquest;* Antonia I. Castañeda, "Engendering the History of Alta California, 1769–1848: Gender, Sexuality, and the Family," *California History* 76, nos. 2/3 (1997): 230–59.

46. Chávez-García, *Negotiating Conquest,* 123. See also further discussion of the decline of the pastoral economy, and drought in relation to land displacement, in Almaguer, *Racial Fault Lines;* Monroy, *Thrown among Strangers;* and Pitt, *Decline of the Californios.*

47. Ian Haney Lopez details this legal paradox wherein Mexicans were defined as White but not granted the rights of whiteness. Ian Haney Lopez, *White by Law: The Legal Construction of Race* (New York: New York University Press, 1996). For example, while schools engaged in practices of public humiliation and corporal punishment for speaking Spanish, and sought to completely segregate Mexicans from Whites, the First National Bank of Oxnard advertised in the newspaper: "Tell Mexicans who cannot speak English that we can talk with them in Spanish. Tell them to come here with their savings, or to send money across into Mexico. They will find us helpful and friendly." *The Oxnard Daily Courier,* July 1, 1920, 3. Similarly, in 1921, Frederick Noble organized a special census in Oxnard to demonstrate they had five thousand Whites residing within city limits—the minimal qualifications for chartering an Elks Club. (The 1920 U.S. Census had counted 4,700). Though they must have counted Mexicans as White to prove this threshold, their records show that only two Mexicans were included among the one hundred charter members of the club—Adolfo Camarillo and Frank A. Camarillo, the sons of Juan Camarillo, one of the only *Californios* in Ventura County to have held on to a large portion of his original rancho land. "It Took a Special Census to Get Elks Lodge Their Charter in 1922," *Oxnard Press-Courier,* September 24, 1948, front page.

48. Almaguer explains that working-class Mexicans "were often denied their legal rights by being categorized as Indians . . . anyone with a dark complexion could be so treated. . . . Although Mexicans were legally accorded the same rights as free white persons, actual extension of these privileges to all segments of this population was quite another matter." Almaguer, *Racial Fault Lines,* 57.

49. See Juan Gómez-Quiñones, *Mexican American Labor, 1790–1990* (Albuquerque: University of New Mexico Press, 1994); Paul S. Taylor, *Mexican Labor in the United States,* vol. 1 (Berkeley: University of California Press, 1930).

50. For early 1900s examples, see Albert Camarillo, *Chicanos in California: A History of Mexican Americans in California* (San Francisco: Boyd & Fraser, 1984), 31–46; for examples from the 1930s, see Taylor, *Mexican Labor in the United States,* 86–89. For examples from the 1940s, see Juan Gómez-Quiñones, *Chicano Politics: Reality and Promise, 1940–1990* (Albuquerque: University of New Mexico Press, 1990), 42–43. On Mexicans as jurists, see Ignacio M. García, *White but Not Equal: Mexican Americans, Jury Discrimination, and the Supreme Court* (Tucson: University of Arizona Press, 2009); Michael A. Olivas, ed., *"Colored Men" and "Hombres Aquí": Hernández v. Texas and the Emergence of Mexican-American Lawyering* (Houston: Arte Público Press, 2006); on residential segregation, see Clemente E. Vose, *Caucasians Only: The Supreme Court, the NAACP, and the Restrictive*

Covenant Cases (Berkeley: University of California Press, 1959); on school segregation, see Wollenberg, *All Deliberate Speed*.

51. See George A. Martinez, "The Legal Construction of Race: Mexican-Americans and Whiteness," *Harvard Latino Law Review* 2, no. 1 (1997): 321–47; Rubén Donato and Jarrod S. Hanson, "Legally White, Socially Mexican: The Politics of de Jure and de Facto School Segregation in the American Southwest," *Harvard Educational Review* 82, no. 2 (2012): 202–25.

52. For example, Tomás Almaguer explains that in Oxnard the Japanese-Mexican Labor Association established "the first major agricultural workers' union composed of newly racialized ethnic populations," and in 1903 they engaged in what became "the first strike successfully against white capitalist interests" in California. Almaguer, *Racial Fault Lines,* 187.

53. For additional examples of this paradox, see José M. Alamillo, *Making Lemonade out of Lemons: Mexican American Labor and Leisure in a California Town 1880–1960* (Urbana: University of Illinois Press, 2006); Sarah Deutsch, *No Separate Refuge: Culture, Class, and Gender on an Anglo-Hispanic Frontier in the American Southwest, 1880–1940* (New York: Oxford University Press, 1987); Molina, *Fit to Be Citizens?*

54. Torsten Magnuson, "History of the Beet Sugar Industry in California," *History Society of Southern California Annual Publication II,* no. 1 (1918): 68–79, 77–79; George W. Shaw, *The California Sugar Industry* (Sacramento, CA: W. W. Shannon, Superintendent State Printing, 1903), 38. See also Barajas, *Curious Unions.*

55. "Beet-Sugar Boom," *Los Angeles Times,* November 4, 1897, 6; Grant W. Heil, "Free Press: Oxnard and Vicinity," *Ventura County Historical Society Quarterly* 19, no. 1 (Fall 1973): 2–6, 2. The word "Beet" in ABSC was changed to "Crystal" in 1934, see chapter 1, n4.

56. Almaguer, *Racial Fault Lines,* 187. Meta Street, near the ABSC, was home to a small Mexican neighborhood, and this street is technically west of the railroad tracks but east of the boulevard. Other neighborhoods grew around and sometimes up against the factories on the east-side corridor. At some point, part of what is now Oxnard Boulevard was also known as Saviers Road. By the 1950s, Saviers Road started south of Wooley Road.

57. "No Protests Filed against City Paving," *Oxnard Courier,* June 25, 1919, front page; see also "Street Paving Started; Will Cover West Side and Circle about City," *Oxnard Courier,* February 16, 1917, front page.

58. See chapter 2 for further discussion and examples of the phrase "first class residence" as part of the restrictions placed on west-side property deeds.

59. Gómez-Quiñones and Vásquez, *Making Aztlán,* xxix.

60. Vicki L. Ruiz, *From out of the Shadows: Mexican Women in Twentieth-Century America* (New York: Oxford University Press, 1998).

61. William Deverell found that in the late 1800s, members of the historical society in Los Angeles discussed archiving White voices and destroying evidence of a Mexican presence in the city. Incomplete historical materials enabled the Whites to invent narratives about Mexicans that served to justify labor segmentation, residential restrictions, and school segregation. Purposeful distortion of historical

records therefore shaped collective memory with a goal of "rendering Mexicans *expressly* visible," while relegating them to actual socioeconomic margins. William Deverell, *Whitewashed Adobe: The Rise of Los Angeles and the Remaking of Its Mexican Past* (Berkeley: University of California Press, 2004), 9–10.

62. Similarly, Deverell identified how racism shaped Los Angeles by "paying attention to the ideas about race and ethnicity, to ideas whites, particularly elite, city-building whites, held about Mexicans." Deverell, *Whitewashed Adobe,* 7.

63. See Jeffery Wayne Maulhardt's picture books on Oxnard in particular. Jeffery Wayne Maulhardt, *Images of America: Oxnard 1867–1940* (Charleston, SC: Arcadia, 2004); Jeffery Wayne Maulhardt, *Postcard History Series: Oxnard* (Charleston, SC: Arcadia, 2009). William Deverell extensively analyzes the ways cultural producers effectively reconstructed a history of Los Angeles for public consumption. Deverell, *Whitewashed Adobe.*

64. Lee Grimes, "Fifty Years Ago Empty Plain on City Site," *Oxnard Press-Courier,* September 24 and 25, 1948, 1, 5. "In the beginning there were the miles of mustard, dotting the treeless plain with yellow, of little interest to the Chumash Indians in the hills or to the Spanish grandees who came after them. Then came the pioneer farmers in the 1890's, mostly from Germany and Ireland, some of them returning to the land after following the gold rush will-o-the-wisp in vain." The banner headline for the fifty-two-page two-day edition of the paper also read: "Sprung from Plain, Oxnard Awaits 50th Birthday."

65. Saviers Road bears his name. "J.Y. Saviers Owned Much of Oxnard Site, Family Californians Nearly 100 Years," *Oxnard Press-Courier,* September 24 and 25, 1948, D4.

66. Over the years, the name of the local newspaper changed. From 1903 to 1910, it was titled *Oxnard Courier,* and was published every Saturday. In 1910, to mark the change from a weekly to a daily paper, it was renamed *The Daily Oxnard Courier.* From 1912 to 1918 it was titled *Oxnard Daily Courier,* with a weekly edition titled *Oxnard Courier.* From 1918 to 1940, the title was *The Oxnard Daily Courier,* and from 1940 to 1959, it was *Oxnard Press-Courier.* From 1959 until the paper was shuttered in 1994, it was titled *The Press-Courier.* For the most part, I researched this paper on microfilm at the Oxnard Public Library and Museum of Ventura County. Some years of publication have been digitized and are available through a subscription to newspaperarchive.com. I offer these details for future researchers, and cite the full name of the paper in the notes because these distinctions are not catalogued.

67. "Oxnard Mexican Murders Girl," *Oxnard Courier,* March 7, 1903, front page; "Mexican Stabbed in Alley Brawl," *The Oxnard Daily Courier,* July 21, 1939, front page; "Mexican Girl Injured in Traffic Jam at Fire," *The Oxnard Daily Courier,* June 19, 1939, front page.

68. I received approval for this research project from the UCLA Institutional Review Board. I conducted some of these interviews in collaboration with Frank P. Barajas or Tara J. Yosso, for an earlier article publication. I also examined existing interviews, which I gathered from various archival collections. Though space restric-

tions have not allowed me to quote from every interview, I have included a full list of interviewees in the appendix.

69. Ignacio S. Carmona, interview by David G. García, February 21, 2015, Oxnard, CA.

70. Mary Valdivia Lamm, interview by David G. García, May 16, 2010, Moorpark, CA.

71. See Raquel Rubio-Goldsmith, "Oral History: Considerations and Problems for Its Use in the History of Mexicanas in the United States," in *Between Borders: Essays on Mexicana/Chicana History,* edited by Adelaida R. Del Castillo (Encino, CA: Floricanto Press, 1990): 161–73.

72. Racially restrictive deeds on school officials' properties (cited in chapter 2) use language specifying covenants to remain in effect "in perpetuity." See also discussion in David G. García and Tara J. Yosso, "Strictly in the Capacity of Servant: The Interconnection between Residential and School Segregation in Oxnard, California, 1934–1954," *History of Education Quarterly* 53, no. 1 (2013): 64–89.

73. See also analysis of the early school board minutes in García, Yosso, and Barajas, "'A Few of the Brightest, Cleanest Mexican Children.'"

74. Jack McCurdy, "School Board Minutes Play Big Role in Oxnard Desegregation," *Los Angeles Times,* January 19, 1975, CC part 2, B1, B3; "Of Children and Chicken Coops," *Los Angeles Times,* January 26, 1975, F2.

75. George Lipsitz has observed, "Events that we perceive as immediate and proximate have causes and consequences that span great distances." George Lipsitz, *Footsteps in the Dark: The Hidden Histories of Popular Music* (Minneapolis: University of Minnesota Press, 2007), viii.

1. THE WHITE ARCHITECTS OF MEXICAN
AMERICAN EDUCATION

Epigraph: "Policewoman Graduate Nurse for City Health," *Oxnard Daily Courier,* January 31, 1917, front page.

1. Richard B. Haydock served as inaugural president of the Oxnard City Board of Trustees and Oxnard's first mayor from 1903 to 1906, and simultaneously as superintendent of Oxnard schools from 1903 to 1907. He left these positions to work as school superintendent for Ventura, California, for four years. In 1911, he was reappointed as superintendent by the Oxnard School Board of Trustees, and held this position until his retirement from public service in June 1939. He also resumed service on the city board of trustees from about 1915 to 1919. See *Oxnard School District Board Members' Terms of Office,* Oxnard Elementary School District, Oxnard, CA, 2012–13; *City of Oxnard Elected Officials History, 1903–2014,* Office of the City Clerk, Oxnard, CA. John Steven McGroarty included Haydock in his volume of biographical sketches, noting that Haydock had served as an elected member of the Ventura County Board of Education in 1888, and had remained in that position for forty-five years. McGroarty further explained that Haydock was a "Royal Arch Mason and was

master of the Oxnard Lodge, F. & A.M. in 1903" and credits Haydock for founding the local chapter of the Red Cross just after World War I. John Steven McGroarty, *California of the South: A History,* vol. 3 (Chicago: S.J. Clarke, 1933), 312–15.

2. "'Our Schools and the Future American': Principal R.B. Haydock Tells Rotary Club What He Thinks on This Subject," *The Oxnard Daily Courier,* December 30, 1921, front page. *The Oxnard Daily Courier* published his speech in four parts on December 29, 30, 31, 1921, and January 3, 1922.

3. I utilize here the concept originally put forward by William H. Watkins in *The White Architects of Black Education: Ideology and Power in America, 1865–1954* (New York: Teachers College Press, 2001).

4. The American Beet Sugar Company (ABSC) became the American Crystal Sugar Company in 1934 and remained in operation until 1958.

5. See, for example, Oxnard local fraternal organizations such as Elks Lodge, Masonic Temple, Knights of Columbus, and Rotary Club.

6. The *Oxnard Courier* often reported on women participating in social, civic, and charity club meetings. I did not find additional archival records for any individual women's clubs. According to newspaper accounts, a series of women's clubs were named after the day of the week they met (e.g., the Oxnard Monday Club held meetings at the Masonic Temple). Other clubs were directly linked to men's associations (e.g., the Women's Auxiliary of the American Legion). Wives of men who worked for the American Beet Sugar Company also figured centrally in Americanization efforts, aimed at Mexican adults, and in mobilizing playground activities for Mexican children. Women also led the Oxnard Parent-Teachers' Association, Catholic Women's Association, Campfire Council, and organized with social-civic organizations such as Oxnard Community Service.

7. These women were most often widowed or unmarried (see, for example, Ventura County superintendent of schools Blanche T. Reynolds, n132). School board records through the 1930s reference an internal policy in the Oxnard School District of encouraging women teachers and principals to resign once they were married.

8. Richard Thompson Ford, "The Boundaries of Race: Political Geography in Legal Analysis," *Harvard Law Review* 107, no. 8 (1994): 1841–1921, 1845.

9. La Colonia was originally known as Colonia Home Gardens, a neighborhood that was bracketed by Third Street and Cooper Road. As it grew, other neighborhoods such as Ramona Home Gardens became connected to La Colonia. In accordance with how my interviewees referred to the neighborhood, I call the entire area by its popular name, La Colonia. See Map 1, page 38.

10. He was elected June 30, 1903. See City of Oxnard Board of Trustees Meeting Minutes, June 30, 1903, folder 07, file no. 00020476. See also a discussion of his role in building city infrastructure and institutions, in Madeline Miedema, "A Giant Step Forward: A History of the Oxnard Public Library, 1907–1992," *Ventura County Historical Society Quarterly* 37, no. 2 (1992): 3–46, 3.

11. Haydock and the city trustees considered west-side infrastructure actions necessary for the public good, in stark contrast to how they viewed the east side. Routine installation of electricity and paved roads exemplified this unequal treat-

ment; for example, 1903 approval of electric lights to be placed in the alleys on blocks K and U, and installation of lights for the downtown plaza (see City of Oxnard Board of Trustees Meeting Minutes, September 29, 1903, folder OXFCC007, file no. 00020484); 1917 placement of light posts at Fifth and B streets, and at the Southern Pacific Railroad Station (City of Oxnard Board of Trustees Meeting Minutes, August 21, 1917, folder OXFCC006, file no. 00021029); 1921 approvals for lighting along north and south Fifth Street, and on A, B, and C streets—all westside residential/business streets (City of Oxnard Board of Trustees Meeting Minutes, October 4, 1921, folder OXFCC006, file no. 00021165); and 1922 street improvement along Wooley Road, from the west line of Saviers Road to the east line of C Street, approved because the "public interest and convenience requires" (City of Oxnard Board of Trustees Meeting Minutes, December 19, 1922, folder OXFCC006, file no. 00021222). The city also approved payment for the costs of paving for the "public benefit" the residential area "Beginning on the west line of Saviers Road at the South east corner of Lot 1, Block 1, Wolff, Hill & Laubacher Subdivision" (City of Oxnard Board of Trustees Meeting Minutes, December 19, 1922, folder OXFCC006, file no. 00021223).

12. Before this time, records indicate the San Pedro School functioned as the city's only school and had been in existence as early as 1870. See Helen Frost, *102 Year History of Oxnard School District* [pamphlet] (Oxnard, CA, 1975). On file with author.

13. The limited integration that did exist in Oxnard schools occurred only at the convenience of Whites and reinforced what Derrick Bell has identified as the "interest convergence" model. Bell conceived of this model in terms of the gains made from civil rights, with the *Brown v. Board* desegregation case as his main example. Applying his analysis to Oxnard, I found examples of "interest convergence" before *Brown* as well. See Derrick A. Bell, "*Brown v. Board of Education* and the Interest-Convergence Dilemma," *Harvard Law Review* 93, no. 3 (1980): 518–33.

14. Ben S. Virden, President, 1916–30; Dr. H. M. Staire, Clerk, 1916–25; Roy B. Witman, Clerk, 1920–34; see *Oxnard School District Board Members' Terms of Office*, Oxnard Elementary School District, Oxnard, CA, 2012–13. The newspaper lists Virden as president of the board in 1939, giving scholarship awards; "Commencement Speaker Urges Graduates to Turn to God to Make Them Stronger in Solving Civilization's Problems," *The Oxnard Daily Courier*, June 10, 1939, front page. Witman also served as chairman of the City Chamber of Commerce; *City of Oxnard Elected Officials History, 1903–2014*, Office of the City Clerk, Oxnard, CA.

15. "Policewoman Graduate Nurse for City Health," *Oxnard Daily Courier*, January 31, 1917, front page.

16. Ibid.

17. Ibid.

18. "Experienced Policewoman Is Chosen," *Oxnard Courier*, February 23, 1917, 3. As a city trustee, Haydock had been authorized to select Thornton, and the chief of police made the official appointment.

19. "Policewoman Graduate Nurse for City Health," *Oxnard Daily Courier*, January 31, 1917, front page. Haydock asserted that the city required a professional

nurse because the city health officer "was under no obligation to treat these people. It would take all his time if he attended to them."

20. Virden served as city treasurer, 1910–20; Haydock's city council service overlapped Virden's, from approximately 1915 to 1919 (see n1). See *City of Oxnard Elected Officials History, 1903–2014*, Office of the City Clerk, Oxnard, CA.

21. "Trustees Name New School Haydock Grammar School," *Oxnard Courier*, March 9, 1917, front page.

22. "Grammar Pupils in New Building," *Oxnard Courier*, March 9, 1917, 3. Haydock School enrollments initially included early elementary grades through eighth grade. By the 1950s, Haydock School was designated an intermediate school, enrolling only seventh- and eighth-grade students. See details of enrollments at each school by year from 1916 through 1950 in "Attendance Registers by Years," Oxnard School District Archives, date unknown.

23. For example, Natalia Molina discusses how the case in Los Angeles of officials characterizing Mexicans as diseased, and treating health problems as a criminal matter, paralleled arguments put forward by proponents of restricting Mexican immigration on the floor of the U.S. Congress in 1924. Natalia Molina, *Fit to Be Citizens? Public Health and Race in Los Angeles, 1879–1939* (Berkeley: University of California Press, 2006).

24. Alfredo Mirandé, *Gringo Justice* (South Bend, IN: University of Notre Dame Press, 1987); Julian Samora, "Mexican Immigration," in *Mexican-Americans Tomorrow: Educational and Economic Perspectives*, edited by Gus Taylor (Albuquerque: University of New Mexico Press, 1975), 60–80.

25. Federal Writers' Project, "Child Labor in California Agriculture," *Monographs Prepared for a Documentary History of Migratory Farm Labor in California* [1938], California Digital Library.

26. "County Seat Notes: Harvest Aid," *Oxnard Daily Courier*, May 25, 1917, 3.

27. "To Make Americans of Foreign-Born," *The Oxnard Daily Courier*, January 10, 1918, front page.

28. "Teaching Foreign Children Our Ways," *The Oxnard Daily Courier*, August 8, 1918, front page.

29. "Oxnard Police Woman to Resign," *The Oxnard Daily Courier*, October 25, 1918, front page.

30. "Policewoman's Work Missed by Trustees," *The Oxnard Daily Courier*, September 3, 1919, front page.

31. Ibid.

32. "Street Paving Started; Will Cover West Side and Circle about the City," *Oxnard Daily Courier*, February 14, 1917, front page. The *Courier* wrote a special front-page note applauding the decision of the trustees, under the title "The Trustees Did Well." Two years later, the newspaper reported some of the ways priorities were also laid out within the west side: "Beside the pavement, which will cover all of the important residence and business streets, the other streets will be covered with crushed rock and made to harmonize with the rest of the city." "No Protests Filed against City Paving," *The Oxnard Daily Courier*, June 25, 1919, front page.

33. "Temporary Hospital Opened," *The Oxnard Daily Courier,* November 4, 1918, front page.

34. Ibid.

35. Ibid.

36. "Firemen Make Clean City Streets," *The Oxnard Daily Courier,* November 4, 1918, front page.

37. "Mexicans Assist City Officers," *The Oxnard Daily Courier,* November 12, 1918, front page.

38. Ibid.

39. In his research observations and oral history interviews throughout California and the Southwest, Paul S. Taylor identified patterns of company neglect fostering unsanitary conditions. He also found extensive evidence of Mexicans taking initiative to improve their living conditions through daily cleaning rituals, including sweeping and cleaning dirt floors, creatively insulating tents and wooden shacks, and taking full advantage of any available bathing facilities. Paul S. Taylor, *Mexican Labor in the United States,* vol. 1 (Berkeley: University of California Press, 1930), 58.

40. "Says Flies Are Bad in This City," *The Oxnard Daily Courier,* October 15, 1919, front page.

41. Ibid.

42. Ibid.

43. Ibid.

44. Ibid.

45. Ibid.

46. Ibid.

47. Molina, *Fit to Be Citizens?,* 2.

48. The Oxnard Monday Club appears to have been a group of women who met regularly on Mondays. In line with nationwide organized efforts to Americanize immigrants, their discussions, according to the newspaper, emphasized local and regional Americanization efforts. "Good Talk on Americanization," *The Oxnard Daily Courier,* October 21, 1919, "Society" page.

49. Ibid.

50. American Beet Sugar Company Agricultural Meeting Minutes, July 22, 1918; thank you to Frank P. Barajas for sharing this memo. Similarly, as Jeffrey Garcilazo explains in his study of Mexican railroad workers, companies such as Southern Pacific Railroad provided a "free-rent" housing incentive and encouraged men to bring their families to elicit a loyal, stable workforce. Jeffrey Garcilazo, "Traqueros: Mexican Railroad Workers in the United States, 1870–1930" (Ph.D. dissertation, University of California, Santa Barbara, 1995).

51. "Good Talk on Americanization," *The Oxnard Daily Courier,* October 21, 1919, "Society" page.

52. Ibid.

53. For further discussion of these laws, see Tomás Almaguer, *Racial Fault Lines: The Historical Origins of White Supremacy in California* (Berkeley: University of California Press, 1994); Molina, *Fit to Be Citizens?* The Chinese Exclusion Act of

1882 established a moratorium on immigration of Chinese workers, a ban that remained in effect until 1943; the 1907–8 Gentlemen's Agreement between the United States and Japan was a treaty wherein the Japanese government agreed to deny Japanese laborers passports to the United States and the latter agreed to end an anti-Asian school ordinance in San Francisco; the Alien Land Acts of 1913 and 1920 aimed to prohibit Asian immigrants from owning land, or leasing it longer than three years in the state of California. For more on the revolution in Mexico, see Devra Weber, *Dark Sweat, White Gold: California Farm Workers, Cotton, and the New Deal* (Berkeley: University of California Press, 1994). The number of Japanese residents in Ventura County decreased from 872 in 1910 to 675 in 1920. Similarly, the number of Chinese residents decreased from 235 in 1910 to 155 in 1920. Mexicans were not disaggregated from the Whites until the 1930 census, though the number of foreign-born from Mexico does provide some insight about immigration during these years. U.S. Bureau of the Census, *U.S. Census of the Population: 1930*, "Population, California, Table 17. Indians, Chinese and Japanese 1910 to 1930 and Mexicans, 1930 for Counties and for Cities of 25,000 or More" (Washington, DC: U.S. Government Printing Office, 1930), 266.

54. U.S. Bureau of the Census, *U.S. Census of the Population: 1930*, "Population, California, Table 4. Population of Counties by Minor Civil Divisions: 1930, 1920, and 1910" (Washington, DC: U.S. Government Printing Office, 1930), 140.

55. U.S. Bureau of the Census, *U.S. Census of the Population: 1950*, "California, Table 4. Population of Urban Places of 10,000 or More from the Earliest Census to 1950" (Washington, DC: U.S. Government Printing Office, 1950), 5–10.

56. Juan Gómez-Quiñones, *Mexican American Labor, 1790–1990* (Albuquerque: University of New Mexico Press, 1994), 104. The U.S. Census counted 33,444 foreign-born Mexicans living in California in 1910, and that number increased to 86,610 by 1920. U.S. Bureau of the Census, *U.S. Census of the Population: 1940*, "California, Table 15. Foreign-Born White, 1910–1940 and Total Foreign-Born, 1850–1900, by Country of Birth, for the State" (Washington, DC: U.S. Government Printing Office, 1940), 533.

57. "Red Cross Makes Move for Better Housing Conditions," *The Oxnard Daily Courier*, October 27, 1920, front page, 2. The city trustees recorded McCulloch's appearance at their meeting on September 21, 1920, with a note that she represented the local Red Cross with a "request for advice and assistance in combating the presence of vermin among some of the Mexican population." The minutes indicate McCulloch was referred to the health officer for action. City of Oxnard Board of Trustees Meeting Minutes, September 21, 1920, folder 07, file no. 00021135. An October presentation by the three women was not found in the city trustee minutes.

58. "Red Cross Makes Move for Better Housing Conditions," *The Oxnard Daily Courier*, October 27, 1920, front page, 2.

59. Ibid.

60. Ibid.

61. Ibid.

62. Ibid.

63. Ibid.

64. Ibid.

65. In contrast to trustee Charles Weaver and Mayor Herbert H. Eastwood, the city health officer, Dr. G. A. Boughton, offered "a word of praise" for the Red Cross women's efforts, noting he had convinced them to present to the city trustees first, before taking the case to the state housing commission. Ibid.

66. Herbert H. Eastwood served as a city trustee from 1909 to 1920 and 1936–42. He served as mayor from 1920 to 1926 and 1942–44. *City of Oxnard Elected Officials History, 1903–2014*, Office of the City Clerk, Oxnard, CA.

67. "Red Cross Makes Move for Better Housing Conditions," *The Oxnard Daily Courier*, October 27, 1920, front page, 2.

68. Ibid.

69. "Mrs. McCulloch Quits Account Her Health," *The Oxnard Daily Courier*, February 2, 1921, front page.

70. "'Our Schools and the Future American': Principal R. B. Haydock Tells Rotary Club What He Thinks on This Subject," *The Oxnard Daily Courier*, December 29, 1921, 2. The Oxnard Rotary Club was founded in 1920 and met weekly for dinner.

71. Haydock's words here echoed those of then–Stanford professor Lewis Terman, who had been applying French psychologist Alfred Binet's intelligence tests to identify the mental age, or intelligence quotient, of school children. In his 1916 book Terman asserted: "Cases . . . which test at high-grade moronity or at border-line . . . represent the level of intelligence which is very, very common among Spanish-Indian and Mexican families of the Southwest and also among negroes. Their dullness seems to be racial, or at least inherent in the family stocks from which they come" (91). Haydock's efforts to segregate Mexicans ran consistent with his words, but he never publicly rationalized his actions explicitly. In contrast, Terman publicly advocated: "Children of this group should be segregated in special classes and be given instruction which is concrete and practical. They cannot master abstractions, but they can often be made efficient workers, able to look out for themselves. There is no possibility at the present of convincing society that they should not be allowed to reproduce, although from a eugenic point of view they constitute a grave problem because of their unusually prolific breeding" (92). Lewis M. Terman, *The Measurement of Intelligence: An Explanation of and a Complete Guide for the Use of the Standard Revision and Extension of the Binet-Simon Intelligence Scale* (Boston: Houghton Mifflin, 1916), 91–92.

72. "'Our Schools and the Future American': Principal R. B. Haydock Tells Rotary Club What He Thinks on This Subject," *The Oxnard Daily Courier*, December 29, 1921, 2.

73. Ibid.

74. Ibid.

75. Ibid., 3.

76. Ibid.

77. Ibid.

78. Ibid.

79. As he described the difficult task of the teachers engaged in mapping out the district into twenty sections, he noted, "In many instances, parents could not speak English, they did not even know the ages of the children, and it was impossible to get absolutely accurate information." "'Our Schools and the Future American': Principal R. B. Haydock Tells Rotary Club What He Thinks on This Subject," *The Oxnard Daily Courier,* December 31, 1921, 6.

80. Ibid. He reported, "716 are classed as White, 8 are classed as Black, 23 are classed as Chinese, 42 are classed as Japanese, 551 are classed as Mexican."

81. Ibid. Of the children, he remarked, "1063 are native born, 282 are foreign born."

82. Ibid.

83. See Molina, *Fit to Be Citizens?,* where she explains that in Los Angeles, public health officials determined "who was healthy enough to work or attend public school . . . [and] not only incorporated their racially charged visions into policies and ordinances that targeted ethnic communities but also helped shape the ways mainstream populations perceived ethnic peoples" (2–3).

84. "Colonia Gardens Folk Petition City Dads to Change City Dump," *The Oxnard Daily Courier,* June 22, 1922, front page. Spelling errors in original (e.g., Joes Martinez was Jose Martinez).

85. Ibid.

86. "Policewoman Graduate Nurse for City Health," *Oxnard Daily Courier,* January 31, 1917, front page.

87. "Colonia Gardens Folk Petition City Dads to Change City Dump," *The Oxnard Daily Courier,* June 22, 1922, front page.

88. The city trustees noted receipt of the petition from the Colonia Gardens residents and indicated deliberation would follow to plan mitigation of the problems identified from the dumping site, but a record of such action was not found. City of Oxnard Board of Trustees Meeting Minutes, June 20, 1922, folder 07, file no. 00021194.

89. "Colonia Home Gardens Being Piped for Water," *The Oxnard Daily Courier,* December 1, 1922, front page.

90. Walter Lathrop served on the city board of trustees from 1914 to 1916. *City of Oxnard Elected Officials History, 1903–2014,* Office of the City Clerk, Oxnard, CA.

91. (Oxnard) Community Service was sponsored by the city government and responsible for community affairs, including the city's parks and recreation activities. "Special Classes in Playground Activity to Be Started Here," *The Oxnard Daily Courier,* May 24, 1923, front page.

92. "Recreation for Women and Girls Is Plan of Community Ser. Here," *The Oxnard Daily Courier,* May 22, 1923, front page.

93. The article specified, "The Americanization group met again just days later to discuss the applicability of Santa Barbara's programming in domestic science and

art . . . cultivating artistic talent in basketry, pottery, clay modeling." "Americaniza-tion Group of Community Service to Meet This Evening," *The Oxnard Daily Courier,* May 29, 1923, front page.

94. "To Include Mexicans in Playground Work," *The Oxnard Daily Courier,* July 17, 1923, front page.

95. "Children Show Great Interest in Community Playground Activities," *The Oxnard Daily Courier,* June 27, 1924, front page. The article discussed A. Martinez's leadership in chairing "the committee for Mexican recreation," which indicates the site attracted Mexican youth and adults well beyond Oxnard as well. For example, the reporter noted plans to install bleachers in advance of a countywide *rebote* contest, from which winners would participate in a Los Angeles state championship. This even aimed to contribute to funds for a playground apparatus. The article also mentioned the formation of several boys' baseball teams, the scheduling of games for a junior playground championship, and the beginning of a class for "the study of community singing and harmony."

96. "City Guests Cleaning 7th Street Playground," *The Oxnard Daily Courier,* June 23, 1927, front page. The article detailed, "A. L. Sexton, caretaker of the community center, is supervising a committee of guests of the city jail in renovating the grounds."

97. See "Mexicans from Many Colonies Organize," *The Oxnard Daily Courier,* May 12, 1924, front page; "Mexicans Offer Aid in Making City Law Abiding Community," *The Oxnard Daily Courier,* May 15, 1924, front page. For more on Mexican participation in recreation and on Americanization for Mexican adults in Oxnard, see Frank P. Barajas, *Curious Unions: Mexican American Workers and Resistance in Oxnard, California, 1898–1961* (Lincoln: University of Nebraska Press, 2012), 111–30.

98. "A labor day for the Mexicans is to be established. . . . [W]ith the aid of the Spanish ladies' lodge they will be served with refreshment while they work." "New Saviers Road Playground Presents Busy Scene Today," *The Oxnard Daily Courier,* January 30, 1924, front page.

99. For example, A. Martinez was elected to the board of directors for Community Service and placed in charge of the Mexican playground. The article notes, "A. Martinez, chairman of the recently organized Mexican central committee was elected a member of the board in place of R. G. Beach . . . Mr. Martinez is well known in Oxnard, particularly among the Mexicans and it is believed he will do good work." "Martinez Takes Place of Beach on Board of Directors Com. Service," *The Oxnard Daily Courier,* December 7, 1923, front page. Another article confirms his role as the "chairman of the central Mexican committee of Community Service." "New Saviers Road Playground, Present Busy Scene Today," *The Oxnard Daily Courier,* January 30, 1924, front page. In 1927, A. Bustamonte is noted as in charge of this playground. "City's Guests Cleaning 7th Street Playground," *The Oxnard Daily Courier,* June 23, 1927, front page.

100. "Former Secretary of Community Service Writes about Oxnard," *The Oxnard Daily Courier,* August 7, 1923, 4.

101. Ibid.

102. "Community Playground Development in Oxnard Received Publicity," *The Oxnard Daily Courier*, February 4, 1924, front page.

103. The local chapter of the Elks had just received its charter two years prior, approved by the national organization after demonstrating that five thousand Whites resided in the area. "It Took a Special Census to Get Elks Lodge Their Charter in 1922," *Oxnard Press-Courier*, September 24, 1948, front page. See also "Elks Liquor License Talks to Continue," *The Press-Courier*, May 22, 1972, 13; "Letters on Elks Liquor License Sent to ABC," *The Press-Courier*, May 24, 1972, 13.

104. Oxnard School Board of Trustees meeting minutes, October 25, 1923.

105. Roosevelt School primarily enrolled children in kindergarten through sixth grade. See "Attendance Registers by Years," Oxnard School District Archives, date unknown.

106. Ibid. Wilson School initially enrolled children in upper elementary, fourth through eighth grades. After 1940, Wilson became a dedicated junior high school, enrolling only seventh and eight grade students. The existing plaque demarcating the now-closed Woodrow Wilson School in Oxnard reads 1928–75. These opening and closing dates do not correspond with school district records.

107. "Parent-Teachers' Association," *The Oxnard Daily Courier*, January 29, 1926, "Society" page.

108. According to Martha Menchaca and Richard Valencia, prior to the opening of the separate facility, Mexican children were forced to take showers before entering school and were then placed into racially segregated classrooms that emphasized English and Americanization. The Canyon School was a schoolhouse of eight classrooms, two bathrooms, and an office for 950 Mexican students from kindergarten through eighth grade. In stark contrast, 667 White students attended the newly constructed Isabel School with twenty-one classrooms, a cafeteria, an auditorium, a training shop, and administrative offices. See Martha Menchaca and Richard R. Valencia, "Anglo-Saxon Ideologies in the 1920s–1930s: Their Impact on the Segregation of Mexican Students in California," *Anthropology and Education Quarterly* 21, no. 3 (1990): 222–49, 238–39; Martha Menchaca, *The Mexican Outsiders: A Community History of Marginalization and Discrimination in California* (Austin: University of Texas Press, 1995).

109. "Parent-Teachers' Association," *The Oxnard Daily Courier*, January 29, 1926, "Society" page.

110. Ibid.

111. Some school officials and scholars questioned the efficacy of segregating students during the 1930s, but such debates are not reflected in the actions of the Oxnard School Board of Trustees. In any case, Charles Wollenberg notes, "The doubts expressed about segregation in the thirties were transformed into new convictions during the forties." Charles M. Wollenberg, *All Deliberate Speed: Segregation and Exclusion in California Schools, 1855–1975* (Berkeley: University of California Press, 1976), 120.

112. "Farmers Here Need a Big Scare to Awaken Them," *The Oxnard Daily Courier*, March 5, 1926, front page.

113. "Our Race Problem," *The Oxnard Daily Courier,* March 10, 1926, 2.

114. Ibid.

115. Ibid.

116. "Supreme Court School Ruling Affects Oxnard," *The Oxnard Daily Courier,* November 22, 1927, front page. Case of *Martha Lum v. Rosedale Consolidated High School in Bolivar County, Mississippi; Gong Lum v. Rice,* 275 U.S. 78 (1927).

117. Ibid.

118. Ibid.

119. Ibid.

120. Ibid. The article goes on to reprint Section 3, Article 10 of the California educational code, establishing the right of school districts to "exclude children of filthy or vicious habits or children suffering from contagious or infectious disease, and to establish separate schools for Indian children and for children of Chinese, Japanese, or Mongolian parentage. When such separate schools are established, Indian children or children of Chinese, Japanese or Mongolian parentage must not be admitted into any other school." The article ends with an overview of the Supreme Court case itself.

121. U.S. Bureau of the Census, *U.S. Census of the Population: 1930,* "Population, California, Table 17. Indians, Chinese and Japanese 1910 to 1930 and Mexicans, 1930 for Counties and for Cities of 25,000 or More" (Washington, DC: U.S. Government Printing Office, 1930), 266.

122. The percentage of Mexican students in Ventura County elementary schools (34.2%) marked the second highest in the state of California, behind only Imperial County, which was 36.8 percent. Paul S. Taylor, *Mexican Labor in the United States,* vol. 6. (Berkeley: University of California Publications in Economics, 1930), 266, "Table 2. Mexican Children Enrolled in Public and Catholic Elementary Schools of California, February 1, 1927; Distribution by Divisions of the State, and by Counties."

123. Ibid., 264.

124. See chapter 2 for further discussion of trustee J. H. Burfeind's written admission that U.S.-born Mexicans possessed the same legal rights as other U.S. citizens.

125. "Supreme Court School Ruling Affects Oxnard," *The Oxnard Daily Courier,* November 22, 1927, front page.

126. "Quota Bill under Fire in the House," *The Oxnard Daily Courier,* February 24, 1928, front page.

127. "Urge Action against Mexican Quota Bills," *The Oxnard Daily Courier,* January 24, 1930, front page.

128. Years prior, the ABSC had expressed a need for factory managers and supervisors to treat the Mexican beet sugar workers well, so they would continue to be "loyal employees." American Beet Sugar Company Agricultural Meeting Minutes, July 22, 1918.

129. Molina, *Fit to Be Citizens?*

130. Wilbur K. Cobb, "Retardation in Elementary Schools of Children of Migratory Laborers in Ventura County, California" (master's thesis, University of Southern California, Los Angeles, 1932), 14.

131. See "El Rio School Pupils to Work in Orchards," *The Oxnard Daily Courier,* September 19, 1922, front page; "Rio School Closes for Walnut Picking," *The Oxnard Daily Courier,* September 18, 1926, front page. Helen Heffernan of the State Department of Education conducted a survey in October 1929 and found that many children attended separate schools for a few hours a day in "cow barns and roadside tents," just a short distance away from "well-ventilated and properly lighted buildings," where "permanent children" received "all the advantages for which California is famous." She identified labor law violations in relation to the placement of children within these facilities; in early release policies, where children would attend school for a few hours and then be released to work in the fields; and in "crop vacations" timed to coincide with the harvest. "36,000 State Pupils Listed as Migratory: Survey Shows Many Have Poor Schooling Because of Parents' Moving," *Oakland Tribune,* January 1, 1929, B23.

132. Blanche T. Reynolds served as the first deputy school superintendent in Ventura County, from 1911 to 1917, under her husband James E. Reynolds's administration. When he left his position to serve with the Red Cross in World War I, she filled in for him, and he then asked in an open letter to voters that her name be written in to replace his on the ballot for Ventura County school superintendent. She served as superintendent from 1918 to 1935. Both she and her husband also served as councilmembers for the city of Ventura at different points in time. See John Allan Rogers, "A History of School Organization and Administration in Ventura County" (Ph.D. dissertation, University of Southern California, Los Angeles, 1961), 124–34.

133. "Education Is of Greater Value than Walnuts Says School Head," *Ventura Free Press,* October 22, 1927, front page.

134. Ibid.

135. "Lecture at School by Dr. Nalder," *The Oxnard Daily Courier,* April 3, 1919, 8.

136. Ibid.

137. See Frank Fielding Nalder, "The American State Reformatory; with Special Reference to Its Educational Aspects" (Ph.D. dissertation, University of California, Berkeley, 1917).

138. "Lecture at School by Dr. Nalder," *The Oxnard Daily Courier,* April 3, 1919, 8.

139. Ibid.

140. Ibid.

141. Ibid.

142. "Education Is of Greater Value than Walnuts Says School Head," *Ventura Free Press,* October 22, 1927, front page.

143. Ibid.

144. "Mexican Costs Are Too High Says Co. Head," *The Oxnard Daily Courier,* January 31, 1928, front page.

145. Ibid.

146. Ibid.

147. "Policewoman Graduate Nurse for City Health," *Oxnard Daily Courier,* January 31, 1917, front page.

148. "Mexican Costs Are Too High Says Co. Head," *The Oxnard Daily Courier,* January 31, 1928, front page.

149. Ibid.

150. "Policewoman Graduate Nurse for City Health," *Oxnard Daily Courier,* January 31, 1917, front page.

151. "Mexican Costs are Too High Says Co. Head," *The Oxnard Daily Courier,* January 31, 1928, front page.

152. Ibid.

153. A Ventura elementary school was named after Blanche T. Reynolds, and she attended the dedication ceremony on October 18, 1956. "Rededication Day Honors Blanche Reynolds Anew," *Ventura County Star–Free Press,* May 29, 1978, A4. This article also credits Reynolds with heading the first Parent Teacher Association in Ventura.

154. Antonia Arguelles DiLiello, interview by David G. García and Frank P. Barajas, June 1, 2010, Oxnard, CA.

155. Ibid.

156. "Community of 3000 Rises at Ranch for Apricot Work," *The Oxnard Daily Courier,* July 17, 1939. The article reported, "With a sprinkling of Americans the workers are mostly Mexican. They are paid 3 cents a box for picking and 12 1/2 cents a tray for pitting, at which jobs the entire family, children and all, may work.... Over 1,400 were registered for work there, the Courier was told, which with children and others unregistered formed a community of over 3,000 people." This statement indicates that children comprised at least half of the apricot "community."

157. Antonia Arguelles DiLiello, interview by David G. García, June 24, 2011, Oxnard, CA.

158. Antonia Arguelles DiLiello, interview by David G. García and Frank P. Barajas, June 1, 2010, Oxnard, CA.

159. Correspondence from Mrs. Ethel Dale, city clerk of the city of Oxnard regarding employee record of Mr. Antonio Arguelles for city of Oxnard, October 7, 1947. Personal collection of Antonia Arguelles.

160. Correspondence from Paul E. Wolven, city manager of the city of Oxnard, regarding reason for retirement of Antonio Arguelles from city of Oxnard, May 4, 1954. Personal collection of Antonia Arguelles.

161. Antonia Arguelles DiLiello, interview by David G. García and Frank P. Barajas, June 1, 2010, Oxnard, CA.

162. W.E.B. DuBois, *The Souls of Black Folk: Essays and Sketches* [1903] (New York: Fawcett, 1961), v.

2. PERNICIOUS DEEDS

Portions of this chapter were adapted and revised from David G. García and Tara J. Yosso, "'Strictly in the Capacity of Servant': The Interconnection between

Residential and School Segregation in Oxnard, California, 1934–1954," *History of Education Quarterly* 53, no. 1 (February 2013): 64–89. Used with permission.
Epigraph: Miguel Espinosa, interview by David G. García and Frank P. Barajas, August 2, 2010, Oxnard, CA.

1. Miguel's family lived in El Rio, a few miles north of and adjacent to La Colonia. The El Rio School District was annexed into the Oxnard School District in 1943. Miguel attended Catholic school in Ventura, and Santa Clara Elementary School, a Catholic school on the west side of Oxnard.

2. Many of the property deeds on the west side of the city contained restrictive language, specifying each lot was to be used only for a "first class residence." See, for example, the deed from school trustee Everett C. Beach, Grant Deed from Adolph J. Carty to Everett C. Beach, November 17, 1930, Ventura County Clerk and Recorder, book 333, p. 245.

3. As Michael Sussman has asserted, "There is no such thing as a racially discriminatory motive in setting housing policies that is discrete from a racially discriminatory motive in education decision-making. Racism is a *pervasive* concept"; emphasis in original. Michael H. Sussman, "Discrimination: A Pervasive Concept," in *In Pursuit of a Dream Deferred: Linking Housing and Education Policy,* edited by john a. powell, Gavin Kearney, and Vina Key (New York: Peter Lang, 2001), 209–28, 209.

4. See further discussion on the subtle, stunning aspects of racism by Chester M. Pierce, who explained: "It is from feelings of superiority that one group of people proceeds to brutalize, degrade, abuse, and humiliate another group of individuals. The superiority feelings and the accompanying contemptuous condescension toward a target group are so rampant in our society. . . . [But] most offensive actions are not gross and crippling. They are subtle and stunning." Chester M. Pierce, "Offensive Mechanisms," in *The Black Seventies,* edited by Floyd B. Barbour (Boston: Porter Sargent, 1970), 265–82, 265–66.

5. David Montejano, *Anglos and Mexicans in the Making of Texas, 1836–1986* (Austin: University of Texas Press, 1987), 167–68.

6. Christopher Ramos has asserted that "residential segregation did not occur by chance, but rather by design." Christopher Ramos, "The Educational Legacy of Racially Restrictive Covenants: Their Long Term Impact on Mexican Americans," *The Scholar* 4 (2002): 149–84, 155.

7. Ramos explains that in Texas "racially restrictive covenants forced Mexican-American families to live in San Antonio's west-side neighborhoods and to send their children to poorly funded schools." Ramos, "Educational Legacy of Racially Restrictive Covenants," 169. Similar separation demarcated by railroad tracks occurred across California and the Southwest. See description of towns in the Imperial Valley, California, in Paul S. Taylor, *Mexican Labor in the United States,* vol. 1 (Berkeley: University of California Press, 1930), 83.

8. W. E. B. DuBois, *The Souls of Black Folk: Essays and Sketches* [1903] (New York: Fawcett, 1961), v.

9. Correspondence from Oxnard resident Alice Shaffer to Mr. Harland Burfeind, clerk of the Oxnard School Board of Trustees, April 21, 1938. The microfilm

of this letter is filed along with the Oxnard School Board of Trustees (OSBT) meeting minutes, at the Oxnard School District Archives, Oxnard, CA.

10. Shaffer to Burfeind, OSBT meeting minutes, April 21, 1938.

11. Ibid.

12. Shaffer owned at least three parcels of land in Oxnard, two that lay in the Wolff Hill Laubacher Subdivision and one located in the Walter H. Lathrop Subdivision. See Indenture between W. H. Gray and Alice Hoey Gray AND Ruth Tash, May 16, 1934, Ventura County Clerk and Recorder, book 418, p. 107. See also Indenture between Ruth Tash AND W. H. Gray and Alice Hoey Gray, May 16, 1934, Ventura County Clerk and Recorder, book 418, p. 110. The Lathrop parcel was clearly encumbered by racially restrictive covenants, evidenced in Indenture between Walter H. Lathrop and Edna Lathrop AND John A. Madison, May 24, 1913, Ventura County Clerk and Recorder, book 138, p. 272, and referenced in Indenture between John A. Madison and Edith Madison AND Alice A. Hoey, October 28, 1924, Ventura County Clerk and Recorder, book 29, p. 420. Evidence strongly indicates that her Hill Street parcels also included racial covenants. See n41 on T. M. Hill, co-owner of Oxnard Land Company. See also the indenture between the Wolff Co. and T. M. Hill referring to two lots in Block 1 within the Wolff Hill Laubacher Subdivision and specifying, "No part of the said premises shall never be sold to Negroes, Japanese, Chinese, Mexicans, or Indians," April 29, 1912, Ventura County Clerk and Recorder, book 133, p. 144. Such racial restrictions were again specified on the indenture between the Wolff Co. and Hill referring to four lots in their co-owned subdivision's Block 2, May 18, 1917, Ventura County Clerk and Recorder, book 155, p. 466.

13. Shaffer to Burfeind, OSBT meeting minutes, April 21, 1938.

14. Ironically, Shaffer is complaining about the enrollment changes initiated by White parents in 1936, who shared her goal of academic and social separation from Mexican children. See OSBT meeting minutes, November 9, 1936, and chapter 3 for further discussion.

15. The board approved the construction of Ramona School in June 1939. OSBT meeting minutes, June 27, 1939.

16. Correspondence from J. H. Burfeind, Clerk of the Oxnard School Board of Trustees to Alice Shaffer, OSBT meeting minutes, April 25, 1938. Capitals/lowercase inconsistencies in original.

17. Burfeind wrote the plan, presented it to Dockstader and Haydock, and signed off on their agreement that it "be put into effect at an early date." OSBT meeting minutes, September 27, 1937. See chapter 3 for further discussion.

18. Burfeind to Shaffer, OSBT meeting minutes, April 25, 1938.

19. Grant Deed from Alice H. G. Shaffer, formerly Alice Hoey Gray, to William M. Carrington and Christina Carrington, August 26, 1940, Ventura County Clerk and Recorder, book 620, p. 653. This deed indicates that by August 1940, Shaffer had established a new permanent address in Ventura. Ten years later, she sold her remaining Wolff Hill Laubacher Subdivision property, including 416 Hill Street, where Burfeind had addressed his response letter. See Grant Deed from Alice H. G.

Shaffer to Raymond F. Gisler and Marion Gisler, December 27, 1950, Ventura County Clerk and Recorder, book 974, p. 306. The house at 416 Hill Street was sold again in 1957, still "subject to all covenants, conditions, restrictions, reservations, rights of way, and all easements of record." See Grant Deed from Raymond F. Gisler and Marion Gisler to James Cannon, Jr. and Siporah Louise Cannon, September 24, 1957, Ventura County Clerk and Recorder, book 1552, p. 539.

20. Madeline Miedema, "A Giant Step Forward: A History of the Oxnard Public Library, 1907–1992," *Ventura County Historical Society Quarterly* 37, no. 2 (1992): 3–46, 3.

21. OSBT meeting minutes, September 22, 1937.

22. I discuss these plans in greater detail in chapter 3.

23. Grant Deed from Hobson Brothers Packing Company to Ben S. Virden, June 17, 1931, Ventura County Clerk and Recorder, book 354, p. 188. Though all the other restrictions expired on March 1, 1946, Virden's deed specified the racial conditions "shall be perpetual."

24. Ibid.

25. Emphasis added. Grant Deed from Los Angeles First National Trust and Savings Bank to Noble A. Powell and Nadine G. Powell and Raymond T. Francis and Evelyn W. Francis, August 20, 1928, Ventura County Clerk and Recorder, book 227, p. 11. Though the other conditions expired on October 1, 1935, the deed specified racial restrictions to be "perpetual and binding forever upon the Grantees, and every successor in interest of the parties hereto."

26. Agreement of Sale between Edwin L. Carty and Doris C. Carty AND R. B. Witman and R. D. Snively, June 11, 1929, Ventura County Clerk and Recorder, book 267, p. 348.

27. See Tomás Almaguer's detailed discussion, "Displacement of the Mexican Ranchero Class in Ventura County," wherein he outlines the ways White immigrants "effectively dispossessed" Mexicans from the land (79–87), undermined their political influence in the county, and transformed the economy from ranching to farming (87–90). He notes, "By 1900 the Mexican male population was securely positioned at the bottom of the county's occupational structure" (102). Almaguer documents the dealings of Thomas A. Scott, a White oil speculator who acquired and partitioned five-sevenths of the land of Rancho Santa Clara O La Colonia through particularly "ruthless" and "callous" means (83). The members of the Gonzales family, who are named as defendants in a partition suit against Scott, held on to the last remaining two-fifths of their land, refusing to sell even at significant financial cost. Later, they sold these lands to members of the Camarillo family, who also struggled against legal and other economic challenges to their lands. These challenges led to the Camarillo family eventually selling much of their lands throughout the county at a drastically reduced price to Thomas R. Bard and other White immigrants. The Camarillo family held on to only a small portion of its original rancho lands. Tomás Almaguer, *Racial Fault Lines: The Historical Origins of White Supremacy in California* (Berkeley: University of California Press, 1994). See also *Scott v. Gonzales,* Supreme Court of the State of California, no. 6507 (1879).

28. Indenture between Hickey Brothers Company and Ray Erwin Dockstader and Nora Belle Dockstader, January 16, 1928, Ventura County Clerk and Recorder, book 151, p. 408. This indenture was "made and accepted SUBJECT TO: Conditions, restrictions and provisions" contained in the deed from Oxnard Land Company to T. J. Childs, February 1, 1912, Ventura County Clerk and Recorder, book 134, p. 85. When Dockstader sold this property in 1966, his grant deed specified that the property remained "subject to covenants, conditions, restrictions, and easements of record." See Grant Deed from Ray E. Dockstader to Oliver A. Folcke and Virginia F. Folcke, March 7, 1966, Ventura County Clerk and Recorder, book 2974, p. 161.

29. Ibid.

30. Grant Deed from E. H. Agee and Annie Boyden Agee to Everett C. Beach, July 8, 1930, Ventura County Clerk and Recorder, book 322, p. 112. Grant Deed from Adolph J. Carty to Everett C. Beach, November 17, 1930, Ventura County Clerk and Recorder, book 333, p. 245. The deed specifies the property is part of Edwin L. Carty's subdivision. The record shows Adolph J. Carty co-owned Carty Tract No. 1 with Edwin L. Carty and his wife Doris C. Carty. See Miscellaneous Record specifying that if breach of conditions and restrictions occurred, property owners would not render mortgage or deed of trust invalid; June 12, 1939, Ventura County Clerk and Recorder, book 592, p. 544. See also Restrictions for Edwin L. Carty and Doris C. Carty Tract No. 2, October 5, 1939, Ventura County Clerk and Recorder, book 601, p. 139, and book 600, p. 366. Both documents bind entire blocks in Carty Tract until 1965. See additional filings to extend time on Carty tract restrictions, n53–n55.

31. "Reservations, Restrictions, and Protective Covenants Applicable to the Eugene H. Agee Subdivision," January 16, 1946, Ventura County Clerk and Recorder, book 736, p. 239. This document specifies covenants "run with the land" until January 1, 1966, and would automatically extend for successive periods of ten years unless a majority of then-owners agreed to change them. See also "Reservations, Restrictions, and Protective Covenants Applicable to the Eugene H. Agee Subdivision," June 18, 1951, Ventura County Clerk and Recorder, book 1005, p. 35, which bound another part of Agee's subdivision until January 1, 1972, with the same racial covenant language and successive ten-year extension periods.

32. Indenture between Walter H. Lathrop and Edna Lathrop AND E. W. Power, April 28, 1913, Ventura County Clerk and Recorder, book 137, p. 366. See further description of Lathrop in n39.

33. Grant Deed from Security-First National Bank of Los Angeles to Elmer W. Power, September 2, 1931, Ventura County Clerk and Recorder, book 360, p. 454.

34. For instance, note from OSBT meeting minutes, September 30, 1937, "Insurance policies expiring October 1 were renewed with E. W. Power, successor to Henry Levy, H. H. Eastwood, E. H. Agee, and John Treher." Again, on September 8, 1938, the minutes state, "It was voted to have school insurance policies changed in accordance with the five-year plan proposed and submitted by Mr. E. H. Agee." See Grant Deed from Leon Lehmann to John D. Treher, December 17, 1930, Ventura County Clerk and Recorder, book 319, p. 271.

35. See chapter 1, n66 for details of Herbert H. Eastwood's specific service dates as city trustee and mayor over the period from 1909 to 1944; Eastwood bought and sold properties in the racially restricted Oxnard Development Company Subdivision. See Indenture between Andrew Hardie and Isabelle Hardie AND Herbert H. Eastwood, November 29, 1919, Ventura County Clerk and Recorder, book 167, p. 234, and Indenture between Herbert H. Eastwood and Irma I. Eastwood AND Nicholas A. Duren, Ventura County Clerk and Recorder October 26, 1920, book 175, p. 228. Anna J. Sells, principal of Wilson and Haydock schools eventually purchased this property, see n47. These indentures refer to the subdivision burdened until January 1, 1970, by the Oxnard Land Development Company. See Walter H. Lathrop, n39, "Restrictions, Covenants and Conditions Imposed upon Oxnard Development Company, Unit No. 3," August 20, 1946, Ventura County Clerk and Recorder, book 760, p. 404. Eastwood also co-owned the racially restricted "Eastwood and Lathrop Subdivision" with Walter H. Lathrop. See, for example, Indenture between H. H. Eastwood and Irma I. Eastwood AND Walter H. Lathrop and Edna Lathrop to Josephine M. Doud, January 15, 1926, Ventura County Clerk and Recorder, book 31, p. 59. See also Indenture between H. H. Eastwood and Irma I. Eastwood AND Walter H. Lathrop and Edna Lathrop to George Brown and Anna Brown, January 19, 1926, Ventura County Clerk and Recorder, book 31, p. 61. Moreover, Eastwood bought property from Lathrop in Ramona Gardens (La Colonia) in 1937, which he sold to the Macias family about one year later. Lathrop's La Colonia subdivision was piped for water at the individual homeowner's expense in 1922 but remained without electricity, gas, or sewage until after World War II. The record does not indicate whether Eastwood made these improvements before selling the property. See Indenture between Walter H. Lathrop and Edna C. Lathrop AND H. H. Eastwood, Ventura County Clerk and Recorder, March 29, 1937, book 393, p. 520. Indenture between H. H. Eastwood and Irma I. Eastwood AND Guadalupe Macias and Ruth Macias, Ventura County Clerk and Recorder, June 24, 1938, book 562, p. 482. Incidentally, the indenture indicates Guadalupe and Ruth Macias already lived in Ramona Gardens, at 141 Hayes Avenue, at the time they purchased this property from Eastwood. By 1938, Antonia Arguelles and her family had also purchased a home and lived at 128 Hayes Avenue.

36. Edwin L. Carty served as city trustee from approximately 1944 to 1947, and mayor, 1948–50. *City of Oxnard Elected Officials History, 1903–2014*, Office of the City Clerk, Oxnard, CA.

37. For further detail on how the local newspaper described the family history of Edwin L. Carty, see "Carty Tract Streets Named for Mayor and His Family," *Oxnard Press-Courier,* September 24, 1948, Sect. E, 6.

38. See, for example, Indenture between Doretta Maulhardt and Edwin L. Carty, March 17, 1920, Ventura County Clerk and Recorder, book 169, p. 261. This indenture refers to "Part of Subdivision nineteen (19) and part of Subdivision twenty (20) as the same are designated and delineated upon that certain map entitled Map of Rancho El Rio de Santa Clara o' La Colonia, partitioned by order District Court 1st Judicial District California, and filed in the office of the County Clerk of Ventura

County in that certain action entitled *Thomas A. Scott, et al., Plffs, vs. Rafael Gonzales, et al., Defts.*, said action brought for the purpose of partitioning said Rancho El Rio de Santa Clara o' La Colonia." These are the subdivisions burdened both by individual lot and by block with long-term racial covenants.

39. Walter H. Lathrop served as a city trustee from about 1914 to 1916, and was a copartner of the Oxnard Development Company with A. J. Dingeman, and burdened these co-owned subdivisions with long-term racial covenants. See "Restrictions, Covenants and Conditions Imposed upon Oxnard Development Company, Unit No. 1," Ventura County Clerk and Recorder, September 20, 1940, book 576, p. 517; "Restrictions, Covenants and Conditions Imposed upon Oxnard Development Company, Unit No. 2," November 22, 1943, Ventura County Clerk and Recorder, book 696, p. 469; and "Restrictions, Covenants and Conditions Imposed upon Oxnard Development Company, Unit No. 3," August 20, 1946, Ventura County Clerk and Recorder, book 760, p. 404. These covenants bound all the lots in the subdivision units until January 1, 1970, and extended the restrictions automatically for periods of ten years unless a majority of then-owners terminated them. Lathrop also bound the properties in his Walter H. Lathrop Subdivision; see Indenture between Walter H. Lathrop and Edna Lathrop AND Kate W. Rice, May 15, 1913, Ventura County Clerk and Recorder, book 138, p. 275.

40. Eastwood, Lathrop, and Lehmann's service as city trustees overlapped from approximately 1914 to 1916, during which time Haydock was also on the city council. Lehmann was city treasurer from 1904 to 1909 and a city trustee from 1914 to 1923. *City of Oxnard Elected Officials History, 1903–2014*, Office of the City Clerk, Oxnard, CA.

41. Hill served on the first city board of trustees from June 1903 until November 1903. He was president of the Oxnard Land Company and co-owned a subdivision in southwest Oxnard encumbered by racial covenants, referred to in the record as the Wolff Hill Laubacher Addition to the City of Oxnard. See Indenture between Oxnard Land Company and Caroline Durr, December 6, 1912, Ventura County Clerk and Recorder, book 134, p. 547.

42. Indenture between Edwin L. Carty and Doris C. Carty AND George M. Pryor and Gertrude E. Pryor, June 10, 1938, Ventura County Clerk and Recorder, book 567, p. 119. Grant Deed from George M. Pryor and Gertrude E. Pryor to Hugh B. Robinson and Oleta Robinson, October 10, 1945, Ventura County Clerk and Recorder, book 728, p. 445.

43. James J. Krouser owned and published the *Oxnard Daily Courier* from 1937 to 1940. See Corporation Grant Deed from W. I. Hollingsworth and Co. to J. J. Krouser, July 25, 1927, Ventura County Clerk and Recorder, book 162, p. 279.

44. Indenture between H. H. Eastwood and Irma I. Eastwood AND Walter H. Lathrop and Edna Lathrop to John Cooluris, January 12, 1926, Ventura County Clerk and Recorder, book 31, p. 63.

45. See, for example, "Elementary Schools to Open Sept. 10, New Teachers Due," *Oxnard Press-Courier*, August 29, 1940, sec. 2, 6. According to this list and school board minutes, Grace C. Noble was hired for the 1940–41 school year at Haydock

School. Grant Deed from Alta E. Diedrich to Lorraine E. Noble and Grace C. Noble, October 23, 1943, Ventura County Clerk and Recorder, book 683, pp. 63–64. See also Declaration of Restrictions, Bank of Italy National Trust and Savings Association, July 9, 1928, Ventura County Clerk and Recorder, book 216, p. 16. These subdivision restrictions utilize the same language found in Virden's deed, specifying the exception to occupancy only "if persons not of the Caucasian race be employed thereon by a Caucasian occupant strictly in the capacity of servant of such occupant" (17). The *Oxnard Press-Courier* also lists Helen C. Deatherage as a first-grade teacher at Roosevelt School in 1940–41. See Joint Tenancy Deed granted from John D. Gastl and Bernice D. Gastl to F. K. Deatherage and Helen C. Deatherage, July 10, 1935, Ventura County Clerk and Recorder, book 457, p. 466. See also deed of trust for same property, July 9, 1935, Ventura County Clerk and Recorder, book 460, p. 196. Both documents refer to her property in the Walter H. Lathrop Subdivision of Oxnard, which was "subject to conditions, restrictions, and provisions" outlined in the Indenture between Walter H. Lathrop and Edna Lathrop AND Kate W. Rice, specifying that "no part of the said premises shall ever be sold to Negroes, Japanese, Chinese, Mexicans or Indians," May 15, 1913, Ventura County Clerk and Recorder, book 138, p. 275.

46. Indenture between Kate J. Dawley and Bernice Curren, January 15, 1937, Ventura County Clerk and Recorder, book 516, p. 162. The indenture specified "that no part of said premises shall ever be sold or rented to Japanese, Chinese, Mexicans, or Indians, and that no part of said premises shall ever be rented to or occupied by Negroes," referring to Kate and Bernice each as widows and detailing that the property was Lot Eight in the John B. Dawley Subdivision.

47. Indenture between Merle F. Skilling and Laura A. Skilling AND Anna J. Sells, January 9, 1924, Ventura County Clerk and Recorder, book 29, p. 195. Grant Deed from Anna J. Sells to Edmund C. Rees and Lottie M. Rees, November 13, 1925, Ventura County Clerk and Recorder, book 85, p. 446. Record of same lot bought and sold by Eastwood. See Indenture between Herbert H. Eastwood and Irma I. Eastwood AND Nicholas A. Duren, October 26, 1920, Ventura County Clerk and Recorder, book 175, p. 228; Duran then sold the lot to Merle F. Skilling and Laura A. Skilling; see Indenture between Nicholas A. Duren and Myrtle Mary Duren AND Merle F. Skilling and Laura A. Skilling, April 2, 1921, Ventura County Clerk and Recorder, book 175, p. 399.

48. Grant Deed from Everett C. Beach and Theresa C. Beach to Clarence A. Brittell and Eva M. Brittell, August 23, 1939, Ventura County Clerk and Recorder, book 595, p. 633.

49. Grant Deed from F. H. Adamson and Lulu E. Adamson to James E. Reynolds and Blanche T. Reynolds, September 23, 1926, Ventura County Clerk and Recorder, book 127, p. 1, which noted the agreement remained "SUBJECT to certain conditions, restrictions, and provisions" as outlined in the Deed from Gilpin W. Chrisman and Jennie M. Chrisman to B. Frank Barr and Homer P. Barr, February 14, 1925, Ventura County Clerk and Recorder, book 34, p. 467.

50. For example, Allen S. Wonn, principal of Ramona School 1946–51, owned property in the Oxnard Park Subdivision, which was burdened by racial covenants.

Grant Deed from Max Glick to Allen S. Wonn, June 1, 1945, Ventura County Clerk and Recorder book 721, p. 316.

51. Judge Albert F. Ross of the Orange County California Superior Court found restrictive covenants against Mexican Americans to be unconstitutional. See *Doss v. Bernal,* Superior Court of the State of California, Orange County, no. 41466 (1943); Robert Chao Romero and Luis Fernando Fernandez, *Doss v. Bernal: Ending Mexican Apartheid in Orange County,* Research Report no. 14 (UCLA Chicano Studies Research Center, University of California, Los Angeles, February 2012).

52. The Federal Housing Administration (FHA) was created in 1934 and officially endorsed and created means to support the enforcement of racial discrimination until the 1948 U.S. Supreme Court decision in *Shelley v. Kraemer.* See also Charles Abrams, *Forbidden Neighbors: A Study of Prejudice and Housing* (New York: Harper & Brothers, 1955). Abrams explains that the FHA also offered a template for suggested phrasing of racial covenants. Abrams, *Forbidden Neighbors,* 230–37. See also underwriting manual, U.S. Federal Housing Administration, *Underwriting and Valuation Procedure under Title II of the National Housing Act* (Washington, DC: U.S. Government Printing Office, 1938). To guide the process of valuation of properties and neighborhoods to determine risk for mortgage insurance, the FHA created a valuation manual, directing local valuators to consider issuing a rating of "reject" if the property was not sufficiently protected from "infiltration of inharmonious racial groups" (sec. 934–35). The FHA manual warned that if children of owners "are compelled to attend school where the majority or a considerable number of pupils represent a far lower level of society or an incompatible racial element, the neighborhood under consideration will prove far less stable and desirable than if this condition did not exist" (sec. 951). The manual also suggested that in undeveloped subdivisions, special considerations should take place to protect the properties from "adverse influences" (sec. 980). High ratings could be considered only for areas with restrictive covenants "imposed upon all land in the immediate environment of the subject location" (sec. 980). Such deed restrictions, the manual recommended, should "be imposed as a blanket encumbrance against all lots in the subdivision and should run for a period of at least twenty-five to thirty years," and should include provision for "Prohibition of the occupancy of properties except by the race for which they are intended" (sec. 980.3). See also directives in *Federal Housing Administration Underwriting Manual* (Washington, DC: U.S. Government Printing Office, 1947), secs. 1320 (1) and 1320 (2).

53. Grant Deed from James E. Weatherall and Dorothy B. Weatherall to John Harlon Burfeind and Mary Elizabeth Burfeind, January 2, 1948, Ventura County Clerk and Recorder, book 821, p. 75. Weatherall and his wife had purchased the property in August 1947, with the condition that the covenants would bind the land until January 1, 1972; see Indenture between Edwin L. Carty and Doris C. Carty AND James E. Weatherall and Dorothy B. Weatherall, August 16, 1947, Ventura County Clerk and Recorder, book 800, p. 333.

54. See, for example, Indenture between Edwin L. Carty and Doris C. Carty AND Elliot B. Thomas and Olinda H. Thomas, December 17, 1945, Ventura County

Clerk and Recorder, book 737, p. 84. On this indenture, the typist struck out the termination date of racial covenants through 1965, and replaced the date with 1970.

55. Grant Deed from Edwin L. Carty and Doris C. Carty to Elliot B. Thomas and Olinda H. Thomas, July 20, 1949, Ventura County Clerk and Recorder, book 883, p. 390. This deed refers to the "Declaration of Establishment of Protective Restrictions, Conditions, Covenants, and Reservations Affecting Certain Property in the City of Oxnard, County of Ventura, State of California," May 13, 1948, Ventura County Clerk and Recorder, book 828, p. 300. Carty also filed a modification of the restrictions to assure lending institutions that a breach of the restrictions and conditions would not render the mortgage invalid. "Modification of Restrictions," June 1, 1949, Ventura County Clerk and Recorder, book 874, p. 474.

56. Grant Deed from Eugene H. Agee and Annie B. Agee to Walter M. Dunning and Effie B. Dunning, October 18, 1950, Ventura County Clerk and Recorder, book 964, p. 146. Grant Deed from Walter M. Dunning and Effie B. Dunning to Daniel M. Tolmach and Jane M. Tolmach, June 5, 1951, Ventura County Clerk and Recorder, book 1007, p. 90. Both refer to the declaration of restrictions outlined by E. H. Agee, January 16, 1946, Ventura County Clerk and Recorder, book 736, p. 239 (see n31).

57. Grant Deed from Paul A. Holmberg and Louise Gallagher Holmberg to Richard M. Clowes and Hannah Z. Clowes, June 7, 1950, Ventura County Clerk and Recorder, book 953, p. 509. Grant Deed from Richard M. Clowes and Hannah Z. Clowes to Floyd M. Rees and Lorraine A. Rees, May 29, 1961, Ventura County Clerk and Recorder, book 2007, p. 488.

58. Antonia Arguelles DiLiello, interview by David G. García and Frank P. Barajas, June 1, 2010, Oxnard, CA.

59. Ibid.

60. Mary Valdivia Lamm, interview by David G. García, May 16, 2010, Moorpark, CA.

61. Joe I. Mendoza, interview by David G. García and Frank P. Barajas, March 26, 2010, Oxnard, CA.

62. Those who were not born at home recalled a private hospital, the Lying-In Hospital and Sanatorium, on Fifth Street and H Street. According to Manuel Espinosa, who was born in Oxnard in 1928, this facility functioned for limited health care needs, mainly for pregnant women and elderly people. "You either went there to have babies or die," he explained. Manuel Espinosa, interview by David G. García and Frank P. Barajas, July 10, 2010, Oxnard, CA.

63. Ernie Carrasco Jr., interview by David G. García and Frank P. Barajas, May 23, 2010, Oxnard, CA.

64. Ibid.

65. Joe I. Mendoza, interview by David G. García and Frank P. Barajas, March 26, 2010, Oxnard, CA.

66. In an article at the city's fiftieth anniversary, one writer noted at least ten social clubs and civic organizations, which had advocated on behalf of the Mexican American community during Oxnard's early history. See H. C. Palomino, "Mexican

Americans Taking Ever Greater Role in City," *Oxnard Press-Courier,* September 24, 1948, sec. E, 7.

67. For further discussion on the daily stress of such segregation, see Chester M. Pierce, "Poverty and Racism as They Affect Children," in *Advocacy for Child Mental Health,* edited by I. N. Berlin (New York: Brunner/Mazel, 1975), 92–109.

68. Antonia Arguelles DiLiello, interview by David G. García, June 24, 2011, Oxnard, CA.

69. Carlos H. Arce, Edward Murgia, and W. Parker Frisbie, "Phenotype and the Life Chances among Chicanos," *Hispanic Journal of Behavioral Sciences* 9, no. 1 (1987): 19–32; Edward E. Telles and Edward Murgia, "Phenotypic Discrimination and Income Differences among Mexican-Americans," *Social Science Quarterly* 71, no. 4 (1990): 682–94.

70. Antonia Arguelles DiLiello, interview by David G. García, June 24, 2011, Oxnard, CA.

71. Dolores Carrasco, interview by David G. García and Frank P. Barajas, May 23, 2010, Oxnard, CA.

72. Ibid.

73. Miguel Espinosa, interview by David G. García and Frank P. Barajas, August 2, 2010, Oxnard, CA.

74. Ibid.

75. Some deeds, as early as 1912 from the Oxnard Land Company, struck out pre-printed racially restrictive language for homeowners with Spanish surnames; see Indenture between the Oxnard Land Company and Alvina Garcia of Oxnard, California, May 25, 1912, Ventura County Clerk and Recorder, book 134, p. 387. This included a strike-out across all restrictions except the section on development of water. Other deeds on purchases of homes within racially restricted areas left the language intact. See Indenture between the Oxnard Land Company and Manuel Jorge of Oxnard, California, February 1, 1912, Ventura County Clerk and Recorder, book 134, p. 273. It remains unclear whether these were Mexicans purchasing homes with restrictions against Mexicans on the grant deed, or if these are perhaps homebuyers of Spanish descent. I also found contradictory evidence regarding Japanese surnames on property deeds in racially restricted subdivisions. For instance, a 1939 deed from Edwin Carty to a married Japanese woman, Sakae L. Morimoto, included additional language not found on other deeds, specifying she was "a native born citizen of the United States of America." See Grant Deed from Edwin L. Carty and Doris C. Carty to Sakae L. Morimoto, November 3, 1939, Ventura County Clerk and Recorder, book 602, p. 636.

76. Melvin Oliver and Thomas Shapiro, *Black Wealth/White Wealth: Toward a New Theory of Inequality* (New York: Routledge, 1994). George Lipsitz also explains, "Net worth is almost totally determined by past opportunities for asset accumulation, therefore is the one figure most likely to reflect the history of discrimination." George Lipsitz, *The Possessive Investment in Whiteness: How White People Profit from Identity Politics* (Philadelphia: Temple University Press, 1998), 13–14.

77. Miguel Espinosa, interview by David G. García and Frank P. Barajas, August 2, 2010, Oxnard, CA.

78. Antonia Arguelles DiLiello, interview by David G. García and Frank P. Barajas, June 1, 2010, Oxnard, CA.

79. Joe I. Mendoza, interview by David G. García and Frank P. Barajas, March 26, 2010, Oxnard, CA.

80. Antonia Arguelles DiLiello, interview by David G. García and Frank P. Barajas, June 1, 2010, Oxnard, CA.

81. Antonia Arguelles DiLiello, interview by David G. García, June 24, 2011, Oxnard, CA.

82. Dolores Carrasco, interview by David G. García and Frank P. Barajas, May 23, 2010, Oxnard, CA.

83. Ibid.

84. Antonia Arguelles DiLiello, interview by David G. García and Frank P. Barajas, June 1, 2010, Oxnard, CA.

85. Ernie Carrasco Jr., interview by David G. García and Frank P. Barajas, May 23, 2010, Oxnard, CA.

86. Antonia Arguelles DiLiello, interview by David G. García, June 24, 2011, Oxnard, CA.

87. Ernie Carrasco Jr., interview by David G. García and Frank P. Barajas, May 23, 2010, Oxnard, CA.

88. Dolores Carrasco, interview by David G. García and Frank P. Barajas, May 23, 2010, Oxnard, CA; emphasis in original.

89. Ibid.

90. Joe I. Mendoza, interview by David G. García and Frank P. Barajas, March 26, 2010, Oxnard, CA.

91. This policing of space in Oxnard reflects the experiences of African Americans in "sundown towns" across the United States, which relied on Blacks for their labor by day while brutally enforcing a Whites-only policy by night. See James W. Loewen, *Sundown Towns: A Hidden Dimension of American Racism* (New York: New Press, 2005).

92. Miguel Espinosa, interview by David G. García and Frank P. Barajas, August 2, 2010, Oxnard, CA.

93. Ibid.

94. Ibid.

95. Dolores Carrasco, interview by David G. García and Frank P. Barajas, May 23, 2010, Oxnard, CA.

96. Antonia Arguelles DiLiello, interview by David G. García, June 24, 2011, Oxnard, CA.

97. George Lipsitz, *How Racism Takes Place* (Philadelphia: Temple University Press, 2011), 6.

98. *Shelley v. Kraemer,* 334 U.S. 1 (1948); *Barrows v. Jackson,* 346 U.S. 249 (1953).

99. The *Los Angeles Times* also failed to report on the case, though it did make the cover story of *Time* magazine. See Chao Romero and Fernandez, *Doss v. Bernal.*

100. The newspaper had a vested interest in not covering these cases. Following James J. Krouser, Dan W. Emmett published the *Oxnard Press-Courier* from 1940

to 1959. Like Krouser, Emmett maintained racial covenants on his property. See Grant Deed from Dan W. Emmett to Harriet A. Brown, March 22, 1937, Ventura County Clerk and Recorder, book 443, p. 302. See also Grant Deed from John H. Burfeind and Mary E. Burfeind to Dan W. Emmett, Ventura County Clerk and Recorder, January 23, 1941, book 633, p. 233.

101. Carty also named streets after his wife, Doris, and his children, Roderick, Robert, and Douglas.

102. Edward W. Soja, *Postmodern Geographies: The Reassertion of Space in Critical Social Theory* (New York: Verso, 1989), 6.

103. Dolores Carrasco, interview by David G. García and Frank P. Barajas, May 23, 2010, Oxnard, CA.

3. "OBSESSED" WITH SEGREGATING MEXICAN STUDENTS

Portions of this chapter were adapted and revised from David G. García, Tara J. Yosso, and Frank P. Barajas, "'A Few of the Brightest, Cleanest Mexican Children': School Segregation as a Form of Mundane Racism in Oxnard, California, 1900–1940," *Harvard Educational Review* 82, no. 1 (Spring 2012): 1–25. Used with permission.

Epigraph: Oxnard School Board of Trustees meeting minutes, November 4, 1936, 2.

1. Blanche T. Reynolds cited Mexican children as comprising 33 percent of the Ventura County school population in 1928. "Mexican Costs Are Too High Says Co. Head," *The Oxnard Daily Courier,* January 31, 1928, front page. Also, correspondence from the clerk of the Oxnard School Board of Trustees (OSBT), John H. Burfeind, to Alice Shaffer in 1938 estimated, "About two-thirds of the youngsters going to our Schools today are of Mexican parentage." OSBT meeting minutes, April 25, 1938.

2. W. E. B. DuBois, *The Souls of Black Folk: Essays and Sketches* [1903] (New York: Fawcett, 1961), 23.

3. See Christopher Ramos, "The Educational Legacy of Racially Restrictive Covenants: Their Long Term Impact on Mexican Americans," *The Scholar,* 4 (2002): 149–84, 169.

4. After examining these 1930s minutes as part of the *Soria v. Oxnard School Board of Trustees* case, Judge Harry Pregerson wrote, "The Board continued to be obsessed with the subject of school segregation plans, and their implementation." 386 F. Supp. 539, 542 (U.S. Dist. 1974).

5. U.S. Bureau of the Census, *U.S. Census of the Population: 1930,* "Population, California, Table 17. Indians, Chinese and Japanese 1910 to 1930 and Mexicans, 1930 for Counties and for Cities of 25,000 or More" (Washington, DC: U.S. Government Printing Office, 1930), 266.

6. Correspondence from Burfeind to Shaffer, OSBT meeting minutes, April 25, 1938.

7. OSBT meeting minutes, August 7, 1934.

8. OSBT meeting minutes, November 4, 1936, 1.

9. As of November 1936, K-6 enrollment at Haydock School was 23 percent White, 73 percent Mexican, and 3.4 percent Asian. OSBT meeting minutes, November 4, 1936, 1.

10. OSBT meeting minutes, November 9, 1936, 1. Unlike the other board meetings, this one took place at Wilson School, and the notes explain that all trustees were present, "together with Mrs. Curren, Mrs. Sells, Miss McEnany, and Superintendent R. B. Haydock." Berenice Curren was the principal of Roosevelt, and Anna J. Sells was principal of Haydock School. Miss McEnany served as the school district nurse.

11. Ibid., 2.

12. Ibid., 1. "The following note, also pencil written, accompanied the parents' report: 'The private opinion of the committee is that the small wooden building at Roosevelt School could be used for the smallest Mexican children with lavatory facilities added to that building and it would meet everyone's approval.'"

13. Ibid.

14. Ibid., 2.

15. Ward A. Leis, "The Status of Education for Mexican Children in Four Border States" (master's thesis, University of Southern California, Los Angeles, 1931), 65.

16. Ibid., 26.

17. Ibid., 27, 29.

18. Ibid., 30.

19. OSBT meeting minutes, November 20, 1936. Unfortunately, this typewritten copy of the "new enrollments" was not appended to the minutes.

20. Ibid.

21. OSBT meeting minutes, April 19, 1937.

22. OSBT meeting minutes, September 22, 1937.

23. Ibid.

24. Quotes and capital/lowercase inconsistencies in original, OSBT meeting minutes, September 27, 1937.

25. OSBT meeting minutes, September 30, 1937.

26. OSBT meeting minutes, November 8, 1937.

27. See further discussion of this exchange in chapter 2. Correspondence from Shaffer to Burfeind, OSBT meeting minutes, April 21, 1938.

28. Burfeind to Shaffer, OSBT meeting minutes, April 25, 1938.

29. Shaffer to Burfeind, OSBT meeting minutes, April 21, 1938.

30. DuBois, *Souls of Black Folk*, 23.

31. Ibid.

32. OSBT meeting minutes, September 13, 1938.

33. OSBT meeting minutes, September 16, 1938.

34. OSBT meeting minutes, December 12, 1938.

35. Ibid.

36. See discussion in chapter 1. "Supreme Court School Ruling Affects Oxnard," *The Oxnard Daily Courier*, November 22, 1927.

37. OSBT meeting minutes, December 21, 1938.

38. According to the records of the federal court, most of the school board meeting minutes from the 1940s through the early 1960s were "lost." The 1930s meeting minutes were "found" during the 1973 school year and became part of the records in the *Soria* case.

39. "Certificates Given Students at Roosevelt," *The Oxnard Daily Courier*, May 27, 1939, "Society" page. See also "Nine Teachers Leave City School System," *The Oxnard Daily Courier*, June 15, 1939, front page.

40. Antonia Arguelles DiLiello, interview by David G. García and Frank P. Barajas, June 1, 2010, Oxnard, CA.

41. This was likely the old San Pedro School building, which had survived the Oxnard Grammar School fire in 1923. Helen Frost, *102 Year History of Oxnard School District*, [pamphlet] (Oxnard, CA, 1975). On file with author.

42. Antonia Arguelles DiLiello, interview by David G. García and Frank P. Barajas, June 1, 2010, Oxnard, CA.

43. Ibid.

44. Ibid.

45. Delia L. Hernandez, interview by David G. Garcia, September 3, 2013, Ventura, CA.

46. Ibid.

47. Ibid.

48. Ibid.

49. Ibid.

50. Ibid.

51. Ibid.

52. William A. Farmer, "The Influence of Segregation of Mexican and American Children upon the Development of Social Attitudes" (master's thesis, University of Southern California, Los Angeles, 1937). Farmer omitted most of the identifying information for the school sites, except for descriptions of racial segregation practices: "Two did not practice segregation; in one the Mexican children were segregated into buildings on the same school grounds; and in the other three, the Mexican children were segregated into schools at some distance from the American school" (7). In his graphs, he identified the different forms of racial separation in the schools as "semi-segregated, non-segregated, segregated, and 90% segregated" (90).

53. Ibid., 90–91.

54. Ibid., 91–92.

55. Ibid., 96–97.

56. Joe I. Mendoza, interview by David G. García and Frank P. Barajas, March 26, 2010, Oxnard, CA.

57. Antonia Arguelles DiLiello, interview by David G. García and Frank P. Barajas, June 1, 2010, Oxnard, CA.

58. Ibid.

59. Joe I. Mendoza, interview by David G. García and Frank P. Barajas, March 26, 2010, Oxnard, CA.

60. Mary Valdivia Lamm, interview by David G. García, May 16, 2010, Moorpark, CA.

61. Ibid.

62. Ibid.

63. Antonia Arguelles DiLiello, interview by David G. García and Frank P. Barajas, June 1, 2010, Oxnard, CA.

64. Ibid.

65. Mary Valdivia Lamm, interview by David G. García, May 16, 2010, Moorpark, CA.

66. Grace Carroll, *Environmental Stress and African Americans: The Other Side of the Moon* (Westport, CT: Praeger, 1998); Chester M. Pierce, "Poverty and Racism as They Affect Children," in *Advocacy for Child Mental Health,* edited by I.N. Berlin (New York: Brunner/Mazel, 1975), 92–109; Chester M. Pierce, "Social Trace Contaminants: Subtle Indicators of Racism in TV," in *Television and Social Behavior: Beyond Violence and Children. A Report of the Committee on Television and Social Behavior, Social Science Research Council,* edited by S.B. Withey and R.P. Abeles (Hillsdale, NJ: Lawrence Erlbaum, 1980), 249–57. Grace Carroll and Chester M. Pierce have analyzed the extreme climate of racism as it pervades society in subtle, stunning, everyday ways that cause African Americans mundane extreme environmental stress (M.E.E.S.). As part of racism, Carroll argues, M.E.E.S. "is so common and is so much a part of our day-to-day experience that we almost take it for granted." Carroll, *Environmental Stress and African Americans,* 4.

67. Burfeind to Shaffer, OSBT meeting minutes, April 25, 1938.

68. Antonia Arguelles DiLiello, interview by David G. García and Frank P. Barajas, June 1, 2010, Oxnard, CA.

69. "Graduation: Largest Grammar School Class Graduates," *The Oxnard Daily Courier,* June 9, 1939, front page, 5. Considering the names recorded in class listings in the newspaper alongside oral accounts, it appears exceptions for Mexican girls to break the color line may have occurred more frequently than for boys.

70. Antonia Arguelles DiLiello, interview, by David G. García and Frank P. Barajas, June 1, 2010, Oxnard, CA.

71. OSBT meeting minutes, September 21, 1938.

72. Ibid.

73. Richard Carballo, interview by David G. García and Frank P. Barajas, May 24, 2010, Oxnard, CA.

74. Ibid.

75. Antonia recalled this practice of placing Spanish-surnamed students in segregated classes: "About two or three kids that I know of . . . they wouldn't say that they were Mexicans, but the name sounded Mexican, or Spanish, or Hispanic. Then, they would be in our class." Antonia Arguelles DiLiello, interview by David G. García and Frank P. Barajas, June 1, 2010, Oxnard, CA.

76. Richard Carballo, interview by David G. García and Frank P. Barajas, May 24, 2010, Oxnard, CA.

77. OSTB meeting minutes, September 23, 1938.

78. See Donna LaRue Ball's online scrapbook for annotated pictures of her life history, including class pictures at Roosevelt and Wilson schools, www .ballandautreyancestry.com/images/sb2.htm (retrieved December 13, 2010).

79. There were 140 eighth-graders promoted in total, including 71 Mexicans, 58 Whites, and 11 Asians. "Graduation: Largest Grammar School Class Graduates," *The Oxnard Daily Courier,* June 9, 1939, front page, 5.

80. Ibid. Mrs. Banner's first name is noted in a later article, "Nine Teachers Leave City School System," *The Oxnard Daily Courier,* June 15, 1939, front page.

81. "Graduation: Largest Grammar School Class Graduates" *The Oxnard Daily Courier,* June 9, 1939, front page, 5.

82. Ibid., 5.

83. "Wilson School 8th Grade Picnics," *The Oxnard Daily Courier,* June 6, 1939, 4. Likewise, there were no Asian surnames listed.

84. Ibid.

85. Antonia Arguelles DiLiello, interview by David G. García, June 24, 2011, Oxnard, CA.

86. Ibid.

87. The newspaper refers to these teachers as Mrs. Owen and Miss Roese [*sic*]. "Certificates Given Students at Roosevelt," *The Oxnard Daily Courier,* May 27, 1939, "Society" page. Later, they are referred to with their first names, Arabella Owen and Charlotte Reebe. "Nine Teachers Leave City School System," *The Oxnard Daily Courier,* June 15, 1939, front page.

88. Antonia Arguelles DiLiello, interview by David G. García and Frank P. Barajas, June 1, 2010, Oxnard, CA. She noted, "Actually, we had some real good teachers. Except for Ms. Owen and Ms. Reebe. I think they were semiretired. [They were there] just because the government said we had to go to school. We didn't really learn much from those two teachers, but the seventh- and eighth-grade teachers were really good. Mr. Hall and Mr. Fox. They were very good." The newspaper later confirmed Owen retired at the end of the 1938–39 school year, and Reebe left the district to take a position in Ventura. "Nine Teachers Leave City School System," *The Oxnard Daily Courier,* June 15, 1939, front page.

89. *Oxnard High School Yearbook, Cardinal and Gold,* 1943. Published by the Senior Class, Oxnard Union High School, Oxnard, CA. Courtesy of Antonia Arguelles DiLiello.

90. Because of the internment of the Japanese during World War II, there were no Japanese students attending Oxnard High School in 1943. In the 1943 OHS yearbook, a Chinese boy with the last name SooHoo is pictured in the sophomore class picture. Ibid. This is likely William D. SooHoo, who was elected to Oxnard City Council in 1962 and then elected mayor for 1966–68. *City of Oxnard Elected Officials History, 1903–2014,* Office of the City Clerk, Oxnard, CA.

91. Mary Martinez was born in Lompoc, California, in 1925. Part of her family immigrated from Spain to Lompoc and then moved to Oxnard around 1927. She attended Santa Clara Catholic School until fifth grade, when she enrolled at

Wilson School, and was placed in White classes. Mary Martinez Carlyle, interview by David G. García and Frank P. Barajas, May 24, 2010, Oxnard, CA.

92. Looking back at her class pictures over the years and her 1943 yearbook, Antonia stated, "Only seven of us, Mexican girls and one boy" graduated. Her recollection is accurate according to who attended the segregated Mexican classes at Wilson; however, it is unclear why she did not count other Spanish-surnamed students, such as Consuelo ("Connie") Diaz. She may not have considered Connie because she was thinking of her actual classmates, but her remark suggests that relying on Spanish surnames may not be the most accurate accounting of students of Mexican descent. The case of Richard Carballo's cousin Mary Martinez, for example, who identified as a Spaniard and was never segregated in Mexican classes at Roosevelt or Wilson, reiterates the complexity of identifying who is Mexican in available historical records.

93. Antonia Arguelles DiLiello, interview by David G. García and Frank P. Barajas, June 1, 2010, Oxnard, CA.

94. Ibid.

95. Antonia Arguelles DiLiello, interview by David G. García, June 24, 2011, Oxnard, CA.

96. Ibid.

97. Natalia Molina, *Fit to Be Citizens? Public Health and Race in Los Angeles, 1879–1939* (Berkeley: University of California Press, 2006), 2–3.

98. At this time, the California educational codes did not make allowance for the segregation of Black children either. See Article 10, Elementary Schools section of the School Law of California 1927 (Sacramento, CA: Office of the Superintendent of Public Instruction, W. M. Cooper, 1927), 132. See also a detailed overview of changes to California's educational codes, from 1870 to 1947, allowing for separate schools to be established for distinct groups of racialized children. David S. Ettinger "Ninth Circuit Review: The History of School Desegregation in the Ninth Circuit," *Loyola Los Angeles Law Review* 12 (1979): 481–504, 481–82.

99. Ettinger, "Ninth Circuit Review." See also chapter 1 for more on the PTA, Haydock, and other school board members discussing the California educational codes particular to segregation. "Supreme Court School Ruling Affects Oxnard," *The Oxnard Daily Courier,* November 22, 1927, front page.

100. For a general history of the Japanese in Oxnard, see Yoshio Fukuyama, "Citizens Apart: A History of the Japanese in Ventura County," *Ventura County Historical Society Quarterly* 39, no. 4 (1994): 3–31.

101. "Japanese Honor R. B. Haydock: Give Educator Gold Loving Cup as Testimonial," *The Oxnard Daily Courier,* June 15, 1939, front page.

102. Ibid.

103. Ibid.

104. Ibid.

105. Ibid.

106. "1,500 Witness O.U.H.S. Graduation Rites," *The Oxnard Daily Courier,* June 9, 1939, front page; "105 'Class of 1939' Students Graduate from O.U.H.S.; Caps

and Gowns Give Dignity to H.S. Graduating Classes" and "O.U.H.S. Class Roll," *The Oxnard Daily Courier,* June 9, 1939, 4–5. See also Nagoa [*sic*] Takasugi, "Valedictory," *The Oxnard Daily Courier,* June 9, 1939, 4–5.

107. As mentioned in the Introduction, scholars most often attribute the construction of the "model minority" myth and subsequent contradictory treatment to the post–World War II and Cold War era.

108. Tom Brokaw, "War Prejudices Show Ugly Side," *Tribune-Democrat* [Johnstown, PA], June 27, 1999, A1, D10. Brokaw highlighted Takasugi in his article series and book, *The Greatest Generation.* He explained that the Quaker group American Friends Service Committee helped Takasugi and four thousand other interned college students apply and pay for completion of their degrees. Takasugi graduated from Temple University and earned a master's degree in business administration from the University of Pennsylvania.

109. Ibid., D10. Brokaw notes that during their internment, Oxnard resident Ignacio Carmona ran the Takasugi family restaurant/fish market, Asahi. After their release, they resumed ownership, and Nao contributed to the business before running for city council. See dates of his city service, *City of Oxnard Elected Officials History, 1903–2014,* Office of the City Clerk, Oxnard, CA. See also the article mentioning Carmona in relation to the Takasugi family and overviewing his biography. Tony Biasotti, "Supervisors Honor Oxnard Man for Community Work, *Ventura County Star,* December 28, 2009, http://archive.vcstar.com/news/supervisors-honor-oxnard-man-for-community-work-ep-370170399–350276271.html (retrieved January 13, 2017).

110. Joe I. Mendoza, interview by David G. García and Frank P. Barajas, March 26, 2010, Oxnard, CA.

111. Antonia Arguelles DiLiello, interview by David G. García and Frank P. Barajas, June 1, 2010, Oxnard, CA.

112. *Soria v. Oxnard School Board of Trustees,* 386 F. Supp. 539, 542 (U.S. Dist. 1974).

113. Ramos, "Educational Legacy of Racially Restrictive Covenants," 155. See further discussion in chapter 2.

4. RAMONA SCHOOL AND THE UNDEREDUCATION OF
CHILDREN IN LA COLONIA

Epigraph: George I. Sánchez, "Bilingualism and Mental Measures: A Word of Caution," *Journal of Applied Psychology* 18, no. 6 (1934): 765–72, 769.

1. Ibid., 770.

2. Ibid.

3. See discussion in chapter 1 of PTA and school trustees' pragmatic efforts to "completely segregate" the Mexican children from the Whites, as reported in the local newspaper, "Supreme Court School Ruling Affects Oxnard," *The Oxnard Daily Courier,* November 22, 1927, front page. See chapter 3 for examination of

school trustees' 1934 and 1936 board minutes using the phrase "complete segregation," Oxnard School Board of Trustees (OSBT) meeting minutes, November 4, 1936, 2.

4. U.S. Bureau of the Census, *U.S. Census of Population: 1950*, "Table 4. Population of Urban Places of 10,000 or More from Earliest Census to 1950" (Washington, DC: U.S. Government Printing Office, 1953), sec. 5, 10.

5. U.S. Bureau of the Census, *U.S. Census of Population: 1950*, vol. 4, *Special Reports*, part 3, ch. C, "Table 7. Citizenship and Country of Birth of White Persons of Spanish Surname, for Counties and Urban Places of 10,000 or More in Selected Southwestern States: 1950" (Washington, DC: U.S. Government Printing Office, 1953), sec. 3C, 43.

6. OSBT meeting minutes, June 27, 1939.

7. Ibid.

8. Ibid.

9. "Cobb Asks Protection on Boulevard Crossings for School Children," *The Oxnard Daily Courier,* May 2, 1939, front page.

10. "Mayor W. Roy Guyer Commended for Quick Action in Safeguarding School Children," *The Oxnard Daily Courier,* May 9, 1939, front page.

11. "New Public School Planned for East Section of Oxnard," *The Oxnard Daily Courier,* July 3, 1939, front page.

12. "Grammar School Board Purchases 6 Acres for East Side School," *The Oxnard Daily Courier,* September 12, 1939, front page.

13. "Plans for New School Approved: Low Cost Revealed by Board of Trustees," *The Oxnard Daily Courier,* December 9, 1939, front page.

14. "Civic Leaders of Oxnard Back Plans for New Colonia School Election on Dec. 15," *The Oxnard Daily Courier,* December 11, 1939, front page.

15. Ibid.

16. "School Bonds Voted," *The Oxnard Daily Courier,* December 16, 1939, front page.

17. "Crossing Guards Authorized," *The Oxnard Daily Courier,* December 13, 1939, front page.

18. "Policewoman Graduate Nurse for City Health," *Oxnard Daily Courier,* Wednesday, January 31, 1917, front page; "Policewoman's Work Missed by Trustees," *The Oxnard Daily Courier,* September 3, 1919, front page.

19. "Names for New School Suggested," *Oxnard Press-Courier,* June 25, 1940, front page.

20. "Plans for New School Approved: Low per Room Cost Revealed by Board of Trustees," *The Oxnard Daily Courier,* December 9, 1939, front page.

21. Ibid.

22. OSBT meeting minutes, January 22, 1942.

23. Ibid.

24. "Elementary Schools to Open Sept. 10; New Teachers Due," *Oxnard Press-Courier,* August 29, 1940, sec. 2, 6.

25. W. E. B. DuBois, *The Souls of Black Folk: Essays and Sketches* [1903] (New York: Fawcett, 1961), 23.

26. Domingo Martinez, "A Comparative Study of the Academic Achievement of the Mexican-American Students in the Wilson Junior High School, Oxnard, California" (master's thesis, Claremont Graduate School, Claremont, CA, 1956), 60–61.

27. Ibid., 3–4. I place the terms "mixed" and "segregated" in quotes to indicate these as labels defined by Martinez. He also referred to Roosevelt as the "non-segregated school," and to Ramona as "the Mexican school." He further explained the term "Segregated School. This is not intended to state, or imply, that Ramona School is a segregated school by edict of the school board. It refers to the Ramona School because it is where most of the Mexican-American pupils attend school" (4).

28. Ibid., 60.

29. "Add Rooms at Ramona," *Oxnard Press-Courier,* July 18, 1941, front page.

30. He explained, "For the larger number of children who attended the kindergarten, a corresponding larger number also attended through the sixth grade." Martinez, "Comparative Study of the Academic Achievement of the Mexican-American Students," 52.

31. Records are unclear in relation to how many classes were offered at each school, and when the pre-first grade/pre-primary classes ended at Ramona. See "Attendance Registers by Years," Oxnard School District Archives, date unknown.

32. Pauline Jeidy, "First Grade Mexican American Children in Ventura County," *California Journal of Elementary Education* 15 (February and May 1947): 200–208, 203.

33. Ibid., 200.

34. Ibid., 203.

35. Ibid., 202.

36. See *Mendez v. Westminster,* 64 F. Supp. 544 (S.D. Cal. 1946); Richard R. Valencia, "The Mexican American Struggle for Equal Educational Opportunity in *Mendez v. Westminster:* Helping Pave the Way for *Brown v. Board of Education,*" *Teachers College Record* 107, no. 3 (2005): 389–423.

37. See further details about California educational codes in chapter 1, n120, and chapter 3.

38. Indeed, in 1957, a federal judge in Texas further found that segregated conditions, including practices of placement in an extra first grade, denied equal treatment to Mexican students. The judge found the grouping of separate classes arbitrary and unreasonable, and ruled for the plaintiffs in *Herminio Hernandez et al. v. Driscoll Consolidated Independent School District,* Civ. No. 1384 (S.D. Tex. 1957); see further analysis in Steven H. Wilson, "Brown over 'Other White': Mexican Americans' Legal Arguments and Litigation Strategy in School Desegregation Lawsuits," *Law and History Review* (2003): 21, 145–94.

39. "Ramona School Decorated to Receive Guests This Week," *Oxnard Press-Courier,* April 10, 1946, 2.

40. Martinez, "Comparative Study of the Academic Achievement of the Mexican-American Students," 61. This practice of placing students without a formal assessment of their actual language ability seems consistent with what Jeidy reported

in 1947. For example, she explained that at Simi Elementary School, "this year for the first time nationality was not considered in grouping first-grade children. All entering children were given the Monroe Reading Readiness test and were grouped according to the results. . . . Twenty-three children, seventeen Mexican-Americans, and five Anglo-Americans constitute the preprimary group." Jeidy, "First Grade Mexican American Children in Ventura County," 205.

41. Martinez, "Comparative Study of the Academic Achievement of the Mexican-American Students," 61.

42. Ibid.

43. Martinez found Mexican American students took 7.1 years to complete elementary school and entered seventh grade 1.3 years over age, at a median of 13.3 years of age. The median grade placement for these seventh-grade students in reading, language, and arithmetic was 6.2, which was 1.2 grades below grade level. Eighth-grade students' median grade placement from reading, language, and arithmetic tests was 6.7, or 1.5 years below grade level. Ibid., 53.

44. U.S. Bureau of the Census, *U.S. Census of Population: 1950*, vol. 4, *Special Reports*, part 3, ch. C, "Table 8. Characteristics of White Persons of Spanish Surname, for Selected Standard Metropolitan Areas, Urbanized Areas, and Urban Places of 10,000 or More in Selected Southwestern States: 1950" (Washington, DC: U.S. Government Printing Office, 1953), sec. 3C, 50. Statewide, in 1950, the median years of schooling for Spanish-surnamed adults were 7.6 for men and 8.0 for women. "Table 3. Characteristics of White Persons of Spanish Surname, for Selected Southwestern States Urban and Rural: 1950," sec. 3C, 16.

45. U.S. Bureau of the Census, *U.S. Census of Population: 1960, Final Report PC(2)-1B, Subject Reports, Persons of Spanish Surname,* "Table 13. Characteristics of White Persons of Spanish Surname, for Selected Standard Metropolitan Statistical Areas and Urban Places in Five Southwestern States: 1960" (Washington, DC: U.S. Government Printing Office), 174.

46. Joe I. Mendoza, interview by David G. García and Frank P. Barajas, March 26, 2010, Oxnard, CA.

47. Ibid.

48. Jack McCurdy, "School Board Minutes Play Big Role in Oxnard Desegregation," *Los Angeles Times,* January 19, 1975, B1, B3.

49. Joe I. Mendoza, interview by David G. García and Frank P. Barajas, March 26, 2010, Oxnard, CA.

50. Ibid.

51. Alex Quiroz, interview by David G. García, September 3, 2013, Oxnard, CA.

52. Ibid.

53. Ibid.

54. Ibid.

55. Ibid.

56. Ibid.

57. Ibid.

58. Ibid.

59. Bedford Pinkard, interview by David G. García, February 25, 2015, Oxnard, CA.

60. Ibid.

61. Ibid. His memory of academic and social segregation echoed in the complaints of a Black mother twenty years later, who in a public forum expressed concern that her daughter and other Black students were "segregated" during PE at Fremont Junior High. Ralph Kaminsky, "Citizens Split over Colonia School: Segregation, Area Boundary Debated," *The Press-Courier*, May 1, 1963, front page, 39.

62. Robert Madrid, StoryCorp interview by Robert Madrid with Robert Cheveres, November 22, 2013, Thousand Oaks, CA. StoryCorp Archive. Interview ID no. MBY011475 (American Folk Life Center, Library of Congress, Washington, DC).

63. Ibid.

64. Ibid.

65. See n3 for sources pertaining to plans for "complete segregation."

66. OSBT meeting minutes, December 12, 1938.

67. Bedford Pinkard, interview by David G. García, February 25, 2015, Oxnard, CA.

68. In 1950, Ventura County counted 114,647 total residents. U.S. Bureau of the Census, *U.S. Census of Population: 1950*, "Table 6. Population of Counties by Minor Civil Divisions: 1930–1950" (Washington, DC: U.S. Government Printing Office, 1953), sec. 5, 18. Mexicans, categorized as White persons of Spanish surname, comprised 21,697, or almost 19 percent, of Ventura County residents. U.S. Bureau of the Census, *U.S. Census of Population: 1950*, vol. 4, *Special Reports*, part 3, ch. C, "Persons of Spanish Surname," "Table 9. Characteristics of White Persons of Spanish Surname, for Selected Counties in Selected Southwestern States: 1950" (Washington, DC: U.S. Government Printing Office, 1953), sec. 3C, 61.

69. Richard Lyttle, "The Largest Labor Camp in Nation in Oxnard," *Oxnard Press-Courier*, March 6, 1958, 11.

70. U.S. Bureau of the Census, *U.S. Census of Population: 1950*, vol. 4, *Special Reports*, part 3, ch. C, "Table 7. Citizenship and Country of Birth of White Persons of Spanish Surname, for Counties and Urban Places of 10,000 or More in Selected Southwestern States: 1950" (Washington, DC: U.S. Government Printing Office, 1953), sec. 3C, 43. The 1950 U.S. Census Bureau used the term "Spanish surname" because it believed the 1930 census word "Mexican" and the 1940 census label "Spanish mother tongue" led to underestimations of the Mexican population. U.S. Bureau of the Census, *U.S. Census of Population: 1950*, vol. 4, *Special Reports*, part 3, ch. C, "Persons of Spanish Surname" (Washington, DC: U.S. Government Printing Office, 1953), sec. 3C, 5–6.

71. "New Elementary School Will Get Name 'Driffill,'" *Oxnard Press-Courier*, April 10, 1946, front page.

72. "School Zones Outlined; Open Sept. 13," *Oxnard Press-Courier*, September 2, 1948, front page. A map of the school zones accompanied the story.

73. Brittell served as the district superintendent from 1939 until his death in 1949.

74. "Juanita School to Open in December," *Oxnard Press-Courier,* November 7, 1951, front page. His remarks are unclear as to whether the kindergarten rooms were included in the total classroom count of eight classrooms. If they were, then each class, kindergarten through second grade, held sixty students. If the kindergarten classrooms were counted separately and indeed the school had ten classrooms, then the first- and second-grade classrooms would have held thirty students each. If the kindergarteners attended only half-day sessions, then each of those classes would have enrolled thirty students. None of this is clear from his statement.

75. "Juanita School to Open in December," *Oxnard Press-Courier,* November 7, 1951, front page.

76. As noted in chapter 2, Curren served as a teacher and principal of Roosevelt School. McKinna served as a school trustee in the 1940s. The original Haydock School remained open until 1952. The name transferred to the new facility in 1954, and has since functioned as a junior high school.

77. "Last Class on Double Sessions Ends," *Oxnard Press-Courier,* November 12, 1954, front page.

78. Clowes estimated an additional three hundred students would likely enroll in Oxnard elementary schools by fall 1954. "Terminaron las Sesiones Dobles de Escuela Juanita," *Oxnard Press-Courier,* November 13, 1954, "Sección en Español: Weekly Press-Courier Spanish Page," 4.

79. Ibid.

80. Dolores Carrasco, interview by David G. García and Frank P. Barajas, May 23, 2010, Oxnard, CA.

81. Ibid.

82. Ibid.

83. Ibid.

84. "Improving Racial and Ethnic Balance and Intergroup Relations: An Advisory Report to the Board of Trustees, Oxnard School District" (California State Department of Education, Division of Compensatory Education, Bureau of Intergroup Relations, April 1969), 14. Data cited as coming from the district director of pupil personnel from November 11, 1968. Oxnard School District Archives, microfilm.

85. "Improving Racial and Ethnic Balance and Intergroup Relations," 15. Blacks and Whites were each approximately 14 percent of the students in the low-math groups. Blacks made up about 13 percent of the low-English groups, and Whites were about 22 percent of students in that track.

86. Dolores Carrasco, interview by David G. García and Frank P. Barajas, May 23, 2010, Oxnard, CA.

87. Ibid.

88. Ibid.

89. Ibid.

90. DuBois, *Souls of Black Folk,* 23.

91. Dolores Carrasco, interview by David G. García and Frank P. Barajas, May 23, 2010, Oxnard, CA.

92. See photograph labeled "Ramona, 1952, Fifth and Sixth Grades, Gloria Martinez, Teacher," Oxnard School District Archives.

93. See photograph labeled "Ramona, Sp. Class, 1952, Barbara Rucker, Teacher." See also photograph "Ramona, 1952," portraying a girl brushing her teeth. The same mirror where the boy brushed his hair is present. Hanging above the sink are sets of hair combs and toothbrushes on a wooden ledge with name labels for each. Oxnard School District Archives.

94. See photographs labeled "Wilson Orchestra, 1943," and "Wilson, 1952," Oxnard School District Archives.

95. See photograph labeled "Juanita Kindergarten," Oxnard School District Archives.

96. Chester M. Pierce, "Offensive Mechanisms," in *The Black Seventies,* edited by Floyd B. Barbour (Boston: Porter Sargent, 1970), 268.

97. Joe I. Mendoza, interview by David G. García and Frank P. Barajas, March 26, 2010, Oxnard, CA.

98. Chester M. Pierce, "Poverty and Racism as They Affect Children," in *Advocacy for Child Mental Health,* edited by I. N. Berlin (New York: Brunner/Mazel, 1975), 92–109. Pierce also wrote about racial microaggressions being assaultive images aimed to belittle the social value of Blacks in society. See Chester M. Pierce, "Social Trace Contaminants: Subtle Indicators of Racism in TV," in *Television and Social Behavior: Beyond Violence and Children. A Report of the Committee on Television and Social Behavior, Social Science Research Council,* edited by S. B. Withey and R. P. Abeles (Hillsdale, NJ: Lawrence Erlbaum, 1980), 249–57.

99. Psychologist Grace Carroll extended Pierce's work to show how racial microaggressions cause extreme mundane environmental stress. Grace Carroll, *Environmental Stress and African Americans: The Other Side of the Moon* (Westport, CT: Praeger, 1998), 4.

100. Pierce, "Offensive Mechanisms," 268.

5. A COMMON CAUSE EMERGES FOR MEXICAN AMERICAN AND BLACK ORGANIZERS

Epigraph: Althea T. L. Simmons, "Voice of the People: On the School Problem," *The Press-Courier,* March 18, 1963, 8.

1. Ibid.

2. Ibid.

3. Ibid.

4. U.S. Bureau of the Census, *U.S. Census of the Population: 1950,* "California, Table 4. Population of Urban Places of 10,000 or More from the Earliest Census to 1950" (Washington, DC: U.S. Government Printing Office, 1950), 5–10; U.S. Bureau of the Census, *U.S. Census of Population: 1970,* "Table 96. General

Characteristics of Spanish Language or Spanish Surname for Areas and Places: 1970" (Washington, DC: U.S. Government Printing Office), sec. 6, 682. Most Mexicans were born in the United States; 5,507 were foreign born; and 18,818 were native (U.S. born). See also "Table 97. Social Characteristics of Persons of Spanish Language or Spanish Surname for Areas and Places: 1970," sec. 6, 689.

5. U.S. Bureau of the Census, *U.S. Census of Population: 1950*, vol. 2, part 5, "Characteristics of the Population: California," "Table 34. General Characteristics of the Population, for Standard Metropolitan Areas, Urbanized Areas, and Urban Places of 10,000 or More: 1950" (Washington, DC: U.S. Government Printing Office, 1950), sec. 5, 101.

6. Voters approved the bond to establish the port in 1937, and on March 9, 1942, it was appropriated under wartime powers to establish the Naval Advanced Base Depot. Ventura County hired more than ten thousand civilian workers and twenty-one thousand military personnel during the 1940s. *Downtown Oxnard Historic Resources Survey: Final Report* (Santa Paula, CA: San Buena Ventura Research Associates, July 2005), 15.

7. Juan Gómez-Quiñones, *Chicano Politics: Reality and Promise, 1940–1990* (Albuquerque: University of New Mexico Press, 1990).

8. Ibid. Mexican Americans comprised 34 percent; Blacks were 6 percent. See U.S. Bureau of the Census, *U.S. Census of Population: 1970*, "Table 96. General Characteristics of Spanish Language or Spanish Surname for Areas and Places: 1970" (Washington, DC: U.S. Government Printing Office, 1970), sec. 6, 682.

9. Chartered as the "Oxnard, California Branch of the NAACP." Correspondence from Ella J. Baker, Director of NAACP Branches, to Theodore R. O. Howard of Oxnard Negro Citizens Committee, March 15, 1945 (Library of Congress, Collection of the National Association for the Advancement of Colored People, Washington, DC, box C17, folder 6). On June 10, 1955, the organization was rechartered as the "Oxnard—Ventura County, California Branch." Memorandum to Miss Suyat from Miss Black, June 8, 1955 (Library of Congress, Collection of the National Association for the Advancement of Colored People, Washington, DC, box 2: C17, folder 6).

10. Leroy A. Gibson Jr., interview by David G. García, March 12, 2014, Oxnard, CA. As a musician, he also went by Buddy Gibson. Founded in 1919, St. Paul's Baptist Church was the first Black church in Ventura County. Tim Pompey, "St. Paul's Baptist Church Celebrates 96th Anniversary," *Tricounty Sentry* [Oxnard, CA], April 2, 2015, front page, http://tricountysentry.com/blog/st-paul-baptist-church-celebrates-96th-anniversary-2/. See also timeline written by Leola Samuel, church historian, m.spbcoxnard.org/about-us/ (retrieved May 10, 2016).

11. Leroy Jr.'s aunt, Cerisa House Wesley, appears to have been the first known African American baby born in the city of Ventura, in 1898. For some time, Cerisa, the oldest of seven siblings, was the only Black student at her elementary school. See Earl J. Carter, "The History of African Americans in Ventura County," in Yvette L. Sutton, *The One Percent Wall: A Retrospective Look at the Contributions of African Americans in Ventura County* [booklet] (Ventura, CA: VET Heritage Productions, 1993). On file with author.

12. Leroy A. Gibson Jr., interview by David G. García, March 12, 2014, Oxnard, CA.

13. "Letters to the Editor: Recreation Center," *Ventura County Star–Free Press,* October 17, 1944, editorial page.

14. Ibid.

15. Ibid.

16. "Colonia Folk Petition City Dads to Change City Dump," *The Oxnard Daily Courier,* June 22, 1922, front page.

17. Ibid.

18. "Letters to the Editor: Recreation Center," *Ventura County Star–Free Press,* October 17, 1944, editorial page.

19. Ibid.

20. "Prejudice in Oxnard Grows; Trouble Brews: Racial Tensions High in Oxnard," *Neighborhood News* [Los Angeles], March 21, 1946 (vol. 16, no. 9, front page) (Bancroft Library, Collection of the National Association for the Advancement of Colored People, Berkeley, CA, region 1, box 86, folder 11).

21. Ibid. "Jim Crow" is printed as one word in lowercase in the original.

22. Ibid.

23. "Four Ejected from Oxnard Theatre as Friction Grows," *California Eagle* [Los Angeles], April 4, 1946, 3 (Bancroft Library, Collection of the National Association for the Advancement of Colored People, Berkeley, CA, region 1, box 86, folder 11). See also https://archive.org/detals/caleagle (retrieved August 11, 2017).

24. Correspondence from Richard Abrams, NAACP Oxnard Branch, to Noel Griffin, NAACP Assistant Field Secretary, April 16, 1946 (Bancroft Library, Collection of the National Association for the Advancement of Colored People, Berkeley, CA, region 1, box 86, folder 11).

25. "Los Guardianes de la Colonia Is Active in Red Cross Drive," *Oxnard Press-Courier,* March 7, 1946, front page.

26. "Red Cross Makes Move for Better Housing Conditions," *The Oxnard Daily Courier,* October 27, 1920, front page, 2.

27. "City Council Will Get Plea to Pave Colonia," *Oxnard Press-Courier,* March 26, 1946, front page.

28. "Hinostro Urged to Get Petition," *Oxnard Press-Courier,* March 27, 1946, front page.

29. In addition to the more formal social and civic organizations, the Mexican community created mutual aid societies which served a number of functions, including providing loans in times of emergencies such as funerals or creating a savings program among community members. These groups were and continue to be an important resource for a community barred from public spaces, including banks. The community cultural wealth fostered among the residents of La Colonia was not just a mode of survival in a segregated city; it was also a way for individuals to prosper while helping their neighbors. Despite the forced relegation of Mexicans to the Colonia area, people did find ways to economically prosper within segregated space by starting their own businesses and recreating Mexican

traditions in the barrio. In her research on Los Angeles, Natalia Molina has examined restaurants in Echo Park, a residential community in Los Angeles, and argues they function "as social spaces that shape the neighborhoods in which they are located in ways that empower those who inhabit the surrounding area" (3). Focusing on these spaces, she reveals how "individuals and groups who do not work explicitly to subvert social norms can nonetheless be place-makers who leave a mark on the urban landscape for generations to come" (3). Natalia Molina, "The Importance of Place and Place-Makers in the Life of a Los Angeles Community: What Gentrification Erases from Echo Park," *Southern California Quarterly* 97, no. 1 (2015): 69–111. Molina's work helps me consider La Central Bakery, located on Meta Street in Oxnard, in the heart of where the Mexican community developed in close proximity to the beet sugar factory. It was originally established in Santa Paula in 1929 when Teofilio and Carmen Rodriquez arrived from Mexico. They relocated La Central to Meta Street in Oxnard in 1948, where it continues to be a mainstay in the city.

30. "Prejudice Discussion Scheduled April 21 at Juanita," *Oxnard Press-Courier,* April 12, 1958, 2.

31. Richard Lyttle, "The Largest Labor Camp in Nation in Oxnard," *Oxnard Press-Courier,* March 6, 1958, 11.

32. Fred Ross cofounded the CSO in East Los Angeles alongside Mexican American organizers and with funding from Saul Alinsky's Industrial Areas Foundation in 1947. Fred Ross, *Conquering Goliath: Cesar Chavez at the Beginning* (Keene, CA: El Taller Gráfica Press, 1989).

33. Gómez-Quiñones, *Chicano Politics,* 53.

34. Margaret Rose, "Gender and Civic Activism in Mexican American Barrios in California: The Community Service Organization, 1947–1962," in *Not June Cleaver: Women and Gender in Postwar America, 1945–1960,* edited by Joanne Meyerowitz (Philadelphia: Temple University Press, 1994), 177–200. For more on the CSO in Oxnard, see Louie Herrera Moreno III, "Labor, Migration, and Activism: A History of Mexican Workers on the Oxnard Plain, 1930–1980" (Ph.D. dissertation, Michigan State University, 2012).

35. Frank P. Barajas, *Curious Unions: Mexican American Workers and Resistance in Oxnard, California, 1898–1961* (Lincoln: University of Nebraska Press, 2012).

36. Ross, *Conquering Goliath.*

37. Julieta Flores Soria Mendoza, interview by David G. García, June 27, 2015, Oxnard, CA.

38. At the same time, the newspaper endorsed candidates with Elks Club and Rotary Club affiliations. "City Council Candidate John Soria Favors Oxnard-Hueneme Consolidation," *The Press-Courier,* March 25, 1960, 3; "Editorials: Tomorrow's Election in Oxnard," *The Press-Courier,* April 11, 1960, 18.

39. Julieta Flores Soria Mendoza, interview by David G. García, June 27, 2015, Oxnard, CA.

40. "Colonia Rebuilding Fight Vowed," *The Press-Courier,* December 1, 1961, front page, 20.

41. Ibid.

42. "U.S. Plan for Colonia: Nason Defends Redevelopment," *The Press-Courier*, December 20, 1961, 7. The CSO's opposition to federal funding for a redevelopment plan also led to its rejection of any city proposal to have a federally funded study of the housing problem in La Colonia. Working with the city-appointed Urban Development Committee, the CSO remained steadfast in placing responsibility for the situation on the city leaders from previous administrations, and requesting local solutions. "Urban Development Unit Rejects Colonia Study," *The Press-Courier*, December 22, 1961, front page.

43. A similarly troubling redevelopment plan had also occurred in nearby Los Angeles, where at least three thousand residents of three neighborhoods comprising an area called Chavez Ravine were permanently displaced after promises of a federal housing project. Despite vigorous, organized protest, the city claimed residents' private property as "eminent domain," for the public good, then canceled the project and ultimately gifted the land to the Dodger Corporation. The evictions of the last remaining families, complete with sheriff's deputies carrying out women to make way for a bulldozer to level their homes, were broadcast via live television in 1959. See Rodolfo F. Acuña, *A Community under Siege: A Chronicle of Chicanos East of the Los Angeles River, 1945–1975*, Monograph no. 11 (Chicano Studies Research Center Publications, University of California, Los Angeles, 1984); Eric Avila, *Popular Culture in the Age of White Flight: Fear and Fantasy in Suburban Los Angeles* (Berkeley: University of California Press, 2006); Ronald Lopez, "The Battle for Chavez Ravine: Public Policy and Chicano Community Resistance in Postwar Los Angeles, 1945–1962" (Ph.D. dissertation, University of California, Berkeley, 1999).

44. Brett Johnson, "Ode to a Neighborhood: Memories of Tortilla Flats Burn Bright at the Museum of Ventura County," *Ventura County Star*, November 1, 2013, 18, 20.

45. Leroy A. Gibson Jr., interview by David G. García, March 12, 2014, Oxnard, CA.

46. "Editorials: Get to the Program," *The Press-Courier*, December 26, 1961, 18.

47. In 1963, a small business owner in La Colonia, Ernesto V. Cen, expressed resentment that city officials, who neglected Colonia as a "mud wallow" until the end of World War II, continued their disrespect for community residents even in their plans for redevelopment. His remarks came in one of a series of articles initiated by an urban renewal plan to destroy seven hundred homes east of the railroad tracks. Don W. Martin, "Long-Time Colonia Resident Is Bitter," *The Press-Courier*, July 20, 1963, 4.

48. "Howlett Urges Slow Approach to Colonia Problem," *The Press-Courier*, January 9, 1962, front page.

49. For example, "Mexicans Assist City Officers," *The Oxnard Daily Courier*, November 12, 1918, front page.

50. "Colonia Home Repairs OK'd," *The Press-Courier*, January 10, 1962, front page, 32.

51. Ibid. See also "Colonia to Begin Cleanup," *The Press-Courier*, January 20, 1962, 32.

52. "City Names New Park for Edwin L. Carty," *The Press-Courier*, January 20, 1962, 32.

53. Ibid.

54. "CSO Blasts Small-Lot Colonia Tract," *The Press-Courier,* February 7, 1962, 3; "Council Voids $6 Million Colonia Plan," *The Press-Courier,* March 14, 1962, 3; "CSO Warns of Colonia Speculators," *The Press-Courier,* March 14, 1962, 11; "CSO Offers Plan for Colonia," *The Press-Courier,* August 29, 1962, 3.

55. "CSO Official Blasts City Policy in Colonia," *The Press-Courier,* October 31, 1962, 36.

56. Ibid. See also "CSO Blasts Small-Lot Colonia Tract," *The Press-Courier,* February 7, 1962, 3.

57. John R. Hatcher III, interview by David G. García, January 27, 2015, Oxnard, CA.

58. Ibid.

59. Joanne Hatcher, interview by David G. García, January 27, 2015, Oxnard, CA.

60. Ibid.

61. John R. Hatcher III, interview by David G. García, January 27, 2015, Oxnard, CA.

62. Albert G. Duff, interview by David G. García and Frank P. Barajas, June 14, 2010, Oxnard, CA.

63. Margaret Tatum Potter, interview with David G. García, February 9, 2015, Oxnard, CA.

64. Ibid.

65. Ibid.

66. William L. Terry, interview by David G. García and Frank P. Barajas, May 8, 2010, Oxnard, CA.

67. Margaret Tatum Potter, interview by David G. García, February 9, 2015, Oxnard, CA.

68. Ibid. At different points in time, Margaret's sister worked as a waitress and Leroy Gibson Jr. performed at the Colonial House.

69. Ibid.

70. Mexie Duff, interview by David G. García and Frank P. Barajas, June 14, 2010, Oxnard, CA. Scholars have pointed out that W. E. B. DuBois publicly shared his optimistic, yet contradictory, feelings about Southern California in particular, writing: "One never forgets Los Angeles and Pasadena: the sensuous beauty of roses and orange blossoms, the air and the sunlight, and the hospitality of all races lingers long. . . . To be sure, Los Angeles is not Paradise, much as the sight of lilies and roses might lead one at first to believe. The color line is there and sharply drawn" (192–94). W. E. B. DuBois, "Colored California," *The Crisis* (August 1913): 192–96. William Deverell explains that cultural productions and practices of historical erasure in the 1800s helped to manufacture such a positive, albeit distorted view. William Deverell, *Whitewashed Adobe: The Rise of Los Angeles and the Remaking of Its Mexican Past* (Berkeley: University of California Press, 2004).

71. The board began closing parts of Wilson in 1958. Oxnard School Board of Trustees (OSBT) meeting minutes, December 3, 1958, 113. The Oxnard School Dis-

trict holds a microfilm copy of the board of trustees meeting minutes for the years before 1939, and a hard copy of the minutes after 1939, organized in binders by year and paginated.

72. "Fremont School Opens Doors to 600 Oxnard Students Next Month," *The Press-Courier*, August 17, 1961, 20.

73. "'Minority Races' in Majority among Oxnard District Elementary Students," *The Press-Courier*, March 13, 1963, 5.

74. The newspaper listed twenty "New Subdivisions," twelve "certain" developments and eight "probable," and pictured each on a map adjacent to this article. Ralph Kaminsky, "Oxnard Students Face Increasing School Shuffle," *The Press-Courier*, April 5, 1962, 21.

75. "Segregation Ruling Doesn't Apply to New Colonia School, Board Agrees," *The Press-Courier*, November 21, 1962, front page.

76. Ibid.

77. Ibid.

78. Ibid.

79. Ibid.

80. Ibid.

81. "It Costs $5,000 for 305 Pupils to Ride to School: $3.2 Million Bond Issue Could Cut Need for Bus Services to Colonia," *The Press-Courier*, January 8, 1963, 6.

82. Ibid.

83. Ibid.

84. Ibid.

85. Ibid.

86. Ibid.

87. As discussed in chapter 4, trustees approved Ramona's construction to alleviate "cramed [*sic*] conditions" at Roosevelt, and to avoid the "hazard" of children having to cross the boulevard and railroad tracks to and from school. OSBT meeting minutes, June 27, 1939.

88. "Mexican Costs Are Too High Says Co. Head," *The Oxnard Daily Courier*, January 31, 1928, front page.

89. "50 Join Committee Backing School Bonds," *The Press-Courier*, January 9, 1963, 3. Reach also wrote an editorial thanking the paper for "fair and accurate coverage of the issues in the coming election," and noting, "It is far more important to put a school where the kids are than to worry about possible discrimination." "Voice of the People: Bonds Are a Must," *The Press-Courier*, January 18, 1963, 8. Reach declared his candidacy for the Oxnard School Board of Trustees the day the bonds election results were announced, and *The Press-Courier* published his picture and accompanying story as front-page news. "Dr. Reach to Run for School Board," *The Press-Courier*, January 23, 1963, front page.

90. "50 Join Committee Backing School Bonds," *The Press-Courier*, January 9, 1963, 3.

91. "NAACP, CSO, to Meet to Air Bond Issue Stand," *The Press-Courier*, January 16, 1963, 33.

92. Ibid.

93. "Principals Fail to Sway CSO Opposition to School Bonds," *The Press-Courier*, January 18, 1963, front page, 20.

94. Ibid.

95. See discussion of his thesis in chapter 4. Domingo Martinez, "A Comparative Study of the Academic Achievement of the Mexican-American Students in the Wilson Junior High School, Oxnard, California" (master's thesis, Claremont Graduate School, Claremont, CA, 1956).

96. "Principals Fail to Sway CSO Opposition to School Bonds," *The Press-Courier*, January 18, 1963, front page.

97. Ibid., 20.

98. Ibid.

99. "NAACP Joins Foes of Bonds," *The Press-Courier*, January 18, 1963, front page.

100. Ibid.

101. "Principals Fail to Sway CSO Opposition to School Bonds," *The Press-Courier*, January 18, 1963, front page.

102. "CSO Fights Colonia School: Weekend Anti-bond Drive Launched," *The Press-Courier*, January 19, 1963, front page.

103. "CSO Officers Live outside Colonia Area," *The Press-Courier*, January 19, 1963, front page.

104. Ibid.

105. "Editorials: A Sorry Mistake," *The Press-Courier*, January 19, 1963, 6.

106. "School Board Head Replies to Foes of Bond Issue," *The Press-Courier*, January 19, 1963, 9.

107. Ibid.

108. Two Southern California cases in particular were being argued, decided, or filed in 1963: *Jackson v. Pasadena City School District*, 382 P.2d 878 (1963); *Crawford v. Board of Education of the City of Los Angeles*, 458 U.S. 527 (1982). *Crawford* was filed in 1963.

109. "Voting Brisk on Elementary School Bonds," *The Press-Courier*, January 22, 1963, front page.

110. Ibid., 14.

111. "Editorials: A Very Important Vote," *The Press-Courier*, January 22, 1963, 6.

112. Ibid.

113. "Bonds Win Heavily; New Schools Rushed," *The Press-Courier*, January 23, 1963, front page. The articles under this front-page banner headline included "District to Push Construction Plans," front page, 3; "Dr. Reach to Run for School Board," front page; "Tale of Two Elections: Voting in Each Precinct," front page; Ralph Kaminsky, "71.9% Vote 'Yes' in Third Election Try," front page.

114. See table under heading "Tale of Two Elections: Voting in Each Precinct," front page; see reporting on table in Ralph Kaminsky, "71.9% Vote 'Yes' in Third Election Try," *The Press-Courier*, January 23, 1963, front page. When the vote counts were officially reconciled the following week, the actual number came out to slightly

above 72 percent. "Oxnard Board Seeks Answer from State: Colonia Area School May Violate Law," *The Press-Courier,* January 30, 1963, front page.

115. "A Heartening Victory," *The Press-Courier,* January 25, 1963, 8.

116. "NAACP Wants Hearing on School Issue," *The Press-Courier,* January 28, 1963, front page.

117. "Segregation Ruling Doesn't Apply to New Colonia School, Board Agrees," *The Press-Courier,* November 21, 1962, front page.

118. "Colonia Area School May Violate Law: Oxnard Seeks Answer from State," *The Press-Courier,* January 30, 1963, front page.

119. "School Board Head Replies to Foes of Bond Issue," *The Press-Courier,* January 19, 1963, 9.

120. "Segregation Ruling Doesn't Apply to New Colonia School, Board Agrees," *The Press-Courier,* November 21, 1962, front page.

121. "Colonia Area School May Violate Law: Oxnard Seeks Answer from State," *The Press-Courier,* January 30, 1963, front page.

122. Ibid. See also OSBT meeting minutes, January 29, 1963, 136–37.

123. "Colonia School May Break Rule, State Says: District Studies Segregation Claim," *The Press-Courier,* February 6, 1963, front page.

124. Ibid.

125. "Oxnard School Board Chief Says NAACP Has 'Point': Colonia Segregation Issue," *The Press-Courier,* February 7, 1963, 3.

126. Ibid.

127. In an editorial, Davis expressed "sincere appreciation" to the newspaper for presenting "clearly and fairly the issues and problems involved in this election." "Voice of the People: Service," *The Press-Courier,* January 22, 1963, 6.

128. Ibid.

129. OSBT meeting minutes, February 5, 1963, 143.

130. "Oxnard School Board Chief Says NAACP Has 'Point': Colonia Segregation Issue," *The Press-Courier,* February 7, 1963, 3. See also OSBT meeting minutes, February 5, 1963, 142–43. According to summaries of two oral histories with John W. Mack, he went on to become the executive director of the Urban League in Flint, Michigan, in 1964, and served as the president of the Urban League in Los Angeles from 1969 to 2005, www.thehistorymakers.com/biography/john-w-mack-41 (retrieved June 23, 2016).

131. "Colonia School May Break Rule, State Says: District Studies Segregation Claim," *The Press-Courier,* February 6, 1963, front page.

132. Ibid. Emphasis added.

133. "Report by Althea T. L. Simmons, Field Secretary, Southern and Southwest Areas. West Coast Region. Period covered by report: September 15 to October 14, 1963," 4 (Library of Congress, Collection of the National Association for the Advancement of Colored People, Washington, DC, box 3: C308, folder 3).

134. OSBT meeting minutes, March 5, 1963, 167–68. See also Ralph Kaminsky, "Juggling Schools Urged to Mix Races: 'Anti-segregation' Plan Faces Study," *The Press-Courier,* March 6, 1963, front page.

135. OSBT meeting minutes, April 30, 1963, 215–19.

136. "Report by Althea T. L. Simmons, Field Secretary, Southern and Southwest Areas. West Coast Region. Period covered by report: May 15 to June 14, 1963," 1, 5 (Library of Congress, Collection of the National Association for the Advancement of Colored People, Washington, DC, box 3: C307, folder 5).

137. "'Minority Races' in Majority among Oxnard District Elementary Students," *The Press-Courier,* March 13, 1963, 5.

138. It remains unclear why, despite the specificity of racial covenants restricting Japanese and Chinese occupancy across the west side, most Asian residents seem to have had their children attending schools and enrolled in classes alongside Whites (see note on this contradiction in residential covenants in chapter 2, n75). The small numbers of Asians, relative to Mexicans or Blacks, may have been a contributing factor to this educational access. For instance, Asians comprised less than 0.9 percent of the city's population in 1950 (there were only 160 Japanese and 29 Chinese residents). See U.S. Bureau of the Census, *U.S. Census of Population: 1950,* "Table 47. Indians, Japanese, and Chinese, by Sex, for Selected Counties and Cities: 1950" (Washington, DC: U.S. Government Printing Office, 1950), 5–179. Over the course of the 1960s, the number of Filipinos living in Oxnard increased, and eventually they were granted their own label in ethnic group distribution charts put out by the district; but Japanese remained the largest subgroup of the Asian population even in 1970. The 1970 U.S. Census counted 1,101 Japanese, 176 Chinese, 591 Filipino, 312 Indian, and 1,176 "all other" nonwhite races in Oxnard (the latter was a new category as of 1970). U.S. Bureau of the Census, *U.S. Census of Population: 1970,* vol. 1, part 6, "California, Section 1. Chapter B. General Population Statistics California," "Table 23. Race by Sex, for Areas and Places: 1970" (Washington, DC: U.S. Government Printing Office, 1970), 6–101.

139. "Editorials: Oxnard Schools and the NAACP," *The Press-Courier,* March 8, 1963, 8.

140. Ibid.

141. Ibid.

142. Ibid.

143. Althea T. L. Simmons, "Voice of the People: On the School Problem," *The Press-Courier,* March 18, 1963, 8.

144. Ibid.

145. Ibid.

146. *Brown v. Board of Education,* 347 U.S. 483 (1954).

147. "Segregation Ruling Doesn't Apply to New Colonia School, Board Agrees," *The Press-Courier,* November 21, 1962, front page.

148. Althea T. L. Simmons, "Voice of the People: On the School Problem," *The Press-Courier,* March 18, 1963, 8.

149. Ibid.

150. Ibid. There was legal precedent for her assertion regarding categorizing Mexican Americans as a "minority group," but in 1963 there was not yet a desegregation case decided at the federal or U.S. Supreme Court level where Mexican Americans

were named as non-White. In *Hernandez v. Texas*, 1954, the U.S. Supreme Court had ruled that Mexican Americans were "a class apart" from Whites, but not quite non-White. They were, in the Court's eyes, "other White." *Hernandez v. Texas*, 347 U.S. 475 (1954). See Michael A. Olivas, ed., *"Colored Men" and "Hombres Aquí": Hernández v. Texas and the Emergence of Mexican-American Lawyering* (Houston: Arte Público Press, 2006). Even this category was inconsistently applied across branches of the federal government and in particular in school segregation law. Guadalupe San Miguel Jr. discusses this in a Texas desegregation case (*Ross v. Eckels*) filed on behalf of Black students in 1956 and ruled on in 1970, wherein the judge ordered integration of Mexican Americans with Blacks, claiming the Mexican Americans were legally White. *Ross v. Eckels*, 317 F. Supp. 512 (S.D. Tex. 1970). See Guadalupe San Miguel Jr., *Brown, Not White: School Integration and the Chicano Movement in Houston* (College Station: Texas A&M University Press, 2001). *Cisneros v. Corpus Christi*, ruled on in 1970, marked the first district court case to extend *Brown* to Mexican Americans and recognize Mexican Americans as an "identifiable ethnic minority." *Cisneros v. Corpus Christi Independent School District*, 324 F. Supp. 599 (S.D. Tex. 1970). The *Keyes v. School District No. 1, Denver, Colorado* case, decided in 1973, is considered the first U.S. Supreme Court case to recognize Mexican Americans as non-White for the purposes of desegregation. See further discussion of *Keyes* in relation to *Soria v. Oxnard School Board of Trustees* in the introduction, n21.

151. Ibid.

152. "Editorials: There Is No Deep South Bias Here," *The Press-Courier*, March 18, 1963, 8.

153. Ibid.

154. Ibid.

155. Ibid.

156. "D.A. Ruling Backs Plan for Colonia Area School: Board Advised to Study Race Issue," *The Press-Courier*, April 3, 1963, front page.

157. Ibid.

158. Ibid.

159. Ibid.

160. In drafting the ruling known as Brown II, Chief Justice Warren wrote, "Decrees in conformity with this decree shall be prepared and issued forthwith by the lower courts," but after conferencing with the other justices he edited his text, changing "forthwith," to "with all deliberate speed." *Brown v. Board of Education*, 349 U.S. 294 (1955), 299. Historian Charles M. Wollenberg writes about how some California school districts questioned the implications of this phrase in the decade after *Brown*: "Was this an order for immediate school integration, integration as soon as was practical, or gradual, evolutionary integration?" Charles M. Wollenberg, *All Deliberate Speed: Segregation and Exclusion in California Schools, 1855–1975* (Berkeley: University of California Press, 1976), 137.

161. OSBT meeting minutes, April 30, 1963, 213–23.

162. Ralph Kaminsky, "Citizens Split over Colonia School: Segregation, Area Boundary Debated," *The Press-Courier*, May 1, 1963, front page, 39.

163. OSBT meeting minutes, April 30, 1963, 216.

164. Ralph Kaminsky, "Citizens Split over Colonia School Segregation, Area Boundary Debated," *The Press-Courier*, May 1, 1963, front page, 39.

165. Ibid.

166. Ibid.

167. Ibid.

168. "Board 'Kills' Colonia School Plan: Segregation Controversy 'Settled,'" *The Press-Courier*, May 22, 1963, front page.

169. Ibid.

170. Ibid.

171. Ibid.

172. Ibid. The meeting minutes refer to this discussion being informed by various prepared statements, which were not found in the archives. Although the discussion was not recorded in the available meeting minutes, the outcome was noted: "There appeared to be general agreement that a junior high should not be built on the Culbert site at this time." OSBT meeting minutes, May 21, 1963, 239.

173. OSBT meeting minutes, June 24, 1963, 263.

174. Chuck Andrews, "Mass Meeting Told No New Junior High: New Grade School Eyed in Colonia," *The Press-Courier*, June 25, 1963, front page.

175. Ibid.

176. OSBT meeting minutes, June 24, 1963, 263. A handwritten note next to the strikeout referenced an attached (unnumbered) page, which included the revised wording and the directive, "See minutes of August 6, 1963, page 16, for correction."

177. Ibid.

178. *Jackson v. Pasadena City School District*, 382 Cal.2d 876 (Cal. 1963).

179. Ibid., 880.

180. "Board 'Kills' Colonia School Plan: Segregation Controversy 'Settled,'" *The Press-Courier*, May 22, 1963, front page.

181. Hank Spier, "Pfeiler Questions Court Decision Outlawing School Segregation," *The Press-Courier*, September 18, 1963, 5.

182. Ibid.

183. Ibid.

184. Ibid. Trustee Kane stood out as disagreeing with his colleagues, noting, "When 95 percent of one school is Mexican-American and Negro, it's de facto segregation and de facto segregation is evil."

185. Ibid.

186. Ibid.

187. Ibid.

188. The *Los Angeles Times* had also covered the September forum but made no mention of the trustees' individual remarks. Instead, the brief story explained, "Oxnard—School officials here will ask the State Commission on Equal Educational Opportunities to investigate what Negro leaders claim is de facto segregation of two elementary schools." "Segregation Probe Asked at Oxnard," *Los Angeles Times*, September 19, 1963, 26.

189. William L. Terry, interview by David G. Garcia and Frank P. Barajas, May 8, 2010, Oxnard, CA.

190. OSBT meeting minutes, October 8, 1963, 77.

191. "Report by Althea T. L. Simmons, Field Secretary, Southern and Southwest Areas, West Coast Region. Period covered by report: September 15 to October 14, 1963," 4 (Library of Congress, Collection of the National Association for the Advancement of Colored People, Washington, DC, box 3: C308, folder 3).

192. In November, Richard Zanders left the NAACP to form a local chapter of the Congress for Racial Equality (CORE) of at least 150 members, and together they threatened aggressive action to force school integration. "Schools Involved: Negro Group Demands Oxnard Integration," *Ventura County Star–Free Press,* November 2, 1963, front page; "Oxnard School Evades Face-to-Face Race Talk," *Ventura County Star–Free Press,* November 6, 1963, B1; "Racial Leader to Protest at Next Oxnard School Meet," *Ventura County Star–Free Press,* November 7, 1963, C4; "'Study-In' Threatened in Oxnard," *Ventura County Star–Free Press,* November 20, 1963, A8; "NAACP Counsel to Give Talk," *Ventura County Star–Free Press,* November 22, 1963, B1; "CORE Gets an Official School Reply," *Ventura County Star–Free Press,* November 29, 1963, B2; "CORE Cancels 'Study-In,'" *Ventura County Star–Free Press,* December 9, 1963, A4; "Trustees Move to End de Facto Segregation," *Ventura County Star–Free Press,* December 11, 1963, front page, A2.

193. Correspondence to Lucille Black, membership Chairman from May L. Davis, Secretary, Oxnard Ventura Branch of the NAACP, October 22, 1965 (Library of Congress, Collection of the National Association for the Advancement of Colored People, Washington, DC, box 3: C10, folder 4).

194. Don W. Martin, "A Man's Passion for Freedom," *PC: The Weekly Magazine of Ventura County,* August 8, 1964, 3.

195. Albert G. Duff, interview by David G. García and Frank P. Barajas, June 14, 2010, Oxnard, CA.

196. Mexie Duff, interview by David G. García and Frank P. Barajas, June 14, 2010, Oxnard, CA.

6. CHALLENGING "A SYSTEMATIC SCHEME OF
RACIAL SEGREGATION"

Epigraphs: (*The Oxnard City Council . . .*) Ron Hosie, "'Perpetuate Segregation': Council, Schools Blasted by MAPA [Mexican American Political Association]," *The Press-Courier,* January 23, 1968, front page. The newspaper referred to Juan Soria as John Soria. (*Segregation has existed . . .*) "Voice of the People: School Desegregation 'Contamination' Theory Hit," *The Press-Courier,* May 6, 1969, 4.

1. Gerhard W. Orthuber, interview by David G. García and Tara J. Yosso, May 4, 2010, Oxnard, CA.

2. Following the records where individual names are listed, I found examples of participation in different community organizations and school/civic committees simultaneously, and a continuity of advocacy over time.

3. For example, Catalina Frazier Soria, Juan's second wife, recalled working with Gary Orthuber during the early stages of conceptualizing the case. She and Fred (Frederick C.) Jones of the NAACP played a key role in organizing the plaintiffs. Catalina and her son, David Frazier, were also named as plaintiffs. Catalina Frazier Soria, interview by David G. García and Tara J. Yosso, May 5, 2010, Newhall, CA.

4. Oxnard School Board of Trustees (OSBT) meeting minutes, December 16, 1969, 113–14.

5. OSBT meeting minutes, February 3, 1970, 138.

6. Gerhard W. Orthuber, interview by David G. García and Tara J. Yosso, May 4, 2010, Oxnard, CA.

7. *Alexander v. Holmes County Board of Education*, 396 U.S. 19 (1969).

8. Matthew F. Delmont, *Why Busing Failed: Race, Media, and the National Resistance to School Desegregation* (Berkeley: University of California Press, 2016), 100–110.

9. "U.S. Officials Concerned about de Facto Segregation in North, West," *Santa Cruz Sentinel*, December 23, 1969, 12; "De Facto Segregation Situation under Attack," *Bakersfield Californian*, December 23, 1969, 8.

10. Delmont, *Why Busing Failed*, 123–24.

11. Complaint for Injunctive and Declaratory Relief for Deprivation of Plaintiff's Rights to Equal Protection of the Laws and Due Process of Law, United States District Court for the Central District of California, Civ. No. 70–396-HP, filed February 20, 1970. Document submitted by Legal Service Center of Ventura County, Estes, Orthuber, Bosshard & Cohen. Signed by Attorneys for Plaintiffs with two signature lines for Gerhard W. Orthuber and Michael Arthur Cohen. Orthuber's typed name and signature were lined-out by hand. Cohen initialed the strike-through. Oxnard School District Archives, microfilm roll 262.

12. Ronald J. Ostrow, "U.S. Tests Busing Ban in Oxnard School Case: Defends New Law in Court for First Time; High Justice Aid to Join S.F. Hearings," *Los Angeles Times*, August 8, 1972, A3; John Willson, "Busing Test: As Oxnard Goes So Goes Nation," *Ventura County Star–Free Press*, August 8, 1972, front page, A8; Helen Reynolds, "Issue of Busing Propels Oxnard into Spotlight," *The Press-Courier*, August 9, 1972, front page, 2.

13. See, for example, Mario T. García and Sal Castro, *Blowout: Sal Castro and the Chicano Struggle for Educational Justice* (Charlotte: University of North Carolina Press, 2014); Juan Gómez-Quiñones and Irene Vásquez, *Making Aztlán: Ideology and Culture of the Chicana and Chicano Movement, 1966–1977* (Albuquerque: University of New Mexico Press, 2014); Louie Herrera Moreno III, "Labor, Migration, and Activism: A History of Mexican Workers on the Oxnard Plain, 1930–1980" (Ph.D. dissertation, Michigan State University, 2012); Laura Pulido, *Black, Brown, Yellow, and Left: Radical Activism in Los Angeles* (Berkeley: University of California Press, 2006).

14. OSBT meeting minutes, October 8, 1963, 77.

15. Quote discussed in chapter 5 by trustee Henry Muller. "Segregation Doesn't Apply to New Colonia School, Board Agrees," *The Press-Courier,* November 21, 1962, front page.

16. Helen Frost, *102 Year History of Oxnard School District,* [pamphlet] (Oxnard, CA, 1975). On file with author.

17. "Ethnic Group Distribution, Oxnard School District, 1965–66" (Oxnard School District Archives, microfilm roll 393). Enrollment information released to court as part of Interrogatories Installments I 52a and II. The original 1966 document header on the right of the page noted, "This Information Will Be Held in a Confidential Manner." See also Interrogatories Installment II, No. 26 (Oxnard School District Archives, microfilm roll 393). In January 1964, the district adopted an "open enrollment" policy, but lack of space was the most common reason for denying student petitions to transfer out of their neighborhood school. Many of these details, including school opening dates and enrollment percentages before and after busing, are detailed in the Appeal from the United States District Court for the Central District of California, Case No. 71–2929, Before: CHOY and GOODWIN, Circuit Judges, and McNICHOLS, District Judge, November 27, 1973, 3–5 (in folder 71–2929, *Oxnard School District et al. v. Debbie;* obtained from the office of Judge Harry Pregerson). See also copy of appeal in binder on *Debbie and Doreen Soria et al. v. Oxnard School District Board of Trustees et al.,* United States District Court, Central District of California, Civ. No. 70–396-HP (Chronology of Events, Oxnard School District Archives). See also *Soria v. Oxnard School Board of Trustees,* 488 F.2d 579 U.S. App. 586 (November 27, 1973).

18. Frost, *102 Year History of Oxnard School District.*

19. "Ethnic Group Distribution, Oxnard School District, 1965–66." Rose Avenue's enrollments changed more significantly than the other two east-side schools in the years but remained unbalanced. By the fall of 1970, Whites comprised 19 percent while Mexican Americans and Blacks together made up 80 percent. "Ethnic Distribution of Students before and after Busing," March 26, 1971, Interrogatory Installment I, Question no. 11, 5 (Oxnard School District Archives, microfilm roll 393).

20. Frost, *102 Year History of Oxnard School District,* 1975.

21. Sierra Linda's enrollments became increasingly White over time and looked like the inverse of Rose Avenue, so that by the fall of 1970 Whites comprised 83 percent while Mexican Americans and Blacks together made up 12 percent. "Ethnic Distribution of Students before and after Busing," March 26, 1971, Interrogatory Installment I, Question no. 11, 5 (Oxnard School District Archives, microfilm roll 393).

22. "Oxnard School Leaders Ponder de Facto Segregation Solutions," *Ventura County Star–Free Press,* October 2, 1968 (Integration/Desegregation 1968, binder 1, Oxnard School District Archives).

23. Ibid.

24. "Improving Racial and Ethnic Balance and Intergroup Relations: An Advisory Report to the Board of Trustees Oxnard School District" (California State

Department of Education, Division of Compensatory Education, Bureau of Intergroup Relations, April 1969) (Oxnard School District Archives, microfilm).

25. Ibid., 13. They cited *Mendez v. Westminster,* 1947; *Brown v. Board,* 1954; *Jackson v. Pasadena,* 1963. The bureau acknowledged that many of the studies about integration had focused on Black children in relation to Whites, but asserted they identified many similarities in the schooling of Mexican Americans. It remains unclear if they further discuss these issues because the microfilm version of the report recovered from the Oxnard School District Archives is missing pages 16 through 43. According to the table of contents, within the "Improving Intergroup Relations" section, there are about four pages dedicated to "Color-blind" or "Color-conscious."

26. Ibid., 14–15.

27. Ibid., 15.

28. Ibid., 44. The bureau simultaneously recommended "a program of master planning by the district staff in terms of the long-range educational, housing, and financial needs of the district."

29. Ibid., 46. It is striking that in the section on "Dissemination of this report," the bureau "recommended that the superintendent arrange for translation of this report, or a comprehensive summary, into Spanish."

30. OSBT meeting minutes, April 29, 1969, 147–49. As noted in the minutes, two representatives of the bureau introduced the report: Eugene S. Mornell and J. Charles Molina.

31. John Willson, "Oxnard School Board Cautious on Plans to Cure Segregation," *Ventura County Star–Free Press,* April 30, 1969, front page, A7.

32. Ibid.

33. Henry J. Johnson, "Busing Pupils Would Result in 'Cultural Contamination,'" *The Press-Courier,* April 30, 1969, 4.

34. Ibid.

35. William (and Margaret) Thrasher, "Racist Society Must Change; School Integration Is Start," *The Press-Courier,* Sunday, May 4, 1969, 4. The original editorial is signed with his wife Margaret's name in parenthesis, though the text makes first-person-singular statements (e.g., "I am sure that as Mr. Johnson says, there are many others who feel the way he does about white superiority"). William Thrasher worked as a history teacher at Oxnard High School and later at Oxnard College.

36. "Voice of the People: School Desegregation 'Contamination' Theory Hit," *The Press-Courier,* April 30, 1969, 4.

37. Ibid. They gave an example of the error in conducting evaluations for Spanish-speaking children in English: "This is one of the faults of the white community, the fact that we base the ability and intelligence of non-whites on their capacity to score on tests."

38. Ibid.

39. Ibid.

40. "Voice of the People: Johnson Theory Disputed," *The Press-Courier,* May 6, 1969, 4.

41. "School Busing Study Shelved until Fall," *The Press-Courier,* June 4, 1969, front page, 2. See also reference to the plans in OSBT meeting minutes, June 3, 1969, 173–74.

42. "Alternative Plans for the Elimination of de Facto Segregation in the Oxnard School District, June 1969" (Oxnard School District Archives, microfilm roll 393). This is a six-page document dated June 3, 1969, which became part of court interrogatories. Each of the twelve alternatives had an accompanying note describing "Best Features" and "Worst Features." For example, alternative 10:

> Redraw all attendance boundaries in the district using a corridor attendance boundary plan as opposed to the more traditional rectangle around a neighborhood school. *Best Features:* Maximum ethnic balance is possible with this plan with the inconvenience shared equally by all sectors of the city. It would be unnecessary for youngsters to move from any given K-6 school once they were originally assigned to that school. *Worst Features:* Maximum dislocation of pupils and extensive transportation for a large number of children. Cost of massive transportation program would be borne indefinitely. (5)

43. "School Busing Study Shelved until Fall," *The Press-Courier,* June 4, 1969, 2. Pfeiler also offered condescending proposals such as ensuring "racially balanced classes" for studying "health and American culture" and suggested the district initiate programming that "proclaimed a war on low achievement," such as requiring underperforming students to attend a summer school session exclusively offered on the east side.

44. Ibid. See also OSBT meeting minutes, June 3, 1969, 174. "Lengthy discussion of the various alternative plans was held. At the conclusion of this discussion, the superintendent was directed to postpone further consideration of this matter until fall."

45. "Oxnard Segregation Issue Boils Anew," *Ventura County Star–Free Press,* September 17, 1969, A2.

46. Ibid.

47. Ibid.

48. "NAACP Head Urges Action on School Racial Imbalance," *The Press-Courier,* September 17, 1969, front page.

49. "School Segregation Talk Asked by State," *The Press-Courier,* September 22, 1969, 2.

50. Ibid.

51. Ibid.

52. OSBT meeting minutes, October 7, 1969, 55.

53. "School Trustees to Study Desegregation," *The Press-Courier,* October 8, 1969, front page.

54. "Oxnard Trustees to Hear de Facto Segregation Issue," *Ventura County Star–Free Press,* October 20, 1969, B1; "De Facto Segregation to Be Aired," *The Press-Courier,* October 21, 1969, front page.

55. Ned MacKay, "Trustees Take 2 Views of School Integration," *The Press-Courier,* October 22, 1969, front page, 2.

56. Ibid., front page.

57. Ibid., 2.

58. Ibid., front page.

59. Some of these letters are acknowledged in OSBT meeting minutes, December 2, 1969, 100.

60. This became Proposition 21, which passed in 1972 with 63 percent of the vote. The NAACP filed a lawsuit to challenge the initiative, and in 1975 the California Supreme Court ruled the operation components, namely the prohibition of school assignment by race, color, or creed, was in violation of state and federal laws. See Daniel Martinez HoSang, *Racial Propositions: Ballot Initiatives and the Making of Postwar California* (Berkeley: University of California Press, 2010), 91–105.

61. "325,173 Signatures Sought to Battle Integration by Bus," *The Press-Courier,* October 18, 1969, 13; "Oxnard Chairman Selected in Busing Initiative Drive," *Ventura County Star–Free Press,* October 19, 1969, A4. See also banner headline, "Petition Prays Parental Consent: Busing Plea Splits Legislators," on same page as small article, "De Facto Segregation to Be Aired," *The Press-Courier,* October 21, 1969, 11.

62. John C. Waugh, "White House Defends Desegregation Rate," *Christian Science Monitor,* October 29, 1969, 6; "No Instant End to Segregation— Government," *Ventura County Star–Free Press,* October 31, 1969, B7.

63. Richard L. Strout, "School Integration Milestone: Burger Court Strengthens 1954 Decision of Warren Court; Nixon Plan Demolished," *Christian Science Monitor,* October 31, 1969, front page, 11 (Integration/Desegregation 1969–70, binder 3, Oxnard School District Archives). See also "Finch Hints Use of Edict to Integrate," *The Press-Courier,* October 31, 1969, 2.

64. See editorial letter from Eleanore Schire, president of the Oxnard Branch of the American Association of University Women, "Voice of the People: Positive Action Urged," *The Press-Courier,* October 31, 1969, 4. See also John Willson, "Women Voters Attack School Segregation," *Ventura County Star–Free Press,* October 16, 1968, E5.

65. Cloene I. Marson, "Voice of the People: Supports Integration," *The Press-Courier,* November 1, 1969, 8.

66. Ibid.

67. Christine E. Kennedy, "Voice of the People: Integration Setting Urged," *The Press-Courier,* November 2, 1969, 4.

68. Ibid.

69. "Oxnard School Trustees Nearly 'Stab' State over Segregation Issue," *Ventura County Star–Free Press,* November 5, 1969, B1. See also observations by reporter John Willson: "Threats of a lawsuit are enough to make many an obdurate man humble, but trustees of the Oxnard Elementary School District do not seem overly concerned by the possibility that the state attorney general's office may bring suit against them for failing to eradicate the de facto segregation in several district schools." John Willson, "De Facto Segregation: The Rush to Delay in Oxnard Schools," *Ventura County Star–Free Press,* November 16, 1969, C8.

70. "NAACP Flays Oxnard Delay in Integration," *Ventura County Star–Free Press,* December 3, 1969, front page; "NAACP Marches for Desegregation," *The Press-Courier,* December 3, 1969, front page, 2.

71. These letters were dated from November 1969 through early January 1970, and a partial list included the NAACP, the American Civil Liberties Union, the Association of Mexican American Educators, the American Association of University Women, Citizens Compensatory Education Advisory Committee, Human Relations Advisory Commission (County of Ventura), and Neighborhood Service Council, as well as letters from Oxnard residents such as Mary and Hugh J. Crawford and Martina McRae (Oxnard School District Archives, microfilm roll 262).

72. Paul Harvey, "Paul Harvey Views: Busing Students for Purpose of Race-Mixing Not Effective," *The Press-Courier,* November 11, 1969, 4.

73. See, for example, Correspondence from S. H. Stewart, Superintendent Oxnard School District, to Dr. William Tinderhughes, Associate Superintendent, Baltimore Public Schools, December 3, 1969; Correspondence from S. H. Stewart, Superintendent Oxnard School District, to James Farmer, Department of Health Education, and Welfare, Assistant Secretary for Administration, December 3, 1969 (Oxnard School District Archives, microfilm roll 389).

74. Ibid.

75. Correspondence from James Farmer, Department of Health Education, and Welfare, Assistant Secretary for Administration, to S. H. Stewart, Superintendent Oxnard School District, January 5, 1970 (Oxnard School District Archives, microfilm roll 389).

76. See Correspondence from S. H. Stewart to James Farmer, December 3, 1969.

77. "Plan to Combat School Bias Okayed in Oxnard," *Ventura County Star–Free Press,* December 18, 1969, A2.

78. Ned MacKay, "School Desegregation Plan Approved," *The Press-Courier,* December 17, 1969, front page, 2.

79. OSBT meeting minutes, January 20, 1970, 130.

80. OSBT meeting minutes, February 3, 1970, 137.

81. Complaint for Injunctive and Declaratory Relief, February 20, 1970, 1, 5.

82. Ibid., 2.

83. Ibid., 4.

84. For more detailed discussion of *Soria* as among the first cases filed jointly by Mexican Americans and Blacks, see the introduction.

85. *Spangler v. Pasadena City Board of Education,* 311 F. Supp. 501 (C.D. Cal. 1970).

86. Complaint for Injunctive and Declaratory Relief, February 20, 1970, 7–8. "Defendant Kane stated that even a skeptic would recognize there was 'an overwhelming amount of evidence available to the effect that a substantial effort is required to solve the segregation problem by the Oxnard School District . . . our thirteen point plan is far less community disruptive than a plan as required by Judge Real of the Pasadena District."

87. Amendment to Complaint, United States District Court for the Central District of California, Civ. No. 70–396-HP, May 22, 1970, 3, signed April 30, 1970, by Ventura County Legal Service Center Attorney for Plaintiffs Michael Arthur Cohen, filed in Court May 22, 1970 (Oxnard School District Archives, microfilm roll 393).

88. *Jackson v. Pasadena City School District,* 382 Cal.2d 876, 880 (Cal. 1963). See further discussion of *Jackson* case in chapter 5.

89. Amendment to Complaint, Civ. No. 70–396-HP, May 22, 1970, 1.

90. Complaint for Injunctive and Declaratory Relief, Civ. No. 70–396-HP, February 20, 1970, 5–7.

91. Ibid., 7.

92. Ibid., 8.

93. Amendment to Complaint, Civ. No. 70–396-HP, May 22, 1970, 2.

94. In the Plaintiffs' Proposed Finding of Fact, a few phrases and words were struck through completely, but only one word—"refused"—was struck out and replaced with another word—"failed"—in no. 61, Stipulated Findings, submitted as part of Exhibit D, p. 33 [handwritten], 1971 (National Archives and Records Administration [Riverside, CA], Civil Case Files, Records of the U.S. District Court, Central District of California, Los Angeles, record group 21, box 31, folder 70–396, vol. 1; obtained from the office of Judge Harry Pregerson).

95. Correspondence from William A. Waters, Assistant County Counsel to Seawright H. Stewart, Superintendent Oxnard School District, June 25, 1970, 5 (Oxnard School District Archives, microfilm roll 262).

96. Ibid., 1.

97. Ibid., 2.

98. Ibid.

99. Ibid., 4.

100. Ibid., 5.

101. Ibid.

102. Ibid., 6. Waters further advised the trustees to be aware of the cost of litigation, referencing the *Crawford* case in particular, where "The Court pointed out the board could have acted with complete impartiality to all of its beneficiaries, could have cooperated to the highest with the court, and could have welcomed a declaration of its duties under the law . . . instead of this, the board defended vigorously at every step of the way." As a result, Waters informed the trustees, the court ordered the defendant school board in Los Angeles to pay the plaintiffs' legal fees.

103. Memorandum Granting Motion for Summary Judgment, United States District Court, Central District of California, Civ. No. 70–396-HP, May 12, 1971, 3–4 (binder on *Debbie and Doreen Soria et al. v. Oxnard School District Board of Trustees et al.,* Chronology of Events, Oxnard School District Archives). See also *Debbie and Doreen Soria et al. v. Oxnard School Board of Trustees,* 328 F. Supp. 155, 157 (C.D. Cal. 1971).

104. Ibid., 3.

105. *Swann v. Charlotte-Mecklenburg Board of Education,* No. 281, 402 U.S. 1 (1971). *Swann* was argued in front of the U.S. Supreme Court five months after *Soria* had been filed in 1970, and was decided in April 1971. The *Swann* case itself had been resubmitted for consideration after the *Green v. County School Board* case in 1968, which found that schools have the responsibility to eliminate segregation "root and branch." *Green v. County School Board,* 391 U.S. 430, 488 (88 S. Ct. 1689, 20 L.Ed.2d 716) (1968).

106. These examples included *Keyes v. School District No. 1,* Memorandum Granting Motion for Summary Judgment, Civ. No. 70–396-HP, May 12, 1971, 3–4.

107. Ibid.

108. Ibid., 4.

109. Ibid., 5.

110. "The Integration Suit, the Court Order, and the Reaction of the Oxnard School District," a two-page statement by Doran W. Tregarthen originally attached along with Correspondence from Doran W. Tregarthen to Oxnard School District Staff Members, May 13, 1971 (binder on *Debbie and Doreen Soria et al. v. Oxnard School District Board of Trustees et al.,* Chronology of Events, Oxnard School District Archives).

111. Ibid.

112. Helen Reynolds, "Oxnard Schools Must Integrate: U.S. Judge Sets June 1, Deadline for Drafting Plan," *The Press-Courier,* May 13, 1971, front page, 3. These directions are not included in the summary judgment but in discussion between the attorneys and Judge Pregerson. See also Gene Blake, "Oxnard Schools Must Integrate U.S. Judge Rules: Workable Plan Ordered within 20 Days; Use of One-Way Bussing Denied," *Los Angeles Times,* May 13, 1971, 3.

113. "Editorials: Wise Words on Integration Effort," *The Press-Courier,* May 14, 1971, 4.

114. See, for example, analysis of desegregation confrontations in Los Angeles: Paul Egly, "*Crawford v. Los Angeles Unified School District:* An Unfulfilled Plea for Racial Equality," *University of La Verne Law Review* 31 (2010): 257–322; David S. Ettinger, "The Quest to Desegregate Los Angeles Schools," *Los Angeles Lawyer* (2003): 55–67.

115. Similarly, Matthew Delmont found that in 1975, television news framed Boston's "busing crisis" as a story about White protesters in conflict with police, which "rendered black Bostonians as bit players in their own civil rights story." Delmont, *Why Busing Failed,* 208.

116. Some Oxnard residents also took up this term, "silent majority." See, for example, editorial by Mrs. Bill R. Corder, "Unconstitutional," *Ventura County Star–Free Press,* July 8, 1971, D8. See further discussion of the term in Delmont, *Why Busing Failed,* 108.

117. A. G. Duff, "Voices of the People: Appeal, Poll Opposed," *The Press-Courier,* June 9, 1971, 9.

118. Memorandum and Order for Judgment, Civ. No. 70–396-HP, July 21, 1971, 1 (binder on *Debbie and Doreen Soria et al. v. Oxnard School District Board of Trustees, et al.,* Chronology of Events, Oxnard School District Archives).

119. Judgment, Civ. No. 70–396-HP, July 21, 1971.

120. Approved Amended Integration Plan, pp. 10–11 of Amended Integration Plan Proposed by the Defendants, Oxnard School District Board of Trustees for Approval by the Court, Civ. No. 70–396-HP, July 7, 1971 (binder on *Debbie and Doreen Soria et al. v. Oxnard School District Board of Trustees et al.,* Chronology of Events, Oxnard School District Archives).

121. Ibid., 28–30.

122. Ibid., 31.

123. Art Kuhn, "300 Turn Out to Oppose Forced Busing of Children: Board Affirms Decision to Appeal," *The Press-Courier,* July 7, 1971, front page, 2.

124. Ibid. Three photos with captions framed the article, including a photo of the meeting, "Forced Busing Draws Packed House," a photo of William Terry as "Against Busing Appeal," and a photo of a Mrs. Robert Willoughby, "Attacks Court Decision."

125. John Willson, "Busing Ultimatum: Foes 'Demand' Court Victory," *Ventura County Star–Free Press,* July 7, 1971, A1, A7. The distinction with how desegregation was covered by the two local papers continued. See, for example, the contrast between "100 Stage Antibusing Rally," *The Press-Courier,* August 28, 1971, front page; and John Willson, "Grim Marchers: Only 60 Protest Oxnard Busing, *Ventura County Star–Free Press,* August 29, 1971, A1.

126. Ibid.

127. Joe D. Olmsted, "Voice of the People: Busing Opposed," *The Press-Courier,* July 12, 1971, 4. The outpouring of protest was not one-sided. See, for example, Richard O. Parks, "Voice of the People: Recall Action Hit," *The Press-Courier,* August 14, 1971, 4; Daniel Philip Goodwin, "Feelings Justified," *The Press-Courier,* August 28, 1971, 4; May L. Davis, "Even Break," *Ventura County Star–Free Press,* July 10, 1971, B12.

128. "Minority Leaders Meet with Cranston," *The Press-Courier,* August 14, 1971, front page, 2.

129. "Where the Voices of Oxnard Leaders?," *Ventura County Star–Free Press,* August 17, 1971, B12. Despite these "local failures," and as in the past, activists and organizations demonstrated leadership. See, for example, the July 1971 report compiled by the League of Women Voters of Ventura County for the purposes of "educating the community about the *Soria* case." League of Women Voters of Ventura County, "Desegregating Oxnard's Schools: Background, Court Decisions, Laws and the Oxnard School Desegregation Plan," July 1971. Oxnard Public Library Special Collections.

130. Notice of Motion for Stay Pending Appeal, *Oxnard School District Board of Trustees v. Debbie and Doreen Soria et al.,* United States Court of Appeals for the Ninth Circuit, September 2, 1971.

131. "Plaintiffs Opposed Oxnard Busing Stay," *The Press-Courier,* September 3, 1971, front page, 2.

132. Delmont, *Why Busing Failed,* 100–13; "Ex-Florida Governor Slated to Speak on Forced Busing," *The Press-Courier,* September 2, 1971, 13; "Kirk Tells of

Plans for Fight on Busing," *The Press-Courier*, September 1, 1971, front page, 2 (photo of Kirk with caption: "Urges Antibusing Unity"). This article is one of four on the front page: Art Kuhn, "Kirk Hits Edict on Compulsory Oxnard Busing," front page, 2; "20,000 S.F. Parents Plan Busing Boycott," front page, 2; "Plaintiffs Oppose Oxnard Busing Stay," front page, 2; "Oxnard Family Kicks Off National Antibusing Trip," front page.

133. "Ex-Florida Governor Slated to Speak on Forced Busing," *The Press-Courier*, September 2, 1971, 13 (photo of Kirk and Mason with caption: "Former Governor Discusses School Busing").

134. In the Oxnard School Board records, Mytinger is listed as serving as a trustee from 1971 to 1973. However, the newspaper reported that he resigned from the board in August 1972. "Mytinger Quits School Post: Trustee Wants Child Out of Local School: Discipline Lack Cited," *The Press-Courier*, August 9, 1972, front page. The article explains that Mytinger resigned and removed his daughter from the district. He purchased a house in Camarillo so she could attend junior high school in that area.

135. "Ex-Florida Governor Slated to Speak on Forced Busing," *The Press-Courier*, September 2, 1971, 13; Art Kuhn, "Kirk Hits Edict on Compulsory Oxnard Busing," *The Press-Courier*, September 1, 1971, front page, 2.

136. A few days later, Mason threatened that he would take his two children out of school if the board were unsuccessful in petitioning a stay of busing. Art Kuhn, "Trustee May Take Children out of School," *The Press-Courier*, September 8, 1971, front page.

137. Art Kuhn, "Kirk Hits Edict on Compulsory Oxnard Busing," *The Press-Courier*, September 1, 1971, front page, 2.

138. Ibid., 2.

139. Ibid.

140. Ibid. Kirk went on to attack trustee Rachel Wong, claiming she may have fraudulently counted herself as a Mexican American. "And the surnames used in integration are an amazing circumstance," the quick-witted politician said. In Florida, Mrs. Wong (school board member Rachel Wong) would be grouped in the Chinese component of such a plan, he quipped, "but it turns out she is Mexican-American. . . . That's not America. It's a strange program and you'd never explain it to us in Florida" (2). Apparently Kirk believed Floridians could not grasp the concept of a woman taking her husband's name without losing her heritage. Rachel Murguía Wong, whose grandparents were Mexican immigrants, had married a Chinese man and added his name to her maiden name. Rachel Murguía Wong, interview by David G. García and Frank P. Barajas, May 30, 2010, Ventura, CA.

141. Index of Supporting Papers attached to Notice of Motion for Stay Pending Appeal, filed with Case No. ——, United States Court of Appeals for the Ninth Circuit, August 30, 1971, 11. The index is a forty-three-page document filed with the notice as part of *Oxnard School District Board of Trustees, Defendants and Appellants, v. Soria et al., Plaintiffs and Appellees*, with the United States Court of Appeals for the Ninth Circuit. There is also a handwritten date of September 2, 1971, and a

blank space (No. ——) for the not-yet-assigned case number. Oxnard School District Archives, microfilm roll 517.

142. Ibid., 8–9.

143. Ibid., 12–13.

144. Ibid., 8. This footnote in the motion was particularly striking as it accused Judge Pregerson of not distinguishing Asian American students from Whites in the comparison of east- and west-side schools, thereby achieving "that which Adolf Hitler didn't," by creating "honorary Aryans." The note goes on to state the defendants "will have more to say on the subject of whether the Constitution is to be color-blind and race-blind or color-conscious and race-activated when they brief the case on the merits." For the purposes of the case, there was indeed very little mention of Asian American students, likely because they comprised a very small percentage of the district total enrollments. This accusation inadvertently points to a continuity in the privileged treatment of Asian Americans by the school board. For example, according to an ethnic census of actual enrollments in the 1970–71 school year, when Asian Americans (noted as "Oriental") made up 1 percent of the district, their enrollment was zero percent at the east-side Juanita, Ramona, and Rose Avenue schools, 5 percent at Sierra Linda, 5 percent at Curren, and 3 percent at Marina West. See "Oxnard School District Ethnic Census: Actual Enrollment after Busing 1970–74" (Oxnard School District Archives, microfilm roll 262).

145. Affidavit of Fred [Frederick C.] Jones, August 31, 1971, filed with United States Court of Appeals for the Ninth Circuit, Case No. 71–2369, Affidavits in Opposition to Stay, September 2, 1971, 7–8 (National Archives and Records Administration—Pacific Region [San Francisco]).

146. Affidavit of Margaret Thrasher, August 31, 1971, filed with United States Court of Appeals for the Ninth Circuit, Case No. 71–2369, Affidavits in Opposition to Stay, September 2, 1971, 17–18; Affidavit of William Thrasher, August 31, 1971, filed with United States Court of Appeals for the Ninth Circuit, Case No. 71–2369, Affidavits in Opposition to Stay, September 2, 1971, 19.

147. Affidavit of Margaret Thrasher, August 31, 1971, 17–18.

148. Affidavit of Barbara Gardner, August 31, 1971, filed with United States Court of Appeals for the Ninth Circuit, Case No. 71–2369, Affidavits in Opposition to Stay, September 2, 1971, 15 (National Archives and Records Administration—Pacific Region [San Francisco]).

149. Affidavit of J. Keith Mason, August 27, 1971, filed with United States Court of Appeals for the Ninth Circuit, Case No. 71–2369, Affidavits Endorsing Petition to Stay (Oxnard School District Archives, microfilm roll 517).

150. Affidavit of Rachel Murguía Wong, August 30, 1971, filed with United States Court of Appeals for the Ninth Circuit, Case No. 71–2369, Affidavits Endorsing Petition to Stay (Oxnard School District Archives, microfilm roll 517); Affidavit of Mary O. Davis, August 27, 1971, filed with United States Court of Appeals for the Ninth Circuit, Case No. 71–2369, Affidavits Endorsing Petition to Stay (Oxnard School District Archives, microfilm roll 517).

151. Affidavit of Mary O. Davis, August 27, 1971. Davis reasoned that "areas in which one race preponderates numerically over others . . . is purely a matter of economics."

152. Ibid.

153. Order, *Soria, appellees, v. Oxnard School Board, appellants*, U.S. Court of Appeals for the Ninth Circuit, Case No. 71–2369, September 13, 1971. Circuit judges Walter Raleigh Ely and Shirley Hufstedler wrote, "The appellant's motion for a stay order pending appeal, filed herein on September 2, 1971, is denied. The appellant should have, in the first instance, presented its application for a stay in the District Court."

154. Art Kuhn, "School Start Due as Planned 'Unless' . . .," *The Press-Courier,* September 5, 1971, front page, 2.

155. "A New Era for Oxnard Schools: Integration Program Begins on September 13th," Special Report of the Oxnard School District, September 1971. Superintendent Tregarthen's statement indicated that the "Report" had been "especially prepared to acquaint every resident with information about the integration plan." The formatting of the document further suggests it was likely sent via U.S. mail. Filed with United States Court of Appeals for the Ninth Circuit, Case No. 71–2929 (National Archives and Records Administration—Pacific Region [San Francisco]).

156. "Attempted School Bus Arson Fails," *The Press-Courier,* September 7, 1971, front page.

157. Judge Harry Pregerson, interview by David G. García and Tara J. Yosso, April 3, 2014, Woodland Hills, CA.

158. Judge Pregerson did not make his presence known to the press. The newspaper also reported that day one occurred without incident. Art Kuhn, "School Busing Starts Smoothly in Oxnard," *The Press-Courier,* September 13, 1971, front page, 2.

159. Helen Reynolds, "Issue of Busing Propels Oxnard into Spotlight," *The Press-Courier,* August 9, 1972, front page.

160. "U.S. Asks Oxnard Busing Case Role," *The Press-Courier,* July 22, 1972, front page.

161. "18-Month Moratorium on Busing Agreed On," *Daily Redlands Facts,* May 17, 1972, front page.

162. Jack McCrudy, "Federal Antibusing Law Faces First Challenge in Oxnard Case," *Los Angeles Times,* July 7, 1972, 3, 22; Ronald J. Ostrow, "U.S. Tests Busing Ban in Oxnard School Case: Defends New Law in Court for First Time; High Justice Aid to Join S.F. Hearings," *Los Angeles Times,* August 8, 1972, A3.

163. John Willson, "Busing Test: As Oxnard Goes So Goes Nation," *Ventura County Star–Free Press,* August 9, 1972, front page, A8.

164. Motion to Enlarge Appellees Brief, United States Court of Appeals for the Ninth Circuit, Case No. 71–2929, submitted June 22, 1972; Order Granting Motion, June 23, 1972, Judge Chambers, United States Court of Appeals for the Ninth Circuit (National Archives and Records Administration—Pacific Region [San

Francisco]; obtained from the office of Judge Harry Pregerson). Appellees had requested and been approved for additional time to submit the brief in May 1972. Appellants had already filed and received approvals to extend their brief as well as time to submit their brief in February and April 1972.

165. Ibid.

166. "Emergency School Assistance Act of 1972 Challenged as Discriminatory to Minorities," *El Chicano Community Newspaper* [Colton, CA], July 12, 1972, 2.

167. Ibid.

168. Helen Reynolds, "Oxnard Bus Decision Weighed by Judges: Right of Congress to Legislate Stays Questioned by Panel," *The Press-Courier,* August 11, 1972, front page, 2.

169. "Antibusing Petition Sent Off," *The Press-Courier,* August 29, 1972, front page; "Douglas Gets Bus Petition," *The Press-Courier,* September 2, 1972, front page. The same day, on the editorial page, an Oxnard resident questioned her tax dollars being spent on busing appeals. Lynn M. Locke, "Voice of the People: Who Pays for Appeal?," *The Press-Courier,* September 2, 1972, 8.

170. Correspondence from Leonard H. Carter, Director, Region I, NAACP, to Attorney Nathaniel Jones, General Counsel, NAACP, August 24, 1972 (Library of Congress, Collection of the National Association for the Advancement of Colored People, Washington, DC, box 5: 139, folder 6).

171. Correspondence from Terry J. Hatter Jr., Executive Director, to Mr. Leonard H. Carter, NAACP Regional Director, September 6, 1972 (Library of Congress, Collection of the National Association for the Advancement of Colored People, Washington, DC, box 5: 139, folder 6; correspondence copied by national counsel Ben James and regional counsel Nat Colley).

172. Ibid.

173. Correspondence from Leonard H. Carter, Regional Director, NAACP to Nathaniel Jones, General Counsel, NAACP, September 8, 1972 (Library of Congress, Collection of the National Association for the Advancement of Colored People, Washington, DC, box 5: 139, folder 6); Correspondence from Nathaniel Jones, General Counsel, NAACP, to Mr. Philip Humer, Howard and Howard Attorneys at Law, September 15, 1972 (Library of Congress, Collection of the National Association for the Advancement of Colored People, Washington, DC, box 5: 139, folder 6).

174. "Court Upholds Oxnard Busing," *Ventura County Star–Free Press,* August 22, 1972, A1; Philip Hager, "U.S. District Court Refuses to Allow Schools in Oxnard to Halt Busing for Desegregation," *Los Angeles Times,* August 22, 1972, 3, 32; "Oxnard to Take Busing Decision to High Court," *Los Angeles Times,* August 25, 1972.

175. "Oxnard Busing: No Problems First Day," *Ventura County Star–Free Press,* September 11, 1972, A4; "Oxnard Busing Stay Turned Down," *Ventura County Star–Free Press,* September 14, 1972, A1; "Chief Justice Petitioned: Oxnard Bus Plea Denied," *The Press-Courier,* September 13, 1972, front page, 2.

176. "Oxnard Bus Plea Denied by Burger: Amendment Emasculated, Sabo Claims," *The Press-Courier,* September 21, 1972, front page, 2.

177. Brief of the Appellants, United States Court of Appeals for the Ninth Circuit, Case No. 71–2929, May 1, 1972, 8 (National Archives and Records Administration—Pacific Region [San Francisco]; obtained from the office of Judge Harry Pregerson).

178. See full copy of David Armor's "The Effects of Busing," dated May 10, 1972, filed with Reply to Opposition for Granting a Rehearing for Clarification of Order Denying Stay, United States Court of Appeals for the Ninth Circuit, Case No. 71–2929, July 13, 1972, Appendix (National Archives and Records Administration—Pacific Region [San Francisco]; obtained from the office of Judge Harry Pregerson). Armor critiqued integration as based on what he determined to be a faulty premise, exemplified by Gordon Allport's "intergroup contact theory," which held that stereotypes, prejudice, and conflict are reduced when groups have sustained contact. He claimed Allport's theory was ineffective in all settings, such as in persistent conflicts between Protestants and Catholics in Northern Ireland and between Israelis and Palestinians.

179. Brief of the Appellants, United States Court of Appeals for the Ninth Circuit, Case No. 71–2929, May 1, 1972, 17–18. See also extensive overview of research on segregation and integration prepared for the appellees by Dr. Audrey J. Schwartz, Brief of Appellees, United States Court of Appeals for the Ninth Circuit, Case No. 71–2929, June 27, 1972, Appendix (National Archives and Records Administration—Pacific Region [San Francisco]; obtained from the office of Judge Harry Pregerson).

180. Index of Supporting Papers attached to Notice of Motion for Stay Pending Appeal, filed with Case No. ——, United States Court of Appeals for the Ninth Circuit, August 30, 1971, 12–13.

181. The brief of the appellants did not explain or define their use of the term "Chicano." They did not follow through on their promised challenge to ethnic/racial identifiers, footnoted in their 1971 notice for motion for a stay, but they did make a footnote reference to the term "Anglo," pointing out that "apparently such use would encompass the Pulaski, Botticini, Goldberg, and Sabo families." Brief of the Appellants, United States Court of Appeals for the Ninth Circuit, Case No. 71–2929, May 1, 1972, 44 (National Archives and Records Administration—Pacific Region [San Francisco]; obtained from the office of Judge Harry Pregerson).

182. Ibid., 17.

183. Reply to Opposition to Granting Rehearing for Clarification of Order Denying Stay, United States Court of Appeals for the Ninth Circuit, Case No. 71–2929, November 27, 1973, 11 (National Archives and Records Administration—Pacific Region [San Francisco]; obtained from the office of Judge Harry Pregerson).

184. *Swann v. Charlotte-Mecklenburg Board of Education,* No. 281, 402 U.S. 1 (1971), 25.

185. Ibid., 26.

186. Ibid., 27.

187. Ibid., 28. "The remedy for such segregation may be administratively awkward, inconvenient, and even bizarre in some situations, and may impose burdens

on some; but all awkwardness and inconvenience cannot be avoided in the interim period when remedial adjustments are being made to eliminate the dual school systems."

188. Brief of the Appellants, United States Court of Appeals for the Ninth Circuit, Case No. 71–2929, May 1, 1972, 8. Emphasis in original.

189. Ibid., 26.

190. Appeal from the United States District Court for the Central District of California, Case No. 71–2929, November 27, 1973, 12.

191. "Trial Ordered on Charge of Oxnard School Segregation," *Los Angeles Times,* November 29, 1972, 3C.

192. Herbert D. Nowlin, interview by David G. García and Frank P. Barajas, May 6, 2010, Ventura, CA.

193. Brief of the Appellants, United States Court of Appeals for the Ninth Circuit, Case No. 71–2929, May 1, 1972, 17–18.

194. "Editorials: A Start toward Solving the Problem," *The Press-Courier,* October 23, 1969, 4.

195. Deposition of Norman R. Brekke, April 1, 1974, 23 (National Archives and Records Administration [Riverside, CA], Civil Case Files, Records of the District Court of the United States, Central District of California, record group 21, box 21–78–0059, 5/54, folder 70–396).

196. Ibid.

197. Ibid.

198. Ibid., 24.

199. Ibid.

200. Brief of the Appellants, United States Court of Appeals for the Ninth Circuit, Case No. 71–2929, May 1, 1972, 8.

201. Ibid., 35–36.

202. Deposition of Thomas Edward Kane, April 16, 1974, 9 (National Archives and Records Administration [Riverside, CA], Civil Case Files, Records of the District Court of the United States, Central District of California, record group 21, box 21–78–0059, 5/54, folder 70–396).

203. Ibid., 10–11.

204. Ibid., 11. Kane claimed that the special programs in the Colonia schools included "reduced class size, special aids, teacher's aides to work with the children, special food training, extra specially qualified personnel who speak two languages, the expenditure of a larger number of dollars per head for special training equipment; overhead viewers, slide projectors, tape recorders, audio-visual equipment, et cetera; whatever tools are available to the profession that they can use to concentrate on the particular deficiencies of these children."

205. Ibid., 30–31.

206. Ibid.

207. "'Our Schools and the Future American': Principal R. B. Haydock Tells Rotary Club What He Thinks on This Subject," *The Oxnard Daily Courier,* December 30, 1921, 3.

208. Deposition of Thomas Edward Kane, April 16, 1974, 31–32.

209. Deposition of Robert Pfeiler, April 16, 1974 (National Archives and Records Administration [Riverside, CA], Civil Case Files, Records of the District Court of the United States, Central District of California, record group 21, box 21–78–0059, 5/54, folder 70–396).

210. Ibid., 5–6. See also overview of family history, "Louis Pfeiler Came in 1868," *Oxnard Press-Courier*, September 24, 1948, sec. F, 6.

211. Deposition of Robert Pfeiler, April 16, 1974, 6.

212. Ibid., 12.

213. Ibid., 6–7.

214. Ibid., 7.

215. Ibid., 13.

216. Deposition of J. Keith Mason, April 16, 1974, 18 (National Archives and Records Administration [Riverside, CA], Civil Case Files, Records of the District Court of the United States, Central District of California, record group 21, box 21–78–0059, 5/54, folder 70–396).

217. Ibid., 7–8.

218. Ibid., 8.

219. Ibid., 14.

220. Ibid., 16.

221. Ibid., 21–25.

222. Complaint for Injunctive and Declaratory Relief, February 20, 1970, 4.

223. Judge Harry Pregerson, interview by David G. García and Tara J. Yosso, April 3, 2014, Woodland Hills, CA.

224. Ibid.

225. Walt Stegmeir, "Integration Ignored, Witness Tells Court," *The Press-Courier*, September 26, 1974, front page, 2.

226. Ibid., 2.

227. Ibid.

228. Ibid.

229. Ibid.

230. Ibid.

231. Ibid.

232. Joel I. Edelman, phone interview by David G. García and Tara J. Yosso, November 3, 2016.

233. Memorandum of Decision Following Ninth Circuit's Remand, Civ. No. 70–396-HP, December 10, 1974, 2 (binder on *Debbie and Doreen Soria et al. v. Oxnard School District Board of Trustees et al.*, United States District Court, Central District of California, Civ. No. 70–396-HP, Chronology of Events, Oxnard School District Archives). See also *Soria v. Oxnard School Board of Trustees*, 386 F. Supp. 539 (U.S. Dist. 1974).

234. Memorandum of Decision Following Ninth Circuit's Remand, Civ. No. 70–396-HP, December 10, 1974, 7.

235. Ibid., 3.

236. Ibid., 8.

237. Ibid., 9–10.

238. Ibid., 11.

239. Ibid., 8.

240. "Of Children and Chicken Coops," *Los Angeles Times,* January 26, 1975, F2.

241. Ibid.

242. See Egly, "*Crawford v. Los Angeles Unified School District*"; Ettinger, "Quest to Desegregate Los Angeles Schools"; *Crawford v. Board of Education of the City of Los Angeles,* 458 U.S. 527 (1982).

243. OSBT meeting minutes, August 7, 1934. See also chapter 3 discussion and Judge Pregerson's characterization of the school board being "obsessed" with school segregation. Memorandum of Decision following Ninth Circuit's Remand, Civ. No. 70-396-HP, December 10, 1974, 5.

244. The plaintiffs' attorneys—with the encouragement of opposing counsel William Waters—had to file a court order to also recover legal fees from the school trustees, which totaled $75,000. Correspondence from Rosalyn M. Chapman, Associate Director, Western Center on Law and Poverty, to William A. Waters, Ventura County Counsel, April 15, 1975; Correspondence from William A. Waters, Ventura County Counsel, to John McDermott, Western Center on Law and Poverty, April 28, 1975 (carbon-copied to Rosalyn Chapman, Herb Nowlin, Norm Brekke, Members of the Board of Trustees); Correspondence from William A. Waters, Ventura County Counsel, to Norman R. Brekke, Superintendent, Oxnard School District, May 19, 1975 (carbon-copied to Members of the Board of Trustees). Oxnard School District Archives, microfilm roll 263.

245. See further discussion of this paraphrasing from Peter Linebaugh and Marcus Rediker in the introduction. Peter Linebaugh and Marcus Rediker, *The Many-Headed Hydra: Sailors, Slaves, Commoners, and the Hidden History of the Revolutionary Atlantic* (Boston: Beacon Press, 2000), 1, 7.

246. Judge Harry Pregerson, interview by David G. García and Tara J. Yosso, April 3, 2014, Woodland Hills, CA.

EPILOGUE

Epigraph: Charles M. Wollenberg, *All Deliberate Speed: Segregation and Exclusion in California Schools, 1855–1975* (Berkeley: University of California Press, 1976), 186.

1. Complaint for Injunctive and Declaratory Relief for Deprivation of Plaintiff's Rights to Equal Protection of the Laws and Due Process of Law, United States District Court for the Central District of California, Civ. No. 70-396-HP, February 20, 1970, 4 (Oxnard School District Archives, microfilm roll 262).

2. Gaye Theresa Johnson, *Spaces of Conflict, Sounds of Solidarity: Music, Race, and Spatial Entitlement in Los Angeles* (Berkeley: University of California Press, 2013), xiv, xix.

3. Ned MacKay, "Colonia Group Hits School Integration Plan," *The Press-Courier*, June 17, 1970, front page. This position resonated with the stance of the local branch of the Brown Berets, a group mobilizing for Chicana/o self-determination. For more on the Oxnard branch of the Brown Berets, see Luis H. Moreno, "¡Ya Basta! The Struggle for Justice and Equality: The Chicano Power Movement in Oxnard, California," in *The Chicano Movement Perspectives from the Twenty-First Century*, edited by Mario T. García (New York: Routledge, 2014), 130–48. Some of my interviewees, such as William L. Terry, contributed to efforts initiated by the NAACP, but viewed the group as "not aggressive enough" in the struggle for justice. In turn, he explained, he and his collaborators, including the Brown Berets, were usually perceived as "too radical."

4. See, for example, W. E. B. DuBois, "Does the Negro Need Separate Schools?," *Journal of Negro Education* 4, no. 3 (1935): 328–35.

5. Scott Steepleton, "Obituaries: Juan Soria, Key Figure in School Desegregation Battle, Dies at Age 65," *Los Angeles Times*, June 15, 1997.

6. Fred Alvarez, "School Named for Justice Marshall," *Los Angeles Times*, August 22, 1998; Marjorie Hernandez, "School Mural Honors Namesake, Juan Soria," *Ventura County Star–Free Press*, August 27, 2009.

7. Wollenberg, *All Deliberate Speed*, 178.

8. Kenneth B. Clark, "Beyond *Brown v. Board of Education*, Housing and Education in the Year 2000," *Minnesota Law Review* 80, no. 4 (1996): 745–48, 746.

9. Richard Delgado and Jean Stefancic, "Derrick Bell's Chronicle of the Space Traders: Would the U.S. Sacrifice People of Color If the Price Were Right?," *University of Colorado Law Review* 62 (1991): 321–29, 328.

10. "Public School Enrollment by Race/Ethnicity 1996–2016," as cited on kidsdata.org, compiled from California Department of Education, California Basic Educational Data System (National Center for Education Statistics, Digest of Education Statistics). See www.kidsdata.org/topic/36/publicschoolenrollment-race/trend#fmt=451&loc=2,363,1626,1&tf=17,88&ch=7,10,9&pdist=73 (retrieved February 28, 2017).

11. Cesar Morales, interview by David G. García, August 29, 2016, Oxnard, CA. For further discussion on the need for an "asset-minded," community cultural wealth approach in schools, see Tara J. Yosso, *Critical Race Counterstories along the Chicana/Chicano Educational Pipeline* (New York: Routledge, 2006).

BIBLIOGRAPHY

SELECTED ARCHIVAL SOURCES AND COLLECTIONS

Carter, Earl J. "The History of African Americans in Ventura County," in Yvette L. Sutton, *The One Percent Wall: A Retrospective Look at the Contributions of African Americans in Ventura County* [booklet]. Ventura, CA: VET Heritage Productions, 1993.

"Desegregating Oxnard's Schools: Background, Court Decisions, Laws and the Oxnard School Desegregation Plan." League of Women Voters of Ventura County, July 1971.

"Improving Racial and Ethnic Balance and Intergroup Relations: An Advisory Report to the Board of Trustees, Oxnard School District." California State Department of Education, Division of Compensatory Education, Bureau of Intergroup Relations, April 1969.

Mexican American Legal Defense and Education Fund Collection, Cecil H. Green Library at Stanford University.

Museum of Ventura County Photographic Collections, Ventura, CA.

National Association for the Advancement of Colored People Collection, Library of Congress, Washington, DC.

National Association for the Advancement of Colored People Region I Collection, Bancroft Library, Berkeley, CA.

"A New Era for Oxnard Schools: Integration Program Begins on September 13th," Special Report of the Oxnard School District, September 1971.

Office of the Clerk of the City, Oxnard, CA.

Online Archive of California, California Digital Library.

Oxnard Public Library Special Collections, Oxnard, CA.

Oxnard School District Archives, Oxnard, CA.

StoryCorp Archive, American Folk Life Center, Library of Congress, Washington, DC.

United States Bureau of the Census, U.S. Census of the Population.

United States Court of Appeals for the Ninth Circuit Records, National Archives and Records Administration, Pacific Region, San Francisco, CA.

United States District Court, Central District of California, Los Angeles Records, National Archives and Records Administration, Riverside, CA.

United States District Court and United States Court of Appeals for the Ninth Circuit Records, Office of Judge Harry Pregerson, Woodland Hills, CA.

Ventura County Clerk and Recorder, Ventura, CA.

Ventura County Surveyor's Office, Ventura, CA.

PRIMARY AND SECONDARY SOURCES

Abrams, Charles. *Forbidden Neighbors: A Study of Prejudice and Housing.* New York: Harper & Brothers, 1955.

Acuña, Rodolfo F. *A Community under Siege: A Chronicle of Chicanos East of the Los Angeles River, 1945–1975.* Monograph no. 11, Chicano Studies Research Center Publications, University of California, Los Angeles, 1984.

———. *Occupied America: A History of Chicanos,* 3rd ed. New York: HarperCollins, 1988.

Alamillo, José M. *Making Lemonade out of Lemons: Mexican American Labor and Leisure in a California Town 1880–1960.* Urbana: University of Illinois Press, 2006.

Alexander v. Holmes County Board of Education, 396 U.S. 19 (1969).

Almaguer, Tomás. "Class, Race, and Capitalist Development: The Social Transformation of a Southern California County, 1848–1903." Ph.D. dissertation, University of California, Berkeley, 1979.

———. *Racial Fault Lines: The Historical Origins of White Supremacy in California.* Berkeley: University of California Press, 1994.

Anderson, James D. *The Education of Blacks in the South, 1860–1935.* Chapel Hill: University of North Carolina Press, 1988.

Arce, Carlos H., Edward Murgia, and W. Parker Frisbie. "Phenotype and the Life Chances among Chicanos." *Hispanic Journal of Behavioral Sciences* 9, no. 1 (1987): 19–32.

Avila, Eric. *Popular Culture in the Age of White Flight: Fear and Fantasy in Suburban Los Angeles.* Berkeley: University of California Press, 2006.

Barajas, Frank P. *Curious Unions: Mexican American Workers and Resistance in Oxnard, California, 1898–1961.* Lincoln: University of Nebraska Press, 2012.

Barrera, Mario. *Race and Class in the Southwest: A Theory of Racial Inequality.* Notre Dame, IN: University of Notre Dame Press, 1979.

Barrows v. Jackson, 346 U.S. 249 (1953).

Bell, Derrick A. "*Brown v. Board of Education* and the Interest-Convergence Dilemma." *Harvard Law Review* 93, no. 3 (1980): 518–33.

———. *And We Will Not Be Saved: The Elusive Quest for Racial Justice.* New York: Basic Books, 1987.

———. *Faces at the Bottom of the Well: The Permanence of Racism.* New York: Basic Books, 1992.

Blanton, Carlos K. "'They Cannot Master Abstractions, but They Can Often Be Made Efficient Workers': Race and Class in the Intelligence Testing of Mexican Americans and African Americans in Texas during the 1920s." *Social Science Quarterly* 81, no. 4 (Winter 2000): 1014–26.

———. "From Intellectual Deficiency to Cultural Deficiency: Mexican Americans, Testing, and Public School Policy in the American Southwest, 1920–1940." *Pacific Historical Review* 72, no. 1 (February 2003): 39–62.

Bowman, J. N. "Prominent Women of Provincial California." *Southern California Quarterly* 39, no. 2 (1957): 149–66.

Brown v. Board of Education, 347 U.S. 483 (1954).

Brown v. Board of Education, 349 U.S. 294 (1955).

Camarillo, Albert. *Chicanos in California: A History of Mexican Americans in California.* San Francisco: Boyd & Fraser, 1984.

Carroll, Grace. *Environmental Stress and African Americans: The Other Side of the Moon.* Westport, CT: Praeger, 1998.

Carter, Thomas P. *Mexican Americans: A History of Educational Neglect.* New York: College Entrance Examination Board, 1970.

Castañeda, Antonia I. "Sexual Violence in the Politics and Policies of Conquest: Amerindian Women and the Spanish Conquest of Alta California." In *Building with Our Hands: New Directions in Chicana Studies,* edited by Adela de la Torre and Beatríz M. Pesquera, 15–33. Los Angeles: University of California Press, 1993.

———. "Engendering the History of Alta California, 1769–1848: Gender, Sexuality, and the Family." *California History* 76, nos. 2/3 (1997): 230–59.

Chao Romero, Robert, and Luis Fernando Fernandez. *Doss v. Bernal: Ending Mexican Apartheid in Orange County.* Research Report no. 14, UCLA Chicano Studies Research Center, University of California, Los Angeles, February 2012.

Chávez-García, Miroslava. *Negotiating Conquest: Gender and Power in California, 1770s to 1880s.* Tucson: University of Arizona Press, 2004.

Cisneros v. Corpus Christi Independent School District, 324 F. Supp. 599 (S.D. Tex. 1970).

Clark, Kenneth B. "Beyond *Brown v. Board of Education,* Housing and Education in the Year 2000." *Minnesota Law Review* 80, no. 4 (1996): 745–48.

Cobb, Wilbur K. "Retardation in Elementary Schools of Children of Migratory Laborers in Ventura County, California." Master's thesis, University of Southern California, Los Angeles, 1932.

Cowan, Robert G. *Ranchos of California: A List of Spanish Concessions 1777–1822 and Mexican Grants 1822–1846.* Los Angeles: Historical Society of Southern California, 1977.

Crawford v. Board of Education of the City of Los Angeles, 458 U.S. 527 (1982).

Delgado, Richard, and Jean Stefancic. "Derrick Bell's Chronicle of the Space Traders: Would the U.S. Sacrifice People of Color If the Price Were Right?" *University of Colorado Law Review* 62 (1991): 321–29.

Delmont, Matthew F. *Why Busing Failed: Race, Media, and the National Resistance to School Desegregation*. Berkeley: University of California Press, 2016.

Deutsch, Sarah. *No Separate Refuge: Culture, Class, and Gender on an Anglo-Hispanic Frontier in the American Southwest, 1880–1940*. New York: Oxford University Press, 1987.

Deverell, William. *Whitewashed Adobe: The Rise of Los Angeles and the Remaking of Its Mexican Past*. Berkeley: University of California Press, 2004.

Donato, Rubén. *Mexicans and Hispanos in Colorado Schools and Communities, 1920–1960*. Albany: State University of New York Press, 2007.

Donato, Rubén, and Jarrod S. Hanson. "Legally White, Socially Mexican: The Politics of de Jure and de Facto School Segregation in the American Southwest." *Harvard Educational Review* 82, no. 2 (2012): 202–25.

Donato, Rubén, and Marvin Lazerson. "New Directions in American Educational History: Problems and Prospects." *Educational Researcher* 29, no. 8 (2000): 4–15.

Doss v. Bernal, Superior Court of the State of California, Orange County, no. 41466 (1943).

DuBois, W. E. B. *The Souls of Black Folk: Essays and Sketches* [1903]. New York: Fawcett, 1961.

———. "Colored California." *The Crisis* (August 1913): 192–96.

———. "Does the Negro Need Separate Schools?" *Journal of Negro Education* 4, no. 3 (1935): 328–35.

Egly, Paul. "*Crawford v. Los Angeles Unified School District:* An Unfulfilled Plea for Racial Equality." *University of La Verne Law Review* 31 (2010): 257–322.

Ettinger, David S. "Ninth Circuit Review: The History of School Desegregation in the Ninth Circuit." *Loyola Los Angeles Law Review* 12 (1979): 481–504.

———. "The Quest to Desegregate Los Angeles Schools." *Los Angeles Lawyer* (2003): 55–67.

Farmer, William A. "The Influence of Segregation of Mexican and American Children upon the Development of Social Attitudes." Master's thesis, University of Southern California, Los Angeles, 1937.

Fukuyama, Yoshio. "Citizens Apart: A History of the Japanese in Ventura County." *Ventura County Historical Society Quarterly* 39, no. 4 (1994): 3–31.

Garber, Elaine K. "Hueneme: Origins of the Name." *Ventura County Historical Society Quarterly* 12, no. 3 (June 1967): 11–15.

García, David G., and Tara J. Yosso. "Strictly in the Capacity of Servant: The Interconnection between Residential and School Segregation in Oxnard, California, 1934–1954." *History of Education Quarterly* 53, no. 1 (2013): 64–89.

García, David G., Tara J. Yosso, and Frank P. Barajas. "'A Few of the Brightest, Cleanest Mexican Children': School Segregation as a Form of Mundane Racism in Oxnard, California, 1900–1940." *Harvard Educational Review* 82, no. 1 (2012): 1–25.

García, Ignacio M. *White but Not Equal: Mexican Americans, Jury Discrimination, and the Supreme Court*. Tucson: University of Arizona Press, 2009.

García, Mario T., and Sal Castro. *Blowout: Sal Castro and the Chicano Struggle for Educational Justice*. Charlotte: University of North Carolina Press, 2014.

Garcilazo, Jeffrey. "Traqueros: Mexican Railroad Workers in the United States, 1870–1930." Ph.D. dissertation, University of California, Santa Barbara, 1995.

Gomez, Laura E. *Manifest Destinies: The Making of the Mexican American Race*. New York: New York University Press, 2007.

Gómez-Quiñones, Juan. *Chicano Politics: Reality and Promise, 1940–1990*. Albuquerque: University of New Mexico Press, 1990.

———. *Mexican American Labor, 1790–1990*. Albuquerque: University of New Mexico Press, 1994.

Gómez-Quiñones, Juan, and Irene Vásquez. *Making Aztlán: Ideology and Culture of the Chicana and Chicano Movement, 1966–1977*. Albuquerque: University of New Mexico Press, 2014.

Gong Lum v. Rice, 275 U.S. 78 (1927).

Gonzalez, Gilbert. "Segregation of Mexican Children in a Southern California City: The Legacy of Expansionism and the American Southwest." *Western Historical Quarterly* 16, no. 1 (1985): 55–76.

———. *Chicano Education in the Era of Segregation*. Philadelphia: Balch Institute Press, 1990.

Green v. County School Board, 391 U.S. 430 (1968).

Greenwood, Roberta S., and R. O. Browne. "The Rise and Fall of Shisholop." *Ventura County Historical Society Quarterly* 12, no. 2 (February 1967): 2–5.

Gregor, Howard F. "Changing Agricultural Patterns in the Oxnard Area of Southern California." Ph.D. dissertation, University of California, Los Angeles, 1950.

Haney Lopez, Ian. *White by Law: The Legal Construction of Race*. New York: New York University Press, 1996.

Heil, Grant W. "Free Press: Oxnard and Vicinity." *Ventura County Historical Society Quarterly* 19, no. 1 (Fall 1973): 2–6.

Hernandez v. Driscoll Consolidated Independent School District, Civ. No. 1384 (S.D. Tex. 1957).

Hernandez v. Texas, 347 U.S. 475 (1954).

Herrera Moreno, Louie, III. "Labor, Migration, and Activism: A History of Mexican Workers on the Oxnard Plain, 1930–1980." Ph.D. dissertation, Michigan State University, 2012.

Jackson v. Pasadena City School District, 382 P.2d 878 (1963).

Jeidy, Pauline. "First Grade Mexican American Children in Ventura County." *California Journal of Elementary Education* 15 (February and May 1947): 200–208.

Johnson, Gaye Theresa. *Spaces of Conflict, Sounds of Solidarity: Music, Race, and Spatial Entitlement in Los Angeles*. Berkeley: University of California Press, 2013.

Johnson, John R., and Sally McLendon. "Cultural Affiliation and Lineal Descent of Chumash Peoples in the Channel Islands and Santa Monica Mountains." Santa Barbara: Santa Barbara Museum of Natural History, 1997.

Keyes v. School District No. 1, Denver, Colorado, 413 U.S. 189 (1973).

King, Chester. "The Names and Locations of Historic Chumash Villages." *Journal of California Anthropology* 2, no. 2 (1975): 171–79.

Lassiter, Matthew D. "Schools and Housing in Metropolitan History: An Introduction." *Journal of Urban History* 38, no. 2 (2012): 195–204.

Lee, Robert G. *Orientals: Asian Americans in Popular Culture.* Philadelphia: Temple University Press, 1999.

Leis, Ward A. "The Status of Education for Mexican Children in Four Border States." Master's thesis, University of Southern California, Los Angeles, 1931.

Linebaugh, Peter, and Marcus Rediker. *The Many-Headed Hydra: Sailors, Slaves, Commoners, and the Hidden History of the Revolutionary Atlantic.* Boston: Beacon Press, 2000.

Lipsitz, George. *The Possessive Investment in Whiteness: How White People Profit from Identity Politics.* Philadelphia: Temple University Press, 1998.

———. *Footsteps in the Dark: The Hidden Histories of Popular Music.* Minneapolis: University of Minnesota Press, 2007.

———. *How Racism Takes Place.* Philadelphia: Temple University Press, 2011.

Loewen, James W. *Sundown Towns: A Hidden Dimension of American Racism.* New York: New Press, 2005.

Lopez, Ian Haney. *White by Law: The Legal Construction of Race.* New York: New York University Press, 1996.

Lopez, Ronald. "The Battle for Chavez Ravine: Public Policy and Chicano Community Resistance in Postwar Los Angeles, 1945–1962." Ph.D. dissertation, University of California, Berkeley, 1999.

Love, Holly, and Rheta Resnick. "Mission Made Pottery and Other Ceramics from Muwu, a Coastal Chumash Village." *Pacific Coast Archaeological Society Quarterly* 19, no. 1 (1983): 1–11.

Magnuson, Torsten. "History of the Beet Sugar Industry in California." *History Society of Southern California Annual Publication II,* no. 1 (1918): 68–79.

Marable, Manning. *Black America.* Westfield, NJ: Open Media, 1992.

Martinez, Domingo. "A Comparative Study of the Academic Achievement of the Mexican-American Students in the Wilson Junior High School, Oxnard, California." Master's thesis, Claremont Graduate School, 1956.

Martinez, George A. "The Legal Construction of Race: Mexican-Americans and Whiteness." *Harvard Latino Law Review* 2, no. 1 (1997): 321–47.

Martinez HoSang, Daniel. *Racial Propositions: Ballot Initiatives and the Making of Postwar California.* Berkeley: University of California Press, 2010.

Maulhardt, Jeffery Wayne. *Images of America: Oxnard 1867–1940.* Charleston, SC: Arcadia, 2004.

———. *Postcard History Series: Oxnard.* Charleston, SC: Arcadia, 2009.

McGroarty, John Steven. *California of the South: A History,* vol. 3. Chicago: S.J. Clarke, 1933.

McWilliams, Carey. *Southern California: An Island on the Land.* Layton, UT: Gibbs Smith, 1946.

Menchaca, Martha. *The Mexican Outsiders: A Community History of Marginaliza-tion and Discrimination in California*. Austin: University of Texas Press, 1995.

Menchaca, Martha, and Richard R. Valencia. "Anglo-Saxon Ideologies in the 1920s-1930s: Their Impact on the Segregation of Mexican Students in California." *Anthropology and Education Quarterly* 21, no. 3 (1990): 222–49.

Mendez v. Westminster, 64 F. Supp. 544 (S.D. Cal. 1946).

Miedema, Madeline. "A Giant Step Forward: A History of the Oxnard Public Library, 1907–1992." *Ventura County Historical Society Quarterly* 37, no. 2 (1992): 3–46.

Mill, Charles. *The Racial Contract*. Ithaca, NY: Cornell University Press, 1997.

Mirandé, Alfredo. *Gringo Justice*. South Bend, IN: University of Notre Dame Press, 1987.

Molina, Natalia. *Fit to Be Citizens? Public Health and Race in Los Angeles, 1879–1939*. Berkeley: University of California Press, 2006.

———. "The Importance of Place and Place-Makers in the Life of a Los Angeles Community: What Gentrification Erases from Echo Park." *Southern California Quarterly* 97, no. 1 (2015): 69–111.

Monroy, Douglas. *Thrown among Strangers: The Making of Mexican Culture in Frontier California*. Berkeley: University of California Press, 1993.

Montejano, David. *Anglos and Mexicans in the Making of Texas, 1836–1986*. Austin: University of Texas Press, 1987.

Moreno, Luis H. "¡Ya Basta! The Struggle for Justice and Equality: The Chicano Power Movement in Oxnard, California." In *The Chicano Movement Perspectives from the Twenty-First Century*, edited by Mario T. García, 130–48. New York: Routledge, 2014.

Muñoz, Laura K. "*Romo v. Laird:* Mexican American School Segregation and the Politics of Belonging in Arizona." *Western Legal History* 26, nos. 1 and 2 (2013): 97–132.

Nalder, Frank Fielding. "The American State Reformatory; with Special Reference to Its Educational Aspects." Ph.D. dissertation, University of California, Berkeley, 1917.

Olivas, Michael A., ed. *"Colored Men" and "Hombres Aquí": Hernández v. Texas and the Emergence of Mexican-American Lawyering*. Houston: Arte Público Press, 2006.

Oliver, Melvin, and Thomas Shapiro. *Black Wealth/White Wealth: Toward a New Theory of Inequality*. New York: Routledge, 1994.

Ong, Paul M., and Jordan Rickles. "The Continued Nexus between School and Residential Segregation." *Berkeley La Raza Law Journal* 15 (2004): 51–66.

Orfield, Gary, and Susan Eaton. *Dismantling Desegregation: The Quiet Reversal of Brown v. Board of Education*. New York: New Press, 1996.

Pierce, Chester M. "Offensive Mechanisms." In *The Black Seventies*, edited by Floyd B. Barbour, 265–82. Boston: Porter Sargent, 1970.

———. "Poverty and Racism as They Affect Children." In *Advocacy for Child Mental Health*, edited by I.N. Berlin, 92–109. New York: Brunner/Mazel, 1975.

————. "Social Trace Contaminants: Subtle Indicators of Racism in TV." In *Television and Social Behavior: Beyond Violence and Children. A Report of the Committee on Television and Social Behavior, Social Science Research Council,* edited by S. B. Withey and R. P. Abeles, 249–57. Hillsdale, NJ: Lawrence Erlbaum, 1980.

Pitt, Leonard. *The Decline of the Californios: A Social History of the Spanish-Speaking Californians, 1846–1890.* Berkeley: University of California Press, 1998.

powell, john a., Gavin Kearney, and Vina Key, eds. *In Pursuit of a Dream Deferred: Linking Housing and Education Policy.* New York: Peter Lang, 2001.

Powers, Jeanne. "Forgotten History: Mexican American School Segregation in Arizona, 1900–1951." *Equity and Excellence in Education* 41, no. 4 (2008): 467–81.

Pulido, Laura. *Black, Brown, Yellow, and Left: Radical Activism in Los Angeles.* Berkeley: University of California Press, 2006.

Ramos, Christopher. "The Educational Legacy of Racially Restrictive Covenants: Their Long Term Impact on Mexican Americans." *The Scholar* 4 (2002): 149–84.

Resnick, Rheta. "Subsistence Patterns at VEN-11, a Coastal Chumash Village." Master's thesis, California State University, Northridge, 1980.

Rice, Richard B., William A. Bullough, and Richard J. Orsi. *The Elusive Eden: A New History of California.* New York: McGraw-Hill, 1996.

Robinson, W. W. *The Story of Ventura County.* Los Angeles: Title Insurance and Trust Company, 1950.

Rogers, John Allan. "A History of School Organization and Administration in Ventura County." Ph.D. dissertation, University of Southern California, Los Angeles, 1961.

Romero v. Weakley, Burleigh v. Weakley, 131 F. Supp. 818 (U.S. Dist. 1955).

Rose, Margaret. "Gender and Civic Activism in Mexican American Barrios in California: The Community Service Organization, 1947–1962." In *Not June Cleaver: Women and Gender in Postwar America, 1945–1960,* edited by Joanne Meyerowitz, 177–200. Philadelphia: Temple University Press, 1994.

Ross, Fred. *Conquering Goliath: Cesar Chavez at the Beginning.* Keene, CA: El Taller Gráfica Press, 1989.

Ross v. Eckels, 317 F. Supp. 512 (S.D. Tex. 1970).

Rubio-Goldsmith, Raquel. "Oral History: Considerations and Problems for Its Use in the History of Mexicanas in the United States." In *Between Borders: Essays on Mexicana/Chicana History,* edited by Adelaida R. Del Castillo, 161–73. Encino, CA: Floricanto Press, 1990.

Ruiz, Vicki L. *From out of the Shadows: Mexican Women in Twentieth-Century America.* New York: Oxford University Press, 1998.

Salinas, Guadalupe. "Mexican Americans and Desegregation." *El Grito: A Journal of Contemporary Mexican-American Thought* 4, no. 4 (1971): 36–58.

Samora, Julian. "Mexican Immigration." In *Mexican-Americans Tomorrow: Educational and Economic Perspectives,* edited by Gus Taylor, 60–80. Albuquerque: University of New Mexico Press, 1975.

San Miguel, Guadalupe, Jr. *"Let All of Them Take Heed": Mexican Americans and the Quest for Educational Equality in Texas, 1910–1981.* College Station: Texas A&M University Press, 1987.

———. *Brown, Not White: School Integration and the Chicano Movement in Houston.* College Station: Texas A&M University Press, 2001.

———. *Chicana/o Struggles for Education: Activism in the Community.* College Station: Texas A&M University Press, 2013.

San Miguel, Guadalupe, Jr., and Richard R. Valencia. "From the Treaty of Guadalupe Hidalgo to Hopwood: The Educational Plight and Struggle for Equity for Mexican Americans in the Southwest." *Harvard Educational Review* 68, no. 3 (1998): 353–412.

Sánchez, George I. "Bilingualism and Mental Measures: A Word of Caution." *Journal of Applied Psychology* 18, no. 6 (1934): 765–72.

———. "The Education of Bilinguals in a State School System." Ph.D. dissertation, University of California, Berkeley, 1934.

———. *Forgotten People: A Study of New Mexicans* [1940]. Albuquerque: University of New Mexico Press, 1996.

Saucedo, Leticia M. "The Legal Issues Surrounding the TAAS Case." *Hispanic Journal of Behavioral Sciences* 22, no. 4 (2000): 411–22.

Scott v. Gonzales, Supreme Court of the State of California, no. 6507 (1879).

Shaw, George W. *The California Sugar Industry.* Sacramento, CA: W. W. Shannon, Superintendent State Printing, 1903.

Shelley v. Kraemer, 334 U.S. 1 (1948).

Shumway, Burgess McK. *California Ranchos: Patented Private Land Grants Listed by County.* San Bernardino, CA: Borgo Press, 1988.

Soja, Edward W. *Postmodern Geographies: The Reassertion of Space in Critical Social Theory.* New York: Verso, 1989.

Soria v. Oxnard School Board of Trustees, 386 F. Supp. 539 (U.S. Dist. 1974).

Spangler v. Pasadena City Board of Education, 311 F. Supp. 501 (C.D. Cal. 1970).

Sussman, Michael H. "Discrimination: A Pervasive Concept." In *In Pursuit of a Dream Deferred: Linking Housing and Education Policy,* edited by john a. powell, Gavin Kearney, and Vina Key, 209–28. New York: Peter Lang, 2001.

Swann v. Charlotte-Mecklenburg Board of Education, No. 281, 402 U.S. 1 (1971).

Taylor, Paul S. *Mexican Labor in the United States,* vol. 1. Berkeley: University of California Press, 1930.

———. *Mexican Labor in the United States,* vol. 6. Berkeley: University of California Publications in Economics, 1930.

Telles, Edward E., and Edward Murgia. "Phenotypic Discrimination and Income Differences among Mexican-Americans." *Social Science Quarterly* 71, no. 4 (1990): 682–94.

Terman, Lewis M. *The Measurement of Intelligence: An Explanation of and a Complete Guide for the Use of the Standard Revision and Extension of the Binet-Simon Intelligence Scale.* Boston: Houghton Mifflin, 1916.

Thompson Ford, Richard. "The Boundaries of Race: Political Geography in Legal Analysis." *Harvard Law Review* 107, no. 8 (1994): 1841–1921.

Torres-Rouff, David. "Becoming Mexican: Segregated Schools and Social Scientists in Southern California, 1913–1946." *Southern California Quarterly* 94, no. 1 (2012): 91–127.

Valencia, Richard R. "The Mexican American Struggle for Equal Educational Opportunity in *Mendez v. Westminster*: Helping Pave the Way for *Brown v. Board of Education*." *Teachers College Record* 107, no. 3 (2005): 389–423.

———. *Chicano Students and the Courts: The Mexican American Legal Struggle for Educational Equality*. New York: Routledge, 2008.

Valencia, Richard R., Martha Menchaca, and Rubén Donato. "Segregation, Desegregation, and Integration of Chicano Students: Old and New Realities." In *Chicano School Failure and Success: Past, Present, and Future,* 2nd ed., edited by Richard R. Valencia, 70–113. London: Routledge, 2002.

Vose, Clemente E. *Caucasians Only: The Supreme Court, the NAACP, and the Restrictive Covenant Cases*. Berkeley: University of California Press, 1959.

Watkins, William H. *The White Architects of Black Education: Ideology and Power in America, 1865–1954*. New York: Teachers College Press, 2001.

Weber, Devra. *Dark Sweat, White Gold: California Farm Workers, Cotton, and the New Deal*. Berkeley: University of California Press, 1994.

Wilson, Steven H. "Brown over 'Other White': Mexican Americans' Legal Arguments and Litigation Strategy in School Desegregation Lawsuits." *Law and History Review* (2003): 21, 145–94.

Wollenberg, Charles M. *All Deliberate Speed: Segregation and Exclusion in California Schools, 1855–1975*. Berkeley: University of California Press, 1976.

Wu, Ellen D. *The Color of Success: Asian Americans and the Origins of the Model Minority*. Princeton, NJ: Princeton University Press, 2013.

Yosso, Tara J. *Critical Race Counterstories along the Chicana/Chicano Educational Pipeline*. New York: Routledge, 2006.

INDEX

Page numbers in *italics* denote photographs and maps.

Americanization: business interests and paternalism of, 19–20, 183n50; leisure activities and, 27, 28, 186–187n93; policewoman nurse and, 16; preprimary classes and, 84–85; Red Cross women on, 21; and Santa Paula school segregation, 188n108; segregation claimed to be in service of, 156; White women and, 27, 180n6, 183n48

American Legion, Women's Auxiliary, 180n6

Anderson, James D., 4

Arguelles Diliello, Antonia, 35–36, 47–53, 63–64, *65*, 66–70, *68*, 72–74, 77, *78*, 95, 196n35, 206n75, 207n88, 208n92

Armor, David, 241n178

Asian Americans: California Education Code allowing school segregation for, 74–75; defendants' claims in *Soria* case about, 238n144; early labor history and racial hierarchy, 171n13; enrollment in White classes, 4, 60, 62, *71*, 74–75, 96, *98*, 224n138, 238n144; enrollments of, 112, 120, *121*; "model minority" myth and, 3, 76, 172n18, 209n107; population of, 183–184n53, 224n138. *See also* Chinese Americans; Japanese Americans; racially restrictive covenants

attrition of Mexican American students (pushout pattern): dress codes and, 73–74; gender and, 66, 73–74, 206n69, 208n92; and high school segregation policy, 58; and kindergarten attendance, 83–84, 211n30; normalization of, 58; retention and, 86; by sixth grade, 58, 59, 99; undereducation and segregation contributing to, 65–67, 73, 99

Ávila Carrasco, Dolores, 49–53, 92–95

Banner, Beatrice (teacher), 72

Barajas, Frank P., 167, 175n44, 178n68, 183n50

Bard, Thomas R., 194n27

Barrows v. Jackson, 54

Beach, Everett C. (school board), 55, 82; racially restrictive covenants on properties of, 43, 44, 45, 192n2, 195n30

Bell, Derrick, 181n13

Bernice Curren School, 91, 113, 116, 120, 238n144

Berzman, William, 158

Binet, Alfred, 185n71

Blacks (African Americans): enrollments in school, 24, 89, 99, 112, 120, *121*, 132, 186n80, 216n11, 229nn19,21; Haydock's views about, 12, 23–24; and junior high proposed for east side, 114; population of, 100, 104, 137; post–World War II expectations and, 101; and race as a relational concept, 3, 172n20; and racial hierarchy, 4–5; and racism in California, 111–112, 220n70; realtors and west-side housing and, 109–112; residential segregation and, 109–111, 220nn68,70; school attendance boundaries as perpetuating segregation of, 125; and school-within-a-school segregation, 64, 94–95; segregated within White classrooms, 89, 90; and social segregation outside classroom, 90, 213n61; "sundown" towns/racial curfews and, 111, 202n91; and "tracking" patterns into junior high, 93, 94, 132, 214n85; White architects of Black education (William H. Watkins), 3–4, 173n29. *See also* mundane racism; NAACP; racially restrictive covenants; racial microaggressions; *Soria v. Oxnard School Board of Trustees*

Boston, MA, 23, 235n115

Boughton, G. A. (city health officer), 185n65

Bracero Program, xi, 90, 105

Braden, Thomas W. (state school board), 118–119

Brekke, Norman (school board), 149–150, 154–155, 156

Brice v. Landis, 142

Brittell, Clarence (superintendent), racially restrictive covenants on properties of, 45

Brittell School (Clarence Brittell School), 91, 120

Brokaw, Tom, 209nn108–109

Broomfield Amendment (busing moratorium), 130–131, 150–151

Brown Berets, 245n3

Brown, Fred, 123, *127*
Brown v. Board of Education: overview, 2–3; and "interest convergence," 181n13; legal application to Mexican Americans, 224–225n150; NAACP and, 122; and school-within-a-school model, 2–3; *Soria* case and, 153, 154; "with all deliberate speed," 123, 225n160
Buena Vista Labor Camp, xi, 70, 105
Bureau of Intergroup Relations report and recommendations, 132–133, 145, 157, 159, 230nn25,28–30
Burfeind, John H. (school board), 41–42, 55, 60, 61, 69, 193nn14,17, 203n1; racially restrictive covenants on properties of, 43, 46, 199n53
Burger, Justice Warren, 152
business interests: Mexican patrons sought by, 176n47; segregation of downtown businesses, 54; unrestricted Mexican immigration favored by, 15, 29, 31–32, 189n128. *See also* agricultural industry; labor market segregation; leisure activities, segregation of
busing: as argument for proposed junior high on east side, 113–114; attempted arson of buses, 150; "forced" busing, 130–131, 146–147, 157; involuntary, 130, 135; Claude Kirk and national campaign against, 130, 146–147, 237n140; local press coverage of, 146, 147, 149–150, 164; Nixon administration moratorium on (Broomfield Amendment), 130–131, 150–151; one-way, 142, 144, 149; poll of parent preferences for, 145; Princeton Plan, 145; *Soria* affidavits against, 149; *Soria* affidavits for, 148–149, 163; *Soria* order for, and attempted stay of, 145, 146–148, 149–153, 154, 164, 237nn134,136, 239n153, 239–240n164; state rule on maximum walking distance to school, 113; two-way, 145, 149, 160–161, 164; "Wakefield Initiative Petition" against, 135, 136–137, 232n60; of White students living east of Colonia, 155

California Educational Code: ethnic composition of area must be considered

for new schools, 112, 122; junior high proposed for east side as violating, 112–113, 116, 117–119, 122, 222n108; removal of racial exclusions from, 85; segregation in, 74–75, 189n120, 208n98; segregation of Black children not allowed, 208n98; segregation of Mexican children not allowed, 31, 74, 85, 208n98
California State Attorney General's Office, 135
California State Board of Education, 118–119, 122
California State Commission on Equal Educational Opportunity, 125–126
California State Department of Education: Bureau of Intergroup Relations report and recommendations, 132–133, 145, 157, 159, 230nn25,28–30; and east-side proposed junior high school, 118–119; on "tracking" patterns, 93, 132
Californios, land grants to: Spanish colonial grants, 6, 8; White acquisition of, 6, 7, 9, 43, 45, 175nn42,44, 176n47, 194n27, 196–197n38
Camacho, Cloromiro, 115, 116–117
Camarillo, Adolfo, 176n47
Camarillo family land holdings, 194n27
Camarillo, Frank A., 176n47
Camarillo, Juan, 175n44, 176n47
Canyon School (Santa Paula), 29, 188n108
Carballo, Gloria, 70, *71*
Carballo, Louis, 70, 72
Carballo, Richard, 70–71, *71,* 110–111, 208n92
Carmona, Ignacio S., 9, 209n109
Carrasco, Ernie Jr., 48, 51–52
Carroll, Grace, 206n66, 215n99
Carter, Leonard H., 151
Carty, Adolph J., racially restrictive covenants on properties of, 44, 192n2, 195n30
Carty, Edwin L., 108, 203n101; racially restrictive covenants on properties of, 44–45, 46, 195n30, 196–197nn36,38,42, 199–200nn53–55, 201n75
Catholic Women's Association, 180n6
Cen, Ernesto V., 219n47

M.E.E.S. *See* mundane extreme environmental stress

Menchaca, Martha, 188n108

Mendez v. Westminster, 85

Mendoza, Joe I., 48–49, 51, 52, 66, 67–69, 76, 87–88, 99

Meta Street, 7, 21, 39, 177n56, 217–218n29

Mexican American Political Association (MAPA), 129, 133, 144, 146, 163–164

Mexican Americans: academic attainment rates, 47–48, 86–87, 212nn43–44; aspirations for the future and, 76–77, 94; classification as a minority group, 122, 136, 224–225n150; classification as non-White, 224–225n150; cultural wealth and, 47–48, 217–218n29; as term, 10; "tracking" patterns in junior high as discriminatory, 93–94, 132, 214n85; U.S. Census identification of, 122, 183–184n53, 213n70. *See also* agricultural workers; Americanization; community activism; criminalization of Mexican Americans; population; segregation; Whites, Mexicans classified as

Mexican playground, 27–28, 187n99. *See also* playgrounds and parks

Mexicans. *See* Mexican Americans

Mexico. *See* immigration from Mexico

microaggressions. *See* racial microaggressions

migratory farmworkers, 32, 34, 190n131. *See also* agricultural workers

military families, segregation and, 50, 101, 103, 109, 111

Millham, Thomas E. (school board), 118, 124

Mills, Charles, 4

Mission San Buenaventura, 6

Mississippi, 30, 129, 130, 137

"model minority" myth, 3, 76, 172n18, 209n107

Molina, J. Charles, 230n30

Molina, Natalia, 3, 19, 172n20, 182n23, 186n83, 217–218n29

Montejano, David, 40

Morales, Cesar (superintendent), 165–166

Mornell, Eugene S., 230n30

movie theater segregation, 51, 103–104

Muller, Henry (school board), 113, 124, 125, 135

mundane extreme environmental stress (M.E.E.S., Grace Carroll), 206n66, 215n99. *See also* racial microaggressions

mundane racism: the color-line as, 39, 40, 44–45, 49, 53–54; community activism to combat, 104, 105; definition of, 5, 162; and diminished enthusiasm for school, 88–89; east-side elementary schools and effects of, 99, 215nn98–99; internalization of discrimination and, 36, 68, 94; oral histories illustrating, generally, 37; and racial myths as origin stories, 8–9, 178nn62,64; school-within-a-school segregation as, 67–69; stereotypes of Mexicans, 35–36; subtle and stunning effects of, 99, 174n36, 192n4, 206n66. *See also* color-line (W. E. B. DuBois); mundane extreme environmental stress; racial microaggressions; segregation strategies

Murray, Police Chief, 18

Mytinger, Kenneth L. (school board), 137, 147, 149, 237n134

NAACP (National Association for the Advancement of Colored People): capacity to consider lawsuits, usefulness of, 104; deep South as linked with local tactics of bigotry, 100, 109; desegregation proposals of, 119–124, 126, 131, 157; integration proposals of, 145, 159; Oxnard–Ventura County, California Branch, 101–104, 216n9; pressure on city council to desegregate, 135–137; Proposition 21 challenged by (1972), 232n60; smeared as outsiders, 116, 120; and *Soria* case, 145, 148–149, 151. *See also* community activism; junior high school proposed for east side

Nalder, Frank Fielding, 32–33

Native Americans ("Indians"): California Educational Code allowing segregation for, 189n120; forced off the land, 6, 45, 174–175n39, 178n64; Mexicans classed as, 176n48; population of, 224n138. *See also* racially restrictive covenants

Perez, Robert, 71, *71*

Pfeiler, Robert E. (school board), 113, 124, 125, 126, 135, 156–157, 231n43

Pierce, Chester M., 99, 174n36, 192n4, 206n66, 215n98

Pinkard, Bedford, 89, 90, 110–111

playgrounds and parks: Mexican community building and organizing and, 27–28, 187nn98–99; naming of, 54, 108; segregation of, 27, 28, 96, 186–187nn91,93,95,96; west side development of, vs. east side, 108

policing: policewoman nurse, 12–16, 18–19, 26, 81, 181–182nn18–19; of "sundown" town/racial curfew rules, 52–53, 111, 202n91. *See also* criminalization of Mexican Americans

Pollack, Henry, 108

Pollock, Mrs. (teacher), 88, 89

population of Oxnard: 1920 census, 176n47; 1930 census, 31, 56; 1940 census, 80, 100; 1950 census, 80, 90, 100; Asian, 183–184n53, 224n138; Black, 100, 104, 137; exponential growth between 1940 and 1970, 100; foreign- vs. native-born Mexicans, 24, 184n56, 215–216n4; growth in, and arguments for east-side junior high school, 112, 221n74; increases following World War II, 100, 104; protests of school board based on, 137. *See also* student enrollments

Port Hueneme (Oxnard), 100, 216n6

Potter, Margaret Tatum, 110, 111, 220n68

Powell, Justice Lewis F. Jr., 152

Powell, Noble A. (school board), racially restrictive covenants on properties of, 43, 194n25

Power, Elmer W. (school board), racially restrictive covenants on properties of, 43, 44, 55, 195nn33–34

Pregerson, Judge Harry (*Soria* case): overview, 11, 131, 142, 161; "Amended Integration Plan" ordered by, 144, 145; decision for the plaintiffs, 159–160, 162–163; as observer of first day of busing, 150, 239n158; on school board as obsessed with segregation, 203n4; stay of the busing order sought during

vacation of, 146; summary judgment of, 143–144, 147, 152–154, 159, 235nn105–106. *See also Soria v. Oxnard School Board of Trustees*

preprimary (pre-first grade) classes, 84–86, 211–212nn31,38,40

Press-Courier, The: advocacy for integration in, 100, 115, 116–117, 121–122, 129, 133–134, 137, 145, 230nn35,37, 240n169; archives of, 178n66; campaign for proposed east-side junior high school, 113–125, 223n127; and city council elections, 106, 218n38; and criminalization of Mexican Americans, 9, 34, 113–114; on housing condition improvement, 107–108; and minutes from 1930s, 154–155; name changes of, 9, 178n66; patterns of omission and distortion rendering Mexicans invisible, 9; racial identifiers and misspellings of names in, 9, 115; racially restrictive covenants challenged in court, lack of coverage of, 54, 202–203n100; racially restrictive covenants on property owned by publishers of, 45, 54, 197n43, 202–203n100; racial myths as origin stories, 8–9, 178n64; and Ramona School campaign, 80–81; on segregation of schools, 29–30, 62; on *Soria* case, 144–145, 146, 147, 149–150, 158

Princeton Plan, 145

Proposition 21 (1972), 136–137, 232n60

Pryor, George (chief of police), 45, 81, 197n42

PTA (Mexican Parent-Teachers Association), 69

PTA (Oxnard Parent-Teachers' Association): and segregation, demand for, 29, 30–31, 62; women as leading, 180n6

public health: Asians portrayed as threat to, 19; California Education Code allowing segregation for, 189n120; Mexicans portrayed as threat to, 4, 12, 13–15, 16, 18–19, 31, 34, 182n23, 183n39, 186n83; policewoman nurse and, 12–16, 18–19, 26, 81, 181–182nn18–19; protests of lack of sanitation infrastructure in La Colonia, 18–19, 20–22, 105, 183n39. *See also*

public health *(continued)*
  criminalization of Mexican Americans;
  health care, segregation of; La Colonia
  (east side), strategic underdevelopment
  of; Red Cross
Puntenney, Harriet (teacher), 72

Quakers, and Japanese internment, 76,
  209n108
Quiroz, Alex, 88–89, 95, 99

race and racism: crime, perilous living
  conditions linked to, 103; internalization of discrimination, 36, 68, 94;
  normalization of disparate treatment
  (*see* mundane racism); as relational
  concept, 3, 172n20. *See also* Americanization; color-line (W. E. B. DuBois);
  criminalization of Mexican Americans;
  gender; geographic racial boundaries;
  population; racial hierarchy as strategy
  of segregation; racially restrictive covenants; racial microaggressions; segregation; social class; "tracking" of students;
  White architects of Mexican American
  education
"racial contract" (Charles Mills), 4, 41, 44
racial hierarchy as strategy of segregation:
  overview, 2, 4–5, 13, 56; early labor
  history and, 171n13; "racial contract"
  among Whites, 4, 41, 44. *See also*
  mundane racism; racially restrictive
  covenants; segregation strategies
racially restrictive covenants: overview, 5, 7,
  50; Asians as exception to enforcement
  of, 224n138; awareness of Mexican
  Americans of, 50, 52, 54; Blacks seeking
  residences and, 109–112, 220nn68,70;
  citywide racial hierarchy created by,
  53–54; and court finding of de jure
  school segregation, 142; Federal Housing Administration (FHA) guidance on
  wording and rationale for, 199n52; "first
  class residences" specified in, 39, 44, 50,
  192n2; Japanese surnames and, 201n75;
  in perpetuity, 10, 43, 179n72; on property bought and sold by city and school
  officials and associates, 43–46,

194nn23,25, 195–200nn28–36,38–50,53–
  57; on property bought and sold by
  owners of *Press-Courier,* 45, 54, 197n43,
  202–203n100; on property owned by
  city contractors, 44, 195n34; and Ramona (east-side) school, 81; servants as
  exception to, 43, 44, 111; *Soria* case
  materials not exposing, 163; Spanish-
  surnamed homebuyers and, 201n75; as
  unconstitutional, 45–46, 54, 199n51;
  and White demands for segregated
  schools, 40–42, 82–83, 193n12; World
  War II returning veterans and workers
  encountering, 101
racial microaggressions (Chester M. Pierce),
  99, 215nn98–99; subtle and stunning
  effects of, 99, 174n36, 192n4, 206n66.
  See also mundane racism
railroad tracks as demarcation, 7, 13, 48,
  177n56, 192n7
Ramona Home Gardens, 180n9
Ramona School: academic achievement of
  students, 86–87, 212nn43–44; age and
  grade placements, 86–87, 212nn43–44;
  attendance boundaries of, 82–83;
  barbed-wire fencing and, 96, *97;* Black
  student enrollments, 89, 99; bond issue
  for, 58, 80, 81; corporal punishment
  used in, 87–88, 89, 90; double sessions
  at, 91; enrollments, 120; establishment
  of, 80–83, 193n15, 221n87, 238n144;
  Juanita school and, as shuffling students
  back and forth, 101; and junior high
  proposed for east side, 113–115, 117,
  119–120, 221n87; and kindergarten, lack
  of, 83–84, 85, 211n30; low quality of
  construction and amenities, 82, 87, 99;
  map showing, *38;* mundane racism in,
  99, 215nn98–99; perceived teacher
  quality, 88–89, 115; portable buildings,
  101, 130, 138; preprimary placements,
  84–86, 211–212nn31,38,40; racially
  restrictive covenants on properties
  owned by staff of, 198–199n50; retention
  rates, 86; safety of children as argument
  for establishing, 80, 81, 114, 221n87;
  segregation within junior high White
  classrooms for graduates of, 89, 90, 99;

describing, 63–69; parents contesting segregation, 69–71, *71*, 72; as pragmatic compromise, 57–58; as preceding *Brown v. Board* decision, 2–3; Ramona School as relieving pressure on, 81–82; Roosevelt School and, 55, 56, 57–58, 60, 61, 63–64, *65*, 67, 204nn10,12, 205n41; social separation outside the classroom, 58, 64, 66, 204n12; and White students shifted away from Haydock School (1936), 40–42, 57–58, 61, 193nn14,17, 204nn10,12; Wilson School and, 55, 56, 57–58, 64–69, *67–68*, 204n10

Scott, Thomas A., 175n44, 194n27, 196–197n38

Scott v. Gonzales, 175n44, 194n27, 196–197n38

segregation. *See* desegregation; geographic racial boundaries; health care, segregation of; integration; labor market segregation; leisure activities, segregation of; neighborhood schools; school segregation; segregation strategies

segregation strategies: overview, 2–3, 4–5, 56, 162; normalization of disparate treatment (*see* mundane racism). *See also* omission of rationale for segregation, as strategy; racial hierarchy as strategy of segregation; residential and school segregation, permanently linked as strategy; school-within-a-school as strategy of segregation

Sells, Anna J. (principal), 204n10; racially restrictive covenants on properties of, 45, 196n35, 198n47

Shaffer, Alice, 40–42, 61, 69, 193–194nn12,14,19, 203n1

Shagaloff, June, 120

Shelley v. Kraemer, 46, 54, 199n52

Sierra Linda School, 132, 229n21, 238n144

"silent majority," 145, 235n116

Simi Elementary School, 211–212n40

Simmons, Althea T. L., 100, 119–120, 121–122, 126

Skilling, Laura S. (teacher), 72

Smith, Lloyd, 71

social class: aspirations for high school graduation, 47–48, 77; aspirations for

the future, 76–77, 94; geographic racial boundaries and differences in, 49, 95, 109, 110. *See also* geographic racial boundaries; racially restrictive covenants; wealth, generational transfer of

social separation outside the classroom: and junior high schools, 89, 90, 213n61; and school-within-a-school segregation, 58, 64, 66, 204n12. *See also* leisure activities, segregation of; school segregation

Soja, Edward, 54

SooHoo, William D., 207n90

Soria, Catalina Frazier, 228n3

Soria, Juan L. ("Big John"): and coalition with NAACP, 127, *127*; and CSO, 106; on de facto segregation, 133; on equal education, 163–164; as leader of Mexican American Political Association, 129; and *Soria* case, 1, 129–130, 144

Soria Mendoza, Julieta Flores, 106

Soria v. Oxnard School Board of Trustees (Debbie and Doreen Soria et al. v. Oxnard School Board of Trustees et al.); overview, 1, 11, 129–131, 163–164; appeal to U.S. Ninth Circuit Court, 147–148, 152–154, 159–160, 240n169, 241–242nn178,181,187; busing order, and denial of stay of, 145, 146–148, 149–153, 154, 164, 237nn134,136, 239n153, 239–240n164; calls for compliance with court mandate, 144–145; cited by U.S. Supreme Court in *Keyes,* 172–173n21; community activist groups as background to, 148–149; decision for the plaintiffs, 159–160, 162–163; depositions of school board members, 155–158; federal government as intervenor in, 150–151; integration plan mandated, 144, 145–146, 150, 159, 160–161, 235n112, 239n155; as joint filing by Mexican American and Black plaintiffs, 3, 129–130, 148–149, 160, 172–173n21, 228n3; legal fees for, 244n244; Mexican American voices as absent from case materials, 163; NAACP support for, 145, 148–149, 151; national issues engaged by, 130–131; original legal complaint for, 129, 130, 139–142, 228n11, 233n86,

Thrasher, William H. (teacher), 133–134, 149, 230n35
Tinklepaugh, Kenneth N. (school board), 135, 136, 149
Title VI of the Civil Rights Act, 159
Tolsten, Fred, 103, 104
Tortilla Flats (Ventura), 107
"tracking" of students: as discriminatory, 93–94, 132, 214n85. *See also* Bureau of Intergroup Relations report
Treaty of Guadalupe Hidalgo, 6
Tregarthen, Doran W. (superintendent), 144–145, 150, 239n155
truancy officer, 19–20, 87–88. *See also* policing: policewoman nurse

Urban League, 102, 223n130
U.S. Census Bureau: identification of Mexican Americans by, 122, 183–184n53, 213n70. *See also* population
U.S. Justice Department, Civil Rights Division, 150–151

Valdivia Lamm, Mary, 9, 48, *65*, 67–69, *68*
Valencia, Richard R., 188n108
Vasquez, Irene, 1
Ventura, CA: community activism in, 102–103; redevelopment in, 107
Ventura County: Chumash peoples and, 174n39; "crop vacations" in academic year, 32, 190n131; Mexican American enrollments in, 165, 203n1; in WWII, 216n6
Ventura County General Hospital, 48
Ventura County Human Relations Committee, 105
Ventura County Legal Service Center, 141–142
Veteran's Administration, 109
Virden, Ben S. (school board), 13, 15, 181n14, 182n20; racially restrictive covenants on properties of, 42–43, 45, 194n23, 197–198n45

Wakefield, Floyd, 136–137
"Wakefield Initiative Petition," 135, 136–137, 232n60
Warren, Chief Justice Earl, 225n160

Waters, William A. (*Soria* defendants' attorney), 142–143, 155, 234n102, 244n244
Watkins, William H., 3–4, 173n29
wealth, generational transfer of (George Lipsitz): net worth as measure of discrimination, 173–174n31, 201n76; racially restrictive covenants as perpetuating, 43, 46; racially restrictive covenants as preventing, for Mexican Americans, 50, 53
Weaver, Charles H., 19, 20, 22, 185n65
Weaver, Mrs. Charles, 27
Webb, Mrs. May (policewoman nurse), 18–19
Wesley, Cerisa House, 216n11
Western Center on Law and Poverty, 141–142, 151, 154
west side: Blacks seeking housing in, 109–112; infrastructure provided by city for properties in, 7, 13, 16, *17*, 26, 39, 180–181n11, 182n32; maps of, *38, 59*; Mexicans seeking housing in, 49–50, 52, 92, 94, 95; Oxnard Boulevard and railroad tracks as demarcation of, 7, 13, 80, 177n56; sanitation and, 18; strategic positioning of schools in, 80; street paving of, 7, 13, 16, *17*, 18, 19, 39, 180–181n11, 182n32. *See also* geographic racial boundaries; La Colonia (east side); leisure activities, segregation of; racially restrictive covenants
White architects of Mexican American education: overview, xii, 3, 162; appointing each other to city council, 12; defined as term, 3–4, 173n29; and fraternal organizations, racially exclusive, 13, 45, 180n5; and leisure activities, segregation of, 28; and naming of streets, schools, and parks, 54, 108, 203n101; as powerbrokers of Oxnard, 12–13; "racial contract" among, 4, 41, 44; studies and plans used as delaying tactic by, 108–109; voice of, as dominating school board minutes, 8; William H. Watkins and concept of, 3–4, 173n29. *See also* business interests; segregation strategies

Made in the USA
Lexington, KY
07 September 2018